"In preparing for the international Synod of Bishops on 'The Word of God in the Life and Mission of the Church,' Pope Benedict XVI reminded the Church that a prayerful study of the Scriptures is at the heart of the Church's renewal. The new Catholic Commentary on Sacred Scripture promises to directly serve that purpose. Drawing on sound biblical scholarship, the commentaries present the reader with the rich harvest of that study, reflecting on the message of the biblical text and engaging the life of faith from a Catholic perspective."

—**Donald Senior, CP**, president, Catholic Theological Union

"This series promises to be spiritually and doctrinally informative, based on careful, solid biblical exegesis. The method and content of this work will be helpful to teachers of the faith at different levels and will provide a reliable guide to people seeking to deepen their knowledge and thereby nourish their faith. I strongly recommend the Catholic Commentary on Sacred Scripture."

—**Cormac Cardinal Murphy-O'Connor**, Archbishop of Westminster

"I welcome with great joy the launch of this new collection of commentaries on the Bible because the project corresponds perfectly to a pressing need in the Church. I am speaking about exegetical studies that are well grounded from a scholarly point of view but not overburdened with technical details, and at the same time related to the riches of ancient interpretation, nourishing for spiritual life, and useful for catechesis, preaching, evangelization, and other forms of pastoral ministry. This is the kind of commentary for which the majority of readers have a great desire."

—**Albert Cardinal Vanhoye, SJ**, Pontifical Biblical Institute, former secretary of the Pontifical Biblical Commission

"When the Scripture is read in the liturgy, it is heard as a living voice. But when expounded in a commentary, it is too often read as a document from the past. This fine new series unites the ancient and the contemporary by offering insight into the biblical text—verse by verse—as well as spiritual application to the lives of Christians today. I particularly like the sidebars inserted into the text called 'Living Tradition' that feature memorable sayings from great Christian teachers or brief explanations of puzzling terms and ideas."

—**Robert Louis Wilken**, University of Virginia

"This new Bible commentary series is based on solid scholarship and enriched by the church's long tradition of study and reflection. Enhanced by an attractive format, it provides an excellent resource for all who are serving in pastoral ministry and for the individual reader who searches the Scriptures for guidance in the Christian life."

—**Emil A. Wcela**, Auxiliary Bishop (retired), Diocese of Rockville Centre; past president, Catholic Biblical Association

"The Catholic Commentary on Sacred Scripture is an ideal tool for living our faith more deeply. This extraordinary resource combines superior scholarship and a vivid, accessible style that will serve the interested layperson and the serious scholar equally well. It feeds both the mind and the heart and should be on the shelf of every committed Catholic believer. I highly recommend it."

—**Charles J. Chaput, OFM Cap**, Archbishop of Denver

"This new commentary series appears to me to be a gift of the Holy Spirit to Catholic clergy, religious, and laity at this historic moment. Pope Benedict has effectively announced the rebirth of Catholic biblical theology, bringing together Scripture, tradition, and the teachings of the Church. This commentary reflects not only biblical criticism but also the unity of the Word of God as it applies to our lives. This is a marvelous and timely introduction."

—**Benedict J. Groeschel, CFR**, author and preacher

"This new commentary series should meet a need that has long been pointed out: a guide to Scripture that will be both historically responsible and shaped by the mind of the Church's tradition. It promises to be a milestone in the recovery of a distinctively Catholic approach to exegesis."

—**Aidan Nichols, OP**, University of Oxford; Fellow of Greyfriars, Oxford

"This series employs the Church's methodology of studying Sacred Scripture in a faithful, dynamic, and fruitful way. With interest in Catholic Bible studies growing rapidly, the repeated question has been, 'can you suggest a reliable commentary?' The Catholic Commentary on Sacred Scripture is now the go-to resource that I can enthusiastically recommend to all my students."

—**Jeff Cavins**, founder, The Great Adventure Catholic Bible Study System

The Gospel of
Mark

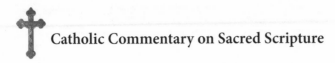 Catholic Commentary on Sacred Scripture

The Gospel of Mark

Mary Healy

B
Baker Academic
a division of Baker Publishing Group
Grand Rapids, Michigan

© 2008 by Mary Healy

Published by Baker Academic
a division of Baker Publishing Group
P.O. Box 6287, Grand Rapids, MI 49516-6287
www.bakeracademic.com

Printed in the United States of America

Library of Congress Cataloging-in-Publication Data

Healy, Mary, 1964–
    The Gospel of Mark / Mary Healy ; Peter S. Williamson and Mary Healy, general editors.
        p.   cm. — (Catholic commentary on sacred scripture)
    Includes index.
    ISBN 978-0-8010-3586-9 (pbk.)
    1. Bible. N.T. Mark—Commentaries. I. Williamson, Peter S. II. Title.
BS2585.53.H43 2008
226.3′077—dc22   2008022352

Nihil Obstat:
Rev. Christopher Begg
Censor Deputatus

Imprimatur:
Rev. Msgr. Barry C. Knestout
Vicar for Administration

Archdiocese of Washington

March 6, 2008

The *nihil obstat* and *imprimatur* are official declarations that a book or pamphlet is free of doctrinal or moral error. There is no implication that those who have granted the *nihil obstat* and the *imprimatur* agree with the content, opinions, or statements expressed therein.

    21   22   23   24   25   26   18   17   16   15   14   13

To Fr. Francis Martin

Contents

Illustrations

Editors' Preface

The Church has always venerated the divine Scriptures just as she venerates the body of the Lord. . . . All the preaching of the Church should be nourished and governed by Sacred Scripture. For in the sacred books, the Father who is in heaven meets His children with great love and speaks with them; and the power and goodness in the word of God is so great that it stands as the support and energy of the Church, the strength of faith for her sons and daughters, the food of the soul, a pure and perennial fountain of spiritual life.

Second Vatican Council, *Dei Verbum* 21

Were not our hearts burning while he spoke to us on the way and opened the scriptures to us?

Luke 24:32

The Catholic Commentary on Sacred Scripture aims to serve the ministry of the Word of God in the life and mission of the Church. Since Vatican Council II, there has been an increasing hunger among Catholics to study Scripture in depth and in a way that reveals its relationship to liturgy, evangelization, catechesis, theology, and personal and communal life. This series responds to that desire by providing accessible yet substantive commentary on each book of the New Testament, drawn from the best of contemporary biblical scholarship as well as the rich treasury of the Church's tradition. These volumes seek to offer scholarship illumined by faith, in the conviction that the ultimate aim of biblical interpretation is to discover what God has revealed and is still speaking through the sacred text. Central to our approach are the principles taught by Vatican II: first, the use of historical and literary methods to discern what the biblical authors intended to express; second, prayerful theological reflection to understand the sacred text "in accord with the same Spirit by whom it was written"—that is, in light of the content and unity of the whole Scripture, the living tradition of the Church, and the analogy of faith (*Dei Verbum* 12).

The Catholic Commentary on Sacred Scripture is written for those engaged in or training for pastoral ministry and others interested in studying Scripture to understand their faith more deeply, to nourish their spiritual life, or to share the good news with others. With this in mind, the authors focus on the meaning of the text for faith and life rather than on the technical questions that occupy scholars, and they explain the Bible in ordinary language that does not require translation for preaching and catechesis. Although this series is written from the perspective of Catholic faith, its authors draw on the interpretation of Protestant and Orthodox scholars and hope these volumes will serve Christians of other traditions as well.

A variety of features are designed to make the commentary as useful as possible. Each volume includes the biblical text of the New American Bible (NAB), the translation approved for liturgical use in the United States. In order to serve readers who use other translations, the most important differences between the NAB and other widely used translations (RSV, NRSV, JB, NJB, and NIV) are noted and explained. Each unit of the biblical text is followed by a list of references to relevant Scripture passages, Catechism sections, and uses in the Roman Lectionary. The exegesis that follows aims to explain in a clear and engaging way the meaning of the text in its original historical context as well as its perennial meaning for Christians. Reflection and Application sections help readers apply Scripture to Christian life today by responding to questions that the text raises, offering spiritual interpretations drawn from Christian tradition or providing suggestions for the use of the biblical text in catechesis, preaching, or other forms of pastoral ministry.

Interspersed throughout the commentary are Biblical Background sidebars that present historical, literary, or theological information and Living Tradition sidebars that offer pertinent material from the postbiblical Christian tradition, including quotations from Church documents and from the writings of saints and Church Fathers. The Biblical Background sidebars are indicated by a photo of urns that were excavated in Jerusalem, signifying the importance of historical study in understanding the sacred text. The Living Tradition sidebars are indicated by an image of Eadwine, a twelfth-century monk and scribe, signifying the growth in the Church's understanding that comes by the grace of the

Holy Spirit as believers study and ponder the word of God in their hearts (see *Dei Verbum* 8).

Maps and a Glossary are located in the back of each volume for easy reference. The glossary explains key terms from the biblical text as well as theological or exegetical terms, which are marked in the commentary with a cross (†). A list of Suggested Resources, an Index of Pastoral Topics, and an Index of Sidebars are included to enhance the usefulness of these volumes. Further resources, including questions for reflection or discussion, can be found at the series web site, www.CatholicScriptureCommentary.com.

It is our desire and prayer that these volumes be of service so that more and more "the word of the Lord may speed forward and be glorified" (2 Thess 3:1) in the Church and throughout the world.

Peter S. Williamson
Mary Healy
Kevin Perrotta

Note to Readers

The New American Bible differs slightly from most English translations in its verse numbering of the Psalms and certain other parts of the Old Testament. For instance, Ps 51:4 in the NAB is Ps 51:2 in other translations; Mal 3:19 in the NAB is Mal 4:1 in other translations. Readers who use different translations are advised to keep this in mind when looking up Old Testament cross-references given in the commentary.

Abbreviations

†	indicates that the definition of a term appears in the glossary
//	indicates where the same account can be found in other Gospels
ACCS	Ancient Christian Commentary on Scripture
b.	Babylonian Talmud
ca.	circa
Catechism	*Catechism of the Catholic Church* (2nd Edition)
JB	Jerusalem Bible
Lectionary	*The Lectionary for Mass* (1998/2002 USA Edition)
LXX	†Septuagint
NAB	New American Bible
NICNT	New International Commentary on the New Testament
NIGTC	New International Greek Testament Commentary
NIV	New International Version
NJB	New Jerusalem Bible
NRSV	New Revised Standard Version
NT	New Testament
OT	Old Testament
PG	Patrologia Graeca. Edited by J.-P. Migne. 162 vols. Paris, 1857–1886
RCIA	Rite of Christian Initiation for Adults
RSV	Revised Standard Version

Books of the Old Testament

Gen	Genesis	Tob	Tobit	Ezek	Ezekiel
Exod	Exodus	Jdt	Judith	Dan	Daniel
Lev	Leviticus	Esther	Esther	Hosea	Hosea
Num	Numbers	1 Macc	1 Maccabees	Joel	Joel
Deut	Deuteronomy	2 Macc	2 Maccabees	Amos	Amos
Josh	Joshua	Job	Job	Obad	Obadiah
Judg	Judges	Ps	Psalms	Jon	Jonah
Ruth	Ruth	Prov	Proverbs	Mic	Micah
1 Sam	1 Samuel	Eccles	Ecclesiastes	Nah	Nahum
2 Sam	2 Samuel	Song	Song of Songs	Hab	Habakkuk
1 Kings	1 Kings	Wis	Wisdom	Zeph	Zephaniah
2 Kings	2 Kings	Sir	Sirach	Hag	Haggai
1 Chron	1 Chronicles	Isa	Isaiah	Zech	Zechariah
2 Chron	2 Chronicles	Jer	Jeremiah	Mal	Malachi
Ezra	Ezra	Lam	Lamentations		
Neh	Nehemiah	Bar	Baruch		

Books of the New Testament

Matt	Matthew	1 Tim	1 Timothy
Mark	Mark	2 Tim	2 Timothy
Luke	Luke	Titus	Titus
John	John	Philem	Philemon
Acts	Acts of the Apostles	Heb	Hebrews
Rom	Romans	James	James
1 Cor	1 Corinthians	1 Pet	1 Peter
2 Cor	2 Corinthians	2 Pet	2 Peter
Gal	Galatians	1 John	1 John
Eph	Ephesians	2 John	2 John
Phil	Philippians	3 John	3 John
Col	Colossians	Jude	Jude
1 Thess	1 Thessalonians	Rev	Revelation
2 Thess	2 Thessalonians		

Introduction

When Mark wrote his †Gospel, to become a follower of Jesus was a radical decision. It could mean incurring disapproval or outright rejection from friends and family. It could entail close fellowship with people one would have previously shunned: the wealthy with slaves, the devout with the formerly decadent, Jewish nationalists with Roman soldiers. For the educated it could mean enduring the ridicule of former colleagues for the absurdity of following a carpenter from a backwater village who had suffered the most ignominious form of capital punishment. And for many, Christian faith would result in imprisonment, torture, and death in the brutality of the Roman arena.

Yet as one reads Mark's work one is impressed with its overflowing joy. Mark is fairly bursting with the good news of Jesus Christ the Son of God, crucified and risen from the dead. For Mark the life and times of Jesus is no mere edifying story. It is an event that has changed the course of world history—that has, in fact, brought history to its culmination. It is what makes sense of and brings to completion all that God did for his people Israel and foretold in their Scriptures. It is good news that has dramatically changed Mark's life.

Mark writes in such a way as to invite his readers to embark on the same adventure that he himself, and Jesus' first disciples, have engaged in: the adventure of encountering Jesus, growing in the knowledge of who he truly is, and committing one's whole life to him. It is nearly impossible to read Mark as a neutral bystander. At every turn he invites his readers to see themselves reflected in the disciples, in the crowds that flock to Jesus for healing, or in the other characters in the story. Like the characters in Mark's Gospel, readers are challenged to respond to the provocative words and astounding deeds of the carpenter from Nazareth.

"Who then is this?" the disciples ask after Jesus calms the storm on the sea (4:41). It is the question at the heart of Mark's Gospel. Jesus himself raises this question when he asks his disciples, "But who do you say that I am?" (8:29). Mark has already provided the answer at the beginning of his work: Jesus is the Messiah, the beloved Son of God (1:1, 11). But it is not enough merely to understand the words; the point is to allow their full reality to come to light through a personal encounter with Jesus. Mark's Gospel is written to enable his readers to do just that.

Who Is Mark?

None of the Gospel authors identify themselves by name in their works. But early Christian tradition ascribed each Gospel to an author who was either an apostle or closely linked with the apostles. The heading "according to Mark" (*kata Markon*) appears in the earliest manuscripts we have of the second Gospel, which date back to the third century. According to ancient tradition, Mark was a disciple of Simon Peter who wrote his Gospel based on Peter's preaching in Rome. This tradition is attested by Papias (ca. AD 60–140), a third-generation Christian:

> This also the elder (John) used to say. When Mark became Peter's interpreter, he wrote down accurately, though by no means in order, as much as he remembered of the words and deeds of the Lord; for he had neither heard the Lord nor been in his company, but subsequently joined Peter.[1]

A few decades later, this tradition is confirmed by Clement of Alexandria (ca. 150–215):

> As Peter had preached the Word publicly at Rome, and declared the Gospel by the Spirit, many who were present requested that Mark, who had followed him for a long time and remembered well what he had said, should write them out. And having composed the Gospel he gave it to those who had requested it. When Peter learned of this, he neither directly hindered nor encouraged it.[2]

Similar testimony is given by Irenaeus (ca. 115–202), a disciple of Polycarp who in turn knew the apostle John; by Tertullian (ca. 155–225); and by Origen

---

1. As quoted in Eusebius, *Ecclesiastical History* 3.39.14–15 (ca. AD 303). Translation is from S. P. Kealy, *Mark's Gospel: A History of Its Interpretation* (New York: Paulist Press, 1982), 12.
2. As quoted in Eusebius, *Ecclesiastical History* 6.14.5–7. Translation is from Oden and Hall, *Mark*, xxiii.

(ca. 185–254).[3] This diverse testimony, from areas as far-flung as France, North Africa, Palestine, and Turkey, is weighty evidence that Peter was indeed Mark's primary source of information about the life of Jesus.

Some indications of Mark's close association with Peter appear in the New Testament. In the First Letter of Peter, Peter sends greetings from "Mark, my son" who is with him in "Babylon," a code name for Rome (1 Pet 5:13). Peter's early preaching as recorded in Acts (Acts 10:36–43) has some close similarities to the structure of Mark. And reading Mark's Gospel one gets the impression of discovering Jesus, day to day, through Peter's eyes (see, for example, 1:29–30, 35–37; 14:27–30). Numerous vivid details unique to Mark—the cushion in the boat (4:38), the nicknaming of James and John (3:17), the wretched condition of the demon-possessed man (5:3–5)—seem to reflect an eyewitness report.[4]

Mark the †Evangelist is traditionally identified with the Mark often mentioned in Acts, whose Jewish name was John (Acts 12:12, 25). If so, he was a Jewish Christian whose mother Mary owned a home in Jerusalem large enough for Christians to use as a meeting place—possibly the "upper room" where the Last Supper was held (Mark 14:15) and where the disciples stayed after the ascension (Acts 1:13). Mark was familiar with not only Peter but also several other great figures of the early Church. He was a cousin of Barnabas (Col 4:10), and served as an assistant on Paul's first missionary journey (Acts 13:5). For some unknown reason, Mark abandoned that mission (Acts 13:13), creating an awkward situation that led to a sharp dispute between Paul and Barnabas. Evidently Mark was later reconciled with Paul, who speaks of him with appreciation as a coworker for the †gospel (Col 4:10; 2 Tim 4:11; Philem 24). Later tradition holds that after serving Peter in Rome, Mark went on to establish the church in Alexandria in Egypt, and became the first bishop of that city.

For Whom Did Mark Write?

Several details corroborate the tradition that Mark's first readers were Roman Christians. Under the Emperor Nero (AD 64–68) the church in Rome suffered brutal persecution. After blaming Christians for the fire that destroyed Rome

---

3. To this list might be added the Anti-Marcionite Prologue, a document attached to the Gospels in many Old Latin manuscripts (ca. AD 160–180), and the Muratorian Canon, an ancient list of the books recognized as authoritative by the Church in Rome (ca. AD 170–190).

4. For further evidence of eyewitness testimony underlying Mark and the other Gospels, see Richard Bauckham, *Jesus and the Eyewitnesses: The Gospels as Eyewitness Testimony* (Grand Rapids and Cambridge: Eerdmans, 2006).

in 64, Nero punished his scapegoats by crucifying them, setting them on fire, and feeding them to wild beasts. Some, under torture or threats, abandoned the faith or even betrayed other believers.

Mark seems to be writing for Christians in crisis. He is the only Evangelist to mention that Jesus was with wild beasts (1:13), a predicament that would have special meaning to the Roman Christians. To the list of rewards promised to Jesus' disciples, Mark adds "with persecutions" (10:30). Only Mark records the saying that "everyone will be salted with fire" (9:49). He emphasizes Jesus' warnings that the disciples will suffer betrayal by relatives and persecution at the hands of authorities (13:9–13).

Mark also portrays the fears, flaws, and failures of Jesus' first disciples—known to his audience as the eminent leaders of the Church—with relentless honesty. The sons of Zebedee were reprimanded for seeking earthly prominence, yet Jesus promises that they will share in his destiny (10:39–40); Peter caved in under pressure (14:29–31), yet Mark's audience knows of his forgiveness and restoration, his courageous leadership, and perhaps his heroic martyrdom. The Evangelist thereby encourages his readers, showing that God's purposes are not foiled by human failure or opposition. The weaknesses of Jesus' followers and the violent hostility of his enemies only play into God's hands.

Another sign of a Roman setting for the Gospel is Mark's frequent use of Latin loan words, including military terms like legion, praetorium, and centurion, and the names of coins. His audience seems to be of mainly †Gentile origin, since he explains such Jewish customs as ritual washings for readers unfamiliar with them (7:3–4). When he occasionally includes an †Aramaic term for vividness, he is careful to provide a translation (3:17; 5:41; 7:11, 34; 15:34).

There is nearly unanimous agreement among scholars that Mark's Gospel was written within a few decades of Jesus' death and resurrection. There is less agreement, however, as to whether the Gospel should be dated before or after the fall of Jerusalem in AD 70. Several factors seem to point to a date prior to this watershed event. First, Jesus' prophecy of the temple's destruction is along the lines of Old Testament prophecies of doom, and contains no details that would suggest a description written after the fact. Second, the content and emphases of the Gospel cohere well with the historical situation of Christians under the persecutions of Nero in the late 60s. Finally, the early postbiblical sources mentioned above describe Mark as written either before the death of Peter (ca. AD 64–67), or shortly thereafter.[5]

---

5. For a fuller discussion, see Donahue and Harrington, *Gospel of Mark*, 41–46.

Mark among the Gospels

For much of Church history Mark has been the neglected Gospel, used only rarely in preaching or doctrinal exposition. Dozens of commentaries on Matthew, Luke, and John were written by the Fathers of the Church, but not one on Mark appears until the early Middle Ages.[6] This was partly due to a view, originating with St. Augustine, that Mark is basically an abbreviated version of Matthew. Indeed, of the 661 verses of Mark, some 90 percent are reproduced in Matthew, and some 55 percent are in Luke. Only a few verses of Mark are not found in the other †Synoptic Gospels (Matthew and Luke), so the Second Gospel did not seem to have much to say that was distinctive.

With the rise of critical biblical scholarship in the nineteenth century, intensive research was done to uncover the stages of oral and written tradition that led to the Gospels in their present form. There was a new surge of interest in what became known as the Synoptic Problem: Why are the three Synoptic Gospels · so different, yet so similar? Is there literary dependence among them? If so, who copied from whom? Which Gospel was composed first? By the twentieth century it was widely accepted that Mark was the most ancient Gospel, used by both Matthew and Luke. The verbal correspondences are too many and too extensive to be explained simply on the basis of common oral traditions. The passages shared by Matthew and Luke but not Mark, consisting mostly of Jesus' teachings, must have come from a different, hypothetical source, which scholars labeled Q (for the German word *Quelle*, "source"). Suddenly Mark had come to center stage: it was thought to be the Gospel closest to the actual events, the one that simply reported them without the theologizing interpretations added by the later Evangelists.

A century of further scholarship has exposed significant defects in that theory. Mark is now recognized as a historian, theologian, and pastor in his own right, whose Gospel displays considerable literary artistry. He does not randomly string episodes one after another, but skillfully weaves them together in pursuit of his distinctive theological and pastoral aims. This does not mean that he is not faithfully reporting what he has received, either from Peter or from other oral or written sources. But it does mean that he recounts the events in such a manner as to reveal a unique dimension of the mystery of Jesus Christ, a dimension that the Church recognizes as an indispensable part of her Scriptures (see the Catechism, 126–27).

---

6. The first commentary on Mark was either that of Venerable Bede (AD 673–735) or that of an anonymous seventh-century monk (once mistakenly attributed to Jerome). See Michael Cahill, "The First Markan Commentary," *Revue Biblique* 101 (1994): 258–68.

Where does that leave the question of the order of the Gospels? Most scholars today hold that Mark was composed first and was used by Matthew and Luke, for reasons that include the following: (1) It is harder to explain why Mark would omit key passages from his source, such as the infancy narratives, the Beatitudes, the Lord's Prayer, and the resurrection appearances, than why Matthew and Luke would add them. (2) It seems more likely that Matthew and Luke would soften Mark's blunt portrayal of the apostles' defects than that Mark would add this theme. (3) Similarly, Matthew and Luke omit some of the more human actions and emotions that Mark attributes to Jesus, which are harder to explain in light of Jesus' divinity. (4) If Mark is writing a digest of Matthew it is hard to see why he would add length and detail to many of the incidents he records. (5) Where the †Synoptics differ in the order of events, Matthew and Luke rarely agree against Mark, suggesting that they copied his work independently. (6) The Greek of Matthew and Luke is more polished than that of Mark; it seems that they consciously improved his style.[7]

A strong minority of scholars, however, contend that the priority of Matthew is more plausible: (1) In many passages Matthew and Luke differ slightly from Mark's wording in exactly the same way, which is hard to explain if they copied him independently. (2) The best explanation for the passages Matthew and Luke share is not a hypothetical document Q (for which there is no evidence), but that one used the other's work, as Luke 1:1 seems to indicate—specifically, that Mark used Matthew, and Luke used both Matthew and Mark. (3) Mark's omission of certain passages is explained by his intention of writing a brief, evangelistic Gospel conveying the essentials of the good news for new converts. (4) Mark's portrayal of the disciples' weaknesses is due to his direct knowledge of these through Peter. (5) Mark accents the human qualities of Jesus in order to show Jesus' human face to the suffering Christians of Rome. (6) Early Christian tradition held that Matthew was written first.[8]

How the Gospels were formed is a complex and fascinating problem that will probably not be solved before Jesus returns in glory. Most works of New Testament scholarship take Markan priority for granted, but it is important to keep in mind that our judgments are always hypothetical. No matter what sources our author used, we must study *his* work in order to understand his theology.

---

7. For more detailed arguments in favor of Markan priority, see C. M. Tuckett, "Synoptic Problem," in *The Anchor Bible Dictionary*, ed. David Noel Freedman, 6 vols. (New York: Doubleday, 1992), 6:263–70. For Markan priority without the Q hypothesis, see Mark Goodacre, *The Case against Q* (Harrisburg, PA: Trinity, 2002).

8. See, for instance, Irenaeus, *Against Heresies* 3.1.1; Fragments of Origen, in Eusebius, *Ecclesiastical History* 6.25.4–5. For more detailed arguments against the priority of Mark, see William Farmer, *The Gospel of Jesus: The Pastoral Relevance of the Synoptic Problem* (Louisville: Westminster John Knox, 1994).

Literary Style

The Gospel of Mark is deceptively simple. Mark writes in a plain, "street language" style of Greek that made his writing accessible to the uneducated but led others to disparage his work as unrefined and vulgar. Yet as modern literary critics have come to recognize, Mark writes with consummate skill. His narrative style is the most vivid of the Gospels. One of his favorite words is *euthys*, "immediately," used over forty times (as compared to six times in Matthew and once in Luke), giving his narrative a sense of urgency and fast-paced action. Mark often switches between past and present tense, as if to bring the action right into the present (a grammatical incongruity that most English translations do not attempt to reproduce). For example, a literal translation of Mark 1:40–44 would read like this:

> A leper comes to him and, kneeling down, begs him and says, "If you wish, you can make me clean." Moved with pity, he stretched out his hand and touched him, and he says to him, "I do will it. Be made clean." The leprosy left him immediately, and he was made clean. Then, warning him sternly, he dismissed him at once. Then he says to him, "See that you tell no one anything."

Although Mark is the shortest Gospel, lacking many of the lengthy teachings recorded by the other Evangelists, he often gives more detailed accounts of the episodes he does include (see, for instance, 2:1–12; 5:1–20). He frequently describes the emotional reactions of Jesus' audience, whether wonder (15:5, 44), astonishment (1:27; 2:12; 10:24), fear (9:6; 10:32), or perplexity (6:20). And he does not hesitate to portray Jesus' emotions: compassion (1:41), indignation (10:14), anger and exasperation (3:5; 7:34; 8:12), distress and sorrow (14:33–34).

Mark sometimes addresses his readers directly. For instance, "that you may know that the Son of Man has authority to forgive sins on earth" (2:10) can be read not only as Jesus' statement to the †Pharisees but also as Mark's comment to the reader. After Jesus' teaching on defilement, Mark adds, "Thus he declared all foods clean" (7:19), helping his readers grasp the full significance of what the Lord has just said. Jesus' long discourse on the Mount of Olives ends with a pointed warning to the reader: "What I say to you, I say to all: 'Watch!'" (13:37). In this way Mark draws his readers into the crisis of decision that faced Jesus' original audience. Who is Jesus? How will I respond to him? Is his death on the cross an abject failure, or is it God's plan of salvation for the world?

Theological Themes

The heart of Mark's theology is the paschal mystery, the paradox of the Messiah who enters into his glorious reign only through the self-abasement of the cross. Mark probably gained this insight through his early mentor, St. Paul (see, for instance, 1 Cor 2:2; Gal 2:19–20; Phil 2:5–11). The cross casts its light and shadow over the whole Gospel, as the destination toward which all Jesus' public ministry—and all Scripture—inexorably leads. But in a more subtle way, the resurrection too sheds its radiant light over the Gospel. Jesus' teachings direct his listeners' attention to the eternal life that he has come to give them (see 8:35b; 9:43; 10:30). His exorcisms and miracles prefigure his definitive victory over sin and Satan; his healings symbolize his raising of the dead on the last day.

Just as the truth of Jesus is found only in the cross, so is the secret of discipleship. To be a follower of Jesus is to share intimately in his life and destiny, as Paul also knew well (see Rom 8:17; Phil 3:8–11). Throughout the Gospel, Jesus' focus is on forming deep bonds of communion with his disciples and preparing them for the ordeal that lies ahead. Ironically, this formation seems not to succeed, since his companions are consistently un-comprehending, hardened, doubting, and inept; they finally abandon their master in his hour of trial. Yet even their failure is part of God's plan, for though they stumble, Jesus remains true, and through his total fidelity to the Father gains forgiveness and restoration for them. Just as in the Old Testament story of Israel, God's love is often met with infidelity and betrayal, yet is constantly renewed, so the Gospel ends with the joyous promise of an encounter with the risen Lord.

Mark offers a bold portrayal of Jesus. He is not afraid to report features that may have stunned, or even scandalized, his audience. He recounts that even Jesus' family thought he was mentally deranged (3:21). Only Mark records Jesus' question to the rich man: "Why do you call me good? No one is good but God alone" (10:18). Where Matthew says that Jesus *did not* do any miracles in his hometown because of the people's unbelief, Mark says he *could not* do any miracles there (6:5). He shows Jesus as ignorant of what his disciples were discussing (9:16, 33) or the time of the end (13:32). He depicts a profoundly human Jesus, who trembled at his approaching death (14:33) and felt abandoned by God (15:34). Yet for Mark these human touches do not in any way diminish Jesus' sovereign majesty as the Father's beloved Son. It is Mark who records the most direct affirmation by Jesus of his divine sonship found in any of the Gospels (see on 14:61–62).

Reading the Gospel of Mark Today

The Gospel of Mark and the three other canonical Gospels are unlike any other kind of literature. They are brief narratives recounting the life, ministry, and teachings of Jesus of Nazareth. In that sense they are roughly analogous to ancient biographies. But they are unique in that they are written from a standpoint of living faith in Jesus Christ, risen from the dead and exalted as Lord over all. For the Gospel writers, because Jesus is alive, all that he said and did in his earthly life is not merely a past event but a present source of grace and power to those who believe in him. They write so as to invite their readers to access that grace and power through faith.

One of the early readers of the Gospel was St. Ignatius, bishop of Antioch (ca. AD 35–110). On his way to martyrdom at Rome, Ignatius wrote, "I flee to the gospel as to the flesh of Jesus Christ."[9] What he meant is that the Gospels do not merely tell him about Jesus but *bring him into living contact with Jesus*. They are in a sense his Real Presence. This is the way the Church has understood the Gospels from ancient times, and it is why the events in Jesus' earthly life are traditionally called "mysteries." As we read or hear the account of these events, especially in the liturgy, we are led into "the invisible mystery of his divine sonship and redemptive mission" (Catechism, 515). That is, the Gospel events become a pattern and effective cause of Jesus' action within the members of his Church *now*. For this reason, interpretation of the Gospels can never be reduced to the application of exegetical methods. Although sound methods are important, ultimately the power of Scripture to bring us into contact with the living Christ is dependent on an ongoing work of the Spirit, bringing to light its deepest meaning and bearing witness to its truth in the mind of the reader.

The Gospels are also unique in that they are written in conscious continuity with the Scriptures of Israel. Indeed, they present Jesus as the culmination of God's whole plan of salvation, who fulfills and reveals the hidden meaning of the Old Testament. All God's dealings with his people Israel prefigure, lead up to, and find their full meaning in Christ. To read the Gospels properly, it is necessary to read them against their biblical background and to pay close attention to their rich tapestry of Old Testament quotations and allusions.

Finally, the Gospels are unique in that they are written in and for the community of believers, the Church. They are intended primarily to deepen the faith of those who have already heard the preaching of the good news and

---

9. *Letter to the Philadelphians* 5.1. Where not otherwise indicated, translations from ancient sources are my own.

responded to it in faith, though for some the Gospels may serve as a first encounter with Jesus.

The setting in which Mark wrote his Gospel is not unlike the situation of Christians today. Those striving to be faithful to Jesus may sometimes feel like a frightened boatful of disciples on the storm-tossed sea of a society that is often hostile to the gospel. As in Mark's day, to be a committed Christian can often mean suffering condescension or hostility from friends or colleagues and exclusion from positions of influence in the world of culture, education, or politics. In many parts of the world, being a Christian puts one at risk of persecution, discrimination, torture, or death. Yet the popes at the beginning of the third millennium have prophetically announced a new evangelization—a new mobilization of the Church to bring the good news once again to the ends of the earth—both to revitalize the lukewarm and to introduce Jesus to those who have never met him before. In such a context, the Gospel of Mark has fresh relevance as a means of evangelization and a source of rich insight on what it means to be a follower of Jesus.

The present commentary has come to birth thanks to the friendship and support of many of my fellow disciples on the way of Jesus Christ. I wish to thank especially my coeditors, Peter Williamson and Kevin Perrotta, for their thorough and incisive comments that greatly improved the manuscript. Jeff Wittung and the capable staff at Baker Academic have been tremendously helpful in guiding this book and series to publication. Thanks also to Fr. Frank Matera, Fr. J. Michael McDermott, Deacon Robert Schwartz, and Eric Sammons for their valuable comments, and to my many friends and family members who have helped bring this work to completion through their encouragement, enthusiasm, and prayers. Finally, this book is dedicated to Fr. Francis Martin, who first brought the words of Scripture to life for me in a summer course on the Gospel of Mark in 1987 and who never tires of preaching the life-giving message of the cross.

Outline of Mark

Prologue: The beginning of the good news (1:1–13)

Part I: "Who is this man?" (1:1–8:26)

  A. Proclamation of the kingdom with deeds of power (1:14–6:32)
- The call of the disciples and Jesus' mighty deeds (1:14–45)
- Controversies with the religious authorities (2:1–3:6)
- A new Israel and a new family of God (3:7–35)
- Parables of the kingdom (4:1–34)
- Jesus' authority over all that threatens us (4:35–5:43)
- Unbelief at Nazareth (6:1–6)
- The mission of the Twelve (6:7–32)

  B. Understanding the bread (6:33–8:26)
- Bread miracle, sea miracle, hardened hearts, healings (6:33–56)
- The new law of the gospel (7:1–23)
- An exorcism and a healing of Gentiles (7:24–37)
- Bread miracle, sea crossing, hardened hearts (8:1–21)
- Gradual healing of a blind man (8:22–26)

Hinge: Peter's confession of faith: "You are the Messiah!" (8:27–30)

Part II: Revelation of the suffering and glorious Messiah (8:31–16:20)

  A. On the way of discipleship (8:31–10:52)
- First passion prediction, inept response, teaching on discipleship (8:31–9:1)
- Transfiguration and an exorcism (9:2–29)
- Second passion prediction, inept response, teaching on discipleship (9:30–10:31)
- Third passion prediction, inept response, teaching on discipleship (10:32–45)
- Instantaneous healing of a blind man (10:46–52)

  B. The Lord comes to his temple (11:1–13:37)
- Jesus' triumphal entry and cleansing of the temple (11:1–26)
- Controversies establishing the basis for Jesus' authority (11:27–12:44)
- End times discourse (13:1–37)

  C. Passion, death, and resurrection (14:1–16:20)
- A woman's anointing; Judas's betrayal (14:1–11)
- The Last Supper (14:12–31)
- Agony, arrest, and desertion in Gethsemane (14:32–52)
- Trials before Jewish and Gentile rulers (14:53–15:15)
- Crucifixion, death, and burial: "Truly this man was the Son of God!" (15:16–47)
- The empty tomb (16:1–8)
- The Longer Ending (16:9–20)

Prologue to the Gospel

Mark 1:1–13

The opening verses of Mark (1:1–13) serve as a prologue, leading into the Gospel and introducing its key themes. What Matthew and Luke take almost four chapters to do, Mark does in thirteen densely packed verses: he introduces the Messiah, Jesus, and recounts the dramatic events that mark the beginning of his public ministry. From the start it is clear that Jesus' mission is both a continuation of and a decisive turning point in the plan of God that has unfolded through the history of Israel. And already in these opening verses, Jesus undergoes a testing, a confrontation, and a victory over †Satan—a prelude to the ultimate victory that will be accomplished at the end of his life.

The Beginning of the Good News (1:1)

---

¹The beginning of the gospel of Jesus Christ [the Son of God].

OT: Gen 1:1; Isa 40:9
NT: Mark 8:29; 15:39; John 20:31; Rom 1:1–4
Catechism: the good news, 422

1:1   The first verse of the Gospel is a title to the whole work. Like Matthew and John, Mark opens with an echo of the book of Genesis. **The beginning** recalls the first line of the creation narrative in Gen 1:1, and suggests that the good news that Mark is about to tell is a new beginning, a new work of God as original and stupendous as the creation of the universe.

What does **gospel** mean here? The Greek word *euangelion* (root of the English word evangelize) means "good news" or "joyful tidings," and often referred to festive public occasions such as a military victory or the coronation of the emperor. An inscription from about 9 BC calls the birthday of Caesar Augustus "good news for the world." For the Old Testament prophets, especially Isaiah, the "good news" is not a past event but a promise that God is coming to save his people:

> Go up onto a high mountain,
>   Zion, herald of glad tidings;
> Cry out at the top of your voice,
>   Jerusalem, herald of good news!
> Fear not to cry out
>   and say to the cities of Judah:
> Here is your God! (Isa 40:9; see Isa 52:7; 61:1)

Mark's announcement of "the beginning of the good news" is a resounding proclamation that now, in Jesus, the long-promised visitation of God has begun. The gospel is something to be preached (1:14; 13:10; 14:9; 16:15) and believed in (1:15). Indeed, so good is this good news that it is worth more than life itself (Mark 8:35; 10:29–30).[1]

What is the content of this good news? In a word, it is that **Jesus** is the **Christ, the Son the God**.[2] Jesus, meaning "†YHWH saves," is the Greek form of Joshua, the name of the ancient leader who led the Israelites into the promised land. Mark gives Jesus two titles—†Christ and Son of God—each of which had profound meaning for Jews. Christ, or Messiah, means "anointed." To declare that Jesus is the Christ is to proclaim that he is the fulfillment of the hopes of Israel, the promised descendant of David who would reestablish the reign of God. Even more, Jesus is the Son of God—a title whose full significance will be unfolded only gradually in the course of Mark's account. From his very first line Mark lets readers in on the secret: Jesus is the long-awaited Messiah, the Son of God in a unique and transcendent way. Yet his readers are invited to

---

1. In later usage, "gospel" also came to mean a written narrative of the life of Jesus, especially one of the four that the Church accepted into the †canon of Scripture.

2. The NAB puts this phrase in brackets to indicate that it is missing in some ancient manuscripts of the Gospel. A scribal error caused this phrase to be dropped from the original, or (less likely) added to it.

The Messiah

BIBLICAL BACKGROUND

Messiah comes from Hebrew *mashiah,* "anointed," which in Greek is *christos,* Christ. In ancient Israel, priests, prophets, and kings were installed in office by being anointed with oil (Exod 29:7; 1 Sam 10:1; 1 Kings 19:16), and the king was often referred to as "the Lord's anointed" (1 Sam 24:7; see Ps 2:2). When the kingship came to an end and Israel was conquered by a succession of foreign rulers, a prophetic expectation grew that God would send a new "anointed one" descended from King David, who would revive the royal dynasty and restore freedom, justice, peace, and prosperity to Israel (see Ps 89:21–38; Isa 61:1–3). For the early Church, the good news was that *Jesus* is this Messiah, the fulfillment of God's promises and the culmination of the ancient roles of priest, prophet, and king in a way that far surpasses the prophetic hopes. The New Testament uses the title Christ so often that it becomes almost a surname for Jesus.

share with the disciples their gradual discovery of the mystery of Jesus. Mark will place these two titles, Messiah and Son of God, on the lips of a Jew and a Gentile, respectively, at key points in his narrative (8:29; 15:39).

Reflection and Application (1:1)

Mark's opening line resonates with his excitement at the glad tidings he is conveying. He sees the coming of Jesus, preceded by that of John the Baptist, as the turning point in history, when God decisively acted to accomplish all that he had promised for so many centuries. At the time Mark wrote, the good news was beginning to explode upon the Mediterranean world, as the apostles and other Christians traveled throughout the empire, evangelizing in synagogues and town squares. Lives were being changed as people who had been lost in spiritual darkness and moral confusion came to know the living Christ and experience his love. Mark's evident joy at the tidings he has to share prompts the questions: Do we realize how good the good news is? Do we recognize that this news fulfills and far surpasses all the deepest longings of the human heart? Or have we settled for a diluted version of the gospel that has little power to impact our daily lives? God's entrance into human history in the person of Jesus Christ is news that is inexhaustibly new, as fresh and potent as on the day it was first proclaimed.

The Precursor (1:2–8)

²As it is written in Isaiah the prophet:
  "Behold, I am sending my messenger ahead of you;
    he will prepare your way.
  ³A voice of one crying out in the desert:
    'Prepare the way of the Lord,
      make straight his paths.'"

⁴John [the] Baptist appeared in the desert proclaiming a baptism of repentance for the forgiveness of sins. ⁵People of the whole Judean countryside and all the inhabitants of Jerusalem were going out to him and were being baptized by him in the Jordan River as they acknowledged their sins. ⁶John was clothed in camel's hair, with a leather belt around his waist. He fed on locusts and wild honey. ⁷And this is what he proclaimed: "One mightier than I is coming after me. I am not worthy to stoop and loosen the thongs of his sandals. ⁸I have baptized you with water; he will baptize you with the holy Spirit."

OT: Exod 23:20; Isa 40:3; Mal 3:1
NT: Acts 13:24–25. // Matt 3:1–12; Luke 3:1–18; John 1:23–28
Catechism: John the Baptist, 523, 717–20; baptism in water and the Spirit, 720
Lectionary: 1:1–8: Second Sunday of Advent (Year B); Mass for the Remission of Sins; 1:7–11: Baptism of the Lord (Year B)

Mark launches into a biblical quotation, showing that Jesus' coming was not out of the blue but was planned and prepared by God for centuries. For Mark, the Old Testament background is crucial for understanding what God is doing now in Jesus. Although Mark mentions only **Isaiah**, his quotation also weaves in phrases from Exodus and Malachi (v. 2). It was not uncommon to cite only the main source when combining related biblical texts. In the Exodus passage, God tells his people that he is sending an angel to guide them through the desert on their way to the promised land (Exod 23:20). Greek *angelos* (like its Hebrew counterpart, *malakh*) means both angel and messenger. Many centuries later, the prophet Malachi prophesied that a **messenger** would "prepare the way" for God's sudden coming on the day of the Lord (Mal 3:1). Malachi identified the messenger with the great prophet Elijah, whose reappearance would signal the events of the last days (Mal 3:23).

    Mark quotes from a section of Isaiah often called the "book of consolation" (Isa 40–55) because it is filled with words of comfort for God's people during their exile in Babylon. Isaiah announces a jubilant **voice, crying out** that the

1:2

1:3

exile will soon come to an end and the Lord will **prepare the way** by removing all obstacles so he can lead his people back through **the desert** to their homeland (Isa 40:3).

In the original passages God was speaking to his people, but Mark has reworked them to portray God speaking to his Son, telling him, Your coming will be prepared by a forerunner, John the Baptist. Thus **the Lord** whose way is prepared is Jesus! His **paths** will be made **straight**—that is, the people's hearts will be made ready for his coming—by the contrition for sin and the †repentance that come about through John's preaching. Mark is saying, in effect, "Israel, here is your God! God's promises are being fulfilled, and a new and greater return from exile is about to take place!"

1:4–5   It was not by chance that **John the Baptist** made his appearance **in the desert**. The desert is a place of deprivation, loneliness, and stripping away of comforts. The Jews would well remember the desert as the place of testing where their ancestors had wandered for forty years after the exodus, often complaining and rebelling against God, discovering God's severity toward sin but also his patience and merciful love. During this formative period, the Israelites were learning to depend on God to guide them and provide for all their needs—though they never learned that lesson completely. Centuries later, through the prophets, God recalled the desert wanderings as a time of intimacy and even of betrothal to his people (Jer 2:1–3; Hosea 2:16–17) and promised to restore the purity of that original relationship.

When John began his ministry the Jews were no longer in exile, but they were under the domination of a foreign power, the Roman Empire. For centuries there had been no prophets to speak God's word to them (see 1 Macc 9:27). In the highly charged atmosphere of the time, filled with conflicting movements, hopes, and expectations for the liberation of Israel, John's **baptism of repentance** made a powerful impact. Repentance (Greek *metanoia*) means literally "a change of mind." Like the prophets of old (see Isa 55:7; Jer 18:11; Zech 1:4), John was calling Israel to a wholehearted return to the Lord, a deep interior conversion through the acknowledgment of their sinful state and their need for **forgiveness**. The time of complacency and human self-sufficiency was over; the time to turn back to God in humble contrition had arrived. Although John's message was hardly a soothing one, it met a spiritual hunger in the people, attracting crowds from throughout †Judea.

"Baptize" was an ordinary Greek word that meant to dip, plunge, or immerse in water. Like the Old Testament prophets, John was proclaiming his message not only in words but in gesture. Why dip people in water? The Jews were familiar with ritual washings that symbolized interior purification (Lev 15; Ps 51:9). But John's invitation to a one-time immersion **in the Jordan River** was more than a cleansing. The Jordan River had great symbolic significance for the Jews. After the exodus Israel had entered the promised land by crossing the Jordan on dry land, led by Joshua (Josh 3). John was interpreting the events of Israel's history as part of a divine plan in which earlier events foreshadow and prepare for God's greater future purposes. John's baptism was a call for the Jews to reaffirm their identity as God's people, to come into the desert with God once more and symbolically reenter the promised land through water. A new exodus was occurring—not from captivity to Pharaoh but from captivity to sin.

Although John's wardrobe and peculiar diet may not have been unusual for desert nomads (see Lev 11:22), they reflected the simplicity and single-mindedness of a man totally focused on God. His lifestyle reinforced his message: put aside all encumbrances to be ready for what God is about to do. The hairy garment and **leather belt** are the same clothing that Elijah wore (2 Kings 1:8)—a signal that John is the new Elijah. The **locusts and wild honey** again evoke the exodus, where they represented God's judgment on sin (the plague of locusts, Exod 10:13–15) and his promises to his people (a land flowing with milk and honey, Exod 3:8; see Ps 119:103).

It is not surprising that some people wondered whether John himself might be the messiah (see Luke 3:15). But John is self-effacing; his whole message is focused on a mysterious One who **is coming after** him,[3] who is **mightier** than he. "Mighty" or the "Mighty One" is a term usually applied to God himself (Deut 10:17; 2 Sam 23:1; Ps 24:8). John sees himself as only a predecessor, not even worthy to perform the task of a slave for the one who is to come, to **loosen the thongs of his sandals.**[4]

John contrasts his own baptism as an outward sign of repentance with that of the mightier One, who **will baptize you with the holy Spirit.** To baptize, or drench, in the Spirit evokes the biblical promise that in the last times God would "pour out" his Spirit like water (Joel 3:1–2; Zech 12:10), bringing about the transformation of heart that would finally enable God's people to respond to him perfectly and experience his blessings (Isa 32:15–18; 44:3–5; Ezek 36:25–27). John's prophecy is one of the most frequently repeated statements in the New Testament (Matt 3:11; Luke 3:16; John 1:33; and on the lips of Jesus in Acts 1:5; 11:16). It reveals that John's water baptism, a bodily immersion, was only

1:6

1:7

1:8

---

3. The JB translation, "Someone is following me," should not be taken to imply that Jesus was a disciple of John the Baptist.

4. Later Jewish sources refer to untying the master's sandals as a task so menial that a Hebrew slave was exempt from it. See *Mekilta* to Exod 21:2; Talmud *b. Ketubboth* 96a.

the symbolic foreshadowing and preparation for an immersion into the very life of God. Mark's first readers, a community of early Christians, undoubtedly understood that the Baptist's prophecy was fulfilled on the day of Pentecost (Acts 2:1–18).

Reflection and Application (1:2–8)

John's prophecy that Jesus would "baptize you with the Holy Spirit" is fulfilled in the life of every new Christian through the sacraments of baptism and confirmation. "Just as the gestation of our first birth took place in water, so the water of Baptism truly signifies that our birth into the divine life is given to us in the Holy Spirit" (Catechism, 694; see 1302). Most Christians receive this unspeakable gift at a very young age; thus to experience its full effects we need to appropriate the gift of the Spirit personally through faith, ongoing conversion, and growth in the knowledge of God.

The phrase "baptism in the Spirit" has also become familiar to millions of English-speaking Christians through the charismatic renewal, which adapted the biblical term to express the life-changing encounter with Christ and outpouring of the power of the Holy Spirit that many experience. "Baptism in the Spirit" in this sense is not a sacrament but a coming alive of the graces received in sacramental baptism. Although the grace of Pentecost is manifested in different ways in every age, it is fundamentally the same grace of which John spoke and which Jesus poured out on the Church after his passion and resurrection.

The Baptism of Jesus (1:9–11)

---

⁹It happened in those days that Jesus came from Nazareth of Galilee and was baptized in the Jordan by John. ¹⁰On coming up out of the water he saw the heavens being torn open and the Spirit, like a dove, descending upon him. ¹¹And a voice came from the heavens, "You are my beloved Son; with you I am well pleased."

OT: Ps 2:7; Isa 42:1–7
NT: Mark 9:7; Luke 4:18. // Matt 3:13–17; Luke 3:21–22; John 1:32–34
Catechism: Baptism of Jesus, 535–37, 1223–25; descent of Spirit on Jesus, 1286
Lectionary: Infant Baptism; Confirmation; Christian Initiation Apart from the Easter Vigil

1:9   Given the exalted baptism that Jesus is going to administer (v. 8), it seems surprising that he now comes in the role of a lowly penitent, to be **baptized in**

the Jordan by John. Mark does not explain why Jesus comes to the Jordan valley from his hometown in **Nazareth of Galilee**, but we can surmise that he does so because he recognizes John's ministry as the prelude to his own (see v. 14). Why does Jesus submit to a "baptism of repentance for the forgiveness of sins" (v. 4)? Not because he himself is a sinner (1:1; see 2 Cor 5:21), but because of his total solidarity with sinful humanity, a solidarity that begins now and will lead inexorably to the cross. Indeed, Jesus' baptism is an anticipation of his passion. Immersion in water is a symbol of death (see Ps 69:2–3; 124:4–5; Jon 2:3–5), and Jesus will later speak of his death as a "baptism" (Mark 10:38). Jesus, like Moses, acts as the ideal intercessor, not standing apart from sinners but in solidarity with them under God's judgment (Exod 32:31–32). In so doing, he acknowledges God's just judgment on sin, while at the same time offering to God the response of perfect †repentance on behalf of the people.

Jesus' **coming up out of the water** (*anabainō*) is answered by a coming down (*katabainō*) of the Spirit from above. According to the Old Testament, sin creates an insuperable barrier, distancing humanity from the holiness of God (see Isa 59:2). God would "come down" to his people only after they had been cleansed of impurity (Exod 19:10–11). The Spirit's descent upon Jesus foreshadows his descent upon the Church at Pentecost, after sin has been removed by the cross.

1:10

Todd Bolen/BiblePlaces.com

Fig. 1. The Jordan River.

Christ Sanctified All Water by His Baptism

"The Lord Jesus came to baptism and willed to have his holy body washed with water. Perhaps someone will say: 'Why did he who is holy want to be baptized?' Listen, then! Christ is baptized not that he may be sanctified in the waters but that he himself may sanctify the waters and purify by his own purification the streams he touches. . . . For when the savior is washed, then all water is cleansed for our baptism and the fount is purified, so that the grace of the washing may be administered to the peoples who would come after. Christ takes the lead in baptism, then, so that the Christian peoples might follow with confidence" (St. Maximus of Turin).[a]

a. *Sermon on Holy Epiphany.*

The whole cosmos is impacted by Jesus' act of humility. The **heavens** are not gently opened but **torn** asunder—a sign that the barrier between God and man is being removed. Israel had pleaded for God to intervene decisively in human events: "Oh, that you would rend the heavens and come down" (Isa 63:19). Now that plea is answered! The same verb "tear" will reappear at a crucial point near the end of the Gospel, when the curtain of the temple is torn from top to bottom at Jesus' death (Mark 15:38), completing the reconciliation of heaven and earth that began at his baptism.

The Spirit's descent in the form of **a dove** recalls the Spirit hovering over the waters at creation (Gen 1:2)[5] and the dove that signaled a new beginning for the world after the flood (Gen 8:8–12). As in his opening line, Mark again hints that, in Jesus, God is bringing about a new creation.

Jesus' baptism is a turning point in his life. With this event he is "anointed" by the Spirit (see Isa 61:1; Acts 10:38) and formally inaugurates his mission as Messiah. By sharing in Israel's baptism of repentance, he has committed himself fully to the Father's call on his life: to be the obedient servant who would be innocent yet "counted among the wicked" because he bears the sins of many (Isa 42:1; 53:11–12).

1:11   In further response to Jesus' baptism is a **voice . . . from the heavens**, obviously that of God the Father. Now we see the whole Trinity involved in this event.[6] God

5. The connection is not as clear in the NAB, which reads "a mighty wind swept over the waters." The Hebrew term *ruah*, like the Greek term *pneuma*, can mean both "wind" and "spirit."

6. Mark does not have an explicitly developed theology of the Trinity, but the fact that he attributes distinct acts to the Father (1:11; 9:7), Jesus, and the Spirit (13:11) shows his implicit awareness of the distinction of Persons in God.

himself puts his stamp of approval on Jesus' mission and delights in his obedient acceptance of it. His words of affirmation, **You are my beloved Son; with you I am well pleased**, are full of scriptural echoes. In Ps 2:7 (RSV), God says to the king of Israel, "You are my son; today I have begotten you," and promises him all the nations of the earth as an inheritance. In Isaiah, God speaks of a servant who would faithfully carry out his will: "Behold my servant, whom I uphold, my chosen, in whom my soul delights; I have put my spirit upon him" (Isa 42:1 RSV). Jesus is the Messiah-King and chosen servant on whom the Spirit rests. And like Isaac, the "beloved son" of Abraham (Gen 22:12), he will willingly offer his life in sacrifice. In Hebrew thought, "beloved son" denotes "only son"; thus, Jesus' relationship with the Father is unlike that of anyone else.

Mark does not indicate that anyone but Jesus saw the Spirit descend or heard the divine voice.[7] Jesus' exalted identity is concealed under the appearance of an ordinary Jewish man coming to John for baptism. But Mark's readers are privy to this secret exchange between the divine Persons.

Reflection and Application (1:9–11)

As God's beloved Son, Jesus embodies Israel, who was called God's son (see Exod 4:22; Hosea 11:1) but could never fully live up to that status. Yet God's words of affirmation and love precede Jesus' accomplishment of his mission and are not a result of it. The New Testament proclaims that all of Jesus' followers have become children of God, participating in his own relationship with the Father (see Rom 8:15–16; 1 John 5:1). Thus these words are spoken to each of us as well: "You are my beloved son," "You are my beloved daughter." Only in accepting our identity as a beloved child of the Father is it possible for us too to embark courageously on the mission to which God has called us.

Temptation in the Desert (1:12–13)

¹²**At once the Spirit drove him out into the desert, ¹³and he remained in the desert for forty days, tempted by Satan. He was among wild beasts, and the angels ministered to him.**

OT: Gen 3:24; Deut 2:7; 8:2
NT: // Matt 4:1–11; Luke 4:1–13

---

7. Compare Matt 3:17, where the heavenly voice speaks to the people about Jesus; and John 1:32–34, where it is John who bears testimony to Jesus.

Catechism: Jesus' temptations, 538–40; Jesus and angels, 333
Lectionary: 1:12–15: First Sunday of Lent (Year B)

1:12–13   Having been anointed by the Spirit, Jesus begins his mission without delay. Since he has associated himself with sinners by undergoing John's "baptism of repentance" (v. 4), the **Spirit** immediately impels him into the consequences of that decision—consequences that will eventually lead to the cross. As Adam and Eve were driven out of the garden (Gen 3:24), Jesus is driven **out into the desert**, the barren wilderness around the Dead Sea. There he remains for **forty days**, a number that signifies a time of testing, as Israel was tested during Moses' forty days on Mount Sinai (Exod 24:18; 32:1), and during the forty years in the desert (Deut 8:2). Jesus relives the story of Israel, but as an obedient Son who is totally faithful in his own trial in the desert.

The desert is depicted in Scripture as the realm of evil powers, symbolized by the predatory beasts that lurk there (Lev 16:10; Isa 35:7–9; Ezek 34:25).[8] Jesus goes there to be **tempted** (or "put to the test," NJB) **by** †**Satan**, that is, to be tested in his resolve to carry out his messianic mission in accord with the Father's will. He faces the same decision as Adam and Eve in the garden (Gen 3:1–6) and Israel in the desert (Exod 15:25; 16:4)—but unlike them, he rebuffs temptation and stands fast in his determination to please the Father. "Satan" means "adversary" and is synonymous with the devil, the prince of †demons (Mark 3:23–26), who will oppose Jesus at every turn. Jesus enters into Satan's territory deliberately, to begin his campaign against the powers of evil. He is looking for a fight! Yet he will confront Satan not with a blast of divine lightning, but in his frail human nature, empowered by the Spirit.

Mark's mention that Jesus was **among wild beasts**, evidently without harm, recalls Isaiah's prophecy that at the coming of the Messiah even wild beasts would be tamed (Isa 11:1–9; see Ezek 34:25–28), restoring God's order to creation. The **angels ministered to him**, just as they had accompanied Israel in the desert (Exod 14:19) and provided food for Elijah (1 Kings 19:5–7).

Reflection and Application (1:12–13)

Christian tradition has always recognized the spiritual battle as an essential part of life in Christ. Indeed, all human history is a story of combat with the powers of evil (Catechism, 409). This combat entails both the struggle against our own tendencies to sin and the rejection of Satan and all his glamorous

---

8. Paradoxically, the desert is also viewed as a place of solitude and withdrawal from human society and thus of special intimacy with God (see on 1:3 above).

Christ's Battle against Satan

St. Lawrence of Brindisi comments, "Christ came into the world to do battle against Satan, to do away with idolatry, and to turn the world to faith and piety and the worship of the true God. He could have accomplished this by using the weapons of his might and coming as he will come to judge, in glory and majesty, just as he manifested himself in his transfiguration. Who would not then have believed in Christ? But in order that his victory might be the more glorious, he willed to fight Satan in our weak flesh. It is as if an unarmed man, right hand bound, were to fight with his left hand alone against a powerful army; if he emerged victorious, his victory would be regarded as all the more glorious. So Christ conquered Satan with the right hand of his divinity bound and using against him only the left hand of his weak humanity."[a]

a. From *A Word in Season: Readings for the Liturgy of the Hours* (Villanova, PA: Augustinian Press, 1999), 7:245.

seductions (Catechism, 2752). Following the example of Jesus and empowered by his Spirit, we are to repel the enemy through prayer and perseverance. We may sometimes feel like singularly feeble warriors. But God never leaves us without the help of the angels in this battle, and through faith we can experience the victory won by Christ on the cross.

A New Teaching with Authority

Mark 1:14–45

The end of John the Baptist's public ministry signals the beginning of that of Jesus. The mission of the precursor—to "prepare the way" for the Son of God (v. 2)—has been accomplished, and Jesus has been anointed for his own mission by the Holy Spirit. Jesus now begins a tour of preaching in his native region of Galilee. His message is not in words only but in deeds of power and authority that will make the kingdom of God an experienced reality.

Jesus Begins to Evangelize (1:14–15)

---

¹⁴After John had been arrested, Jesus came to Galilee proclaiming the gospel of God: ¹⁵"This is the time of fulfillment. The kingdom of God is at hand. Repent, and believe in the gospel."

OT: Isa 52:7; 61:1–2
NT: // Matt 4:12–17; Luke 4:14; John 4:1–3
Catechism: proclamation of the kingdom, 543–46
Lectionary: 1:14–20: Common of Pastors; Admission to Candidacy for the Diaconate and the Priesthood

1:14–15   Mark notes here only that **John had been arrested**; later he will provide full details about the Baptist's fate (6:14–29). The Greek word for arrested (*paradidōmi*) literally means "handed over," and is the same word translated "betrayed" when applied to Jesus in the passion narrative (14:10–11, 18). The shadow of the cross looms over the beginning of Jesus' mission, since John's

Galilee

Galilee, the northern part of the promised land, was populated by several of the tribes of Israel when they entered the land in the fifteenth century BC. But after the Assyrians invaded Israel in 722 BC (see 2 Kings 15:29), they deported the ten northern tribes and forcibly planted foreign ethnic groups in their place. Because of its mixed population, the region came to be called "Galilee of the Gentiles," and its inhabitants were looked down on by other Jews as an impure race. Yet the prophet Isaiah announced that one day God would manifest himself in Galilee, and that a "great light" would shine "upon those who dwelt in the land of gloom" (Isa 8:23–9:1). The fact that Jesus began his public ministry there was a sign of the fulfillment of that hope.

own sufferings in accord with God's plan prefigure those of Jesus. Jesus' followers, in turn, will share his destiny of being "handed over" to their enemies (13:9–12).

Jesus' preaching is about **the gospel of God**, that is, the good news of salvation that is both from God and about God. Verse 15 sums up the core of his message. The **time of fulfillment** means that now, in Jesus, God is breaking into history to fulfill his promises and bring his whole plan to completion. It is a decisive moment, a turning point. This moment, fixed and determined long ago by God, marks the beginning of the definitive stage in salvation history.

The †**kingdom of God** is a favorite theme in the †Synoptics and the most characteristic term Jesus uses to signify what he is about. Later he will unfold its meaning in a series of parables (4:1–32). Although this phrase never appears in the Old Testament, it sums up Israel's yearning for the full manifestation of God's authority in Israel and in the whole world: "The LORD of hosts will reign" (Isa 24:23; see 52:7; Zech 14:9).

Jesus' announcement that the kingdom is **at hand** suggests both a present and a future quality, like a sunrise below the horizon. The kingdom is already present, embodied in Jesus' own person. Indeed, throughout his ministry it will become evident that the "foreign occupation" of sin, Satan, disease, and death is being overthrown. Yet the kingdom is incipient and partly veiled; like seeds sown in the ground, it will keep growing until it reaches its consummation (4:26–29).

The arrival of the kingdom calls for a twofold human response: to **repent, and believe in the gospel**. Jesus is taking up a theme of the prophets: God's continual call for his people to repent or "turn back" to him with all their hearts (Neh 1:9; Isa 44:22; Hosea 14:2). The Baptist had already begun to sound this call (v. 4). But Jesus adds a new accent with the invitation to *believe*, that is, trustingly accept and yield to what God is doing in him. The kingdom is near enough that anyone who so chooses can reach out and lay hold of it through faith.

Reflection and Application (1:14–15)

The prayer Jesus taught his disciples, although not recorded by Mark, provides the most concise interpretation of the meaning of the kingdom of God: "Your kingdom come, your will be done, on earth as in heaven" (Matt 6:10). The kingdom of God is wherever God's will is done, which already takes place fully in heaven but begins on earth in every heart that surrenders to him. As Paul observes, whoever chooses to live in this kingdom experiences "peace, and joy in the Holy Spirit" (Rom 14:17).

The Call of the First Disciples (1:16–20)

> [16]As he passed by the Sea of Galilee, he saw Simon and his brother Andrew casting their nets into the sea; they were fishermen. [17]Jesus said to them, "Come after me, and I will make you fishers of men." [18]Then they abandoned their nets and followed him. [19]He walked along a little farther and saw James, the son of Zebedee, and his brother John. They too were in a boat mending their nets. [20]Then he called them. So they left their father Zebedee in the boat along with the hired men and followed him.

OT: 1 Kings 19:19–21; Jer 16:14–16
NT: John 1:35–42. // Matt 4:18–22; Luke 5:1–11
Catechism: Jesus and his disciples, 520, 787–88; vocation, 863–65

1:16–17   Now that Jesus' ministry has begun, his call to repent and believe quickly becomes personal. As he passes by the **Sea of Galilee**, he sees two brothers, **Simon** and **Andrew**, going about their daily business, which happens to be commercial fishing. What is striking about Jesus' call is the authority with which it is issued. He is asking these men to accept a complete and permanent change of lifestyle for the sake of a totally new destiny. It was not unusual for †disciples to gather around a learned rabbi to spend a period of time studying the †law with him. But here Jesus takes the initiative, choosing whom he wishes. Later in the Gospel, Mark will portray the prominent role of Simon,

Who Is a Disciple?

LIVING
TRADITION

St. Basil, a fourth-century doctor of the Church, wrote this about becoming a Christian: "A disciple is, as the Lord himself taught us, whoever draws near to the Lord to follow him—to hear his words, to believe and obey him as Lord and king and doctor and teacher of truth. . . . So, whoever believes in the Lord and presents himself ready for discipleship must first learn to set aside every sin and everything that distracts from the obedience owed to the Lord."[a]

a. *On Baptism* 1.2.

---

whom Jesus renames Peter, as leader and spokesman of the disciples (3:16; 8:29; 14:37; 16:7).

The call to be **fishers of men** evokes a prophecy of Jeremiah in which God promised to send out "many fishermen" to gather in the Israelites who had been scattered among the nations (Jer 16:14–16; see Mark 13:27). Jesus' first disciples may have recalled this prophecy with a dawning sense of excitement as they began to realize the momentous significance of the vocation into which they were entering.

Mark emphasizes the prompt and radical obedience of these ordinary fisher-men: immediately **they abandoned their nets and followed him**. The Greek text includes the term *euthys*, "immediately," which is left untranslated in the NAB. Now that "the time of fulfillment" has come (v. 15) there is no time for dillydallying. Just as when God called their forefather Abraham (Gen 12:1–4), there is no hesitation, no discussion, no questions. Elijah's call of Elisha (1 Kings 19:19–21) had also interrupted his daily work—but whereas Elisha begged for permission to take leave of his family first, the disciples drop everything to follow Jesus (see Mark 10:28).

1:18

The pattern is repeated with **James** and **his brother John**, who are **mending their nets**, probably in preparation for the next night's fishing. The presence of **hired men** and a **boat** indicates that the fishing business of Zebedee and sons enjoyed some prosperity. But in response to Jesus' call, there is a complete abandonment of both occupation and **father**. To part so suddenly with their father would have been shocking in the social context of the day, where family obligations were paramount (see Sir 3:16). It illustrates the absoluteness of Jesus' claim, taking precedence over even the closest human bonds (Mark 10:29–30).

1:19–20

These four, especially Peter, James, and John, become Jesus' most intimate friends (1:29; 13:3; 14:33). Mark never hesitates to display their failures as disciples (8:32–33; 10:35–40; 14:66–72). Yet the force of that initial call endured and eventually matured into a heroic conformity to Christ and courage in spreading the gospel. Peter, leader of the apostles (Matt 16:18; Mark 16:7), stood up on the day of Pentecost and "caught" three thousand souls for Christ (Acts 2:38–41). According to tradition, both he and his brother Andrew were later martyred by crucifixion. James, traditionally known as James the Greater, became one of the earliest Christian martyrs, executed by Herod (Acts 12:2). John is regarded by tradition as the longest-lived disciple and author of the Fourth Gospel.

Reflection and Application (1:16–20)

Prior to Jesus' call, the four fishermen were what some might call "nobodies." There was no unusual aptitude, talent, or prominence to explain Jesus' choice. Indeed, they were hardly auspicious recruits for one who intended to gather in God's people from among the nations and inaugurate the reign of God. Yet that is equally true for most of Jesus' subsequent followers. Every Christian is chosen by him personally and is given an irreplaceable role in the advance of the kingdom, along with all the resources needed to carry it out.

Mark will repeatedly emphasize the high cost of discipleship—and its even greater rewards (see 10:29–30). Following Jesus means a break with the past and a willingness to let go of all other attachments. Not everyone is called literally to abandon their profession or family, but all are called to put everything in second priority to him. Saying yes to that call is the first step in a lifelong adventure.

The Demons' Demise Begins (1:21–28)

²¹Then they came to Capernaum, and on the sabbath he entered the synagogue and taught. ²²The people were astonished at his teaching, for he taught them as one having authority and not as the scribes. ²³In their synagogue was a man with an unclean spirit; ²⁴he cried out, "What have you to do with us, Jesus of Nazareth? Have you come to destroy us? I know who you are—the Holy One of God!" ²⁵Jesus rebuked him and said, "Quiet! Come out of him!" ²⁶The unclean spirit convulsed him and with a loud cry came out of him. ²⁷All were amazed and asked one another, "What is this? A new teaching with authority. He commands even the unclean spirits and they obey him." ²⁸His fame spread everywhere throughout the whole region of Galilee.

NT: Acts 16:18. // Luke 4:31–37
Catechism: exorcisms, 550, 1673; sabbath, 345–49

The call of the first disciples is followed by Jesus' first miraculous work, an exorcism. By this act Jesus' announcement of the kingdom (v. 15) becomes dramatically perceptible and concrete. Throughout the public ministry Mark shows Jesus' progressive dismantling of the powers of darkness, the advancement of his assault on Satan's kingdom that began with the temptation in the desert (1:13; see 3:23–27).

Jesus proceeds with his new disciples to **Capernaum**, a small fishing village on the northwest shore of the Sea of Galilee and the home base of his ministry in Galilee. According to Mark, Capernaum was the hometown of at least two disciples (v. 29), and Jesus took up residence there (2:1). By the first century AD most towns with a sizable Jewish population had a †**synagogue** where the faithful gathered for prayer, readings, and instruction in the Law and Prophets. As a Jew faithful to the religious customs of his people, Jesus regularly observed **the †sabbath** by attending the synagogue services (see 3:1; 6:2).

1:21

Since any man conversant with the Scriptures could be invited to comment on the readings (see Acts 13:14–15), Jesus takes the occasion to teach. Mark says nothing here about the content of Jesus' teaching. What is most important

1:22

Fig. 2. Ruins of a fourth-century synagogue at Capernaum.

Todd Bolen/BiblePlaces.com

is its effect. First, the people are **astonished**, for he teaches with **authority**. Mark will repeatedly emphasize the wonder, awe, and astonishment of Jesus' listeners at his words and deeds (6:2; 7:37; 10:26; 11:18). In contrast to **the** †**scribes**, Jesus is not merely offering his opinions or handing on traditions of biblical interpretation. He speaks as one who has authority *in himself* to reveal the definitive meaning of the Scriptures.

1:23–24   Second, Jesus' teaching has the intrinsic effect of exposing evil so that it can be expelled.[1] Mark does not explain whether the **man with an** †**unclean spirit** was a regular synagogue attendee or whether he came specifically to disrupt Jesus' sermon. But in the presence of Jesus, the grip of evil on the man comes to light and he cries out in fear and rage, **What have you to do with us?** The spirit is challenging Jesus' encroachment on the demons' formerly uncontested territory, evidently aware that his coming portends their downfall. The spirit claims hidden knowledge of Jesus' identity, a frequent demonic tactic (3:11; 5:7) that may be intended to catch Jesus off guard or gain some control over him. But the attempt is futile.

"Holy One" is a term usually reserved for God (1 Sam 2:2; Hosea 11:9) but is occasionally used for those who are consecrated in his service as priests or prophets (Num 16:5–7; 2 Kings 4:9; Ps 106:16). **Holy One of God** is an accurate title for Jesus (see John 6:69), but not one that he wants publicized at this point in his mission. He will reveal his identity on his own terms and in his own time, to ensure that it will be rightly understood.

1:25–26   Jesus sternly rebukes the spirit: **Quiet!** (literally, "Be muzzled!") **Come out of him!** In a final show of defiance, **the unclean spirit** convulses the man as it departs, helpless before Jesus' word of command. Already the Baptist's prophecy of a "mightier one" to come (v. 7) is being fulfilled before the people's eyes. The demon's tyranny is over and the possessed man is set free.

1:27–28   The people react with amazement: **What is this? A new teaching with authority.** They recognize an intrinsic connection between Jesus' teaching and his power to dispel evil. Jesus' teaching is "new" not only because it has never been heard before, but because it has power to accomplish what it communicates (see Isa 55:11). The teaching itself—the revelation of the good news of God and his plan—frees human beings from their captivity to evil (see 1:39; 6:12–13). As a result of this first manifestation of divine authority Jesus' **fame** spreads **everywhere** throughout Galilee.

1. The NAB loses something of the dramatic tension by eliminating Mark's term *euthys*, "immediately," used three times in this passage (vv. 21, 23, 28). Here the demon-possessed man comes on the scene "immediately" as Jesus teaches.

The Sabbath

The sabbath (Hebrew *shabbat*) is the seventh day of the week, on which God "rested" after the creation of the world (Gen 2:2–3) and commanded a day of rest for his people (Exod 20:10–11; Lev 23:3). In the Old Testament, the sabbath was the sign of humanity's special dignity, setting us apart from the rest of creation.[a] The sabbath was also a sign of God's irrevocable †covenant with Israel (Exod 31:16) and a memorial of their liberation from bondage in Egypt (Deut 5:15). Jesus never fails to respect the holiness of this day. He initiates many works of healing and deliverance on the sabbath[b] as a sign of the renewal of the covenant and the restoration of human dignity that had been marred by the fall.

a. See Pope John Paul II, apostolic letter *Dies Domini* (1998), 11–12; Abraham Joshua Heschel, *The Sabbath: Its Meaning for Modern Man* (New York: Farrar, Straus, and Giroux, 1951), 16–18.
b. Mark 1:29–31; 3:1–5; Luke 13:10–17; 14:1–4; John 5:1–9; 9:1–14.

Reflection and Application (1:21–28)

The story of Jesus' first exorcism portrays the forces of evil in a way that may appear to readers today as strikingly personal. For Mark, as for the whole New Testament, evil is not an impersonal force but is concentrated in invisible, malevolent beings who are bent on destroying human beings and hindering God's plan of salvation. These evil spirits are responsible for various mental and even physical maladies (7:25; 9:17–27; see Matt 12:22; Luke 13:11). Some exegetes, noting that the Gospels do not always clearly distinguish between illness and demonic possession, have concluded that the references to demons

Unclean Spirits

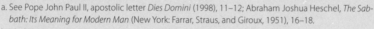

"Demon" and "unclean spirit" are synonymous terms in the Gospels for invisible, supernatural beings who wreak havoc in human life and are sometimes able to control an individual of whom they take possession (Matt 12:43–45; Mark 5:2–5). They are designated as "unclean," using an Old Testament term for a person or thing that is ritually defiled and therefore prohibited from taking part in worship. Because Jesus came to destroy the works of Satan (1 John 3:8), casting out demons and undoing their effects was a central aspect of his public ministry.

Exorcisms in Church Tradition

Following the example of Jesus, Catholic tradition has always recognized the need for exorcisms to free those possessed by evil spirits. Although sensationalized by movies like *The Exorcist*, exorcisms are done only in strictly defined cases and according to rigorous guidelines. The Catechism states: "In a simple form, exorcism is performed at the celebration of Baptism. The solemn exorcism, called 'a major exorcism,' can be performed only by a priest and with the permission of the bishop. The priest must proceed with prudence, strictly observing the rules established by the Church. Exorcism is directed at the expulsion of demons or to the liberation from demonic possession through the spiritual authority which Jesus entrusted to his Church. Illness, especially psychological illness, is a very different matter; treating this is the concern of medical science. Therefore, before an exorcism is performed, it is important to ascertain that one is dealing with the presence of the Evil One, and not an illness" (1673).

are simply a mythical way of symbolizing the misfortunes to which human beings are prone. The Church has always taught, however, that demons are real spiritual beings, fallen angels who were created by God but became evil by their own free choice (Catechism, 391–95). Anyone tempted to dismiss accounts of demons as fables does not have to look far to see evidence of their influence today. Such phenomena as "racial cleansing," group suicides, and the sexual abuse of children show a more than merely human malice at work, seeking to destroy the image of God in man. But as frightening and real as is the power of demons, the authority of Christ is infinitely superior. Through his cross and resurrection, Christ definitively conquered the powers of hell. For the present time, however, their malicious actions are permitted by God, who is able to work good out of every evil (Rom 8:28). The grace of baptism affords us protection from demons and the strength to resist their seductive influence.

The Healing of Peter's Mother-in-Law (1:29–34)

²⁹On leaving the synagogue he entered the house of Simon and Andrew with James and John. ³⁰Simon's mother-in-law lay sick with a fever. They immediately told him about her. ³¹He approached, grasped her hand, and helped her up. Then the fever left her and she waited on them. ³²When it was evening, after sunset, they brought to him all who were ill

or possessed by demons. ³³The whole town was gathered at the door. ³⁴He cured many who were sick with various diseases, and he drove out many demons, not permitting them to speak because they knew him.

OT: Jer 17:24
NT: Mark 15:41; Luke 10:40; John 12:2. // Matt 8:14–17; Luke 4:38–41
Catechism: Christ the physician, 1503–5

The first exorcism is directly followed by the first physical healing—another visible manifestation of the presence of the kingdom. For the Gospels, illness is closely related to demonic oppression, as part of the condition of fallen humanity and a sign of Satan's domination over human beings, from which Jesus came to liberate us (see Matt 12:22; Mark 9:20, 25; Luke 13:16).

After the **synagogue** service, Jesus enters **the house of Simon and Andrew**. **1:29**
Archaeologists have unearthed the probable remains of this house near the synagogue in Capernaum, under the ruins of an ancient church that was built on the site. The house consists of a cluster of small rooms built of basalt rock, surrounding an open courtyard that was probably shared by the extended family. Now that the disciples have committed themselves to share the life and destiny of Jesus, he enters their home and takes interest in the intimate concerns of their family life.

Simon's wife is not mentioned here, but she later accompanies him on his **1:30**
missionary journeys (1 Cor 9:5). Her mother is bedridden by **fever**, which at the time was often caused by malaria and could be life-threatening. The severity of the illness is shown by the woman's inability to carry out the demands of hospitality for her honored guest. The disciples demonstrate the Christian response to troubles: they **immediately** tell Jesus about it, even without knowing what he is going to do.

Jesus' healings often involve his physical contact with the patient, a personal **1:31**
and consoling touch. In this case he **grasped her hand** and **helped her up** (literally "raised her up," the same word used for his own resurrection, 16:6). This woman's recovery from illness is a foreshadowing of the resurrection on the last day (12:24–26). Her immediate reaction is a model of discipleship: **she waited on them**. The Greek verb, *diakoneō*, later becomes a standard term for Christian ministry (Acts 6:2), from which we derive the word "deacon." It is what Jesus himself said he came to do: "not to be served but to serve" (Mark 10:45). The right response to an experience of Jesus' healing power is to begin to spend oneself in service to him and his disciples, that is, to the Church. Women exemplify this service in a particular way in the Gospels (Mark 15:41; Luke 10:40; John 12:2).

1:32–34   The first exorcism and first healing spark the first gathering of crowds around Jesus. He is now a public figure, sought after by all who labor under the debilitating effects of sin. The people wait until **after sunset** because of the sabbath regulations prohibiting the carrying of burdens (Jer 17:24). In Jewish reckoning, the day begins at sunset (Gen 1:5; Lev 23:32), so the sabbath runs from sundown on Friday to sundown on Saturday. The people seek Jesus' help for their most basic, practical needs—health for themselves and their loved ones—and he responds without a hint of reproach. The work of healing, in all its senses, is at the heart of his messianic mission. The Greek verb for **cured**, *therapeuō*, is the root of the English word therapy, and often implies treating or taking care of the sick. The implication may be that Jesus spent time ministering tenderly to each afflicted person. **Many** does not imply that some were not healed, but simply that a large number is involved. The exorcism in the synagogue earlier that day (1:27) was the start of a rout, as the demons flee helplessly before Jesus' command. Again he forbids **them to speak**, because they would disclose his identity at an inopportune time and in the wrong way.

For Mark, healing and casting out demons are of central importance in Jesus' ministry. They serve as his audiovisual aids, making the presence of the kingdom real and perceptible, and as such they are inseparably linked to the proclamation of the gospel, both for Jesus and for his disciples (6:12–13; 16:15–18). Jesus calls himself the physician (2:17) and his mission is to seek and save the lost (Luke 19:10; see John 3:17; 12:47).

Alone with the Father in Prayer (1:35–39)

[35]Rising very early before dawn, he left and went off to a deserted place, where he prayed. [36]Simon and those who were with him pursued him [37]and on finding him said, "Everyone is looking for you." [38]He told them, "Let us go on to the nearby villages that I may preach there also. For this purpose have I come." [39]So he went into their synagogues, preaching and driving out demons throughout the whole of Galilee.

OT: Ps 57:9; 88:14; 92:2; Song 3:2–4
NT: 1 Thess 5:17. // Luke 4:42–43
Catechism: Jesus as the model of prayer, 520, 2599–606
Lectionary: Institution of Readers

1:35   Given the stunning displays of power just recounted, there is a note of simplicity and humility in the report that Jesus rose early to go off and pray. Although he speaks and acts with divine authority, Jesus seeks guidance from God like an ordinary man. Both the time and the place chosen by him are especially suited to prayer. Mark emphasizes the early hour, **very early before dawn**, as if, like the psalmist, Jesus desires to precede the sunrise in giving glory to God: "Awake, my soul; awake, lyre and harp! I will wake the dawn" (Ps 57:9; see 88:14; 92:2). The **deserted place** recalls the desert in 1:3–13, a place of solitude conducive to intimate communion with God. Aware that crowds will always be flocking to him from this point on, Jesus is determined to find the time he needs to renew his communion with the Father in prayer (see Mark 6:46; 14:32–42).

Simon Peter acts on behalf of the many who are **looking for** Jesus because they perceive in him the answer to their deepest longings. Jesus had taken the initiative in calling the disciples (1:16–20), but now they pursue him, or "track him down." There may be an allusion here to the bride's pursuit of her beloved in the Song of Songs, interpreted by the ancient Jews as an image for Israel's spousal love for God: "in the streets and crossings I will seek him whom my heart loves. I sought him but I did not find him" (Song 3:2–4). In a real sense, "*everyone* is looking for" Jesus, whether they know it or not.   **1:36–37**

Upon their "finding him," Jesus replies with a solemn declaration of the purpose of his mission (see John 18:37 for a similar declaration). **Have I come** suggests more than Jesus' appearance in public; it alludes to his being sent into the world by the Father, and thus implies his preexistence (see Mark 9:37). He has come to **preach**, that is, proclaim the kingdom (1:14), on an increasingly wider scale. And his preaching, as is evident from the episodes already narrated (1:15–34), consists not merely of words but of a power that has a dramatic impact on his listeners, making the kingdom a reality in their lives. By saying "**let us go**" Jesus includes his disciples in that mission. His time alone with his Father has confirmed him in his self-understanding and prepared him for the whirlwind of ministry to follow.   **1:38**

Mark concludes by summing up Jesus' Galilean ministry (as in 3:10–12): he was **preaching** the kingdom of God (see 1:14–15) and **driving out demons**, that is, releasing people from the kingdom of darkness. The preaching comes first, and as the truth of the gospel begins to enlighten people's minds the demons can no longer maintain their hold. Jesus focuses his ministry in the **synagogues**, where people are already gathered to seek God in common prayer and worship.   **1:39**

Cleansing of a Leper (1:40–45)

40A leper came to him [and kneeling down] begged him and said, "If you wish, you can make me clean." **41**Moved with pity, he stretched out his

hand, touched him, and said to him, "I do will it. Be made clean." ⁴²The
leprosy left him immediately, and he was made clean. ⁴³Then, warning
him sternly, he dismissed him at once. ⁴⁴Then he said to him, "See that you
tell no one anything, but go, show yourself to the priest and offer for your
cleansing what Moses prescribed; that will be proof for them." ⁴⁵The man
went away and began to publicize the whole matter. He spread the report
abroad so that it was impossible for Jesus to enter a town openly. He remained outside in deserted places, and people kept coming to him from
everywhere.

OT: Lev 13–14
NT: // Matt 8:1–4; Luke 5:12–16
Catechism: Jesus hears our prayer, 2616; Christ the physician, 1503–5

1:40   Few afflictions in biblical times were more hideous and terrifying than that
of leprosy. "Leprosy" could refer to a variety of severe skin disorders, including actual leprosy (Hansen's disease), in which a bacterial infection causes the
skin to ulcerate, resulting in oozing sores, disfigurement, loss of limbs, and
occasionally blindness. In ancient times leprosy was incurable and its diagno-
sis virtually a death sentence. Besides the physical ravages, there was the total
ostracism from human society imposed by the law: "The one who bears the
sore of leprosy shall keep his garments rent and his head bare, and shall muffle
his beard; he shall cry out, 'Unclean, unclean!'. . . He shall dwell apart, making
his abode outside the camp" (Lev 13:45–46). Even worse, a leper was ritually
unclean and thus barred from entering the temple, God's holy dwelling place,
to participate in the liturgy of Israel. The law could do nothing to help a leper;
it could only protect the community from the spreading of the disease.

By approaching Jesus, this **leper** makes a bold move. Not only does he
violate the strictures of the law, but he risks encountering the familiar re-

action of horror and revul-
sion at the sight of a leper.
He kneels, a sign of both
supplication and reverence
(Ps 22:30; 95:6). His plea, **If
you wish**, shows his utter
confidence in Jesus' power.
Significantly, he does not ask
Jesus to *heal* him but to make

Fig. 3. The anguish of leprosy.

Christoph von Toggenburg

him **clean**. His deepest desire is to be free once again to partake in the worship of God's people.

At the sight of this wretched man, Jesus is **moved with pity**, a verb denoting a strong emotional reaction. As the bystanders look on with astonishment, Jesus stretches out **his hand** and touches him. But Jesus is not defiled by the leprosy; instead, his touch and word instantly make the man **clean**. The power of Jesus' cleanness—his holiness—is invincible. Because no defilement can contaminate him, he is able to remove defilement from all those who approach him in faith.

1:41–42

Verse 43 could be interpreted to mean that Jesus **sternly** charged and **dismissed** (literally, "cast out") not the leper but a demon, presumably one that caused the leprosy. His command, **See that you tell no one anything**, seems surprising. Why would he not want this healing to be publicized, since he himself is traveling around

1:43

The Messianic Secret

One of the most striking features of the Gospel of Mark is the theme of the "messianic secret." Although Jesus does mighty works of healing and deliverance, he repeatedly insists that these works not be publicized (1:44; 5:43; 7:36; 8:26; 9:9) and forbids both people (8:30) and demons (1:25, 34; 3:12) to reveal his true identity. Why? The key to the puzzle is found only after Peter's confession of faith (8:27–30). Jesus' messianic identity is a deeper mystery than any of his followers yet fathom, and it must be unveiled gradually. The messiah of popular expectation was a political and military leader who would liberate Israel from Roman domination and usher in a new world of peace and prosperity. But Jesus had come to bring a much greater liberation—from the domination of sin, Satan, and death—and his mission was inseparably linked with the laying down of his life on the cross. Until that mystery was revealed, the risk was that sensational reports about his miracles would generate a false and distorted messianic enthusiasm.

Although it is easy for us in hindsight to disparage Jesus' contemporaries for their worldly expectations, his twenty-first century followers are just as prone to misinterpret him on an earthly, superficial level—for instance, in some forms of liberation theology or in the "prosperity gospel." The gradual disclosure of the messianic secret has to happen for every Christian, as we learn from Jesus the paradox of the cross. As we are purified of our limited human ideas of what God's kingdom should be, we are led into the reality that is far greater: what "eye has not seen, and ear has not heard . . . what God has prepared for those who love him" (see 1 Cor 2:9).

proclaiming the good news of the kingdom? It is the first clear instance of what biblical scholars have called the "messianic secret" in Mark: Jesus' insistence on concealing his identity and mighty works during the time of his public ministry.

1:44–45   Jesus tells the cleansed man to show himself to a **priest** and offer the sacrifice prescribed for cleansing from leprosy (see Lev 14), showing his respect for the law of **Moses** (Mark 7:10; 10:3; see Matt 23:2–3). A priest's pronouncement of a clean bill of health will allow the man to reenter society and participate once again in temple worship. The prescribed rite was to take two clean birds, one to be sacrificed and the other, dipped in the blood of the first, to fly away free (Lev 14:3–7). If the man complied with Jesus' word, he might have discovered a symbolic image foreshadowing Jesus' own sacrifice and helping him understand more deeply what Jesus had done for him. But for now, he is unable to contain his delight. Ignoring Jesus' injunction, he begins to **publicize the whole matter** and **spread the report**. Mark uses Christian terminology, literally "preach a lot" and "spread the word," drawing an unmistakable parallel with the joyful evangelistic preaching of Christians who have been cleansed by Christ in baptism.

As a result, it becomes **impossible for Jesus to enter a town openly**. Ironically, Jesus has now taken on himself the leper's previous status: the healed man is free to return to human society, but Jesus must remain **outside in deserted places** to avoid being mobbed by people seeking to benefit from his miraculous powers. He has healed the man with leprosy at a cost to himself—just as later in the Gospel he will take on Barabbas's status as a condemned criminal, while Barabbas goes free (15:15).

Reflection and Application (1:40–45)

Although leprosy has been virtually wiped out in developed nations, the loneliness and social stigma attending various physical or interior afflictions—for instance, AIDS or mental illness—is as widespread as ever. Indeed, leprosy is only an outward sign of the inner uncleanness experienced by *all* fallen human beings. The defilement of sin often causes a deep inner shame, even when a person is not consciously aware of it, that makes a person hesitant to turn to God. But as this man's boldness in approaching Jesus was richly rewarded, so is the prayer of all those who approach him with confidence in his cleansing power, especially through the sacrament of reconciliation. Jesus is not dismayed, scandalized, or contaminated by any human defilement. He willingly removes it by the power of his own holiness, restoring our communion with others and making us fully qualified to enter into God's presence.

Physician, Bridegroom, and Lord of the Sabbath

Mark 2:1–3:6

By this point in Mark's narrative, Jesus has been proclaiming the kingdom of God and graphically demonstrating its reality by healing the sick and casting out demons all over Galilee. His mission seems to be an unbroken string of successes until, at this point, there is a turn in the story. Beginning with the healing of a paralyzed man, Jesus encounters opposition in the form of disapproval, suspicion, and contention on the part of the religious authorities. This incident is the first in a series of five conflict stories in which Jesus faces increasing resistance, culminating in a plot to kill him. At the same time, each episode is a further illustration of the "new teaching with authority" (1:27) and an occasion for a deeper revelation of his identity.

Healing of a Paralytic (2:1–12)

¹When Jesus returned to Capernaum after some days, it became known that he was at home. ²Many gathered together so that there was no longer room for them, not even around the door, and he preached the word to them. ³They came bringing to him a paralytic carried by four men. ⁴Unable to get near Jesus because of the crowd, they opened up the roof above him. After they had broken through, they let down the mat on which the paralytic was lying. ⁵When Jesus saw their faith, he said to the paralytic, "Child, your sins are forgiven." ⁶Now some of the scribes were sitting there

asking themselves, [7]"Why does this man speak that way? He is blaspheming. Who but God alone can forgive sins?" [8]Jesus immediately knew in
his mind what they were thinking to themselves, so he said, "Why are you
thinking such things in your hearts? [9]Which is easier, to say to the paralytic, 'Your sins are forgiven,' or to say, 'Rise, pick up your mat and walk'?
[10]But that you may know that the Son of Man has authority to forgive sins
on earth"—[11]he said to the paralytic, "I say to you, rise, pick up your mat,
and go home." [12]He rose, picked up his mat at once, and went away in the
sight of everyone. They were all astounded and glorified God, saying, "We
have never seen anything like this."

OT: Exod 34:6–7; 2 Sam 12:13; Isa 43:25
NT: // Matt 9:1–8; Luke 5:17–26
Catechism: healing and forgiveness, 1421, 1441–42, 1484, 1502; Jesus and the Pharisees, 574, 589
Lectionary: Anointing of the Sick

2:1–2   After completing his first preaching tour around the villages of Galilee (1:39),
Jesus returns to his adopted hometown of **Capernaum**. This time, his presence
and his message attract so many **that there was no longer room for them** (see
1:33). Jesus takes the occasion to carry out the purpose for which he has come,
and which his disciples will continue after his resurrection (16:20): to preach
the word (1:38; see 1:15).

2:3–5   As Jesus is speaking, **four men** struggle through the crowd, carrying their
paralyzed friend. Often those who desire to draw near to Jesus have to overcome obstacles (7:27; 10:13, 48). In this case there is a double barrier, since the
helpless man not only needs to be carried but his faithful entourage is **unable
to get near Jesus** because of the overflowing crowd. Undaunted, they hit on
an ingenious solution. Hoisting their friend up to **the roof**, a flat roof probably
made of beams covered with thatch and packed clay (see Luke 5:19), they break
through it and begin to lower him down to the room below. It must have been
more than a little distracting to Jesus' sermon as the listeners felt bits of falling
clay and watched a stretcher being slowly lowered into their midst. But Jesus'
response is unambiguously affirming. Neither he nor Peter (whose house it
presumably was) reproach the men for damaging the roof. Instead, Jesus takes
notice of **their faith**. It is not clear whether the paralytic himself has faith, but
the faith of his friends is sufficient to carry him in his paralyzed condition. Jesus
gently reassures him, **Child, your sins are forgiven**.
            This response is probably far from what the man expected to hear. It goes
to the root of a deeper paralysis, the interior crippling that comes from sin.
In linking illness with sin, Jesus is drawing on a biblical theme familiar to his

listeners: although illness is contrary to God's intention, it is one of the evils that afflict humanity as a consequence of sin (2 Chron 26:16–21; Ps 38:2–18; 107:17). In fact, sickness is prominent among the punishments threatened by God for his people's infidelity to the covenant (Deut 28:21–35). This does not mean that all illness can be directly attributed to personal fault; the examples of Job and the suffering just man in the Psalms show that the innocent also suffer. But in this case Jesus evidently sees into the man's heart and releases him from a burden of guilt that he had borne, perhaps unconsciously, for years. It is the precondition to his being freed of his physical handicap.

Jesus' word is what philosophers call a "performative statement," a statement that brings about what it says.[1] He is not merely telling the man that God has forgiven him; he is *effecting* that forgiveness. The significance of this stunning claim is not lost on the audience, some of whom are †**scribes** trained in the law. They know well that forgiveness of sins is a prerogative of **God alone** (see Ps 51; Isa 43:25). Understandably, they are discomfited, and think to themselves, **He is blaspheming**. By perceiving these unspoken misgivings, Jesus gives the first evidence that his claim is legitimate, for it is God who reads the human heart (1 Sam 16:7; Jer 11:20; Sir 42:18).

2:6–8

Which is easier? At first glance, surely it is easier to claim something about an interior state of affairs than publicly to call forth a miracle. Anyone could say, **Your sins are forgiven**, but there would be no way to prove or disprove the efficacy of those words. But the claim to work a miracle could be verified on the spot. Jesus will do what is "harder" as a sign of his authority to do what is "easier." Verse 10 can be interpreted not only as part of Jesus' reply to the scribes but also as Mark's aside to his readers: that *you* **may know**. It is a phrase often used in the Old Testament when a display of God's power will demonstrate that he is God (Exod 8:6; 10:2; 16:12; Isa 45:3). Jesus applies it to himself: his works of healing are a revelation of his divine identity and his power to take away sins. For the first time he refers to himself as the †**Son of Man**, a title that will become increasingly prominent in the Gospel, especially as he speaks of his coming passion. Perhaps, after all, healing a paralytic *is* easier because of the high cost that forgiveness of sins will exact from Jesus.

2:9–11

At the word of Jesus, the man **rose**, the same word that will be used for Jesus' resurrection (16:6). Like the early Christian audience of Mark's Gospel, this man has begun a new life. His physical healing is a proof that he is indeed forgiven—it is an outward sign of the interior liberation brought about by the

2:12

---

1. Other examples of performative statements would be "I do" in a wedding, or "I bequeath my car to my brother."

forgiveness of his sins (see John 5:14). As often happens in Mark, the crowd reacts with astonishment and praise of God. The scribes, however, do not share the excitement but begin to nurse a grudge against Jesus.

Reflection and Application (2:1–12)

If a paralyzed man is an image of someone who cannot help himself—who needs the help of others to carry out some of the basic tasks of life—then all human beings are paralyzed in relation to God! None of us can approach God with self-sufficiency, relying on our own strength alone. All have been incapacitated in one way or another by sin and need the faith of others—whether parents, teachers, friends, or even strangers—to "carry" us to Jesus, especially in times of spiritual darkness, confusion, or fatigue. The faith of this man's loyal friends was the catalyst for Jesus to work a healing that changed his whole life, physically and spiritually. In a similar way, Christians are often called to bring to Jesus those who cannot come by themselves. Indeed, parents do so whenever they baptize an infant. Intercessory prayer, offered in tenacious faith that lets no obstacles block the way, is another powerful way to bring others to Jesus.

The Call of Levi (2:13–17)

¹³Once again he went out along the sea. All the crowd came to him and he taught them. ¹⁴As he passed by, he saw Levi, son of Alphaeus, sitting at the customs post. He said to him, "Follow me." And he got up and followed him. ¹⁵While he was at table in his house, many tax collectors and sinners sat with Jesus and his disciples; for there were many who followed him. ¹⁶Some scribes who were Pharisees saw that he was eating with sinners and tax collectors and said to his disciples, "Why does he eat with tax collectors and sinners?" ¹⁷Jesus heard this and said to them [that], "Those who are well do not need a physician, but the sick do. I did not come to call the righteous but sinners."

OT: Deut 12:7; Jer 3:22; 17:14; Hosea 14:5
NT: Matt 11:19; Luke 15:1–2. // Matt 9:9–13; Luke 5:27–32
Catechism: invitation to sinners, 545, 588–89; Jesus and the Pharisees, 574

2:13   The second controversy is occasioned by the call of Levi, the only disciple besides the fishermen whose vocation story is recorded by Mark. As Jesus walks **along the sea**, his favorite setting for teaching (see 3:7; 4:1–2; 6:34), crowds gather once more to listen to him. Mark again declines to tell us the content of Jesus' teaching; instead he focuses on its effect—in this case a sudden and radical transformation of life.

Like the four fishermen (1:16–20), **Levi** is in the midst of his workday, just   2:14
"minding his own business," when Jesus passes by and speaks the words that will change his life forever: **Follow me.** In contrast to the fishermen, who would have been regarded as upstanding if simple Jews, Levi (identified as Matthew in Matt 9:9; see Mark 3:18) was a disreputable figure. His occupation was one of the most despised in Jewish society, since tax collectors drained the poor of their livelihood on behalf of the Roman government, and the tax system lent itself to fraud and extortion. Levi's **customs post** was strategically located on a major trade route that ran through Capernaum. Perhaps he had been listening curiously with one ear to Jesus' teaching as he counted change at his post. It probably came as a complete surprise that this famous wonder-working rabbi would invite the likes of Levi into his intimate circle (see Luke 19:2–7). But like the fishermen, his response is unhesitating.

Levi's new relationship with Jesus is followed by what would be considered   2:15–16
its natural consequence: fellowship **at table**. In Jewish culture, there was no greater way to solidify a relationship than to share a common meal (Gen 26:30; 31:54; 1 Sam 9:24). Even Israel's covenant relationship with God was celebrated by eating and drinking in his presence (Exod 24:11; Deut 12:7), and expectation of the messiah often centered on the rich banquet he would provide (Isa 25:6; 55:1–2). Mark does not tell us in whose **house** the meal was held, perhaps deliberately. Although it is reasonable to infer that Levi hosted the banquet (see Luke 5:29), on another level it is Jesus who hosts at this celebration of renewed covenant fellowship. Levi and many other **tax collectors and sinners** enjoy Jesus' company, and he theirs. It is the first of several meals in the Gospel (Mark 6:41–42; 8:6–8; 14:3) leading up to the climactic meal, the Last Supper (14:18; see 16:14).

Mark notes that by this time not only those specifically called by Jesus but **many** others **followed him**—that is, became his **disciples**. †Disciple (Greek *mathētēs*) means a student or follower who attaches himself personally to a teacher to learn from both his doctrine and his example. That Jesus accepts sinners as his disciples is a sign of his power to call people to †repentance (see 1:15) and to forgive sin, as demonstrated in the preceding story of the paralytic. But the religious authorities are scandalized by his association with such undesirable people. Apparently lacking the courage to confront Jesus directly, they demand an explanation from his disciples.

Pharisees, Guardians of Jewish Identity

BIBLICAL BACKGROUND

The Pharisees were members of a small but highly influential renewal movement in ancient Judaism who practiced strict piety and regarded themselves as guardians of the †Torah. The term "Pharisee" meant "separated" and reflected their zeal to maintain the distinctive identity of the Jewish people during a period of foreign occupation and blending of cultures. To insulate themselves from Gentile defilement, they developed elaborate rules for devotion and ritual purity (Mark 2:18; 7:1–5).

Jesus at times sharply admonished the Pharisees for hollow religiosity and a zeal that rested on self-reliance rather than surrender to God (Mark 8:15; 12:15; see Matt 23). Yet if Jesus is severe toward the Pharisees, it is because he is closer to them than to other contemporary Jewish groups. He affirms some of their doctrines, including the resurrection of the dead, the existence of angels, and forms of piety like prayer, fasting, and almsgiving. His warnings against their errors are recorded in the Gospels because they are warnings to Christians as well.

The Pharisees often appear in the Gospels opposing Jesus, seeking to ensnare him in a misstep (Mark 3:2, 6; 8:11; 10:2; 12:13). But not all Pharisees rejected the gospel (John 3:1–2); some became Christians (see Acts 15:5). The most famous Pharisee was St. Paul, who considered his being a Pharisee a mark of honor (Acts 23:6; Phil 3:5–6), although he regarded his former righteousness under the law "rubbish" in comparison with Christ (Phil 3:8). After the destruction of Jerusalem in AD 70, the Pharisees survived and became the forerunners of rabbinic Judaism.

2:17   In response, Jesus utters a proverbial saying that gives a crucial insight into his messianic mission: he is a **physician** and his mission is to heal. On one level this is evident from the many cures he has performed. But **the sick** referred to here are the tax collectors and sinners. Thus the most debilitating ailment that he came to heal is sin. Jesus is assuming the role of God himself: God is the physician (Exod 15:26; Sir 38:1–15), and he heals his people first and foremost of their chronic rebellion (Jer 3:22; 17:14; Hosea 14:5).

Jesus clarifies further: **I did not come to call the righteous but sinners.** His "call" is the invitation to the messianic banquet, the joyful restoration of divine fellowship that the tax collectors and sinners are enjoying at that moment. But does this saying mean that Jesus did *not* come to call the morally upright? Is he excluding the scribes and Pharisees from his call? The answer is clear in light of the biblical testimony concerning who "the righteous" are. In the fullest sense of righteousness, "*None* is righteous, no, not one" (Rom 3:10 RSV; see

Ps 14:1–3). All are sinners. The only difference is that some admit their lack of righteousness and some do not (see 1 John 1:8–10), thus refusing Jesus' messianic invitation (see Matt 22:3) and his medicinal grace. Jesus is recasting the people's whole understanding of the messiah. His mission is not to vindicate those who keep the law, and condemn the rest; rather, it is to offer the healing of which *all* people are in need: healing from the devastation of sin. Even sins of pride and judgmentalism are among the sicknesses he came to heal.

The Bridegroom and the New Wine (2:18–22)

---

[18]The disciples of John and of the Pharisees were accustomed to fast. People came to him and objected, "Why do the disciples of John and the disciples of the Pharisees fast, but your disciples do not fast?" [19]Jesus answered them, "Can the wedding guests fast while the bridegroom is with them? As long as they have the bridegroom with them they cannot fast. [20]But the days will come when the bridegroom is taken away from them, and then they will fast on that day. [21]No one sews a piece of unshrunken cloth on an old cloak. If he does, its fullness pulls away, the new from the old, and the tear gets worse. [22]Likewise, no one pours new wine into old wineskins. Otherwise, the wine will burst the skins, and both the wine and the skins are ruined. Rather, new wine is poured into fresh wineskins."

OT: Jdt 8:5–6; Isa 54:5; 62:4–5; Hosea 2:20–22; Joel 4:18
NT: Matt 11:19; 22:2; 25:1; Luke 18:12; John 3:29. // Matt 9:14–17; Luke 5:33–39
Catechism: fasting, 1434, 1438; Christ the Bridegroom, 796

Jesus' supper with sinners in the previous episode provokes another expres-　2:18
sion of pious disapproval in the form of a question about fasting. In Hebrew literary patterns the middle element in a series is often the focus of attention. This third conflict story in a series of five, in which Jesus refers to himself as the bridegroom, provides the key to interpreting the rest. In veiled language, Jesus reveals something about the true significance of the meal just enjoyed and the purpose of his coming.

As a devout Jew and authoritative teacher, Jesus was naturally expected to hold his followers to the discipline of fasting, one of the three basic practices of Jewish piety (see Tob 12:8; Matt 6:3, 6, 16). Although Jewish law required fasting only once a year, on the Day of Atonement (Lev 16:29), **the Pharisees** practiced it twice a week as a mark of devotion (Luke 18:12). **The disciples of John** the Baptist apparently imitated John's ascetic lifestyle (Mark 1:6) and fasted as a sign of †repentance (see Joel 2:12–13). Yet Jesus and his disciples, in contrast, are seen not only feasting with sinners but failing to observe days of fasting (see Matt 11:19). Once again, those voicing criticism aim it indirectly, as if seeking to drive a wedge between Jesus and his followers. Whereas the previous question about Jesus had been addressed to his disciples (Mark 2:16), now a question about his **disciples** is addressed to Jesus.

2:19   Jesus replies, as he often does, with a rhetorical question inviting his questioners to a deeper level of understanding. This reply reveals something new and unexpected about his identity: he is a **bridegroom** (see Matt 22:2; 25:1; John 3:29). And the meal just enjoyed was no ordinary gathering of friends: on a symbolic level it was a wedding feast celebrated by Jesus the bridegroom with his **wedding guests**. For Jews steeped in the Scriptures, this imagery was familiar. God had revealed his love for his chosen people as a spousal love: "For he who has become your husband is your Maker; his name is the LORD of hosts" (Isa 54:5). Yet Israel, in return, had often behaved like an adulterous wife: "Like a woman faithless to her lover, even so have you been faithless to me, O house of Israel, says the LORD" (Jer 3:20). A central theme of the messianic promises was that God would one day fully restore the nuptial bond between himself and his people: "I will espouse you to me forever: I will espouse you in right and in justice, in love and in mercy; I will espouse you in fidelity, and you shall know the LORD" (Hosea 2:20–22; see Isa 62:4–5).

2:20   Jesus is alluding to the fulfillment of that promise, the time of uncontainable joy when God would finally bring about the intimate communion with himself for which his people had longed. And in a veiled way, Jesus is identifying *himself* as the God who desires to wed his people. His presence, walking among the villages of Galilee, was a signal that Israel's infidelities were about to be washed away and the wedding covenant renewed once and for all. The practice of fasting, a sign of mourning (see Jdt 8:4–6), would be out of place in such a celebration. But Jesus also hints forebodingly at a blot on the festivities, **when the bridegroom** would be **taken away** (see Isa 53:8)—a veiled reference to his passion. Since Jesus will no longer be visibly present on earth, his disciples will rightly resume the practice of fasting, though on a different basis than before. From then on, fasting will be a way to prepare for and heighten the full joy of the messianic banquet in which we will one day share.

2:21   Jesus further elucidates his meaning with two parable-type images, both based on everyday household life. First, **no one sews a piece of unshrunken cloth on an old cloak**. It was common knowledge that a patch made of new fabric would shrink during washing and pull away from the sewn edges, causing

Fasting in Christian Tradition

Following the biblical tradition, the early Church developed customs of fasting as a way to intensify prayer and practice self-denial. By the late second century, there was a tradition of fasting for forty hours from Good Friday afternoon through Easter morning to commemorate the Lord's passion. Lent later developed as a fast of forty days. "The Fathers held fasting in high esteem. In their view, the practice of fasting made the faithful ready for nourishment of another kind: the food of the Word of God (cf. Matt 4:4) and of fulfillment of the Father's will (cf. John 4:34). Fasting is closely connected to prayer, it strengthens virtue, inspires mercy, implores divine assistance and leads to conversion of heart."[a]

Christian tradition has always closely linked fasting with charity to the poor. St. Augustine wrote, "Do you wish your prayer to fly toward God? Give it two wings: fasting and almsgiving."[b]

a. Office of Papal Liturgical Celebrations, Dec. 14, 2001.
b. *Enarrations on the Psalms* 42.7.

---

a worse tear.[2] Later in the Gospel, clothing signifies both the **old** life that is put off when someone encounters Jesus (10:50; 13:16) and the **new** life that Jesus bestows (5:15; see Rom 13:14; Gal 3:27).

Second, **no one pours new wine into old wineskins**. Leather wineskins would   2:22
become dry and brittle with age. They could safely contain old wine, but new wine, still in the process of fermenting, would release gasses that could **burst the skins**. New wineskins would have some elasticity and be able to expand with the fermenting process. The contrast of new and old provides the key to these sayings. Jesus is bringing about the kingdom of God, a completely new life, a new way of salvation that cannot be contained within the institutions and observances of the old covenant. The old cloak and wineskins had fulfilled their role. Jesus did not come merely to "patch up" or rectify his people in their devotional practices; he came to give them a total inner transformation. The "new wine" is the wine of God's abundant blessings that were to be poured out on Israel (Isa 25:6; 55:1; Joel 4:18)—ultimately, the Holy Spirit (see Acts 2:15–17; Eph 5:18). At the Last Supper, wine will be explicitly linked with the covenant in Christ's blood (Mark 14:24–25). Now Jesus reveals that room must

---

2. The NAB translates the Greek *plērōma* literally as **fullness** (NJB "patch"). *Plērōma* probably refers to the way a patch fills the space made by a tear, but in context it could also allude to the fulfillment of God's plan brought about by Jesus (see Gal 4:4; Eph 1:10).

be made for that new wine in **fresh wineskins**, that is, human hearts that are transformed, pliable, and ready to be expanded in accord with the hidden growth of the kingdom (see 4:26–27, 32).

Lord of the Sabbath (2:23–28)

> [23]As he was passing through a field of grain on the sabbath, his disciples began to make a path while picking the heads of grain. [24]At this the Pharisees said to him, "Look, why are they doing what is unlawful on the sabbath?" [25]He said to them, "Have you never read what David did when he was in need and he and his companions were hungry? [26]How he went into the house of God when Abiathar was high priest and ate the bread of offering that only the priests could lawfully eat, and shared it with his companions?" [27]Then he said to them, "The sabbath was made for man, not man for the sabbath. [28]That is why the Son of Man is lord even of the sabbath."

OT: Gen 2:2–3; Exod 20:8–11; Lev 24:5–9; Deut 23:26; 1 Sam 21:2–7
NT: Matt 12:1–8; Luke 6:1–5
Catechism: sabbath, 345–49, 2168–73; Jesus and the law, 547–82, 2173

2:23   The fourth controversy, like the second, involves a meal—but this time it is a meal on the go, the ancient equivalent of fast food. Mark notes several occasions when Jesus and his disciples are so busy ministering to the throngs of people that they have no time even to eat (3:20; 6:31; 8:1). Here, on the way to their next mission stop, the hungry disciples take advantage of their route through a **field of grain** to snack on raw wheat. Plucking off the **heads of grain**, they rub off the husks in their hands and eat the ripe kernels. Such an action was explicitly permitted by Jewish law, as long as one did not use a reaping tool to help oneself to someone else's harvest: "When you go through your neighbor's grainfield, you may pluck some of the ears with your hand, but do not put a sickle to your neighbor's grain" (Deut 23:26).

2:24   But †Pharisees are lurking nearby to watch for a misstep—in this case an apparent violation of the **sabbath**. They notice the snacking disciples and immediately pounce on Jesus: **why are they doing what is unlawful on the sabbath?** The law of Moses clearly prohibits work, including reaping, on the sabbath (Exod 34:21). In the Pharisees' stringent interpretation, even hand-plucking to ease one's hunger on the road counted as reaping and therefore as forbidden work.

Jesus neither affirms nor disputes their interpretation of what counts as work.   2:25–26
Instead, he brings the discussion to a different level, answering their question
with a counterquestion. He refers to an incident recorded in 1 Sam 21:2–7, when
David and his **companions** were fleeing for their lives from the murderous King
Saul. En route, David stopped at the **house of God** (which at that time was the
meeting tent, since the temple had not yet been built) to beg some bread for
himself and his hungry men. Since there was no ordinary bread on hand, the
priest, Ahimelech, responded by giving David some of **the bread of offering**,
the holy bread that was kept on a special altar and that priests alone could eat
(Exod 25:30; Lev 24:5–9).[3] The fact that the holy bread was available suggests
that that incident too took place on the sabbath (Lev 24:5–9).

In drawing this comparison, Jesus is declaring that the requirements of his
messianic mission (here, his disciples' need for nourishment on the road) take
precedence over the prescriptions of the law. But he is also saying more than
this. Jesus is likening himself to David, and his disciples to David's loyal band
of soldiers. David was the "anointed one" who had been chosen by God to lead
Israel (1 Sam 16:13), but who spent years being hunted down by Saul before
finally taking up his royal throne. Like David, Jesus is the Lord's anointed one,
his Messiah, pursued and persecuted by the leaders of Israel until the day when
he will take up his throne. Those who share in his divinely appointed mission
are doing God's work and therefore are granted a priestly dispensation from the
sabbath regulations, just as David's men had been granted a priestly privilege
regarding the holy bread.[4]

Having established this dispensation, Jesus declares a deeper principle that   2:27–28
underlies it: **The sabbath was made for man, not man for the sabbath.** The
whole purpose of the sabbath was to raise human beings above the routine of
earthly labors each week, to fulfill their unique privilege of living in covenant
relationship with God. Any sabbath observance that hinders rather than en-
hances the fulfillment of that purpose is a contradiction to the sabbath itself.
Jesus concludes by asserting, **the Son of Man is lord even of the sabbath.** This
does not mean that Jesus is abrogating the sabbath laws. Rather, he is pointing to his divinity in a veiled way, asserting the authority that belongs to God

---

3. The phrase **when Abiathar was high priest** is apparently incorrect, since it was not Abiathar but
his father, Ahimelech, who was priest at the time. A possible solution to the discrepancy is that sometimes a section of a biblical scroll was named for a prominent individual or event in that section (as in
Mark 12:26). The phrase, which is literally "concerning Abiathar the high priest," was then intended to
locate the relevant section of 1 Samuel, in a way similar to modern biblical chapter divisions. See Lane,
Gospel of Mark, 115–16. In return for his pains in helping David, Ahimelech was killed by Saul, and his
son Abiathar took over as priest in his place.

4. See Tim Gray, *Mission of the Messiah* (Steubenville, OH: Emmaus Road, 1998), 79–83.

alone, the Creator who instituted the sabbath (Gen 2:2–3). Moreover, Jesus is declaring that his mission is the fulfillment of the sabbath and the revelation of its deepest meaning. What this means will be spelled out in the fifth and final conflict story.

Withered Hand, Withered Hearts (3:1–6)

[1]Again he entered the synagogue. There was a man there who had a withered hand. [2]They watched him closely to see if he would cure him on the sabbath so that they might accuse him. [3]He said to the man with the withered hand, "Come up here before us." [4]Then he said to them, "Is it lawful to do good on the sabbath rather than to do evil, to save life rather than to destroy it?" But they remained silent. [5]Looking around at them with anger and grieved at their hardness of heart, he said to the man, "Stretch out your hand." He stretched it out and his hand was restored. [6]The Pharisees went out and immediately took counsel with the Herodians against him to put him to death.

OT: 1 Macc 2:27–41; Ezek 3:7
NT: Mark 2:28. // Matt 12:9–14; Luke 6:6–11
Catechism: the sabbath, 345, 348, 2168–73; Jesus and the law, 547–82, 2173

3:1–2   The fifth controversy is the climax of the series and a concrete illustration of what Jesus has just declared: that he is Lord of the sabbath. By now the opposition of the Pharisees has become open hostility. The presence of a man with **a withered hand** in the synagogue, instead of arousing their compassion, becomes an opportunity to bring a legal charge against Jesus. As soon as he enters, they are watching suspiciously **to see if he would cure him on the sabbath**. A hand that was withered (literally, "dried up") was atrophied and probably paralyzed—a severe disability in a society where most men made a living by manual labor. Jesus' opponents take for granted that he is able to cure and they guess, rightly, that the sight of the disabled man will move him to do so. But their only interest is in whether he will again violate their interpretation of sabbath law. In their view, unless there is a life-threatening condition, healing counts as medical treatment prohibited on the sabbath (see Luke 13:14).[5]

3:3   Far from being intimidated by their scrutiny, Jesus ensures that what he is about to do will be in full public view. The verb for **come up**, *egeirō*, can also be translated "rise up," and is the same word used for Jesus' resurrection in 16:6.

5. For this common interpretation, see the Mishnah, *Shabbat* 14.3–4.

Mark often uses it in healing stories (1:31; 2:9–12; 5:41; 10:49) to indicate that Jesus is bringing about not only physical cures but a restoration to fullness of life.

Jesus' rhetorical question about what is **lawful** recalls the Pharisees' earlier charge against the disciples (2:24). On one level the answer is obvious: of course it is right to **do good** rather than evil and to **save life** rather than kill on the sabbath, as on any day of the week. But Jesus may also be alluding to an exception to sabbath law that the Pharisees themselves recognized as legitimate. During the time of the Maccabean revolt, the Jews' strict sabbath adherence, to the point of even refusing to fight in self-defense on the sabbath, had resulted in a disastrous slaughter. Afterward they decided, "Let us fight against anyone who attacks us on the sabbath, so that we may not all die as our kinsmen died in the hiding places" (1 Macc 2:41). Jesus' argument amounts to saying: If you recognize a right to wage war on the sabbath to defend life, how much more ought you to recognize the legitimacy of a good deed like restoring health to this man?[6]

3:4

The Pharisees' refusal to come to terms with this argument is signaled by their stony silence. As often in Mark, Jesus looks around at his audience with a searching gaze that penetrates to the heart (3:34; 10:21, 23; 11:11), the inner place of decision that only God can see (1 Kings 8:39). Unlike Matthew and Luke, Mark gives us a glimpse of Jesus' interior reaction: he is angry and deeply **grieved at their hardness of heart**. "Hardness of heart" signifies a stubborn refusal to be open to God (Jer 11:8; Ezek 3:7; Eph 4:18), a condition that will at times characterize even his disciples (Mark 6:52; 8:17). Jesus' **anger** is more than merely a human emotional response. "Anger" is often used in the Old Testament to describe God's holy indignation at human evil (Exod 32:10; Num 11:1; Isa 60:10), which will be fully disclosed on the "day of wrath" (Zeph 1:15; Rom 2:5). The kingdom of God, made present in Jesus' words and deeds, evokes responses that disclose the true state of each person's heart in preparation for God's final judgment (see John 3:19).

3:5–6

At Jesus' word, the man stretches out his crippled **hand**, and in this very act it is **restored**. The Pharisees' response to this deed of mercy is swift. Ironically, they answer Jesus' question by their actions: rather than choosing to do good on the sabbath, they choose to do evil and destroy life by conspiring **to put him to death**. So fierce is their wrath that they join forces with political opportunists whom they would normally avoid at all costs: the **Herodians**, supporters of †Herod Antipas (see Mark 12:13). Jesus' fate is thereby linked with that of John the Baptist, who will be killed by Herod (6:14–29).

6. See Marcus, *Mark 1–8*, 248.

This incident raises the question: Why did Jesus deliberately heal on the sabbath, knowing that it would provoke such furious antagonism? Note that in all four Gospels, every one of the healings initiated by Jesus takes place on the sabbath.[7] On other days, the sick themselves or their relatives or friends approach Jesus to seek healing, but only on the sabbath does Jesus takes the initiative. Why does Jesus apparently prefer to heal on the sabbath? The declaration given in 2:28 and illustrated in 3:1–6 provides the answer. The Son of Man is Lord of the sabbath, and he exercises his lordship by undoing the effects of sin and inaugurating the new creation by which humanity is restored to the fullness of life that God intended from the beginning. Jesus thereby fulfills the original purpose of the sabbath: to bring humanity into communion with God.

7. Matt 12:8–14; Luke 13:10–17; 14:1–4; John 5:1–9; 9:1–14. See sidebar on the sabbath, p. 47.

A New Israel and a New Family

Mark 3:7–35

The previous chapter showed conflict brewing between Jesus and the religious authorities, to the point where the Pharisees began to plot his death (3:6). In response, Jesus withdraws to the sea and countryside (see 1:45). From this point on he will be more elusive, avoiding the synagogues and traveling back and forth across the lake, often at night. For now he continues his ministry of teaching, healing, and exorcisms in Galilee. But there is a new element in place: Jesus now begins to take steps to establish a new Israel and a new family of God. Whereas the previous section entailed a deepening revelation of the identity of Jesus, this section begins to shed light on the identity of the community he is gathering about him.

Lakeside Healings (3:7–12)

⁷Jesus withdrew toward the sea with his disciples. A large number of people [followed] from Galilee and from Judea. ⁸Hearing what he was doing, a large number of people came to him also from Jerusalem, from Idumea, from beyond the Jordan, and from the neighborhood of Tyre and Sidon. ⁹He told his disciples to have a boat ready for him because of the crowd, so that they would not crush him. ¹⁰He had cured many and, as a result, those who had diseases were pressing upon him to touch him. ¹¹And whenever unclean spirits saw him they would fall down before him and shout, "You are the Son of God." ¹²He warned them sternly not to make him known.

OT: Zech 8:23
NT: Mark 6:56; Acts 5:15
Catechism: Christ the physician, 1503–5

69

3:7–8   This passage stands in sharp contrast to the previous, where the only recorded reaction to Jesus' act of healing is the smoldering fury of his opponents. Here his popularity among ordinary people skyrockets. Mark stresses the fact that people are flocking to Jesus from every corner, not only from Jewish lands but from among the Gentiles as well.

Aware that violent plans are fermenting, Jesus withdraws **toward the sea**. The verb **withdrew** suggests a desire for seclusion in areas removed from human activity (as in 1:35; 3:13; 6:31–32). Perhaps Jesus sought some time for prayer or for privately instructing his disciples. But as usual, just the opposite occurs. His fame as a healer and exorcist has spread far beyond the bounds of his home region. Crowds come from **Judea**, the area south of Galilee and Samaria, including **Jerusalem** the capital city. Beyond these predominantly Jewish regions, Mark lists foreign areas in a geographic circle (see map, p. 349). People come from **Idumea** more than one hundred miles to the south (in present-day southern Israel and the West Bank), from the eastern regions **beyond the Jordan** River (in present-day Jordan and Syria), and from the area of **Tyre and Sidon** on the Mediterranean coast to the northwest (in present-day Lebanon). The reader of the Gospel begins to get the impression that the whole world is coming to Jesus.

3:9–10   The frailty of Jesus' human nature stands out in ironic contrast to his mighty works. Although he cures the infirmities of others by a mere touch, his own

Fig. 4. The "Jesus Boat," a first-century fishing boat discovered in 1986 buried in the mud along the shore of the Sea of Galilee.

body is at risk of being crushed by the crowds mobbing him. He tells his disciples to **have a boat ready** so that, if necessary, he can put out a bit from the shore and continue to minister to the sick without being trampled (see 4:1). The crowds seem to be less interested in Jesus himself than in what he can do for them. They come in their desperation, some having endured years of debilitating illness and perhaps having given up hope of health and vitality. From their native places far away they have heard rumors of the wonder worker from Nazareth who just might be able to provide the wholeness for which they long. He **cured many** ("many" signifies a large number and does not imply that some were left uncured; see Matt 8:16), so that the afflicted **were pressing upon him** (literally, "falling on him") **to touch him**. Jesus does not reprimand them but simply allows the physical contact with himself that makes the sick well (Mark 5:27–31; 6:56).

Some of the afflictions involve possession by **unclean spirits**. Unlike either the religious authorities or the crowds, these supernatural beings have clear and certain knowledge of who Jesus is. Their prostration before him is not a sign of genuine worship but an obeisance compelled by Jesus' irresistible authority (as in 5:6). Nor is their clamorous shout a confession of faith, but a futile attempt to render him harmless, in accord with the common view that one could acquire mastery over another by using the individual's proper name (see 1:24; 5:7). But Jesus' conquest of the kingdom of Satan, which began in the desert (1:13, 25–26, 34), is unstoppable. He **sternly** forbids the demons to publicize their superhuman knowledge.

3:11–12

The Appointment of the Twelve (3:13–19)

---

¹³**He went up the mountain and summoned those whom he wanted, and they came to him. ¹⁴He appointed twelve [whom he also named apostles] that they might be with him and he might send them forth to preach ¹⁵and to have authority to drive out demons: ¹⁶[he appointed the twelve:] Simon, whom he named Peter; ¹⁷James, son of Zebedee, and John the brother of James, whom he named Boanerges, that is, sons of thunder; ¹⁸Andrew, Philip, Bartholomew, Matthew, Thomas, James the son of Alphaeus; Thaddeus, Simon the Cananean, ¹⁹and Judas Iscariot, who betrayed him.**

OT: Exod 19:3
NT: Matt 19:28; John 15:16; Rom 10:15. // Matt 10:1–4; Luke 6:12–16
Catechism: apostles, 551–52, 765, 858–60; bishops as their successors, 861–62, 1577

3:13–15   Jesus has come to a crucial moment in his ministry, and he acts with solemn deliberateness. Now it becomes clear that he does not intend to carry out his mission on his own, but to form a chosen company to collaborate with him and to continue his work after he is "taken away" (2:20). Mark highlights the solemnity of this act by noting that Jesus **went up the mountain**, just as Moses went up Mount Sinai (Exod 19:3) where God gave the law and forged the twelve tribes of Israel into his chosen people. From among his disciples, Jesus **summoned those whom he wanted**, a phrase that indicates a sovereign choice not dependent on human initiative, as in John 15:16: "It was not you who chose me, but I who chose you and appointed you to go and bear fruit." It is no coincidence that he **appointed twelve**, the number of the sons of Jacob from whom the twelve tribes of Israel were descended (see Matt 19:28; Rev 21:14). Jesus is establishing a new leadership for a new Israel (see Mark 10:42–43), in preparation for the renewal and fulfillment of the covenant at his passion (14:24). That the early Church recognized a crucial significance in this number is shown by the appointment of Matthias to fill the place left by Judas after his betrayal and death (Acts 1:15–26).

The commissioning of the Twelve is different from the call of the disciples recounted earlier (Mark 1:16–20; 2:14). Whereas the call to discipleship is a universal invitation to follow Jesus (2:15; 3:7; see Matt 11:28–29), the †apostles are a special group chosen from among the disciples to participate in Jesus' mission in a unique way (see Mark 6:7). Apostle (Greek *apostolos*) means "one sent out," that is, an authorized representative or envoy. Jesus sums up their duties in two simple phrases: to **be with him** and that **he might send them forth**. To "be with him" means that the apostles' task is first and foremost to have close personal fellowship with Jesus. Without intimacy with him, there will be no effectiveness to their mission (see John 15:4–7). Luke later portrays the impact of "being with Jesus" where he recounts the Jewish leaders' astonishment at the fearless preaching of the apostles: "Now when they saw the boldness of Peter and John, and perceived that they were uneducated, common men, they wondered; and they recognized that *they had been with Jesus*" (Acts 4:13 RSV; emphasis added).

Second, the apostles are "sent forth" by Jesus and entrusted with the same twofold mission as his own (see Mark 1:39): **to preach** and **to drive out demons**. To preach is to be a herald announcing the good news that the kingdom of God is at hand (see 1:14–15). St. Paul characterizes preaching the gospel as the primary function of an apostle (1 Cor 1:17). As in Jesus' own ministry, preaching the gospel is inseparable from casting out demons (see Mark 1:27), who hold sway over human beings through falsehood and deceit. That Jesus gives the apostles **authority** to drive out demons indicates that an exorcist succeeds not by special techniques or talents, but only by the authority delegated from the One who has already conquered the demons (as the incident recounted in Acts 19:13–16 vividly illustrates). Like Jesus, the apostles are to proclaim the reign of God in words together with mighty deeds that demonstrate its reality.

Mark now provides the official roll call of the Twelve. What is striking about   **3:16**
this list is what a motley crew they are. Yet Jesus is forming a community from these diverse men, and calling them to be just as closely bound to one another as they are to him (see John 17:21–23). Their mission will be carried out not independently but in fellowship with one another. **Simon, whom he named Peter**, is always listed first among the apostles, signifying his role as their chief and spokesman (see Mark 8:29; 10:28; 14:37; 16:7). In the Old Testament, to confer a new name is a divine act expressing a change in a person's destiny and the call to a decisive role in God's plan of salvation: Abram becomes Abraham (Gen 17:5); Sarai becomes Sarah (Gen 17:15); Jacob becomes Israel (Gen 32:29). Peter (Greek *petros*, from which is derived the English "petrify") was a translation of the †Aramaic *kepha*, rock, and signified Peter's role as a solid foundation on which Jesus would build his new community of faith (Matt 16:18; see John 1:42). The New Testament sometimes uses the Aramaic form of the name (John 1:42; 1 Cor 9:5).

The two sons of Zebedee, **James** and **John**, are affectionately nicknamed **sons**   **3:17**
of thunder by Jesus, perhaps reflecting their stormy temperaments (see Mark

Exorcisms and the Proclamation of the Gospel

LIVING
TRADITION

For the early Church, the remarkable success of Christian exorcisms was among the most powerful testimonies to the truth of the gospel. In the second century St. Justin Martyr wrote, "Jesus was born by the will of God the Father for the salvation of believers and the destruction of demons. And now you can learn this by what you see with your own eyes. For throughout the whole world and in your city [Rome] there are many demoniacs whom all the other exorcists, sorcerers and magicians could not heal, but whom our Christians have healed and do heal, disabling and casting out the demons who possessed them in the name of Jesus Christ who was crucified under Pontius Pilate."[a]

a. *Second Apology* 6.5–6.

The Apostles and Their Successors

LIVING
TRADITION

From the earliest days of the Church the apostles appointed other men to succeed them to ensure that the mission Jesus entrusted to them would continue after their death (Acts 1:15–26; 1 Tim 3:1; 2 Tim 1:6). In Catholic tradition bishops are by definition the successors of the apostles. "The bishops have by divine institution taken the place of the apostles as pastors of the Church, in such wise that whoever listens to them is listening to Christ and whoever despises them despises Christ and him who sent Christ" (Catechism, 862, quoting *Lumen gentium*, 20, 2). But in another sense, "The whole Church is apostolic, in that she remains, through the successors of St. Peter and the other apostles, in communion of faith and life with her origin: and in that she is 'sent out' into the whole world. All members of the Church share in this mission, though in various ways" (863).

9:38; 10:35–41; Luke 9:54). These first three apostles, to whom Jesus gives new names, will be associated with him in a special way (Mark 5:37; 9:2; 14:33).

3:18   **Andrew**, along with his brother Simon, was one of the first fishermen called to discipleship (1:16), and occasionally joins Jesus' most intimate circle (1:29; 13:3). **Philip** bears a popular Greek name, and is mentioned nowhere else in the †Synoptics but frequently in John (1:43–48; 6:5–7; 12:21–22; 14:8–9). **Bartholomew** (Aramaic for "son of Talmai") has traditionally been identified with the Nathaniel mentioned by John (John 1:45–49).[1] Mark does not tell us anything about **Matthew**, though the Gospel of Matthew identifies him as a tax collector (Matt 9:9). **Thomas** (meaning "twin" in Aramaic) appears as the doubting apostle in John 20:24, and is revered in postbiblical tradition as the apostle to India. **James the son of Alphaeus** may be a brother of Levi the tax collector (Mark 2:14). **Thaddeus** has been traditionally identified with the Judas (or Jude) son of James mentioned by Luke (Luke 6:16; Acts 1:13). **Simon** is surnamed **the Cananean** (from an Aramaic word meaning "zealous"; see Luke 6:15), indicating his zeal for the honor of God and the Jewish nation.

3:19   Finally, **Judas Iscariot** is mentioned last as the apostle who later **betrayed** Jesus (14:10, 43). "Judas" is the Greek form of "Judah," one of the twelve sons of Jacob. Iscariot is of uncertain meaning, but could mean a man from the village of Kerioth (Josh 15:25). The ominous note sounded by the mention of Judas's treachery signals that being an apostle is not a guarantee of holiness or lifelong fidelity. It also indicates that for the rest of this little band, accepting Jesus' call

1. Hence the Gospel reading for the feast of St. Bartholomew is John 1:45–51.

means more than an exciting ministry of evangelization: it means "being with him" (Mark 3:14) also in the pain of rejection and betrayal.

Jesus Is Misunderstood by His Own (3:20–21)

---

²⁰He came home. Again [the] crowd gathered, making it impossible for them even to eat. ²¹When his relatives heard of this they set out to seize him, for they said, "He is out of his mind."

NT: Mark 6:3; John 1:11; 7:5; 10:20

One of Mark's signature techniques is to "sandwich" one story inside another   3:20
so that each sheds light on the other. In this case, he arranges the three scenes in vv. 20–35 into one block of material. In the first and the third units Jesus is misunderstood by his own family; the second (vv. 22–30) involves a far more serious charge from the religious authorities.

After the appointment of the Twelve, Jesus comes **home** to the house of Peter and Andrew at Capernaum, which he had made his home base (1:29; 2:1). This time the press of people is so great that Jesus and his disciples find it impossible to care for their own needs, **even to eat** (as will happen again in 6:31; 8:1).

To understand the reaction of Jesus' **relatives**, it is important to recognize   3:21
what family bonds meant in the social context of the time. For the ancient Jews, as for many non-Western cultures today, an individual existed only as part of an extended family unit, whose authority structure, obligations, and customs governed every aspect of life. Any action by an individual was a reflection on the whole family, and any breach of family honor would usually meet with severe discipline. Since Jesus' foster father Joseph was presumably no longer alive (see 3:31), Jesus' uncles and senior cousins would have considered him under their charge and answerable to them for his conduct.

Hearing of all the commotion surrounding him, these relatives feel duty bound to **set out**, probably from his native village of Nazareth twenty miles away, to **seize** him—the same verb used later for his arrest (14:46). From their perspective, Jesus ought to be back home making tables and chairs instead of attracting throngs of sick and demon-possessed people, not to mention arousing the hostility of the religious leaders. Their action was probably motivated in part by a desire to protect him. **For they said** is better translated "for people were saying" (RSV), since the subject is left vague. Word was getting around that Jesus was **out of his mind** (or "beside himself," RSV), meaning that his wonder-working activity seemed evidence of mental imbalance. Since mental illness was often associated with demonic influence (John 10:20), these suspicions could be seen as a lesser version of the charge leveled by the scribes in the next episode.

Reflection and Application (3:20–21)

Based on their reaction, it appears that Jesus' relatives do not see anything in him other than the ordinary young kinsman they have known all their lives. The whole town of Nazareth will later display a similar response (6:1–3). As the Gospel of John notes, "even his brothers did not believe in him" (John 7:5 RSV). The Son of God suffered misunderstanding even from those closest to him: his family and, on a wider scale, his people (John 1:11). So too his followers often experience the pain of misunderstanding or even mockery from family members who do not understand a life of radical commitment to Jesus. In contemporary secular culture, faithfulness to the gospel sometimes entails being willing to appear to the world as "fools for Christ."

Diabolical Accusations (3:22–30)

---

²²The scribes who had come from Jerusalem said, "He is possessed by Beelzebul," and "By the prince of demons he drives out demons."

²³Summoning them, he began to speak to them in parables, "How can Satan drive out Satan? ²⁴If a kingdom is divided against itself, that kingdom cannot stand. ²⁵And if a house is divided against itself, that house will not be able to stand. ²⁶And if Satan has risen up against himself and is divided, he cannot stand; that is the end of him. ²⁷But no one can enter a strong man's house to plunder his property unless he first ties up the strong man. Then he can plunder his house. ²⁸Amen, I say to you, all sins and all blasphemies that people utter will be forgiven them. ²⁹But whoever blasphemes against the holy Spirit will never have forgiveness, but is guilty of an everlasting sin." ³⁰For they had said, "He has an unclean spirit."

OT: Isa 5:20; 49:24–25
NT: John 7:20; 10:20. // Matt 12:22–32; Luke 11:14–21
Catechism: Jesus' defeat of Satan, 539, 550, 2850–54; blasphemy against the Spirit, 1864

3:22   Inserted in the middle of the account of family misunderstanding is this episode involving a far more sinister accusation. For the first time in the Gospel, †**scribes** from **Jerusalem** appear, big guns perhaps sent by the authorities in the capital to check out the rumors concerning the miracle worker from Nazareth. The Jerusalem scribes were experts in the Mosaic law whose authority was more weighty than that of the Galilean Pharisees, and who emerge as Jesus' fiercest opponents in the Gospel (7:1, 5; 10:33; 11:18, 27; 14:1). Their verdict is categorical: **"He is possessed by Beelzebul," and "By the prince of demons he drives out demons"** (see John 10:20 for a similar accusation). Beelzebul is a name for †Satan, probably derived from a title of the false god of the Canaanites, "Baal the Prince."[2] For readers of the Gospel, who are privy to Jesus' divine identity and have followed his ministry of healing and liberation of the oppressed, such a charge is chilling.

Instead of taking umbrage, Jesus responds with patience and serenity, using †**parables** or analogies to refute the allegations step by step. His **summoning** of the scribes suggests that they were spreading the rumors behind his back, but he wishes to confront them face to face. He answers the twofold charge, that he is possessed by Satan and that he performs exorcisms by demonic sorcery, in reverse order.

3:23–26

First, the claim that Jesus is using demonic power to cast out demons is disproved by its logical absurdity. **How can Satan drive out Satan?** In three parallel statements Jesus likens Satan to the ruler of a **kingdom** or **house**, who would naturally act in self-interest. What ruler would instigate a revolt against his own rule? Everyone knows that civil war in a kingdom or internal strife in a household spells destruction.[3] If Satan were making war on his own subordinates through Jesus' exorcisms, Satan's dominion would have quickly collapsed.

Jesus then uses a burglary analogy, this time to explain what he *is* doing. Satan is compared to a **strong man** self-assuredly guarding his possessions—that is, possessed human beings. By referring to demon-possessed people as Satan's **property**, Jesus suggests that the evil one has obtained a real though illicit foothold in their souls. No one can release them from such captivity except by first "tying up" the strong man. Only then can he **plunder his house**. Jesus has broken into the domain of evil, incapacitating its ruler so he can then despoil his possessions. This analogy evokes a prophecy of Isaiah: "Thus says the LORD: Can booty be taken from a warrior? or captives be rescued from a tyrant? Yes, captives can be taken from a warrior, and booty be rescued from a tyrant; Those who oppose you I will oppose, and your sons I will save" (Isa 49:24–25). As John the Baptist

3:27

---

2. Some ancient manuscripts of Mark read "Beelzebub" (see NIV), which is close to the mocking distortion of Baal's name, Baalzebub ("lord of the flies") in 2 Kings 1:3, 6.

3. Jesus' listeners might have perceived in 3:24–25 an allusion to Herod the Great, whose household and kingdom both were divided after his death in 4 BC and "came to an end." See Donahue and Harrington, *Mark*, 130.

The Sin against the Holy Spirit

LIVING TRADITION

In his encyclical on the Holy Spirit, Pope John Paul II explained that the blasphemy against the Holy Spirit "does not properly consist in offending against the Holy Spirit in words; it consists rather in the refusal to accept the salvation which God offers to man through the Holy Spirit, working through the power of the Cross." It is "the sin committed by the person who claims to have a 'right' to persist in evil—in any sin at all—and who thus rejects Redemption."[a] The Catechism adds: "There are no limits to the mercy of God, but anyone who deliberately refuses to accept his mercy by repenting, rejects the forgiveness of his sins and the salvation offered by the Holy Spirit. Such hardness of heart can lead to final impenitence and eternal loss" (1864).

a. *Dominum et vivificantem*, 46.

had announced, Jesus is the "mightier one" (Mark 1:7) who alone has power to bind Satan and release those suffering under his tyrannical rule.

3:28–29   Finally, Jesus addresses the scribes' first charge, that he is "possessed by Beelzebul," not with a parable but with a somber warning. †**Amen** means "truly" or "so be it" in Hebrew, and is used at the end of prayers to express agreement (see Neh 8:6). Jesus' custom of saying "Amen" to *preface* a solemn affirmation is a completely new usage. Its closest parallel is the divine oath, "As I live, says the LORD . . . ," often used to introduce God's most solemn warnings (Num 14:28; Isa 49:18; Ezek 5:11). Here the affirmation is, first and foremost, that **all sins** are forgivable, even **all blasphemies**, which are most serious since they are committed against God himself. To blaspheme is to insult or abuse the name of God. However, whoever blasphemes **against the holy Spirit will never have forgiveness**. What does it mean to blaspheme against the Holy Spirit? In the context of this passage it is to harden one's heart so completely that one defiantly refuses to recognize the action of God and even attributes to evil the good works done by Jesus in the power of the Spirit (Mark 1:10; see Isa 5:20). It is therefore to close the door to the Holy Spirit's inner work of conversion. The point is not that there is any exception to God's mercy. Rather, the point is that persons who persist in such willful blindness refuse to repent and thus choose to *close themselves* to the forgiveness that God offers through Jesus.

3:30   Mark explicitly connects this blasphemy against the Holy Spirit with the scribes' accusation. Jesus is not declaring that the scribes *have* committed the everlasting sin, but is warning them of the grave peril they are in, unless they open their hearts to the Spirit and repent.

The True Family of Jesus (3:31–35)

³¹His mother and his brothers arrived. Standing outside they sent word to him and called him. ³²A crowd seated around him told him, "Your mother and your brothers [and your sisters] are outside asking for you." ³³But he said to them in reply, "Who are my mother and [my] brothers?" ³⁴And looking around at those seated in the circle he said, "Here are my mother and my brothers. ³⁵[For] whoever does the will of God is my brother and sister and mother."

OT: Exod 24:7; Ps 40:9; 143:10
NT: Mark 10:29–30; Luke 9:61–62; Rom 8:29. // Matt 12:46–50; Luke 8:19–21
Catechism: brothers of Jesus, 500; family of God, 2790
Lectionary: Common of Pastors; Consecration of Virgins and Religious Profession

After the incident with the scribes, Mark resumes the account of Jesus' rela-   **3:31–32**
tives who had set out to "seize him" (3:21). This time **his mother and his broth-ers** are specifically mentioned (some ancient manuscripts also include **sisters**). So densely packed is the crowd sitting around Jesus that, like the friends of the paralyzed man in 2:4, they find it impossible to get near him. Mark highlights the contrast between Jesus' family and the audience surrounding him by twice not-ing that his family members stood **outside** (3:31, 32). They send word through the crowd, naturally expecting that when Jesus hears that his family is calling he will immediately interrupt his discourse to answer their summons.

The Brothers and Sisters of Jesus

BIBLICAL BACKGROUND

Who are the brothers and sisters of Jesus mentioned here and through-out the New Testament (John 2:12; Acts 1:14; 1 Cor 9:5; Gal 1:19)? Some commentators have contended that they refer to Jesus' full siblings. But the ancient Church unanimously held that Mary remained a virgin throughout her life. That Mark is not referring to full siblings of Jesus is indicated by his later mention of James and Joses as sons of a dif-ferent Mary (Mark 6:3; 15:40; see Matt 27:56). Moreover, the brothers' authoritative behavior toward Jesus (Mark 3:31–32) suggests that they are older than he, although Jesus is Mary's firstborn (Luke 2:7). Both Hebrew and Aramaic, lacking a word for "cousin," used "brother" to refer to a range of kinship relationships (see Gen 13:8; 2 Kings 10:13–14; Rom 9:3). The Greek term *adelphos* also admitted a wider meaning than full sibling. Catholics have tradition-ally interpreted Jesus' brothers to refer either to his cousins, as St. Jerome held, or to children of Joseph by an earlier marriage (see Catechism, 500).

This is the only time in Mark that Mary the **mother** of Jesus appears on the scene, although she is mentioned by name in 6:3. Mark does not indicate that she shares the opinion of those who think Jesus is "out of his mind" (3:21). But the episode does suggest that she does not yet fully comprehend the scope and significance of her son's mission. She, like others, has to grow in understanding of the divine mystery that only faith can penetrate (see Luke 1:29, 34; 2:19, 50–51). Here, as in the finding of Jesus in the temple (Luke 2:49) and at the cross (John 19:26–27), she is called to undergo a certain detachment in her earthly relationship to Jesus so that her faith can be stretched to encompass her far greater role in the new family that Jesus is establishing.[4]

3:33–34   Jesus' reply must have sounded shocking in the cultural context of first-century Judaism. It is the first indication of a principle that will become clearer as the Gospel progresses: all earthly ties take second place to the kingdom of God (10:29–30; see Luke 9:61–62; 14:26). Even the closest of human bonds—familial bonds, which in Jewish society were all-important—are of lesser priority than Christian discipleship. Jesus looks at those seated around him with a gaze of affection and intimacy: **Here are my mother and my brothers.** He thereby elevates them to a completely unexpected status: they are not merely his followers, they are his *family*. He is establishing a new family, the family of God, whose members are united around Jesus in a bond of love, familiarity, and loyalty far stronger than any blood relationships (see John 1:12; Rom 8:29; Eph 2:19; Heb 2:10–11). In so doing, he is not rejecting his earthly family; rather, he is establishing a new basis for their claim on him. That his brothers did eventually accept this new basis for kinship with Jesus is shown by their active presence in the early Church (Acts 1:14; 1 Cor 9:5; Gal 1:19).

3:35   With his final statement Jesus explains the foundation for the new messianic family. The absolute priority in the heart of Jesus is to please his Father (14:36; John 4:34; 8:29), the perfect expression of the covenant relationship (Exod 24:7–8; Ps 40:9; 143:10). Thus the only condition for entering God's family is to do God's **will**, just as Jesus did (see Matt 7:21). And to do God's will one must first learn what it is, by sitting and listening to Jesus as the crowd is doing. The inclusion of "mother" in his list of kin means that members of the family of God are not merely adopted as younger siblings of Jesus; by doing God's will they in a real sense *bring Jesus forth into the world* (see Gal 4:19). But there is no "father" in the list, since Jesus has only one, heavenly Father.

---

4. Mary's maternal role in the new family of God is suggested in Mark 3:35, further developed in Luke 1:43; 2:34–35; John 19:26–27; Rev 12:1–6, and elaborated theologically in early Christian tradition.

Parables of the Kingdom

Mark 4:1–34

Up to this point, Mark has strongly emphasized the centrality of teaching in Jesus' ministry but has said very little about what he actually taught.[1] Now he gives us an extended discourse in which Jesus begins to unfold the meaning of the kingdom of God whose arrival he has proclaimed (1:15). By analogy with Matthew's Sermon on the Mount (Matt 5–7) and Luke's Sermon on the Plain (Luke 6:17–49), this lengthy teaching could be called Mark's "Sermon on the Sea."[2] As will become evident, the key word in this discourse is "to hear," and the underlying theme is the human response to Jesus' proclamation of the kingdom.

The Parable of the Sower (4:1–9)

[1]On another occasion he began to teach by the sea. A very large crowd gathered around him so that he got into a boat on the sea and sat down. And the whole crowd was beside the sea on land. [2]And he taught them at length in parables, and in the course of his instruction he said to them, [3]"Hear this! A sower went out to sow. [4]And as he sowed, some seed fell on the path, and the birds came and ate it up. [5]Other seed fell on rocky ground where it had little soil. It sprang up at once because the soil was

---

1. Although Mark cites less of the actual teaching than any other Gospel, he accents Jesus' role as teacher more than any other Gospel: see 1:21–22, 27; 2:13; 4:1–2; 6:2, 6, 34; 8:31; 9:31; 10:1; 11:17; 12:14, 35; 14:49.
2. See Martin, *Gospel according to Mark*, 79.

not deep. ⁶**And when the sun rose, it was scorched and it withered for lack of roots.** ⁷**Some seed fell among thorns, and the thorns grew up and choked it and it produced no grain.** ⁸**And some seed fell on rich soil and produced fruit. It came up and grew and yielded thirty, sixty, and a hundredfold.**" ⁹**He added, "Whoever has ears to hear ought to hear."**

OT: Gen 26:12; Deut 6:4
NT: 1 Pet 1:23. // Matt 13:1–9; Luke 8:4–8
Catechism: parables, 546
Lectionary: Mass for the Laity; 4:1–10, 13–20: Common of Doctors of the Church

4:1–2   Once again Jesus begins to teach in his favorite auditorium—the open air **by the sea** of Galilee—as the ever-increasing **crowd** continues to flock around him. This time he does not just instruct his disciples to have a boat ready (3:9),

---

What Is a Parable?

BIBLICAL BACKGROUND

Perhaps the most distinctive and well-known characteristic of Jesus' teaching is his use of parables. A parable is a short, memorable story or image, usually drawn from nature or daily life, that conveys profound spiritual truths. Through his parables, Jesus "shows how the divine light shines through in the things of this world and in the realities of our everyday life."[a] Jesus' parables have three significant traits:

1. On the surface they are simple enough for a child to understand. They make spiritual realities accessible by conveying them in concrete images instead of theoretical abstractions.
2. Paradoxically parables also have a mysterious dimension, a hidden depth of meaning that is not always easy to grasp, and that comes to light only upon thoughtful, open-minded reflection.
3. Thus the parables both conceal and reveal the mystery of the kingdom, depending on the disposition of the hearer (see Mark 4:10–13). One cannot remain neutral in the face of a parable; it provokes thought and challenges the listener to a decisive response to Jesus and his message.

In a broad sense, the Greek word *parabolē* means a "placing side by side" or comparison. It can include almost any kind of figurative speech: a metaphorical saying (Mark 3:23–27), allegory (4:13–20; 13:34–37), maxim (2:21–22), lesson or illustration (13:28), or enigmatic saying or riddle (7:15–17). Parables were sometimes used in the Old Testament (see Judg 9:7–15; 2 Sam 12:1–6).

a. Joseph Ratzinger (Pope Benedict XVI), *Jesus of Nazareth*, trans. Adrian J. Walker (New York: Doubleday, 2007), 192.

he actually gets into the **boat** and sits down, using it as an outdoor pulpit. Since sound carries well over water, Jesus' unaided voice could have reached thousands of people seated on the shore sloping down to the sea. He **taught them at length** according to his preferred method, as recorded in the †Synoptics: through the use of **parables**.

Jesus begins his instruction with an exhortation to pay close attention to what he is saying. The beginning of verse 3 reads literally, "Listen! Look!" He is asking his listeners to both hear his words and use their imaginations to picture the scene he is describing. The setting would be thoroughly familiar to his audience, many of whom made their living by farming. In Galilean agriculture, plots usually consisted of a thin layer of topsoil over a shelf of limestone. The seeds were sown by hand, using every available space, then plowed into the ground afterward. Thus this **sower** who lets seed fall **on the path**, **on rocky ground**, and **among thorns** is not as careless as he may seem. The seeds scattered on the rough path that villagers have trod through the fields will be plowed back in. Likewise the seed scattered among last year's withered thorns. The sower cannot tell by sight where the underlying rock lies close to the surface; he scatters liberally, knowing that some seeds will miss the mark.

But the results of this farmer's sowing labor are initially disappointing. Many of the seeds fare badly. Those sown on the path are quickly pecked away by **birds** before he has had a chance to plow them in. Those sown on rocky ground get a little further. Since they remained near the surface even after plowing, the little sprouts quickly appear but are **scorched** by the sun and wither **for lack of roots**. Those sown among thorns get further still: they grow into mature plants but then are **choked** by the fast-growing thornbushes around them before they are able to produce any grain. But the surprising conclusion is that, despite these failures, the sowing ends up producing a spectacular result. For a farmer working the fields of ancient Galilee, a thirtyfold yield is a plentiful harvest. Sixtyfold is a bumper crop, and a **hundredfold** is nearly miraculous (see Gen 26:12).

Jesus concludes the parable with another solemn call to attention, forming a frame with verse 3: **Whoever has ears to hear ought to hear.** This summons echoes the famous command of Deut 6:4, known to Jews as the Great Shema (from the Hebrew word for hear, *shema*): "Hear, O Israel!" To hear means far more than to take in with the ears: it means to absorb, to appropriate deeply into one's heart, to allow the message to sink in and change one's whole life. In fact, with this parable Jesus is illustrating what he himself is doing in proclaiming the kingdom of God. Jesus, seated in the boat and speaking to the crowds

4:3–8

4:9

on the hillsides, is the sower scattering his seed. Some of the seed has fallen on deaf ears; some has met with stony resistance (see Mark 2:7; 3:1–6). Yet all the while it is producing a stupendous yield among those who listen with open ears, a yield that may not be evident now but will come to light at the future time of the harvest. That is why the parable of the sower provides the key to the others that follow (see 4:13).

The Mystery of the Kingdom (4:10–12)

---

¹⁰**And when he was alone, those present along with the Twelve questioned him about the parables. ¹¹He answered them, "The mystery of the kingdom of God has been granted to you. But to those outside everything comes in parables, ¹²so that**

'they may look and see but not perceive,
**   and hear and listen but not understand,**
**   in order that they may not be converted and be forgiven.'"**

OT: Deut 30:10; Isa 6:9–10; Amos 3:7
NT: Matt 11:25–26; John 12:37–40. // Matt 13:10–15; Luke 8:9–10
Catechism: parables, 546

4:10–11   Mark now provides an interlude in the series of parables, with a private conversation that takes place at another time, **when he was alone** with his disciples. It seems paradoxical that Jesus was "alone" with more than twelve other people present! Those **present** (literally, "around him"), as in 3:34, are those individuals who have left the crowd to stay close to Jesus and continually learn from him—that is, those who have become his disciples. Unsure of the meaning of the parable, they ask Jesus to explain. In reply, he draws a contrast between his disciples, to whom **the mystery of the kingdom** has been granted, and **those outside**, to whom **everything comes in parables**. This pronouncement is one of the most difficult in the Gospel. Taken at face value it sounds as if Jesus has deliberately excluded some people from the kingdom by cloaking his words in mystery to avoid being understood. How are we to interpret this cryptic statement?

The key lies in understanding "mystery," a word that is used only here in the Gospels (see Matt 13:11; Luke 8:10), but often in the teaching of St. Paul. In the Old Testament, mystery refers to God's plans that are secret, yet revealed to the prophets for the sake of God's people (Dan 2:19, 28; Amos 3:7). They are a mystery not because God wants them unknown, but because they become known only by revelation. Similarly, in the New Testament the mystery is the whole plan of salvation that was eternally hidden in the heart of God, but has now been revealed in Christ (Rom 16:25–26; 1 Cor 2:7; Eph 3:3–9). God's hidden purposes are not a puzzle to be figured out, nor can they be grasped by any human intellectual methods. Like the secrets of any person's heart, they can be known only if one freely chooses to disclose them. That is why Jesus says elsewhere that his gospel is "hidden from the wise and the learned" but "revealed to little children" (Matt 11:25; Luke 10:21). Jesus is calling his disciples to recognize that they have been granted an immense privilege (see Matt 13:17): to them the mystery of the kingdom, present in the person and teaching of Jesus, has been unveiled. The parable of the sower has prepared them to understand the mystery that he will later teach explicitly: his kingdom will be established in a hidden and unexpected way—not through a triumphant conquest, but by way of suffering, setbacks, and seeming failure. It is a mystery that will culminate in the cross.

But what about those outside? Jesus describes their predicament with a quotation from Isaiah (Isa 6:9–10).[3] In the context of the passage, God forewarns Isaiah that he would be called to preach judgment to Israel at a time when the people were mired in sin and injustice, and so his message would meet with stubborn resistance. The forceful language does not mean that God himself will block the people's ears and eyes. Rather, the prophet's message will cause the people to blind and deafen *themselves* to avoid hearing it, in order to persist in their rebellion. Jesus, likewise, is addressing a wayward generation, many of whom will harden themselves to avoid grasping the implications of his words. His parables, by their hidden depths veiled in simplicity, will cause a separation by the response they evoke in listeners' hearts. For those who ponder the parables with sincere openness, the mystery of the kingdom will be gradually unveiled. But for those who prefer to persist in their own rebellious ways, the parables will remain opaque: **so that they may look and see but not perceive, and hear and listen but not understand**. Their obstinacy hinders them from attaining the goal of all Jesus' teaching: that they **be converted and be forgiven**. The tone of Jesus' words expresses a longing in the heart of God, as if God were saying: "If only you would listen, my people!" (see Deut 30:10; Ps 81:13–14; Luke 19:42). Yet his pronouncement hints at a theme that Paul will later develop in great detail (Rom 9–11): even the hardening of part of Israel—the refusal of many

4:12

3. The New Testament often quotes or alludes to this passage: Matt 13:13–17; Mark 8:17–18; Luke 8:10; John 9:39; 12:40; Acts 28:26–27.

Jews to accept the gospel—is within God's plan and will in the end contribute to the full and glorious accomplishment of his mysterious purposes.

Interpretation of the Parable of the Sower (4:13–20)

[13]Jesus said to them, "Do you not understand this parable? Then how will you understand any of the parables? [14]The sower sows the word. [15]These are the ones on the path where the word is sown. As soon as they hear, Satan comes at once and takes away the word sown in them. [16]And these are the ones sown on rocky ground who, when they hear the word, receive it at once with joy. [17]But they have no root; they last only for a time. Then when tribulation or persecution comes because of the word, they quickly fall away. [18]Those sown among thorns are another sort. They are the people who hear the word, [19]but worldly anxiety, the lure of riches, and the craving for other things intrude and choke the word, and it bears no fruit. [20]But those sown on rich soil are the ones who hear the word and accept it and bear fruit thirty and sixty and a hundredfold."

NT: James 1:21; 1 Pet 1:23–25. // Matt 13:18–23; Luke 8:11–15
Catechism: attitudes to God, 29

4:13　　　Jesus proceeds to fulfill his disciples' request (4:10) for a comprehensive explanation of the parable of the sower. **This parable**, he indicates, provides a clue for understanding all **the parables**; it is a parable about the parables. Yet here, as will often happen, the disciples are slow to grasp Jesus' meaning (7:18; 8:17–21; 9:32). Readers of the Gospel might wonder: how can they be blamed for their lack of understanding when Jesus had declared above (4:11) that understanding comes only as a gift? But there is no contradiction. By themselves they cannot grasp the mystery of the kingdom; Jesus has to open their eyes to it. But they must allow themselves to be drawn into the dynamic of the parable and its radical implications for their lives. Their slowness to understand only highlights the greatness of the revelation that has been granted to them.

4:14–15　　Jesus interprets the parable as an allegory, an extended metaphor in which each detail has a symbolic meaning. Mark has narrated this explanation such that it applies both to Jesus' own ministry and to the Church's ministry after his resurrection. The **sower** is not identified but clearly it is Jesus himself and, by extension, all preachers of the gospel. The **word** he **sows** is his proclamation of the kingdom (1:15), which will later become the Church's message of salvation in Christ (Col 1:5; 1 Thess 1:6; James 1:21; 1 Pet 1:25). The parable then focuses on four types of human response. These do not necessarily represent completely distinct categories of people; they may describe the responses of the same individual at different times. The **ones on the path** are those in whom the word meets with no interest or receptivity. Like seed on a hard-trodden path, the gospel has no chance to sink in. †**Satan** swoops down like a greedy bird and snatches it away, perhaps through distractions, fears, or faulty human reasoning. Indeed, this is what will occur when Jesus sows "the word" about his coming passion (Mark 8:31–33): Peter vehemently rejects this word, and Jesus immediately refers to him as Satan.

The second category are those who enthusiastically **receive** the word for what it is: good news bringing salvation. But there remains an underlying hardness of heart that prevents the word from penetrating deeply. As a result, their allegiance to Christ is too shallow to sustain them in times of **tribulation** or religious **persecution**. Such trials are an inevitable part of the Christian life (Mark 10:30; 13:9), as the early Church knew well by experience (Acts 8:1; 2 Cor 12:10; 1 Pet 4:12–14). But instead of persevering, these people quickly **fall away** (*skandalizomai*), a word that means to stumble or be tripped up. This is precisely what will occur with the disciples when Jesus is arrested (Mark 14:27, 50). **4:16–17**

Those **sown among thorns** are those who do let the word sink in, but also allow other preoccupations to begin to crowd in and compete for priority. **Worldly anxiety** is literally "the cares of this age." Daily cares are an unavoidable part of life in this world, especially for those who are married and raising families (see 1 Cor 7:32–34). But the danger is to allow these legitimate concerns to take over and suffocate one's devotion to Jesus and zeal for the age to come. The deceptive **lure of riches** and the **craving for other things** such as power, possessions, and prestige likewise prove fatal to discipleship (Mark 10:37; 12:38–40). Later in the Gospel a rich man will exemplify this pitfall (10:17–22). Tragically the good news that has germinated within such people **bears no fruit**. Their spiritual life is sterile. **4:18–19**

After spelling out these negative responses to the gospel, Jesus describes in the briefest of terms those who allow the seed of the word to produce its marvelous effect. Like **rich soil**, they **hear the word**, **accept it**, and **bear fruit**. Although it is the seed itself that is actively at work (as Jesus will explain further in 4:26–29), each step requires an intensely personal cooperation. It is not enough to listen to Jesus' words: one must ponder and understand them, take them into one's heart, and allow them to transform one's whole life. **4:20**

The contrast between the soil that produces a rich yield and the soil that fails to bear fruit parallels the contrast between Jesus' disciples and "those outside" (4:11)—although the disciples sometimes exhibit the characteristics of poor soil. The good and bad soil are in turn subdivided into three categories. The barren ground includes the hard pathway, the rocky soil, and the thorny soil. The fruitful ground includes those who bear **thirty and sixty and a hundred-fold**. Jesus is exhorting his listeners to examine their response to his call, and honestly evaluate what interior obstacles may be hindering them from bearing the abundant harvest that God desires.

Reflection and Application (4:13–20)

The explanation of the parable of the sower would have resonated with Mark's audience as a powerful word of encouragement. If even Jesus' preaching seemed to meet with so much initial resistance and failure, how could it not be the same for his followers in the early Church, who were trying to spread the gospel of the kingdom in an indifferent and sometimes violently hostile society? Despite the many seeds apparently sown in vain, God is at work to produce what will finally be revealed as a stupendous harvest. The parable illustrates the "mystery of the kingdom" that Jesus mentioned in 4:11. The reign of God will not come about through unmitigated success and uninterrupted growth. An unexpected but necessary part of the plan is the setbacks and failures that give Jesus' disciples a share in the mystery of his own suffering.

The parable of the sower is particularly illuminating for those who teach RCIA or are involved in other evangelistic or catechetical activities. It can lead the participants, and indeed all of us, to reflect on the dangers in our lives that threaten the fruitfulness of the word. What kind of soil am I? Has the word of God been fruitful in me? If not, what obstacles are there, and how will I overcome them?

The Light That Must Be Seen (4:21–25)

---

²¹He said to them, "Is a lamp brought in to be placed under a bushel basket or under a bed, and not to be placed on a lampstand? ²²For there is nothing hidden except to be made visible; nothing is secret except to come to light. ²³Anyone who has ears to hear ought to hear." ²⁴He also told them, "Take care what you hear. The measure with which you measure will be measured out to you, and still more will be given to you. ²⁵To the one who

has, more will be given; from the one who has not, even what he has will
be taken away."

NT: John 1:9; 8:12. // Matt 5:15; 10:26; Luke 8:16–17; 11:33; 12:2; 19:26

The parable of the sower and its explanation are followed by four cryptic
sayings, which Matthew and Luke also record but in different contexts. Jesus
probably spoke these sayings many times in various settings over the course of
his public ministry. Mark has combined them here in two pairs (vv. 21–22 and
24–25), with the solemn admonition of verse 9 repeated in between: "Anyone
who has ears to hear ought to hear."

Jesus is continuing to instruct his disciples in private, although at an unspeci-   **4:21**
fied point the setting will shift back to the crowds by the sea (see 4:33). He asks
a rhetorical question: **Is a lamp brought in** (literally, "Does the lamp come")
only to be hidden **under a bushel basket** or **a bed**? The obvious answer is: Of
course not! The implication is that the lamp is Jesus, who has come into the
world to bring humanity the light of revelation (see Luke 2:32; John 1:9; 8:12).
Jesus wishes to prevent a mistaken interpretation of his earlier words about
the mystery of the kingdom (Mark 4:11). Despite the obscurity of the parables

and the difficulties people
have in understanding his
teaching, his purpose is not
to hide the kingdom but to
make it known.

Verse 22 clarifies the   **4:22**
point. What is **hidden** and
secret is the mystery of the
kingdom that is present in
Jesus. It is hidden in the ordinariness of his life (see 6:3),
in the apparent simplicity of
the parables (4:11), and in
the disappointments and
hindrances he has encoun-
tered (2:7; 3:6, 21–22). But it
is hidden only for a time, for
the sake of eventually being

Fig. 5. First-century Palestinian lamp.

fully revealed. Just as Jesus' identity cannot be prematurely publicized, because to do so would lead to a false understanding of his messiahship, so the mystery of the kingdom has to germinate and sprout deep within human hearts before its full splendor can **come to light**. On one level this saying alludes to the fact that the time of hiddenness has ended with Jesus' resurrection. Now the mystery of his messianic identity and mission is fully revealed, and his followers are to take that light into the whole world (see 13:10). How senseless it would be to be given such a bright light only to conceal it under a bushel basket or a bed! On another level the kingdom is still hidden in the trials and setbacks that accompany the Church's mission of evangelization. But in the end, all that God wishes to reveal is destined to come to light.

4:23 Jesus stresses the importance of taking time to consider and reflect on this mystery of hiddenness by twice reminding his audience to carefully heed his words.

4:24–25 The second pair of cryptic sayings expands on the consequences of hearing well or poorly. Jesus is telling his audience: You will profit from my teachings in the **measure** you pay attention to them—and if you do strive to understand, God will give you **still more** understanding than you could attain by your own efforts. The last saying, which occurs elsewhere in the context of the parable of the talents (Matt 25:29; Luke 19:26), seems to conflict with our idea of fairness, and even other biblical statements about the poor being made rich (Mark 9:35; Luke 1:53; 6:20, 24). What could it mean here? In this context it signifies that whoever responds to Jesus with openness and a desire to learn **will be given** even **more** insight; whoever does not will lose even the little understanding he has. God's revelation is a gift, but it is a gift that must be freely accepted.

The Parable of the Growing Seed (4:26–29)

---

²⁶He said, "This is how it is with the kingdom of God; it is as if a man were to scatter seed on the land ²⁷and would sleep and rise night and day and the seed would sprout and grow, he knows not how. ²⁸Of its own accord the land yields fruit, first the blade, then the ear, then the full grain in the ear. ²⁹And when the grain is ripe, he wields the sickle at once, for the harvest has come."

OT: Joel 4:11–16
NT: 1 Cor 3:6–7; 1 Pet 1:23–25; Rev 14:14–15
Lectionary: Mass for Productive Land

These verses recount another seed parable, one that is found only in Mark.   4:26–29
This time the focus is on the seed's intrinsic power to grow **of its own accord**.
The sower liberally scatters his seed, then goes on with the routine of his daily
life. Slowly, imperceptibly, the seed begins to sprout. The farmer does not know
how this happens; even today, with the tremendous advances in microbiology,
life remains a mystery. Nor can the farmer control the process. According to its
natural stages **the land yields fruit, first the blade, then the ear, then the full
grain**. The farmer can water, weed, and fertilize the ground as the months go
on, but he cannot make the ripe grain appear a day before its appointed time.
Farming requires an element of trust and patience. Yet the moment **the harvest**
has arrived, the farmer is ready with his **sickle** to reap without delay. The harvest
is a biblical image for the final judgment (Joel 4:13; Rev 14:14–15).

With this parable Jesus explains that the kingdom of God is a divine work,
not a human achievement. God brings about its growth, which at times is
imperceptible. We cooperate, but we cannot control or hasten the arrival of
the kingdom by our efforts any more than the farmer can harvest his grain
in January. St. Paul knew this principle well: "I planted, Apollos watered, but
God caused the growth. Therefore, neither the one who plants nor the one who
waters is anything, but only God, who causes the growth" (1 Cor 3:6–7). Every
member of the kingdom is being made ready for the harvest by our inner growth
in holiness and virtue, which *God* brings about through our cooperation with
his grace. The parable serves as an encouragement for those who think their
efforts for the kingdom are fruitless, and a warning for those who think they
can bring about the kingdom by their own projects and programs.

The Parable of the Mustard Seed (4:30–32)

> ³⁰**He said, "To what shall we compare the kingdom of God, or what
> parable can we use for it? ³¹It is like a mustard seed that, when it is sown
> in the ground, is the smallest of all the seeds on the earth. ³²But once it is
> sown, it springs up and becomes the largest of plants and puts forth large
> branches, so that the birds of the sky can dwell in its shade."**

OT: Ezek 17:23; 31:6; Dan 4:9
NT: // Matt 13:31–32; Luke 13:18–19

It is as if Jesus is thinking aloud, searching for ways to help his listeners   4:30–32
to grasp the mystery of the kingdom (see 4:11). Because **the kingdom** is a
divine reality, it cannot be defined or contained in human categories. It can

be understood only by using analogies, word pictures that force the listener to think and ponder at a deeper level. Once again, the earthly reality most suitable as an analogy to the kingdom is, of all things, a tiny seed. In this third seed parable, the emphasis is on the seed's smallness. For Jesus' Jewish audience, the idea of the kingdom as a seed must have been quite a surprise. A more predictable comparison would be a mighty army (see Isa 13:4; Joel 2:11) or a cataclysmic earthquake (Isa 29:6). But no, the kingdom is like a **mustard seed**, which Jesus describes (using the device of hyperbole, or exaggeration, for effect) as **the smallest of all the seeds on the earth**. But once sown, it **springs up and becomes the largest of plants** (another hyperbole).

In mentioning **large branches** that shelter many **birds**, Jesus is evoking the Old Testament image of a lofty, shady tree, symbolizing an empire that grants protection to peoples of different races and tongues (Ezek 17:23; 31:6; Dan 4:9). The parable of the mustard seed thus points to the future worldwide reach of the kingdom of God. From its humble, inauspicious beginnings in Jesus' itinerant preaching in Galilee with a small band of followers, the kingdom will mature to an immense tree in whom the Gentiles will find a home. This growth will not be due to human methods but to God's hidden power. Jesus speaks with utter assurance of the future success of the kingdom, urging his disciples to persevere with hope and patience.

The Purpose of the Parables (4:33–34)

---

[33]**With many such parables he spoke the word to them as they were able to understand it. **[34]**Without parables he did not speak to them, but to his own disciples he explained everything in private.**

OT: Deut 6:4
NT: // Matt 13:34–35
Catechism: parables, 546

4:33   Mark's final word on the parable discourse is another affirmation that Jesus **spoke** in **parables** not to obfuscate (as vv. 11–12 might suggest), but to adapt the mystery of the kingdom to the capacity and openness of his listeners. The end of verse 33 reads literally, "as they were able to hear it," repeating the key verb "hear" for the thirteenth time in this chapter. The disposition Jesus seeks from his followers is the same demanded by God of his chosen people: "Hear, O Israel!" (Deut 6:4). To hear means not only to listen or even to understand, but to accept with a willing heart—that is, to obey. A person's understanding of

92

the kingdom grows as one reflects on the parables and embraces their implications, enlarging one's capacity to "hear."

Although Jesus spoke to the crowds only in parables, **to his own disciples he explained everything in private**. Who are these privileged disciples? Mark 3:32–35; 4:10 make clear: not just the Twelve, called to a special mission, but all "those present along with the Twelve"—that is, all those who choose to be disciples by staying close to Jesus to listen to his teachings, and by doing the will of the Father.

4:34

Reflection and Application (4:33–34)

A distinctive characteristic of Jesus' teachings is their inescapable demand for personal engagement. Jesus speaks in such a way that you cannot "get it" simply by hearing homilies, listening to recorded talks, studying works of theology, or even reading biblical commentaries. The only way to attain full understanding is by coming to Jesus personally and asking *him* to reveal the meaning. Even today, Jesus welcomes any disciple who comes to him in prayer and says, "Lord, explain the parable," or, "Explain the meaning of this scripture passage that seems obscure to me." As saints of every stripe, educated and uneducated, have attested over the ages, the Lord will reveal profound mysteries to hearts that approach him in humble faith.

Authority over Nature, Demons, Disease, and Death

Mark 4:35–5:43

Following the day of teaching in parables Mark places a group of miracle stories that reveal Jesus' awesome power over all the elements that cause fear and distress in human life. These mighty deeds are part of the continued training of his apostles in preparation for their being sent out on mission (6:7). By the end of this section they will have seen firsthand Jesus' authority over all that could threaten them, and they will be ready to be granted a share in that authority. Also in this section, Jesus' mission expands for the first time into pagan territory outside the borders of Israel—a prelude to the Church's mission to the Gentiles.

The Calming of the Storm (4:35–41)

---

³⁵On that day, as evening drew on, he said to them, "Let us cross to the other side." ³⁶Leaving the crowd, they took him with them in the boat just as he was. And other boats were with him. ³⁷A violent squall came up and waves were breaking over the boat, so that it was already filling up. ³⁸Jesus was in the stern, asleep on a cushion. They woke him and said to him, "Teacher, do you not care that we are perishing?" ³⁹He woke up, rebuked the wind, and said to the sea, "Quiet! Be still!" The wind ceased and there was great calm. ⁴⁰Then he asked them, "Why are you terrified? Do you not yet have faith?" ⁴¹They were filled with great awe and said to one another, "Who then is this whom even wind and sea obey?"

OT: Ps 4:9; 65:8; 89:10; 107:28–30; Jon 1
NT: // Matt 8:23–27; Luke 8:22–25
Lectionary: Anointing of the Sick; Mass in Time of Earthquake, or For Rain, or For Good Weather, or To Avert Storms, or For Any Need

Jesus had been teaching the multitude in parables from a boat anchored just   **4:35–36**
offshore (4:1). Concluding his "Sermon on the Sea" as **evening** approaches, he
asks his disciples to **cross to the other side**. The eastern side of the Sea of Galilee,
across from Capernaum, was a predominantly Gentile area (5:1). This voyage
is Jesus' first extension of his ministry into Gentile territory (later repeated in
6:45; 7:31; 8:13). Disciples accompany him in several boats, **leaving the crowd**
behind on the shore. They cast off with Jesus **just as he was**, still seated in his
floating pulpit, without his first going ashore.

The Sea of Galilee is known for the **violent** storms that can arise without   **4:37–38**
warning, as wind is funneled through the steep valleys among the hills surrounding the lake. In this instance the gale is so fierce that it terrifies even seasoned
fishermen. **Waves** come crashing **over the boat**, swamping it and threatening
to sink it. Yet in the midst of this fury, Jesus is **in the stern, asleep**. Anyone
who has ever been in a violently storm-tossed boat has reason to think that
this ability to sleep through the storm was the first miracle! Jesus exemplifies
the perfect trust in God that is often signified in Scripture by a peaceful and
untroubled sleep (see Job 11:18–19; Ps 4:9; Prov 3:24).

But his serenity is not shared by the disciples, who awaken Jesus with a stinging reproach: **Teacher, do you not care that we are perishing?** It is the first
time in the Gospel that Jesus has been called "Teacher," having just completed
a day of teaching (Mark 4:1–34). This time there will be a powerful lesson of
faith, learned by experience. The tone of the disciples' question suggests that
they have a vague idea that Jesus can do something about the storm, but they
think he is indifferent to their desperate plight, as if he has no concern for their
safety or survival. How often God's people reproach him this way, from the Old
Testament (see Exod 14:10–11; Num 14:3) to this day.

The Sea of Galilee

**BIBLICAL
BACKGROUND**

The Sea of Galilee, called the Sea of Chinnereth (meaning "lyre-
shaped") in the Old Testament (Num 34:11), is actually a freshwater
lake about seven miles wide and thirteen miles long, lying between
Galilee to the west and the region of the Decapolis (today, the Golan
Heights) to the east. From its southern end, the Jordan River flows
toward the Dead Sea. In the first century the lake provided a thriving
commercial fishing industry for the villages that dotted its shoreline.
It is still known for the violent gales that can arise suddenly and pose
a danger to small boats.

4:39   Jesus does not leave his disciples in their panic but immediately awakens and rebukes the raging elements. He does not pray that God would calm the storm, but commands it himself with sovereign authority: **Quiet! Be still!** (literally, "Be muzzled!"). **Rebuked** is the same word used to describe his casting out of unclean spirits (1:25; 3:12), suggesting that demonic powers somehow instigated the squall that threatens to deflect him and his disciples from their mission. In the Old Testament the sea is often viewed as a symbol of chaos and the habitation of evil powers (Job 26:12–13; Ps 74:13–14; Isa 27:1). Jesus exorcises these adverse forces of nature with the same authority with which he freed human beings from demonic oppression. Instantly the howling **wind** subsides and the choppy waters become **calm**. The wording parallels Ps 107:28–29: "In their distress they cried to the LORD, who brought them out of their peril, Hushed the storm to a murmur; the waves of the sea were stilled."

4:40–41   The moment the danger has passed, Jesus chides his disciples for their feeble faith. **Why are you terrified? Do you not yet have faith?** Certainly, they had turned to him in their moment of terror and dismay. But they did not yet grasp who he really is: sovereign Lord over all creation. Jesus was forming a band of followers who were to be confident in their mission on earth: to bring the peace and authority of the kingdom into all the troubles of humanity. He had called them to complete a task on the other side of the sea; would he have done so only to let them perish in the waves (see Exod 14)? As the disciples knew well, God alone has power to subdue the seas: "You rule the raging sea; you still its swelling waves" (Ps 89:10; see Job 38:8; Ps 65:8). Indeed, from the Exodus on, God's control of the sea has signified his tender care for his people (Exod 15; Isa 51:10). So it is no wonder that after Jesus calms the storm, **they were filled with great awe** (literally, "they feared a great fear"). Their abject terror of the forces of nature has been replaced by reverent fear of the presence of God in Jesus. Jesus' subduing of the sea is an †epiphany, a manifestation of his divine authority. **Who then is this?** is a question that not only Jesus' contemporaries but all the readers of the Gospel are meant to ask (see Mark 8:29).

Reflection and Application (4:35–41)

Mark narrates this story not only to recount the memorable event of the storm, but also to reflect the experience of the early Christians. The boat bearing the disciples and the sleeping Jesus is an image of the Church (see Eph 4:14). The small and struggling early Church, storm-tossed on the seas of the

Christated Asleep in Us

LIVING TRADITION

St. Augustine comments: "When you are insulted, that is the wind. When you are angry, that is the waves. So when the winds blow and the waves surge, the boat is in danger, your heart is in jeopardy, your heart is tossed to and fro. On being insulted, you long to retaliate. But revenge brings another kind of misfortune—shipwreck. Why? Because Christ is asleep in you. What do I mean? I mean you have forgotten Christ. Rouse him, then; remember Christ, let Christ awake within you, give heed to him. . . . 'Who is this, that even the winds and sea obey him?'"[a]

a. *Sermon* 63.1–3.

---

vast Roman Empire, must have sometimes wondered why their Lord seemed to be asleep in the stern—absent, unaware, or unconcerned about the mortal perils that threatened them. How often have his disciples through the ages felt that way in the midst of "storms" of persecution, natural disasters, or personal troubles? But Jesus' authority is without limit, and though he allows trials, in the end nothing can truly harm those who trust in him (see Luke 10:19). His reproach in verse 40 is an invitation for all Christians to awaken their faith in his presence and in his absolute authority over the cosmos. The true antidote to fear of earthly dangers is the faith that comes from "fear of the Lord," the reverent awe of God that Scripture calls the beginning of wisdom (Job 28:28; Ps 111:10; Prov 1:7). "He who fears the Lord is never alarmed, never afraid" (Sir 34:14). Indeed, the most repeated command in Scripture is "Do not fear!" Why? Because to refuse to give in to fear disables the enemy's strategy, which is to dissuade Jesus' followers from their mission. When we have no fear, the enemy trembles in fear.

Liberation of a Man Tormented by Demons (5:1–13)

---

¹They came to the other side of the sea, to the territory of the Gerasenes. ²When he got out of the boat, at once a man from the tombs who had an unclean spirit met him. ³The man had been dwelling among the tombs, and no one could restrain him any longer, even with a chain. ⁴In fact, he had frequently been bound with shackles and chains, but the chains had been pulled apart by him and the shackles smashed, and no

one was strong enough to subdue him. ⁵Night and day among the tombs and on the hillsides he was always crying out and bruising himself with stones. ⁶Catching sight of Jesus from a distance, he ran up and prostrated himself before him, ⁷crying out in a loud voice, "What have you to do with me, Jesus, Son of the Most High God? I adjure you by God, do not torment me!" ⁸[He had been saying to him, "Unclean spirit, come out of the man!"] ⁹He asked him, "What is your name?" He replied, "Legion is my name. There are many of us." ¹⁰And he pleaded earnestly with him not to drive them away from that territory.

¹¹Now a large herd of swine was feeding there on the hillside. ¹²And they pleaded with him, "Send us into the swine. Let us enter them." ¹³And he let them, and the unclean spirits came out and entered the swine. The herd of about two thousand rushed down a steep bank into the sea, where they were drowned.

OT: Deut 14:8
NT: Matt 12:43; Mark 3:27. // Matt 8:28–32; Luke 8:26–33
Catechism: exorcisms, 550, 1673

This episode is Jesus' first excursion into non-Jewish territory, and it begins in the same way as his public ministry among the Jews (1:21–27): with immediate confrontation and decisive victory over evil. Just as the stilling of the storm showed his power over the forces of destruction in nature, so the exorcism of the demoniac shows his power over the forces of destruction within the human person.

5:1   The **territory of the Gerasenes**, on the east side of the Sea of Galilee,¹ would have been an eerie place even in daylight. To this day numerous caves dot the shoreline, many of which were used to bury the dead. Then as now, tombs were popularly regarded as a favorite haunt of demons. The lifestyle and customs of this Gentile region would have seemed alien to Jews, since the inhabitants did not observe the Jewish moral or dietary laws. Indeed, this particular vicinity would be viewed as doubly unclean, containing as it did both tombs (see Num 5:2) and pigs (see Lev 11:7). As Jesus steps ashore, he is immediately challenged by the demonic powers that seem to hold sway in the area, as if they are jealous of their territorial rights.

1. The exact location of this site is unknown, since the city of Gerasa (modern Jerash) is actually some thirty miles southeast of the lake. A few ancient manuscripts have "Gadarenes" instead of "Gerasenes" (in accord with Matt 8:28), but Gadara is about five miles from the shore, with no steep cliffs nearby. Other manuscripts attempt to resolve the problem by substituting "Gergesenes," a site nearer the lake. Most likely Mark had in mind a general area between Gerasa and the lake.

The moment Jesus sets foot on land, the demon-possessed man comes out   5:2–3
to him **from the tombs**, wild-eyed, shouting, and bearing the marks of self-
mutilation. Mark's description of the demon-possessed man is vivid, including
more elaborate detail than the descriptions by Matthew and Luke. This is a
man who experiences a "violent squall" (4:37) not in nature but in himself. The
unclean spirit has taken over the center of his personality, resulting in a life of
unbearable torment and alienation. Unable to function in human society, he
lives **among the tombs**, that is, in the realm of the dead. The scene seems to
echo Isaiah's indictment of rebellious Israel: "people who provoke me continually
. . . living among the graves and spending the night in caverns, Eating swine's
flesh" (Isa 65:3–4). But paradoxically, the tomb is the very place where, at the
end of the Gospel (Mark 16:5–6), Jesus' ultimate victory will be manifested in
his resurrection from the dead.

Mark's description is designed to show how demonic influence distorts and   5:4–5
destroys the image of God in humans. The man's behavior is a picture of despair
and self-hatred: **he was always crying out and bruising himself with stones**.
He is evidently more of a danger to himself than to anyone else. Thwarting
every attempt to subdue him with **shackles and chains**, he demonstrates the
preternatural strength that has sometimes been verified in cases of demonic
possession. We learn later that he is unclothed (v. 15), another indication of
his loss of human dignity.

Mark emphasizes the futility of society's efforts to solve the demoniac's problem. The most they can do is attempt to restrain the man physically, and even
that has proven totally ineffective. The verb for **bound** in verse 4 (*deō*) is the
same word used in Jesus' parable of the strong man (3:27). The parable has
prepared the reader to recognize that Jesus alone is **strong enough** to bind
Satan and thus set the man free. The exorcism that is about to occur is a visible
enactment of the parable.

It may seem surprising that the demon-possessed man **prostrated himself**   5:6
before Jesus. But here as in 3:11 the gesture does not reflect an attitude of worship but rather a submission compelled by Jesus' irresistible authority. The man's
contradictory actions (running to Jesus, prostrating himself, yet assuming Jesus
will destroy him) may indicate either the demon's panic and desperation, or
the interior conflict in the man whose voice and personality have been com-
mandeered, but who longs for liberation.

Just as at the exorcism in Capernaum (1:24), the man fiercely demands, **What**   5:7
have you to do with me? The demon is fully aware of Jesus' divine identity,
but his use of the title **Son of the Most High God** is not a confession of faith.

Rather, it is a desperate attempt to gain control over Jesus (see the same tactic in 1:24; 3:11–12). The "Most High" is a title often used by Gentiles to denote the God of Israel (Num 24:16; Isa 14:14). In the New Testament, "Most High" is used mostly by those under demonic influence (Luke 8:28; Acts 16:17), perhaps because it is an acknowledgment of greater power by lesser spiritual powers.

Ironically this spirit opposed to God attempts to get control of the situation by adjuring Jesus—whom he has just acknowledged as God's own Son—in the name of God, using a formula found in Jewish exorcisms. But the tactic is futile. The arrival of Jesus has precipitated a crisis in which the evil spirit senses that its reign of terror over human beings has come to an end and its **torment** (probably referring to eternal punishment; see Matt 8:29; 18:34) is about to begin. From the start it is evident to both parties that Jesus has the upper hand, and the demon is quickly reduced to pleading for terms (Mark 5:10). There is a double irony in that the demon begs reprieve from torment, the very thing it has been imposing on its victim.

5:8   Jesus had already begun to pronounce the words of exorcism, **Unclean spirit, come out of the man!** He now turns the tables on the demon by demanding to know its name. In the Bible, as in much of the ancient world, a name is far more than a label; it expresses the core of a person's identity (see Gen 3:20; Exod 2:10; 1 Sam 1:20). To know the name of a demon was thus in a certain sense to have authority over it, to be able to make it act. Jesus' ability to extract the demon's name underscores his absolute authority.

5:9–10   The demon's answer is **Legion**, a Latin term for a regiment of about six thousand men. This reply could represent the demon's attempt to be evasive, or to impress Jesus with a show of power. The term would have struck a chord with the Jews of Jesus' time, who were longing for liberation from the Roman legions. But Jesus' concern is a much deeper liberation—from the bondage of sin and Satan. The demons' plea not to be driven **away from that territory** suggests that demons are in some way territorial; though immaterial beings themselves, they maintain power by attaching themselves to certain regions, objects, or individuals (see Matt 12:43–45; Tob 8:3).

5:11–13   There is nothing unusual in a **herd of swine** grazing on the hillside in Gentile territory, though for Jews the sight of these unclean animals (Deut 14:8) would have been repugnant. Although the demons seem to win a concession from Jesus, it proves to be their downfall. Unable to control their new hosts, they inadvertently send them careening down the bank in a deadly stampede. Like the ancient enemy of Israel, Pharaoh and his army (Exod 14), the demons meet a watery demise. The sea is often portrayed in Scripture as the abode of evil (Dan 7:3; Rev 13:1; 21:1).

Neither Jesus nor his disciples are troubled by the loss of the swine or the economic damage it entails. Infinitely more important is the man's restoration to human dignity. The incident is a concrete illustration of God's preferential love and compassion for humanity, as possessing value far above any other creatures: "You are worth more than many sparrows" (Luke 12:7; see Matt 12:12).

Reflection and Application (5:1–13)

The Gerasene demoniac is a graphic example of the dehumanizing effect of evil and the tyranny it gives demons over human beings. It is evident that what is needed for this man's salvation is not merely conversion and reform of life, but deliverance: the expulsion of evil spirits and their influence that only the Son of God can accomplish. Although this is obvious in his case, it is also true to a lesser degree in every human life. Because of original sin, Satan has acquired a certain domination over all human beings (Catechism, 407; see John 8:34; Rom 5:12–19); in all of us the image of God is defaced to some degree. Thus the Rite of Baptism is always preceded by an exorcism, banishing any evil spirits that may have insinuated themselves into a person's life (Catechism, 1237). Jesus' exorcism of the demoniac gives us an insight into what his work of redemption has accomplished for every one of us.

Bearing Witness to Christ (5:14–20)

[14]The swineherds ran away and reported the incident in the town and throughout the countryside. And people came out to see what had happened. [15]As they approached Jesus, they caught sight of the man who had been possessed by Legion, sitting there clothed and in his right mind. And they were seized with fear. [16]Those who witnessed the incident explained to them what had happened to the possessed man and to the swine. [17]Then they began to beg him to leave their district. [18]As he was getting into the boat, the man who had been possessed pleaded to remain with him. [19]But he would not permit him but told him instead, "Go home to your family and announce to them all that the Lord in his pity has done for you." [20]Then the man went off and began to proclaim in the Decapolis what Jesus had done for him; and all were amazed.

NT: // Matt 8:33–34; Luke 8:34–39
Catechism: evangelization, 905, 2044, 2472
Lectionary: 5:18–20: Mass in Thanksgiving to God

5:14–17   Not surprisingly, the event that has just transpired is a matter of sensational local news, so the **swineherds** immediately begin to spread the report. As the crowds begin to gather, they are met with the sight of the former demoniac now in a completely different condition, an image of tranquility. Mark emphasizes the man's transfigured state with three Greek participles in a row: **sitting, clothed, in his right mind**.

"Sitting" conveys the restfulness that has come to this formerly frenzied man who is now at peace with himself and with God. Clothing is significant in Scripture as an extension of the person (Mark 1:6; 9:3) and a symbol of human dignity (Luke 15:22; Rev 19:8). Conversely, being unclothed signifies the shame caused by sin (Gen 3:10; Isa 20:4; Mark 14:52). It is God who, in his tender kindness, clothes human beings whose transgressions have stripped them of dignity (Gen 3:21; Zech 3:3–5; Luke 15:22). Thus the man's being clothed signifies not only that he is now sane and in full possession of his faculties, but also that he is restored to a state of uprightness before God. Now he is able to see things clearly, that is, not only to identify Jesus but also to relate to him in the appropriate attitude of gratitude and devotion.

The participles "sitting" and "clothed" reappear in Mark 16:5, again in the setting of a tomb, where it describes the young man who announces Jesus' resurrection. With these verbal parallels Mark hints that the exorcism of the Gerasene demoniac, like all Jesus' miracles in the Gospel, is an anticipation of the power of his resurrection, already at work in the lives of human beings.

There is irony in Mark's account of the reaction to this wondrous event. Rather than the amazement and praise that might be expected (see 1:27; 2:12), the people are **seized with fear** (the same verb, *phobeō*, was used for the apostles' reaction to Jesus' calming of the storm in 4:41). Now that the demon-possessed man is no longer running around naked, cutting himself, and howling in the hills, they are afraid. What explains this odd reaction? Perhaps the people recognize that in the face of this stunning manifestation of power they cannot remain neutral toward Jesus. The exorcism of the possessed man represents a challenge to their lives, a call to a decision. Rather than face the uncomfortable question of who Jesus is and what claim he might make on their lives, they **beg him to leave their district**. They would prefer to have life go on as it is, without any divine interruptions to rock the boat. In mentioning the swine again (v. 16), Mark suggests that financial considerations stemming from the ruin of such a large herd may also have influenced the locals.

5:18   As Jesus is concluding his brief visit to the land of the Gerasenes, turned away by the inhabitants, the exorcised man makes the opposite request: he pleads

to remain with him. To remain with (literally, "to be with") Jesus signifies becoming his disciple, the same phrase used of the Twelve in 3:14. This response shows his gratitude to Jesus, his liberator.

Jesus' reply is not a rejection but rather a commissioning. The man is told to **go** and **announce** to others **all that the Lord** has done for him—that is, to become an evangelist! The phrase is literally, "Go to your house, to your own [people]," those from whom the man had been estranged and who will now be astounded at his transformation. His personal experience of God's mercy through Jesus' act of deliverance is the only credential he needs.

This command makes the exorcised man the first "Christian" missionary to the Gentiles, anticipating the Gentile mission that will begin in earnest after the resurrection (16:15). It is in striking contrast to the messianic secret, the injunctions to silence following Jesus' works of healing among the Jews (1:44; 5:43; 7:36; 8:26). Indeed, it is the only occasion in Mark where Jesus tells a healed person to spread the news. The man is not asked to proclaim the identity of Jesus, but rather what Jesus did for him. Yet Jesus' use of "the Lord" in place of his own name is a veiled reference to his divinity. The Lord (*ho Kyrios*) is the title used in the Greek Old Testament to substitute for the unutterable divine Name. On the surface Jesus' command is to proclaim what *God* has done for him, but the man seems to grasp the connection, since he obeys by going off to proclaim **what Jesus had done for him**.

The **Decapolis** (literally, Ten Cities) was a federation of independent cities, mostly Greek in culture, comprising a large area east of the Jordan River. The seemingly inauspicious missionary, a former demoniac, faithfully carries out Jesus' command by broadcasting throughout the entire region his story of deliverance—the kind of proclamation that is impossible to refute. Indeed, the success of his efforts appears later from the very different reception Jesus meets on his second visit to the area (7:31–8:9).

Reflection and Application (5:14–20)

At first sight, this first mission of Jesus and his disciples to the Gentiles looks like a near-total failure. Only one person has been won over, and not a very reliable one at that. The rest of the people have made clear their desire to have no further contact with Jesus. The disciples might well have concluded at that point that Jesus should simply give up on the Decapolis and keep his ministry within the bounds of Israel. Yet in the context of the Gospel, we can see the kingdom of God breaking in on this evil-infested area. This man's demons had cast a pall over the whole region (see v. 10), and now they are banished. The tomb-covered hills have lost their power to intimidate. The next time Jesus comes, the whole region responds to him differently, and a way is opened for the healing of others.

So often Jesus chooses a person we would be least likely to choose. Surely the Lord could find a more respectable, upright man to be his witness in the Decapolis! Yet he chose this man, previously known throughout the region for his degradation, now visible to all as healed and full of joy. The message he had to offer would have been very simple: "See the scars? I was the guy who cut myself and howled at night. I don't do it any more!" But it would be hard to imagine a more eloquent witness to Jesus' identity and saving mission. A living witness is Jesus' secret weapon, a powerful means to begin opening people's hearts to his teaching and his works of mercy. Hearing the man's testimony, people could conclude, "If Jesus can deliver this wretched man, surely he can set me free too." The episode is an example of the demonstration of power that accompanies any effective proclamation of the good news (see 1 Cor 2:4; 2 Cor 12:12). It reminds us that the most important qualification to bring people into an encounter with the living Christ is not a theology degree but rather the ability to tell "all that the Lord has done for you."

A Father's Plea (5:21–24)

> [21]When Jesus had crossed again [in the boat] to the other side, a large crowd gathered around him, and he stayed close to the sea. [22]One of the synagogue officials, named Jairus, came forward. Seeing him he fell at his feet [23]and pleaded earnestly with him, saying, "My daughter is at the point of death. Please, come lay your hands on her that she may get well and live." [24]He went off with him, and a large crowd followed him and pressed upon him.

NT: Mark 16:18; John 11:25–26. // Matt 9:18–19; Luke 8:40–42

5:21   Jesus' return to the Jewish side of the Sea of Galilee is immediately followed by two more miracles: the raising of a girl from the dead and the cure of a hemorrhaging woman. In his characteristic literary technique Mark sandwiches one story in the middle of the other. There are several points of correspondence between the two. The woman has suffered bleeding for as long as the girl has lived, twelve years. The woman reaches out her hand to Jesus (v. 27), whereas

Jesus takes the girl by the hand (v. 41). The healing of the woman who lived with the slow encroachment of death anticipates the healing of the girl who actually experienced death.

The narrative begins with Jesus once more pressed to the edge of the sea by teeming crowds (as in 2:13; 3:9; 4:1). A **synagogue** official named **Jairus** makes his way to the front and falls at Jesus' feet with a poignant appeal: **My daughter is at the point of death.** A synagogue official was an eminent layman whose duties included oversight of the synagogue's activities and finances. This man's humble posture—a gesture of petition or homage (see Acts 10:25)—is remarkable in view of the fact that Jesus' last visit to a synagogue ended with a plot to kill him (Mark 3:6). Jairus's desperation has made him unconcerned for others' negative opinions of Jesus and even his own poise in the presence of others. His only concern is that Jesus heal his daughter before it is too late. The request that Jesus **lay hands on her** reflects the Jewish sense of the capacity of the human body to mediate God's grace and power. Healings in Scripture often occur not by word only but by physical contact.[2]

Jairus's request is that his little girl may **get well** (literally, "be healed" or "be saved")[3] and **live**—verbs often used for the fullness of salvation and eternal life that Jesus came to give (8:35; 13:13; 16:16; see John 11:25–26). The man's desire that his daughter be restored to physical health reflects a deeper human longing for ultimate deliverance from death. Jesus cannot remain indifferent to his earnest pleading; as often in the Gospels, he is moved by the plea of parents for their children (Mark 7:25–30; 9:17–27; Luke 7:12–15).

5:22–24

Triumph over Disease (5:25–34)

> [25]There was a woman afflicted with hemorrhages for twelve years. [26]She had suffered greatly at the hands of many doctors and had spent all that she had. Yet she was not helped but only grew worse. [27]She had heard about Jesus and came up behind him in the crowd and touched his cloak. [28]She said, "If I but touch his clothes, I shall be cured." [29]Immediately her flow of blood dried up. She felt in her body that she was healed of her affliction. [30]Jesus, aware at once that power had gone out from him, turned around in the crowd and asked, "Who has touched my clothes?" [31]But his disciples said to him, "You see how the crowd is pressing upon you, and yet you ask, 'Who touched me?'" [32]And he looked around to see who had

---

2. See 2 Kings 4:34; Mark 1:31, 41; 5:28, 41; 6:5; 7:33; 8:22–23; Acts 9:17; 28:8.
3. The Greek verb is *sōzō*, which means both heal and save. See below at v. 34.

done it. [33]The woman, realizing what had happened to her, approached in fear and trembling. She fell down before Jesus and told him the whole truth. [34]He said to her, "Daughter, your faith has saved you. Go in peace and be cured of your affliction."

OT: Lev 15:19–33
NT: Mark 6:56; Acts 19:12. // Matt 9:20–22; Luke 8:43–48
Catechism: Jesus' response to faith, 548

5:25–26　　At this point the story is interrupted by another distressing predicament, this time of a woman **afflicted with hemorrhages**. Since blood is the seat of life (Lev 17:11), this woman has experienced her life draining away, with the weakness and fatigue that usually accompany chronic bleeding. Worse, her discharge has left her in a perpetual state of ritual impurity, according to the law of Moses. Anything she touches or sits on becomes unclean, and others avoid contact with her since touching her would make them unclean (Lev 15:25–27). If she is married, sexual union is forbidden to her and her husband (Lev 20:18). Worst of all, she is prohibited from entering the temple to worship with God's people (Lev 15:31–33). Mark magnifies her plight by noting that she had **spent all** her financial resources on **doctors**, whose painful treatments failed to alleviate the condition and only increased her suffering.

5:27–29　　But what she has **heard about Jesus** has stirred her to faith, despite all her disappointments over the years. Mark makes us privy to her inner soliloquy: **If I but touch his clothes, I shall be cured** (literally, "be healed" or "be saved," as in v. 23). Even garments can be vehicles of Jesus' healing power, if touched in faith (see Mark 6:56; Acts 19:12). The moment she does so, she senses that she is **healed of her affliction**.

5:30　　Jesus, too, senses the flowing forth of his healing **power**. But he does not want the recipient to slip away with only a physical healing. The fullness of healing, spiritual as well as physical, occurs only in a personal encounter with himself. So he turns to seek out the recipient of his healing power.

5:31–32　　**Who touched me?** The disciples think Jesus' question is absurd, given the thronging crowds. As on other occasions where he is about to display his sovereign power, they completely miss the point. They even feel obliged to help their Lord gain some common sense and realism (as in 6:35–37; see John 11:12, 39). But their perplexed reaction only reveals how much they still have to learn. What made the woman's touch unlike that of all the others in the crowd was her faith. She had wanted to touch Jesus' garment lightly, without attracting any attention to herself, whereas others were jostling roughly against him. Yet her touch was more efficacious than all the rest, because through faith it came into contact with the person of Jesus and his healing power. Jesus **looked around**, desiring that she meet his gaze and enter into a relationship with him.

As soon as the woman realizes Jesus is seeking her out, she is afraid. And no wonder, because by deliberately touching another person she has just breached the rules regarding ritual impurity. But as the leper discovered (1:41), it is impossible to make Jesus unclean; rather, his touch makes the unclean clean. The woman's **fear and trembling** expresses not merely timidity but human awe at the mighty deeds of God, as at the calming of the storm (4:41; see Exod 15:16; Ps 2:11; Jer 33:9). She already knows she has been healed (Mark 5:29) but perhaps at a deeper level now, she realizes what has **happened to her**: she has come into contact with the Lord. She falls down **before Jesus** (a gesture of homage, as in v. 22), and confesses her daring act.

Far from reprimanding her for her boldness, Jesus reassures her, addressing her affectionately as **daughter**. Like all those who "do the will of God" (3:35), she is welcomed into his family. Jesus will later commend Bartimaeus with the same words: **Your faith has saved you** (10:52). The Greek verb *sōzō*, used here in verses 23, 28, and 34, means both "save" and "heal." The woman's faith has opened her to receive not only physical healing but also the ultimate salvation of body and soul that it prefigures.

Jesus dismisses the woman with a traditional parting blessing: **Go in peace** (Exod 4:18; Judg 18:6). The biblical understanding of peace (in Hebrew, *shalom*) is not merely the absence of conflict but total harmony and well-being. She is healed of her **affliction** and enabled once again to participate fully in the covenant life of God's people.

Reflection and Application (5:25–34)

The afflicted woman in this episode is a model for approaching Jesus. While crowds of people were bumping into him as he walked along, she *touched* him. Her faith brought her into living contact with Jesus, and as a result she experienced a dramatic healing. The difference between the crowds and the woman prompts the question: How often do we merely bump up against Jesus—for instance, when we receive him in the Eucharist? Do we half-consciously jostle against him amid all the other preoccupations of the day, or do we come to him determined to *touch* him personally, with a lively awareness of the grace and power that can flow forth from him into our lives?

Mark notes that this woman had "heard about Jesus," a reminder of the Christian obligation to tell others about him (see 13:10; Rom 10:17). Recently an Indian priest told me the story of another woman who had "heard about Jesus." She was a Sikh woman from the Punjab whose legs had been paralyzed for twelve years. Hearing reports that Jesus was healing people at a Catholic retreat center in southern India, she came. There she met the priest and told him of her painful past, how she had been abused by her husband and finally in despair had jumped off a balcony, breaking her back. The priest was moved to speak to her about Jesus' teachings on forgiveness, and invited her to forgive her husband. She immediately challenged him: "If I forgive my husband, will your Jesus heal me?" After a quick prayer, he answered, "I don't know if it is Jesus' will to heal you, but I do know that if you forgive, you will experience a peace and a joy that you have never known before." The next day, a retreat speaker invited everyone to stand up and thank God for his goodness. The woman later told the priest what happened: "I thought to myself, I have so much to thank God for. I am alive, I have two sons who take care of me. I must praise God!" She stood, raised her hands to God, and was instantly and completely healed of her paralysis. The woman stayed at the retreat center for several months to go through RCIA. She and her sons were baptized, and they went home to "tell everybody about Jesus."

Triumph over Death (5:35–43)

---

³⁵While he was still speaking, people from the synagogue official's house arrived and said, "Your daughter has died; why trouble the teacher any longer?" ³⁶Disregarding the message that was reported, Jesus said to the synagogue official, "Do not be afraid; just have faith." ³⁷He did not allow anyone to accompany him inside except Peter, James, and John, the brother of James. ³⁸When they arrived at the house of the synagogue official, he caught sight of a commotion, people weeping and wailing loudly. ³⁹So he went in and said to them, "Why this commotion and weeping? The child is not dead but asleep." ⁴⁰And they ridiculed him. Then he put them all out. He took along the child's father and mother and those who were with him and entered the room where the child was. ⁴¹He took the child by the hand and said to her, "Talitha koum," which means, "Little girl, I say to you, arise!" ⁴²The girl, a child of twelve, arose immediately and walked around. [At that] they were utterly astounded. ⁴³He gave strict orders that no one should know this and said that she should be given something to eat.

OT: 1 Kings 17:21; 2 Kings 4:34
NT: Acts 9:40. // Matt 9:23–26; Luke 8:49–56
Catechism: restoring the dead to life, 994; Jesus hears our prayer, 2616

At this point the narrative quickly shifts back to Jairus. The woman's bold **5:35–36** initiative stands in sharp contrast to the dismissive attitude of the messengers: **Your daughter has died; why trouble the teacher any longer?** But as the Gospel has already clearly established, Jesus wants to be troubled! And those who "trouble" him are the ones who will experience his healing power. At their message Jairus's heart must have filled with anguish at the fatal delay caused by the hemorrhaging woman. But Jesus ignores the unbelieving messengers and reassures him, **Do not be afraid; just have faith** (literally, "only believe"). With this word he is calling Jairus to lay hold of a deeper faith than he has had so far. The situation has worsened since he first approached Jesus. Then his daughter was merely sick, but now he is asked to believe that Jesus can conquer death itself. As Jesus indicated a moment ago (v. 34), faith is the disposition that opens the way for his mighty works to be accomplished (see 6:5–6).

Jesus brings with him only the inner circle of disciples, the three who will **5:37–38** accompany him at other key events: at the Transfiguration (9:2), on the Mount of Olives (13:3), and at the agony in Gethsemane (14:33). Their presence here is a signal that what is about to happen is another key moment in Jesus' mission, giving a glimpse of his divine identity. When they arrive at the house they meet with **a commotion, people weeping and wailing loudly**. The tumult may indicate the presence of hired mourners, a common practice among the ancients. Unlike stoic modern Westerners, the ancient Jews mourned the death of a loved one with elaborate rituals, including loud groans and wailing (Jer 9:17), dirges (Jer 9:17; Matt 11:17), flute playing (Matt 9:23), even shaving the head and stripping off clothes (Jer 16:6; Ezek 24:16–24).

Jesus' response to the hubbub is enigmatic: **The child is not dead but asleep.** **5:39–40** Was he denying that she had really passed away? No, sleep is his characteristic way of referring to death (John 11:11–14; see Dan 12:2), which continued into early Christian usage (1 Cor 15:51; 1 Thess 5:10). Jesus is calling his listeners to recognize that death is not the ultimate end of human life; it is only a temporary phase from which all will be awakened at the resurrection. His raising of the dead girl would be a sign that despair and terror at the finality of death are no longer an inevitable part of human life (see Heb 2:14–15). But in response to his call to faith the mourners **ridiculed him**, a verb that suggests scornful laughter. The child's tragic death has no solution, in their limited view. Jesus **put them all out**, since unbelief creates a climate that hinders his mighty works (see Mark 6:5–6).

Mark records the actual words spoken by Jesus in †Aramaic, indicating the **5:41–43** memorable impression this event made on the eyewitnesses. Taking the child

by the hand, as he had done for Peter's mother-in-law (1:31), Jesus speaks with authority: **Little girl, I say to you, arise!** The verb for arise, *egeirō*, is the same word used for Jesus' resurrection (16:6), and often appears in his healings as a sign that they foreshadow his ultimate victory over sickness, death, and all the effects of sin. The girl **arose immediately**. In reaction to this breathtaking demonstration of power, the greatest miracle that Jesus has performed so far, the witnesses are **utterly astounded**. They recognize that the overcoming of death itself is something only God can do, a sign of the new creation promised in Scripture (Isa 25:8; Ezek 37:13).

Jesus' command that she **be given something to eat** adds a note of tenderness and realism; he knows that the little girl's body needs nourishment to recover strength. The episode concludes with **strict orders** that the miracle not be disclosed. Considering the mourners and the crowd that have been following Jesus, that would be a difficult command to carry out. But perhaps Jesus means that they should avoid undue publicity and celebrate their joy within the privacy of their home. A rumor that he has raised a dead child to life could lead to a superficial acclaim that would only hinder the understanding of his messiahship.

The raising of Jairus's daughter is the climax of the series of miracles recounted in this section of Mark (Mark 4:35–5:43). Each one increasingly reveals Jesus' power to overcome death. He has rescued his disciples from near-certain death in the storm on the lake, delivered a man whose existence was a living death among the tombs, restored to health a woman whose life was draining away, and raised a dead girl to life. In each case the way to experience Jesus' saving power is to reject fear and yield to faith, a deeply personal faith that comes into living contact with him. Mark is preparing his readers to grasp the magnitude of Jesus' ultimate conquest of death in his resurrection, the prelude to the resurrection of all believers to eternal life.

Jesus Comes to His Own

Mark 6:1–32

By the end of Mark 5, an enormous momentum has been created. Jesus has traveled throughout Galilee and beyond, proclaiming the kingdom and demonstrating its presence with healings, exorcisms, a spectacular feat subduing the elements of nature, and even the raising of a dead child. Despite some fierce opposition from the religious authorities, the advance of the kingdom still looks like a triumphal march. Crowds of people have experienced liberation, healing, and the tender compassion of Jesus. But at the beginning of chapter 6, this activity suddenly comes to a grinding halt. The mighty works that hostile opponents, demons, diseases, and even death could not stop, are blocked—temporarily—by a greater obstacle: unbelief. It is not that Jesus' power is limited, but people are hindered from *experiencing his power* by their refusal to believe in him.

Yet the meager results of the mission in Jesus' own hometown are more than outweighed by the abundant fruit of the mission on which he now sends his apostles. By the end of this section, no longer Jesus alone but now his apostles bring healing, freedom, and new life to multitudes of people. It is the debut of the mission of the Church.

Unbelief at Nazareth (6:1–6)

¹He departed from there and came to his native place, accompanied by his disciples. ²When the sabbath came he began to teach in the synagogue,

and many who heard him were astonished. They said, "Where did this man get all this? What kind of wisdom has been given him? What mighty deeds are wrought by his hands! ³Is he not the carpenter, the son of Mary, and the brother of James and Joses and Judas and Simon? And are not his sisters here with us?" And they took offense at him. ⁴Jesus said to them, "A prophet is not without honor except in his native place and among his own kin and in his own house." ⁵So he was not able to perform any mighty deed there, apart from curing a few sick people by laying his hands on them. ⁶He was amazed at their lack of faith.

He went around to the villages in the vicinity teaching.

NT: Mark 3:20–21, 31–35; John 6:42; 7:5. // Matt 13:54–58; Luke 4:16–30
Catechism: brothers of Jesus, 500; laying on hands, 699; prayer with faith, 2610

6:1–2   Jesus returns for the first time in the Gospel to **his native place**, Nazareth (1:9, 24). Nazareth was a small, insignificant village (see John 1:46) of not more than a few hundred inhabitants. In this place where one might expect the warmest welcome and most enthusiastic acclaim, he meets a very different response. According to his usual custom (Mark 1:21, 39; 3:1), on **the sabbath** Jesus enters **the synagogue to teach**. At first the villagers seem to react in the same way as other audiences: they are **astonished** at his wisdom and authority (1:22; 11:18). But in this case it is an astonishment at what seems inappropriate and out of place to them. To their minds Jesus is just "one of the guys," someone they have known all their lives. They had never seen anything extraordinary about him. All this itinerant preaching and miracle-working seems to them to be putting on airs. **Where did this man get all this?** Their questions display not a sincere pursuit of truth but rather indignant skepticism. They are asking the right questions, which all the readers of the Gospel are meant to ask, but with the wrong attitude. They cannot accept that the answer might be "from God." **Wisdom** and **mighty deeds** (*dynameis*) are attributes of God himself (Jer 10:12; 51:15; Dan 2:20), and Scripture often refers to the great deeds accomplished by God's "hand" (Exod 32:11; Deut 4:34; 7:19). But the people cannot bring themselves to draw the logical conclusion of their reasoning.

6:3   The villagers deem that Jesus' hands would be put to better use by returning to his former occupation: woodworking (the Greek word for **carpenter**, *tektōn*, can also mean builder or craftsman). Their reference to Jesus' family members by name shows their close familiarity with his background. Only in Mark is Jesus referred to as the **son of Mary**, an unusual designation since Jews customarily referred to sons in relation to their fathers (Matt 16:17; Mark 10:35). It may have been a veiled slur, alluding to the fact that Mary was not yet married at the time of Jesus' conception (see John 8:41), or perhaps simply an indication that Joseph was deceased. Their questions suggest that they have pigeonholed Jesus: they are confident that they know all there is to know about him. So **they took offense** at him (*skandalizomai*, meaning to stumble over an obstacle). The idea that their hometown carpenter, Jesus, could be inaugurating the kingdom of God was scandalous; it did not conform to their preconceived ideas about how God would and could act. And their attachment to their preconceived ideas became an obstacle to faith. Like the "outsiders" described earlier, they "look and see but do not perceive, and hear and listen but do not understand" (Mark 4:12).

Jesus replies to their outburst with a proverbial saying that, in one form or another, was current in his time: **A prophet is not without honor except in his native place and among his own kin and in his own house** (Luke 4:24; John 4:44). By referring to himself as a †prophet Jesus links his destiny to that of the long line of Old Testament prophets who suffered rejection or violence because of the unpopularity of their message.[1] He is held without honor in circles of increasing intimacy: among his townspeople, his relatives, and even his household. Their failure to accept him is symbolic of the rejection of his people: "He came to what was his own, but his own people did not accept him" (John 1:11; see Luke 13:34–35). **6:4**

So acute is the people's unbelief that Jesus is unable **to perform any mighty deed**, apart from **curing a few sick people**. Unlike Matthew and Luke, Mark does not soften or omit this statement that seems to limit the power of the Son of God. Mark wishes to highlight the necessity of faith—at least a basic openness to God's power at work in Jesus—as the proper disposition for receiving his healing. Despite the atmosphere of unbelief in Nazareth, however, Jesus cures a few people, once again by his personal touch (see 1:31, 41; 5:23, 28). He is **amazed** at the people's **lack of faith** (or "unbelief," RSV)—ironically, he shows the same emotion that characterizes others' positive reaction to his miracles (5:20; see Luke 8:25). Few things cause as strong a human reaction in Jesus as a lack of faith, or conversely, great faith (see Matt 8:10; 15:28). Faith is his door into human hearts, but it can be opened only from within. **6:5–6**

Following this episode, Jesus continues his ministry in the surrounding **villages**. Mark emphasizes Jesus' mission of **teaching**, but by now his readers understand it is a "teaching with authority" that includes healing the sick and expelling demons (see Mark 1:27).

---

1. See 2 Chron 24:19; 36:16; Neh 9:26, 30; Jer 35:15; Ezek 2:5; Dan 9:6, 10; Hosea 9:7.

Reflection and Application (6:1–6)

It would be easy to judge the townspeople of Nazareth. How could they have been so blind as to fail to recognize the Messiah in their midst? But it is impossible to say who would not have reacted similarly in the same circumstances. This incident reveals the "extraordinary ordinariness" of the Son of God. He lived a life so lowly, unassuming, and unremarkable that the possibility that the omnipotent God was present in him was simply incomprehensible to many who knew him. It is not the first time that the lowly ways of God have perplexed and disconcerted his people (Judg 6:14–15; 1 Kings 19:11; Mic 5:1). Isaiah had prophesied a Suffering Servant of God who, before his great work of atonement, would grow up unrecognized in the midst of the people (Isa 53:2). God desired his work of redemption, the reconciliation of humanity with himself, to come not from without but from within: our redeemer is one of us (see Heb 2:11, 17).

The Mission of the Twelve (6:7–13)

7He summoned the Twelve and began to send them out two by two and gave them authority over unclean spirits. 8He instructed them to take nothing for the journey but a walking stick—no food, no sack, no money in their belts. 9They were, however, to wear sandals but not a second tunic. 10He said to them, "Wherever you enter a house, stay there until you leave from there. 11Whatever place does not welcome you or listen to you, leave there and shake the dust off your feet in testimony against them." 12So they went off and preached repentance. 13They drove out many demons, and they anointed with oil many who were sick and cured them.

NT: 2 Cor 9:8; Phil 4:11–13; James 5:14–15. // Matt 10:1–15; Luke 9:1–6
Catechism: mission of the apostles, 2, 551, 858–60, 1122; anointing of the sick, 1499–523

6:7 The initial phase of the training of the Twelve is now complete, and they are ready to participate actively in the mission of Jesus—to become fishers of men (1:17). Their first task as †apostles was "to be with him" (3:14); the second is to be "sent out" (*apostellō*, from which "apostle" is derived) and carry out the same works Jesus himself has been doing. They have "been with" Jesus for some time and have witnessed his serene response to opposition (3:21–30; 6:1–6), his teaching in parables (4:1–34), and his prodigious miracles (4:35–5:43). By this point they must have trembled at the tall order given to them: to do the same mighty deeds. That Jesus **began to send them out** suggests that he did not send all twelve at once, but took time with each pair, ensuring that they were fully prepared and had confidence to begin their mission.

They were not to go alone but **two by two**, as little units of Christian community (see Matt 18:20), since their mission was to gather God's people into a new community centered on Jesus (see Mark 3:34; John 11:52). The Church's experience over the ages has confirmed the wisdom of this approach (see Acts 13:1–3; 15:39–40). A lone missionary is at risk of discouragement, danger, and temptation; but a pair of missionaries can pray together, encourage and support each other, correct each other's mistakes, and discern how to deal with problems together. Moreover, in the law of Moses the testimony of two witnesses is necessary to sustain a criminal charge (Num 35:30; Deut 19:15); how much more the testimony to the gospel, on which eternal life is at stake (Mark 6:11). Again there is a strong emphasis on their task of expelling **unclean spirits** (3:15)—in fact, it is the only task mentioned here, suggesting that it sums up their whole ministry. They are granted a share in Jesus' divine **authority** so as to advance his conquest of the realm of evil.

Jesus' instructions regarding their traveling gear may strike us as rather   **6:8–9** austere. The apostles are to **take nothing** with them other than the clothing on their backs, **sandals** on their feet, and a **walking stick**.[2] A stick, or staff, is a biblical symbol for authority (Exod 4:20; Mic 7:14). The lack of a **sack** meant that they could not even accept provisions from others for the journey. Why is this poverty so important to their mission? Mark does not explain, but several reasons can be surmised. First, the apostles had to learn not to rely on their own resources but on God's all-sufficient providence (see 2 Cor 9:8–10; Phil 4:11–13). Because they were occupying themselves with God's work, God would occupy himself with their daily needs. Their bare simplicity of life, like that of John the Baptist (Mark 1:6), would help them stay free of distractions and focus wholly on their mission. Moreover, their need for food and shelter would call forth hospitality in those to whom they ministered, an important principle of early Church life (see Acts 16:15; Rom 12:13; 3 John 5–8). Finally, their lack of material possessions lent credibility to their message, since it demonstrated that they were preaching the gospel out of conviction rather than desire for gain. Peter was later able to say to the cripple at the temple gate, "I have neither silver nor gold, but what I do

---

2. The accounts in Matthew (10:10) and Luke (10:4) differ slightly in not allowing the Twelve even sandals or a walking stick for their mission. Mark may include these items to emphasize his theme of Jesus' disciples on a continuous journey, walking with him on "the way" of Christian discipleship.

have I give you: in the name of Jesus Christ the Nazorean [rise and] walk" (Acts 3:6).

6:10   In the Jewish tradition of hospitality (see Gen 18:1–8; 19:1–3; Job 31:32), it was common for travelers to be welcomed spontaneously into homes along their way, especially since not every village boasted an inn. Jesus instructs the Twelve to stay in whatever **house** they **enter**, not moving about from house to house. The reason may be to avoid any rivalry or jockeying for prestige that could arise among villagers wishing to host them. Nor may the apostles upgrade their accommodations. Like Jesus, they were likely to be besieged by crowds once they began the ministry of healing and exorcism in a given town (see Acts 8:6), and staying in one place would limit unnecessary distractions.

6:11   The stakes involved in accepting or refusing the gospel are high. Jesus equates the response given to his apostles with a response to himself (see 9:37). To welcome them is to welcome him. And to refuse to listen is to forfeit his invitation to eternal life (see 8:38; 16:16; John 3:18). To **shake the dust off** one's **feet** was a symbolic gesture of repudiation (Acts 13:51), meant as a solemn warning to those who rejected the apostles' message. For Jews, the soil of Israel was holy (see 2 Kings 5:17; Isa 52:2); upon reentering the land after a journey they would shake the pagan dust off their feet as a sign of separating themselves from Gentile ways. This gesture would serve as a **testimony against** such unreceptive villages on the day of judgment. It is also a reminder to the apostles not to be discouraged by the resistance they will sometimes encounter. Their job is to carry out their mission obediently; success is in the hands of God. No one can be compelled to accept their message.

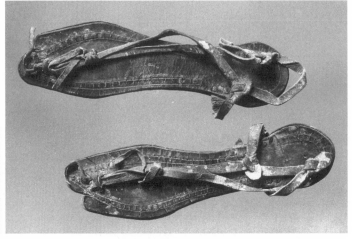

Fig. 6. Ancient sandals found at Masada.

Zev Radovan/www.BibleLandPictures.com

The Sacrament of the Sick

The Church recognizes Mark 6:13 as part of the biblical basis for the Sacrament of the Sick, through which the Church continues to minister Jesus' healing power to those in need of it. "Among the seven sacraments there is one especially intended to strengthen those who are being tried by illness, the Anointing of the Sick: 'This sacred anointing of the sick was instituted by Christ our Lord as a true and proper sacrament of the New Testament. It is alluded to indeed by Mark, but is recommended to the faithful and promulgated by James the apostle and brother of the Lord'" (Catechism, 1511, quoting the Council of Trent).

Mark describes the apostles' preaching in the simplest of terms: like John the Baptist (1:4), they **preached** †**repentance** (*metanoia*), the call to turn away from sin and toward God in a complete change of heart. The fullness of the Christian gospel, the victory of the crucified and risen Lord, can be proclaimed only after the resurrection. But their message, like that of Jesus, carries authority (6:7); it is accompanied by works of power that serve as visible signs confirming its truth. This is the only time in the Gospels that anointing with **oil** is mentioned in conjunction with curing the **sick**, although it later becomes a practice of the early Church (James 5:14). Oil was used for medicinal purposes (Luke 10:34), but here its sacramental value as a vehicle for divine healing is emphasized.

6:12–13

The Beheading of John the Baptist (6:14–29)

¹⁴King Herod heard about it, for his fame had become widespread, and people were saying, "John the Baptist has been raised from the dead; that is why mighty powers are at work in him." ¹⁵Others were saying, "He is Elijah"; still others, "He is a prophet like any of the prophets." ¹⁶But when Herod learned of it, he said, "It is John whom I beheaded. He has been raised up."

¹⁷Herod was the one who had John arrested and bound in prison on account of Herodias, the wife of his brother Philip, whom he had married. ¹⁸John had said to Herod, "It is not lawful for you to have your brother's wife." ¹⁹Herodias harbored a grudge against him and wanted to kill him but was unable to do so. ²⁰Herod feared John, knowing him to be a righteous and holy man, and kept him in custody. When he heard

him speak he was very much perplexed, yet he liked to listen to him. ²¹She
had an opportunity one day when Herod, on his birthday, gave a banquet
for his courtiers, his military officers, and the leading men of Galilee.
²²Herodias's own daughter came in and performed a dance that delighted
Herod and his guests. The king said to the girl, "Ask of me whatever you
wish and I will grant it to you." ²³He even swore [many things] to her, "I
will grant you whatever you ask of me, even to half of my kingdom." ²⁴She
went out and said to her mother, "What shall I ask for?" She replied, "The
head of John the Baptist." ²⁵The girl hurried back to the king's presence
and made her request, "I want you to give me at once on a platter the
head of John the Baptist." ²⁶The king was deeply distressed, but because of
his oaths and the guests he did not wish to break his word to her. ²⁷So he
promptly dispatched an executioner with orders to bring back his head.
He went off and beheaded him in the prison. ²⁸He brought in the head
on a platter and gave it to the girl. The girl in turn gave it to her mother.
²⁹When his disciples heard about it, they came and took his body and laid
it in a tomb.

OT: 1 Kings 19:2; Sir 48:9–12; Mal 3:23–24
NT: Mark 9:11–13. // Matt 14:1–12; Luke 3:19–20; 9:7–9
Catechism: John the Baptist, 523, 717–20
Lectionary: Martyrdom of St. John the Baptist

Between the accounts of the apostles setting out on their mission and returning from it, Mark inserts an interlude: the sordid story of Herod's banquet
and his execution of John the Baptist. The placement of this episode is by no
means accidental. As Mark already hinted in 1:14, John's life is in a mysterious
way patterned on that of Christ; his death foreshadows Jesus' death. The passion of John recounted here coincides with the first mission of the apostles, as
the passion of Jesus will give birth to the Church's mission in which the gospel
is proclaimed to the whole world.[3] With this parallel Mark suggests that John's
self-offering shares, in a hidden way, in the spiritual fruitfulness of the sacrifice
of Christ.

6:14–16   **Herod heard about** the apostles' mission, because Jesus' **fame** (literally, his
name) **had become widespread**. Like the seed that falls on the path (4:15),
Herod's hearing of the word about Jesus will be fruitless, since it does not take
root in him. The rumors circulating about Jesus, later repeated in 8:28, illustrate
widespread spiritual confusion. Some people held that Jesus was a resurrected

---

3. See Wilfrid Harrington, *Mark*, New Testament Message 4 (Wilmington, DE: Michael Glazier,
1985), 83.

Herod and Herodias

BIBLICAL BACKGROUND

The Herod who reigned during Jesus' public ministry was Herod Antipas, client ruler under the Roman emperor of the regions of Galilee and Perea. Antipas was one of the many sons of Herod the Great, who had been known for his great building projects (including the renovation of the temple) and his brutal murders (including the slaughter of the innocents, Matt 2:16). After his father's death in 4 BC, Antipas was appointed "tetrarch," or ruler, over a quarter of the kingdom.

The Herodian family history reads like an ancient soap opera. Antipas was a half-uncle to Herodias, daughter of his half-brother. She was originally married to a different half-uncle, Herod Philip (Mark 6:17; Luke 3:1). Her daughter Salome was born of that union. Both Antipas and Herodias divorced their first spouses to marry each other, after living for some time in open adultery. Besides the execution of John, this act also precipitated a war between Antipas and his first wife's father, leading to Antipas's downfall and exile in AD 39.[a]

a. See Josephus, *Antiquities* 18.109–19.

John the Baptist, a strange opinion since Jewish tradition accepted belief in a general resurrection at the end of the age, not in a dead individual returning to earth. The view that **mighty powers are at work in him** attributes paranormal or occult phenomena to Jesus, as if he is inhabited by good powers just as demoniacs are inhabited by evil ones. Others held that he was **Elijah**, not recognizing in Jesus the transcendent fulfillment of all that Elijah and John the Baptist had prophesied. Yet another opinion maintained that Jesus was **a †prophet like any of the prophets**. Indeed he was (6:4), but not merely another of the Old Testament prophets; he was the definitive prophet promised by Moses (Deut 18:18), who would impart all that God wanted to reveal to his people. All these opinions remain fixated in the wise words and wondrous works done by Jesus, and fail to arrive at the person revealed through those words and deeds. Perhaps Herod, plagued with a guilty conscience for his execution of the innocent John, was susceptible to superstitious fears and thus opted for the first opinion, that Jesus is actually **John** whom he **beheaded**.

At this point Mark gives his readers a flashback describing in detail how the Baptist met his demise. John had incurred the wrath of the ruling family by publicly denouncing their adulterous conduct. **Herod** had divorced his first wife to marry his brother's wife **Herodias**, and John boldly admonished them for this unlawful union (see Lev 20:21). His baptism of †repentance (Mark 1:4) was no mere ritual; it was a call for the whole people to radically turn away

6:17–18

from sin. John recognized that the behavior of political leaders had a powerful impact on the moral environment of the country at large. The Herodian scandal would dull the consciences of the people and put obstacles in the way of the "straight path" God was preparing for the Messiah (1:3). Like the prophets of old, John was willing to risk his life for his message.

6:19–20   John's admonition earned him the bitter resentment of Herodias, who **wanted to kill him**. Herod, however, was ambivalent. He had a mild religious curiosity and **liked to listen** to John but did not actually take his words seriously. To placate his wife, Herod had John arrested but still listened to his preaching in fascination and perplexity. Ironically the powerful ruler living in decadent luxury was afraid of the austere prophet from the desert. Herod's reaction to John was remarkably similar to that of King Ahab to John's predecessor Elijah many centuries before. Like John, Elijah had publicly rebuked the king for a sin urged on him by his wife, Queen Jezebel (1 Kings 21:1–29). Although Ahab gave Elijah a hearing, Jezebel furiously plotted to kill him (1 Kings 19:1–3).

6:21–23   Unlike Jezebel, Herodias found the **opportunity** to destroy the man she hated. To celebrate his birthday (a secular rather than a Jewish custom), Herod invited his **courtiers** (top government officials), **military officers**, and **the leading men of Galilee** (social elites, probably the Herodians mentioned in 3:6; 12:13). It became a banquet of death, in contrast to the banquet of life Jesus had celebrated with the outcasts and repentant sinners of Galilee (2:15). Herodias's **daughter**, Salome, **performed a dance**—probably a seductive display that would have been highly unusual for a royal princess but not implausible in an all-male party that doubtless included abundant alcohol. In an excess of delight, Herod attempted to impress his guests by making grandiose promises and even "oaths" to the young girl. Offering **half** his **kingdom** was merely an expression of extravagance (see Esther 5:6; 7:2); Herod, as a client of Rome, did not have power to subdivide his kingdom.

6:24–29   Prompted by her mother, whom she seemed to take after, the girl made her gruesome request: **I want . . . the head of John the Baptist**. Her enthusiasm for this request is shown by her own additional touches—**at once, on a platter**—to guarantee that the macabre deed would be carried out before her stepfather had time to change his mind. Herod instantly realized the foolishness of his **oaths**. But valuing the admiration of his **guests** more than an innocent man's life, he acceded to the girl's request. The **executioner**, having efficiently carried out his orders, brought in **the head on a platter**, as if it were the next course in Herod's birthday banquet. When they heard what happened, the Baptist's disciples **took his body** and gave him an honorable burial, foreshadowing the proper burial given to Jesus (15:46).

Reflection and Application (6:14–29)

Readers might wonder why Mark has spent so much time on this chilling episode, the only sustained narrative in his Gospel that is not directly about Jesus. Perhaps it is to highlight the passion of John as a foreshadowing of the passion of Christ. Herod's actions show the snowball effect of unchecked sin, a common biblical theme (see Gen 4:5–8; 2 Sam 11; James 1:14–15). From adultery Herod progressed to debauchery and ultimately, via his rash oaths, to murder. Like Pilate later in the Gospel, Herod holds no malice toward his victim, yet cowardice and excessive concern for his own reputation lead him to bloodshed. Each player in the drama is complicit in the evil: his scheming wife, her lascivious daughter, the ruthlessly efficient executioner, and even Herod's dissipated guests, who raise no protest against the death of the innocent. Similarly, all the players in the passion of Jesus—and by extension, all of sinful humanity—are complicit in the death of the Son of God. Jesus, like John, will meet his end because he confronts people with the hard but salutary truth about God's claim on our lives and the call to †repentance that is the doorway to salvation. The success of the apostles' first mission, which immediately follows John's death, is a symbolic anticipation of the countless multitudes who will enter the kingdom as a fruit of the death of Christ—and of the witness of Christian martyrs, who testify to the gospel at the cost of their lives (see Mark 10:45; 14:24; Rev 12:11).

The Return of the Twelve (6:30–32)

> ³⁰The apostles gathered together with Jesus and reported all they had done and taught. ³¹He said to them, "Come away by yourselves to a deserted place and rest a while." People were coming and going in great numbers, and they had no opportunity even to eat. ³²So they went off in the boat by themselves to a deserted place.

OT: Exod 33:14; Deut 12:10; Isa 40:31
NT: 2 Cor 11:27. // Luke 9:10–11
Catechism: rest, 2184
Lectionary: 6:30–34: Mass for a Council or Synod or a Spiritual or Pastoral Meeting

After the interlude on the death of John the Baptist, Mark picks up where he left off with the mission of **the †apostles** (6:7–13), who now return to Jesus and report to him **all they had done and taught**. Although Jesus' recent instructions

6:30

(6:7–11) did not mention teaching, it was part of the ministry for which he had appointed them (3:14). This brief passage serves as a hinge, concluding the mission of the Twelve and preparing for the theme of nourishment and bread on which the next major section will focus.

6:31–32   Jesus recognizes that after their period of intense apostolic labors, the Twelve need to be refreshed once again in his presence and in their fellowship with one another. To "be with him" remains a requirement of fruitful apostleship that must be constantly renewed (3:14; see John 15:4). The **deserted place** recalls the desert of 1:3–13, a place of testing but also a place of solitude and retreat where God's people withdraw from the world for special intimacy with him. Jesus' desire to give them **rest** evokes the rest that God pledges to give his people in the promised land (Exod 33:14; Deut 12:10; see Heb 4:9–11). It also shows his concern for the practical, physical needs of those who spend themselves in his service.

From the fact that **people were coming and going in great numbers** it may be inferred that the apostles' preaching of †repentance (6:12) had hit the mark. More people than ever were being drawn to Jesus and prepared to receive his teaching and his healing power. Once again Mark notes that the apostles' ministry was so demanding that they **had no opportunity even to eat** (see 3:20). They are taking on the character of Jesus, who subordinates his personal needs to his ministry to his people. This remark prepares for the miracle of the loaves that is about to occur. Jesus and the apostles go off to **a deserted place** that, as we will soon see, turns out to be not so deserted after all.

Reflection and Application (6:30–32)

This brief passage illustrates the rhythm of Christian apostolic activity, which ought to alternate between periods of intense labor and periods of simply "being with" Jesus (see 3:14). Here we can imagine him taking time with each disciple to listen to the reports of their successes and failures, to encourage, counsel, and redirect them where necessary. What spiritual refreshment they must have found in this "debriefing" conversation. It is true that the demands of apostolic activity, both then and now, will occasionally preempt the need for physical and mental rest (see 6:33–34). But the temptation for those of us who work in Christ's vineyard is to get so caught up in the busyness of ministry that we repeatedly ignore the need for prayer, rest, and stillness in God's presence. When that happens it is all too easy to begin imperceptibly substituting our own agenda for the Lord's. Authentic Christian ministry is rooted in prayer, since apart from him we can do nothing (John 15:1–8). How can we carry out the Lord's work except in the Lord's strength (see 1 Pet 4:11)? And how can we be renewed in that strength except by waiting in his presence (see Isa 40:31)?

Understanding the Bread I

Mark 6:33–7:37

The return of the Twelve is followed by a part of the Gospel known as the "Bread Section" (6:33–8:26), in which bread, *artos*, appears no less than seventeen times.[1] Mark has carefully arranged this section to show a deepening revelation of the mystery of Jesus, centering on the theme of bread. Twice Jesus miraculously feeds a multitude with a few loaves and fish, each time followed by a crossing of the lake, a conflict with Pharisees, a healing, and finally a confession of faith. It is as if Jesus had to repeat the sequence for its full significance to dawn on his disciples. At the middle and end of the section he heals a deaf man and a blind man, symbolizing his opening of the spiritually deaf ears and blind eyes of his disciples.

Throughout the section, bread serves as a keyword for an understanding of Jesus and his mission, which the disciples often lack (6:52; 8:14–21). Through the events recounted here Mark prepares the reader to grasp the significance of the climactic bread event in the Gospel, the eucharistic banquet. Ultimately the bread signifies the passion and glory of the Son of Man, who will give his life for us as spiritual food (14:22).

The Compassion of Jesus (6:33–34)

---

[33]**People saw them leaving and many came to know about it. They hastened there on foot from all the towns and arrived at the place before them.**

---

1. *Artos* is sometimes translated "loaf" or left untranslated, so its occurrence is not always apparent in English translations.

³⁴**When he disembarked and saw the vast crowd, his heart was moved with pity for them, for they were like sheep without a shepherd; and he began to teach them many things.**

OT: Sir 15:3; Isa 40:11; Jer 31:10; Ezek 34:11–16
NT: 1 Pet 2:25. // Matt 14:13–14; Luke 9:11
Catechism: the Good Shepherd, 754
Lectionary: 6:34–44: Mass in Time of Famine

The previous scene ended with Jesus and his disciples going off to a "deserted   **6:33**
place" for some much-needed rest. The moment word gets out that Jesus is taking off by boat the people anticipate where he will go and run there **on foot**,
arriving **before them**. By the time the boat lands the shore is no longer deserted
but lined with a "vast crowd."

The hoped-for retreat has been sabotaged. But instead of reacting with exas-   **6:34**
peration Jesus is **moved with pity** at the sight of the needy crowds. This is one
of the few occasions where Mark gives us a glimpse into the emotions of Jesus,
here using a verb that connotes a deeply felt, gut reaction (see 1:41; 8:2). Pity,
or compassion, is one of the most distinctive attributes of God (Ps 86:15; Isa
54:7–8; Hosea 11:8). Jesus recognizes that the people are **like sheep without a
shepherd**, a phrase often used to describe the condition of God's people in the
absence of sound leadership.[2] As shepherdless sheep are likely to scatter, get
lost, and quickly become vulnerable to predatory beasts, so when leadership
fails, God's people are likely to stray away from fidelity to him and become
prey to their enemies. After Israel had experienced centuries of incompetent,
self-seeking, and corrupt leadership (as exemplified by Herod Antipas), there
was a growing recognition that ultimately only God himself can adequately
guide his people and provide for their needs. The prophets had announced a
great promise: "Thus says the Lord GOD: I myself will look after and tend my
sheep. . . . I myself will pasture my sheep; I myself will give them rest" (Ezek
34:11, 15; see Isa 40:11; Jer 31:10). Mark hints that Jesus himself is the divine
Shepherd (see John 10:1–18), the fulfillment of God's promise to care for his
people directly and no longer through an intermediary.

In Matthew's version of this incident, Jesus responds to the people's need by
healing the sick (Matt 14:14). But for Mark, Jesus exercises his saving power
first and foremost by teaching. Indeed his teaching *is* healing, since it liber-
ates people from their captivity to evil (see Mark 1:27). At the same time, his
teaching is feeding, since by proclaiming the good news of the kingdom Jesus

---

2. Num 27:17; 1 Kings 22:17; 2 Chron 18:16; Jdt 11:19; Ezek 34:5; Zech 10:2.

is satisfying their spiritual hunger. Often in Scripture receiving divine wisdom is symbolized by eating and drinking (Prov 9:1–5; Sir 15:3; 24:18–22; Amos 8:11). Even before Jesus multiplies the loaves, the people are already feasting on a banquet of wisdom—a point made explicitly in John, where the "bread" is Jesus' teaching (John 6:35–50).

The Feeding of the Five Thousand (6:35–44)

---

³⁵By now it was already late and his disciples approached him and said, "This is a deserted place and it is already very late. ³⁶Dismiss them so that they can go to the surrounding farms and villages and buy themselves something to eat." ³⁷He said to them in reply, "Give them some food yourselves." But they said to him, "Are we to buy two hundred days' wages worth of food and give it to them to eat?" ³⁸He asked them, "How many loaves do you have? Go and see." And when they had found out they said, "Five loaves and two fish." ³⁹So he gave orders to have them sit down in groups on the green grass. ⁴⁰The people took their places in rows by hundreds and by fifties. ⁴¹Then, taking the five loaves and the two fish and looking up to heaven, he said the blessing, broke the loaves, and gave them to [his] disciples to set before the people; he also divided the two fish among them all. ⁴²They all ate and were satisfied. ⁴³And they picked up twelve wicker baskets full of fragments and what was left of the fish. ⁴⁴Those who ate [of the loaves] were five thousand men.

OT: Num 11:13, 22; 2 Kings 4:42–44; Isa 55:1–2
NT: Mark 14:22. // Matt 14:15–21; Luke 9:12–17; John 6:5–13
Catechism: the miracles of the loaves, 1335

6:35   The feeding of the five thousand is one of the most memorable events in Jesus' public ministry—in fact, the only miracle attested in all four Gospels (Matt 14:14–21; Luke 9:11–17; John 6:5–13). Mark recounts this dramatic event, like the earlier supper with sinners (Mark 2:15–17), as not only a meal but also a revelation of Jesus' identity and messianic mission. Almost every line echoes the Old Testament, providing clues to the meaning of Jesus' action. In contrast to the opulent Herodian banquet just recounted (6:14–30), which ended in a death, here Jesus feeds ordinary people with very simple fare, leading to life.

Verses 35–39 contain the most extended conversation in Mark, which begins with the disciples recommending that Jesus "dismiss" the people for supper. This seems like a reasonable suggestion, but in reality it shows that they fail to perceive the significance of what is happening, a failure that will recur several times in the bread section (see 6:52; 7:18; 8:17, 21). What have they missed? They remind Jesus that they are in a **deserted place** (*erēmos topos*), but in the Old Testament, the desert or wilderness (*erēmos*) is the very place where God himself provides superabundantly for his people. In the desert God had shown his goodness by feeding the people with manna (Exod 16), the "bread from heaven" (Ps 78:24–25) and "food of angels" (Wis 16:20–21). By letting the Israelites experience hunger and then providing for their physical needs, God had taught them that he would satisfy their spiritual hunger as well: "not by bread alone does man live, but by every word that comes forth from the mouth of the LORD" (Deut 8:3).

The disciples have overlooked the significance of these biblical events for their present situation. By asking Jesus to send the people away, they are suggesting that he let the sheep fend for themselves—as if by leaving Jesus, the people will get something they cannot get from him! Ironically the disciples advise that the people **buy themselves something to eat**, unaware that Jesus is already fulfilling God's promise to provide a food that no money can buy: "You who have no money, come, receive grain and eat; Come, without paying and without cost, drink wine and milk! Why spend your money for what is not bread; your wages for what fails to satisfy? Heed me, and you shall eat well, you shall delight in rich fare" (Isa 55:1–2). **6:36**

Jesus' reply is startling—it seems deliberately to intensify the predicament: **Give them some food yourselves.** Knowing exactly what he is about to do, he is seeking first to awaken his disciples' faith by calling them to handle a situation that is clearly beyond their own resources. Even more, he is calling for their active participation in his own divine work of providing for the needs of the people. **6:37**

The disciples' response has a tone of astonishment and even sarcasm. Their perplexity recalls Moses' complaint to God in the desert: "Where can I get meat to give to all this people? . . . Can enough sheep and cattle be slaughtered for them? If all the fish of the sea were caught for them, would they have enough?" (Num 11:13, 22; see Ps 78:19). Jesus does not answer directly, but instructs them to bring to him the little they have, which turns out to be **five loaves and two fish**. It is significant that he insists on beginning with what they have to offer. Jesus does not want to create bread out of stones (see Matt 4:3; Luke 4:3), or out of thin air, but to take and miraculously multiply what his disciples are able to give out of what they have—a principle that will bear on all their future apostolic labor. **6:38**

6:39–40   In preparation for the miracle Jesus instructs the people to **sit down in groups**. The word for groups, *symposia*, suggests the image of guests reclining at a dinner party. Jesus is hosting a banquet in the desert! It is the messianic banquet foretold by Isaiah (Isa 25:6; 55:1–2). The **green grass** is not an accidental detail, but an allusion to the "green pastures" in which the Lord, the Good Shepherd, gives his people repose and sets a table before them, in the well-known psalm (Ps 23:2, 5). It also evokes the prophetic promise that God would transform the desert into a place of refreshment and life (Isa 35:1; Ezek 34:25–31). The people's orderly seating **in rows by hundreds and by fifties** recalls the arrangement of the tribes of Israel as they camped in the desert (Exod 18:21–25). Once again (as in 1:2–8) Mark hints that what is occurring is a new exodus, in which God is feeding his people with a new "bread from heaven" (see Exod 16:4).

6:41   Mark describes Jesus' actions with a string of verbs that his readers would immediately recognize as a foreshadowing of the Last Supper (14:22): he *took . . . blessed . . . broke . . .* and *gave* the **loaves** to his disciples to distribute to the people, along with the **fish**. The word for loaves is the plural of *artos*, bread. **Looking up to heaven** was a traditional gesture of prayer (see 7:34); for Jesus, it expresses the orientation of his whole being to the Father. The **blessing** was probably the customary Jewish thanksgiving before a meal: "Blessed are you, O LORD our God, King of the universe, who brings forth bread from the earth." Unlike the other verbs, **gave** is in a form that signifies a continuing action: Jesus *kept giving* his disciples the bread to distribute to the people. The way for them to participate in his miraculous provision for the people is to continually receive from him. To **set before** is a verb often used to express hospitality at table (Gen 18:8; 1 Sam 28:22; Luke 11:6), and accents Jesus' welcome of the people in contrast to the disciples' request to send them away (Mark 6:36).

6:42   The miracle itself happens in a quiet, unobtrusive way, as if the extraordinary increase of the loaves and fishes escapes the notice of some of the people. Unlike most of Jesus' miracles, this one is not followed by exclamations of amazement and wonder. What is most important is that **all ate and were satisfied**. Just as in the miracle of the manna in the desert, there is more than enough to satiate the hunger of all (Exod 16:18; Hosea 13:5–6). As the psalmist proclaims, "You open wide your hand and satisfy the desire of every living thing" (Ps 145:16). By providing superabundantly for his people, Jesus has taken on the role of God himself, fulfilling the prophecy of Isaiah: "The Lord will give you the bread you need and the water for which you thirst. No longer will your Teacher hide himself, but with your own eyes you shall see your Teacher" (Isa 30:20). The physical feeding on bread and fish is an outward sign of an interior feasting on the revelation of God that alone can fully satisfy the human heart.

The extraordinary abundance is highlighted by the leftovers far exceeding the original amount, verifying that no one went away hungry: **twelve wicker baskets full**. Jesus' miracle overwhelmingly surpasses that of the prophet Elisha, who had fed a hundred men with twenty barley loaves (2 Kings 4:42–44). The enormous crowd includes **five thousand men**, which could amount to some twenty thousand people with the inclusion of women and children (see Matt 14:21). The disciples carefully gather up what remains, letting nothing go to waste. The number twelve, corresponding to the twelve tribes, is an oblique reminder that Jesus is gathering around himself a new Israel.

6:43–44

Reflection and Application (6:35–44)

Not only Jesus' teachings but even his actions are parables, signs that point beyond themselves to a deeper mystery. The early Church recognized in the miracle of the loaves a symbolic anticipation of the Eucharist, when Jesus would share both word and food with his people. In fact, the structure of the eucharistic liturgy follows the same pattern seen in this miracle. First, in the Liturgy of the Word, Jesus nourishes us with his teaching through the Scripture readings and the homily that breaks open their meaning. Then, in the Liturgy of the Eucharist, he nourishes us with the Bread of Life, his own body and blood given for us. Vatican Council II teaches, "The Church . . . especially in the sacred liturgy, unceasingly receives and offers to the faithful the bread of life from the table both of God's Word and of Christ's Body" (*Dei Verbum* 21). As the basketfuls of leftovers vividly symbolize, when God feeds his people there is always more than enough to satisfy all. How could it be otherwise, since the gift is God himself?

Jesus' startling command, "Give them some food yourselves," is a word for all those called to pastoral ministry in the Church. Jesus cares for his people's needs, physical as well as spiritual, and summons us to do so for others. Like the disciples, when confronted with a glaring need we might be tempted to say: Lord, I don't have what it takes to feed all these people! And indeed, we don't. Yet if we offer him the few "loaves and fishes" we do have—whether in leading a Bible study, volunteering in an outreach to the poor, or even making a financial contribution—we can ask and expect him to multiply it and make it part of his superabundant provision for all the needs of his people.

Walking on the Water (6:45–52)

---

⁴⁵Then he made his disciples get into the boat and precede him to the other side toward Bethsaida, while he dismissed the crowd. ⁴⁶And when he had taken leave of them, he went off to the mountain to pray. ⁴⁷When it was evening, the boat was far out on the sea and he was alone on shore. ⁴⁸Then he saw that they were tossed about while rowing, for the wind was against them. About the fourth watch of the night, he came toward them walking on the sea. He meant to pass by them. ⁴⁹But when they saw him walking on the sea, they thought it was a ghost and cried out. ⁵⁰They had all seen him and were terrified. But at once he spoke with them, "Take courage, it is I, do not be afraid!" ⁵¹He got into the boat with them and the wind died down. They were [completely] astounded. ⁵²They had not understood the incident of the loaves. On the contrary, their hearts were hardened.

OT: Job 9:8, 11; Ps 107; Isa 43:15–16
NT: // Matt 14:22–33; John 6:15–21
Catechism: Jesus at prayer, 1502

Here the Gospels of Matthew, Mark, and John all follow the same order of events: after the feeding of the five thousand, and closely linked to it, is the mysterious incident of the walking on water. The feast of bread and fish that Jesus hosted in the desert (v. 32) was a moment of revelation, a renewal of Israel's experience of God's tender care for her in the desert (Exod 16). It was meant to evoke the question in the disciples' minds—Who is this? (see Mark 4:41; 8:29)—and to give them a deeper glimpse into the meaning of Jesus' mission. But as the present episode will make clear, the disciples have not yet grasped the significance of the miracle of the loaves.

6:45   After the miracle, Jesus has the disciples **precede him** toward **Bethsaida**, a fishing village at the north end of the lake, just east of the mouth of the Jordan River. Now that the crowd has been nourished in spirit and body, Jesus can dismiss them. As will soon be seen, he is subjecting his disciples to a test that will prepare the way for yet further revelation.

6:46   Meanwhile, Jesus departs by himself **to pray**, resuming the pursuit of solitude that had been interrupted by the crowds (vv. 31–34). Mark mentions Jesus alone at prayer three times in the Gospel (see 1:35; 14:32–42). In each case he is at a defining point in his ministry, where the underlying question is: What is the true nature of his messiahship as willed by the Father? Here he has just done a miracle that reveals something essential about his messianic role, and is about to do another. As verse 48 suggests, Jesus spends most of the night in prayer, seeking to confirm his understanding of and total obedience to the Father's will. His chosen setting for prayer, **the mountain**, again recalls the exodus, when Moses had gone up Mount Sinai to receive God's law (Exod 19:3). A mountain is a privileged place of encounter with God (Gen 22:14; Exod 3:1; Ps 3:5; 68:17). In Mark, key events in Jesus' public ministry take place on a mountain: the commissioning of the apostles (Mark 3:13), the transfiguration (9:2), the discourse on the end times (13:3), and the agony in Gethsemane (14:26).

In Jesus' absence, the disciples are once again in distress in the boat (as in 4:35–41). This time there is no mention of a storm, but they are laboring against a contrary wind and have made frustratingly little headway in their voyage. Jesus, looking far out across the lake, sees the boat **tossed about**, battling a headwind. It is by now the **fourth watch of the night**, between 3 and 6 AM (see 13:35). **6:47–49**

Jesus comes **toward them walking on the sea**. This action can be fully understood only in light of the Old Testament, where God's power to tread the waves is a sign of his sovereignty over all creation: "I am the LORD, your Holy One . . . who opens a way in the sea and a path in the mighty waters" (Isa 43:15–16; see Job 38:16; Ps 77:20). That Jesus **meant to pass by them** seems strange in view of the disciples' distress, but Mark is deliberately using the language of a †theophany, a manifestation of God's awesome presence and power. God had revealed himself to Moses and Elijah by "passing by" them (Exod 34:6; 1 Kings 19:11), and there is an especially close parallel in Job: "He alone stretches out the heavens and treads upon the crests of the sea. . . . Should he come near me, I see him not; should he pass by, I am not aware of him" (Job 9:8, 11).

The disciples display the typical human response when confronted with the majesty of God: they are **terrified** (Exod 20:18; Job 23:15; Luke 2:9). Seeing the figure coming toward them over the waves in the dead of night, understandably "they thought it was a ghost" (Greek *phantasma*) and "cried out" in panic. It was not a case of hyperactive imagination, since they **all** saw him. Unlike the previous boat incident, it is not the turbulent sea but Jesus himself who causes their alarm. They still lack the faith to recognize who he really is. But he immediately calms their fear with a threefold reassurance: **Take courage, it is I, do not be afraid!** Biblical theophanies are often accompanied by an encouragement not to fear, so overwhelming is the presence of God or his angels.[3] But the key to the episode is in the middle statement: "It is I" (*egō eimi*), which can also be translated "I AM," the divine name revealed at the burning bush (Exod 3:14). It is a veiled reference to the divinity of Jesus. Indeed, his reassurance echoes the **6:50–51**

---

3. Gen 15:1; Exod 20:20; Judg 6:23; Mark 16:6; Luke 1:13, 30; 2:10.

divine words of consolation: "Fear not, I am with you; be not dismayed; I am your God" (Isa 41:10). Jesus gets **into the boat with them**, and his presence alone is enough to make the wind cease, confirming his absolute mastery over the elements. As often occurs following a demonstration of Jesus' authority, the disciples are completely **astounded** (see 2:12; 5:42).

6:52   Mark's conclusion to this episode is unique among the Gospels. What does the disciples' fear at seeing Jesus have to do with their lack of understanding about **the loaves**? They have seen Jesus' mighty deeds, but have not yet fully grasped their meaning. They missed the fact that in spreading a banquet for his people in the desert, Jesus is acting as Shepherd-Messiah of his people— indeed he is fulfilling a role that belongs to God alone. Had they pondered the praises of God in Psalm 107, they might have seen the connection: "For he satisfied the thirsty, filled the hungry with good things. . . . He spoke and roused a storm wind; it tossed the waves on high. . . . Hushed the storm to a murmur; the waves of the sea were stilled" (Ps 107:9, 25, 29). That their **hearts were hardened** (like the Pharisees in Mark 3:5) seems to indicate that it was not a case of simple ignorance but a willful blindness, a reluctance to open their hearts fully to what God was doing in Jesus.

Touching the Tassel of His Cloak (6:53–56)

> [53]After making the crossing, they came to land at Gennesaret and tied up there. [54]As they were leaving the boat, people immediately recognized him. [55]They scurried about the surrounding country and began to bring in the sick on mats to wherever they heard he was. [56]Whatever villages or towns or countryside he entered, they laid the sick in the marketplaces and begged him that they might touch only the tassel on his cloak; and as many as touched it were healed.

OT: Num 15:37–39
NT: Acts 19:11–12. // Matt 14:34–36
Catechism: Christ the physician, 1503–5

6:53   This summary of Jesus' healing activity illustrates once again his compassion for the sick and the people's profound attraction to him.[4] Mark earlier noted that the disciples were to cross toward Bethsaida at the northeast corner of the lake (6:45), but now they come to **land at Gennesaret**, a region of fertile

4. See similar summaries in 1:28, 39, 45; 2:13; 3:7–12; 4:33; 6:6.

plains along the western shore. They may have wondered why Jesus sent them toward Bethsaida only to end up on the opposite side of the lake. Perhaps it is meant to serve as a reminder that Jesus knows what he is about: even when he seems to lead his followers in one direction only to have them change course, there may be a purpose in the journey itself that is even more important than the destination.

Upon arrival Jesus is **immediately recognized** by the people, who seize the opportunity by running to bring **the sick on mats** (just as the friends of the paralytic had done, 2:4). The mention of hearing suggests that all who come into contact with Jesus become heralds of his presence, telling others about him. He enters into every sphere of Galilean society—**villages**, **towns**, and **countryside**—and everywhere the people beg him for healing.[5] The **market-places**, the open areas that were the center of commercial and political activity, now become places of encounter with Jesus. As in the story of the woman with a hemorrhage (5:28), all that is needed is a **touch**, since even his garments can mediate his healing power.

The tassel on his cloak is no mere decoration. It is the long fringe (Hebrew *tzitzit*) that Jewish men wore on the corners of their prayer shawl, in accord with the law of Moses: "Speak to the Israelites and tell them that they and their descendants must put tassels on the corners of their garments. . . . When you use these tassels, let the sight of them remind you to keep all the commandments of the LORD" (Num 15:38–39; see Deut 22:12; Matt 23:5). Jesus is the model of faithfulness to the covenant, who perfectly fulfills the Father's commands. All who **touched it were healed**—not because of any magical power in the tassel itself, but because of their faith in him who wore it. Here, as often in Mark's healing narratives (Mark 5:23, 34; 10:52), physical healing is an anticipatory sign of salvation in the full sense, since the same verb, *sōzō*, can be translated "heal" or "save."

Reflection and Application (6:53–56)

Readers of the Gospel might sometimes be tempted to envy Jesus' contemporaries, who had the privilege of seeing him, hearing his voice, and even touching him to receive his healing power. But Christian tradition has always held that later generations have no less privilege than they. Because Jesus is alive and risen from the dead, the mighty works he did on earth are accessible even

---

5. The verb "to beg" (*parakaleō*) literally means "call to the side of," and is the root of *paraklētos* (advocate), Jesus' title for the Holy Spirit in the Gospel of John (John 14:16).

now to those who draw near to him in faith. The Catechism, citing our passage, states, "The sick try to touch him, 'for power came forth from him and healed them all.' And so in the sacraments Christ continues to 'touch' us in order to heal us" (1504). Jesus is still the great Physician of our souls and bodies. In the power of the Holy Spirit he continues his work of healing and salvation through the Church, especially in the two sacraments of healing: Penance and the Anointing of the Sick (1421).

Clean Hands, Distant Hearts (7:1–8)

---

¹Now when the Pharisees with some scribes who had come from Jerusalem gathered around him, ²they observed that some of his disciples ate their meals with unclean, that is, unwashed, hands. ³(For the Pharisees and, in fact, all Jews, do not eat without carefully washing their hands, keeping the tradition of the elders. ⁴And on coming from the marketplace they do not eat without purifying themselves. And there are many other things that they have traditionally observed, the purification of cups and jugs and kettles [and beds].) ⁵So the Pharisees and scribes questioned him, "Why do your disciples not follow the tradition of the elders but instead eat a meal with unclean hands?" ⁶He responded, "Well did Isaiah prophesy about you hypocrites, as it is written:

'This people honors me with their lips,
  but their hearts are far from me;
⁷In vain do they worship me,
  teaching as doctrines human precepts.'

⁸You disregard God's commandment but cling to human tradition."

OT: Exod 30:17–21; Isa 29:13
NT: Luke 11:39–41; Heb 9:10. // Matt 15:1–3, 7–9
Catechism: Jesus and the law, 577–82

7:1–2   At the center of the first part of the Bread Section (6:30–7:37) Mark places a lengthy dispute over Jewish legal customs (7:1–23). This discussion returns to a theme that was prominent earlier in the Gospel: the religious authorities' hostility to Jesus (2:1–3:6; 3:21–30). Whereas the earlier disputes became an occasion for a deeper revelation of Jesus' identity and mission, this one becomes an occasion to reveal a transformation in God's covenant relationship with his people.

134

As Jesus is going about his ministry of healing, **Pharisees** team up with **scribes from Jerusalem** (see 3:22) to pose an accusatory question. †Pharisees were members of a renewal movement that sought to restore God's favor to Israel by advocating strict observance of the law and total separation from all Gentile defilement. †Scribes were professional copyists and scholars of the law, some of whom were also Pharisees. Those from the capital, Jerusalem, probably carried an extra weight of authority. Together they are scandalized to observe how some of Jesus' disciples **ate their meals**. The phrase is literally "eat breads," linking this dispute with the miracle of the five thousand who "ate breads" in 6:35–44. Perhaps it was Jesus' miraculous provision of bread in the desert (where the crowds had no opportunity to wash their hands) that occasioned the religious leaders' pious disapproval. The controversy also bears on the postresurrection Church for which Mark is writing, where the burning question was: Are Christians obliged to follow the law and traditions of the Jews? (see Acts 15). The question is especially urgent in regard to the Church's mission among the Gentiles, a theme to which the Bread Section often alludes.

The gist of the accusation is that Jesus' followers eat "with unclean, that is, un- **7:3–4** washed, hands." The problem in view is not hygiene but ritual purity. "Unclean" (*koinos*) literally means "common" or "profane," the opposite of holy or set apart for God. To grasp the point of the accusation it is necessary to understand the background of these Jewish practices, which Mark proceeds to explain for the benefit of his Gentile readers (7:3–4). The law of Moses had prescribed rules for the cultic purity of priests, including the **washing** of **their hands** and feet before offering sacrifices (Exod 30:17–21) and ritual purity (which usually entailed washings) before eating their share of a sacrifice (Num 18:11–13). These

Fig. 7. Ancient Jewish pottery found at Qumran.

Zev Radovan/www.BibleLandPictures.com

The Tradition of the Elders

BIBLICAL BACKGROUND

Like any law, the law of Moses requires interpretation: how, when, for whom, and in what circumstances are these regulations to be applied? Over the centuries, an oral tradition of legal interpretation had developed, handed down by generations of leading rabbis. For the Pharisees, this oral tradition was just as binding as the written Torah. It prescribed numerous and detailed rules of conduct for daily life, so much so that carrying it out had become a burden that sometimes obscured the purpose of the law (see Matt 23; Luke 11:46; Acts 15:10). By the end of the sixth century AD, the oral traditions were fixed in writing in the Mishnah and its accompanying commentary known as the Talmud.

biblical rules apply only to priests serving at the altar, but the oral **tradition** developed by the Pharisees had extended them to govern the behavior of *all* Jews at *all* meals—making every meal a religious act and a symbolic expression of Jewish identity (see Acts 10:28). Moreover, any contact with potentially unclean persons or products in **the marketplace** necessitated a ritual washing, and all items used to prepare or serve food, such as **cups and jugs and kettles**, also needed purification. Some manuscripts of the Gospel include **beds**, which could become unclean due to various causes (see Lev 15:2–5, 19–27). Although not all Jews kept this oral tradition, by the time of Christ it was expected of all, and those who failed to keep it were despised by the Pharisees as the "accursed" ordinary folk who were ignorant of the law (see John 7:49).

The Septuagint

BIBLICAL BACKGROUND

The Septuagint (meaning "seventy," often abbreviated LXX) was a translation of the Old Testament into Greek done in the third or second century BC for the benefit of Jews living in Egypt who were no longer familiar with Hebrew. Its name comes from a legend that seventy scholars worked on the translation. New Testament authors often follow the Septuagint version when quoting the Old Testament. The Fathers of the Church considered the Septuagint inspired because its wording was an apt preparation for the gospel. For instance, in the messianic oracle of Isa 7:14, the Septuagint translated the Hebrew word for "young woman" with the more specific Greek term "virgin"—making it an explicit prophecy of the virgin birth (Matt 1:23).

After this parenthesis Mark returns to the question of the Pharisees and   7:5
scribes: Why do some of Jesus' disciples "eat breads" **with unclean hands?** Not
only do these disciples apparently flout the requirements of ritual purity, but they
also ignore the **tradition of the elders** that the Pharisees consider binding.

Jesus' response must have taken them aback. Rather than citing grounds for   7:6–7
an exception for his disciples, he levels a countercharge challenging the entire
edifice of Pharisaic legalism. His accusers are **hypocrites** (literally, "stage ac-
tors"), people whose outward conduct does not correspond with the true state
of their heart. To explain what he means Jesus invokes a prophecy of Isaiah
(29:13). It is important to understand the context of this prophecy (which Mark
quotes in a form close to the †Septuagint version).

Isaiah is speaking to Israelites who have lost an intimate contact with God,
and serve him with an empty formalism devoid of authentic love. Their **worship**
is mere lip service, consisting of inherited rituals that are not rooted in interior
conversion of the heart. In fact, they are promoting their own superficial religiosity as a substitute for true obedience to God's will (see Isa 29:10–12). But
God's response, through Isaiah, is not so much a threat as a promise. He will
once again intervene in the lives of his people with acts so wondrous that they
will be moved to acknowledge him as the God of the covenant and honor him
with authentic worship (Isa 29:14–24). Jesus' invocation of this prophecy is a
veiled proclamation that the promise is now being fulfilled in their midst. For
that very reason, the warning implied in the prophecy is all the more urgent.

The punch line of Jesus' countercharge is the last line, which he will repeat in   7:8
different forms in vv. 9 and 13: **You disregard God's commandment but cling to
human tradition.** It is a scathing indictment of his questioners' whole approach
to religion, in which the key contrast is between "God's" and "human." They
have neglected what is truly of God in favor of their own human agendas.

Reflection and Application (7:1–8)

This passage regarding "human tradition" is sometimes cited against the
Catholic understanding of the authority of Tradition together with Scripture
as the rule of faith. But it is crucial to note that Jesus is not rejecting tradition
per se, which becomes an important term in the early Church for the handing
on of authoritative apostolic teaching (1 Cor 11:2, 23; 2 Thess 3:6). Rather, he
is rejecting *merely human* traditions that are not based in God's word, that in
fact negate the intent of God's word. Paul himself exhorted Christians to "stand
firm and hold fast to the traditions which you were taught, either by an oral

statement or by a letter of ours" (2 Thess 2:15). The apostles handed down what they received from Jesus and the Holy Spirit first in oral form through their teaching and example, and later in the written form of the New Testament (see Catechism, 96–100). Indeed, the formation of the †canon of Scripture was itself an exercise of apostolic tradition.

This passage is also sometimes cited in disparaging Catholic liturgical and devotional practices as mere "human traditions." This misunderstanding is due in part to a real problem: religious practice is often superficial and routine among those who have not been adequately evangelized and whose faith fails to impact their choices and behavior in any significant way.[6] Jesus is speaking about an attitude toward God that he saw in the scribes and Pharisees and that can be found among Christians in every church: the tendency to substitute religiosity for genuine obedience to God and his word. What is needed is a personal encounter with Jesus leading to a deep transformation of heart. When that occurs, religious practices come to life and serve their true purpose.

An Example of Hypocrisy (7:9–13)

---

[9]He went on to say, "How well you have set aside the commandment of God in order to uphold your tradition! [10]For Moses said, 'Honor your father and your mother,' and 'Whoever curses father or mother shall die.' [11]Yet you say, 'If a person says to father or mother, "Any support you might have had from me is qorban"' (meaning, dedicated to God), [12]you allow him to do nothing more for his father or mother. [13]You nullify the word of God in favor of your tradition that you have handed on. And you do many such things."

OT: Exod 20:12; 21:17; Num 30:3; Sir 3:1–16
NT: 1 Tim 5:4. // Matt 15:3–6
Catechism: the fourth commandment, 2196–200; duties of children to parents, 2214–20

7:9–10   To ensure that his point made above (vv. 6–8) is understood, Jesus provides a concrete example. The statement in verse 9 might be better translated as a question:[7] "Is it right for you to **set aside the commandment of God in order to uphold your tradition?**" Jesus is inviting his questioners to examine their interior motives and ask themselves whether what they teach and prac-

---

6. See John Paul II, *Catechesi tradendae*, 19–20; *Christifideles laici*, 59.
7. Donahue and Harrington, *Mark*, 222. Since the original Greek manuscripts had no punctuation, sometimes the translator has to conjecture the author's intended syntax.

tice is truly consistent with the law of God. His example involves the fourth commandment, **Honor your father and your mother** (Exod 20:12). The severe penalty prescribed for one form of its violation (Exod 21:17) indicates how serious is the obligation to respect one's parents. In the Old Testament wisdom tradition honoring one's father and mother is linked with fear of the Lord, and is a prerequisite to receiving God's blessings (Sir 3:1–16).

In contrast to the clear intent of God's law is the casuistry of the Pharisees   **7:11–12** and scribes: **Yet you say. . . .** Jesus is referring to a custom whereby a person could vow to set aside a sum of money as a deferred gift to the temple. **Qorban** is a Hebrew word for an offering or gift **dedicated to God** (see Lev 1:2), or by extension, to the temple treasury (Matt 27:6). If a person had made this vow while his parents were still alive, the money thus dedicated could not be used to support them. Since the law of Moses contains strict injunctions for the fulfillment of vows (Num 30:3; Deut 23:22–24), apparently the vow was considered binding even when it conflicted with the solemn obligation of the fourth commandment.[8] However, Jesus' criticism is not primarily about when to dispense people from vows. Rather, the problem is making the *qorban* vow in the first place in a way that interferes with the obligation to care for one's parents. What may lie behind Jesus' criticism is a practice in which a person pledges an impressive temple donation out of showy religiosity, and says in effect to his aging or even destitute parents, "I will honor you by making this donation instead of by providing you with the necessities of life." Such a person thus obeys the fourth commandment in outward appearance only while neglecting to care for the actual material needs of his parents.[9]

By allowing and encouraging this hypocritical practice the Pharisees and   **7:13** scribes **nullify the word of God in favor of** their **tradition**. This is Jesus' third repetition of essentially the same charge (see 7:8, 9), each time in stronger terms. To "nullify" is a legal term meaning to invalidate or repeal. His indictment could hardly have been more forceful. To these learned scholars and upholders of tradition, who considered themselves the exemplars of Jewish piety and guardians of the law, he exposes the truth that they have actually emptied the law of its spirit and authentic meaning. The *qorban* practice is not an isolated example, for they **do many such things**, including their sabbath interpretations critiqued earlier in the Gospel (2:24; 3:2–4). The "word of God" here refers to the Scriptures, especially the †Torah. In early Christian tradition the word of

8. Later rabbinic teaching specifically forbids this kind of abuse: Mishnah, *Nedarim* 9.1.

9. This is the interpretation offered by St. Jerome, *Letter 123, To Ageruchia*. It differs from that of most modern interpreters, who hold that the main point is that vows made for an unworthy purpose (for example, to withhold support from one's parents) should not be considered binding.

God came to mean the gospel, God's plan as fulfilled in Christ and handed on in the preaching of the apostles (Acts 6:7; 8:14; 1 Thess 2:13)—thus Mark wants his readers to understand Jesus' admonition as also aimed at the Church. Whereas human beings can be prone to nullify the word of God with a legalistic and hollow piety, Jesus in his life and mission fulfills it.

What Comes from Within (7:14–23)

¹⁴He summoned the crowd again and said to them, "Hear me, all of you, and understand. ¹⁵Nothing that enters one from outside can defile that person; but the things that come out from within are what defile." [¹⁶]

¹⁷When he got home away from the crowd his disciples questioned him about the parable. ¹⁸He said to them, "Are even you likewise without understanding? Do you not realize that everything that goes into a person from outside cannot defile, ¹⁹since it enters not the heart but the stomach and passes out into the latrine?" (Thus he declared all foods clean.) ²⁰"But what comes out of a person, that is what defiles. ²¹From within people, from their hearts, come evil thoughts, unchastity, theft, murder, ²²adultery, greed, malice, deceit, licentiousness, envy, blasphemy, arrogance, folly. ²³All these evils come from within and they defile."

OT: Lev 11
NT: Acts 10–11, 15; Rom 14; Gal 5:19–21. // Matt 15:10–20
Catechism: Jesus and Israel, 574–82; the heart, 2517–19, 2563; capital sins, 1866

7:14   The third section is the climax, in which the point of the whole discussion (7:1–23) comes to light. After his lengthy criticism of the "traditions of the elders" (vv. 6–13), Jesus now goes back to answer the question about his disciples eating with unwashed hands (v. 5). As will become clear it is no mere matter of lax discipline. So significant is the following pronouncement that Jesus summons **the crowd** so that all might hear it. He prefaces it with a solemn injunction that highlights the enigmatic nature of what he is about to say and the need to ponder it carefully: **Hear me, all of you, and understand**. He had given similar admonitions in 4:3, 9, 23, 24, but now there is a more direct emphasis on his own authority: "Hear *me*." "All of you" may be to emphasize that his next pronouncement is intended not only for his immediate audience, but for all Christians in all generations.

7:15   Jesus first states his point in parable form to the crowds, before giving an explanation privately to his disciples (see 4:34). **Nothing** that enters **from outside**

can defile a person. This statement broadens the discussion far beyond ritual washings or even oral traditions; it alters the status of a large portion of the †Torah itself, the written law that is the foundation of Judaism. The verb "defile" is a legal term in the Torah (related to "unclean" in v. 2), meaning to render something unclean, unfit for worship of God or any sacred use. Much of the law of Moses concerns the distinction between clean and unclean, how a person or object becomes unclean, and what to do about it (see especially Lev 11–15; Deut 14). Jesus is radically recasting the whole meaning of clean and unclean: external things cannot **defile** a person; rather uncleanness comes **from within**, from the deep inner wellspring of a person's words and actions. Already in the Old Testament the prophets had decried merely ceremonial, external practices of devotion (see Isa 1:11–17; Hosea 6:6; Amos 5:21–27) and taught that the true defilement is evil conduct (Ezek 36:17). But Jesus is going far beyond this to set aside the whole system of ceremonial cleanness—because in him its purpose is now fulfilled.[10]

Understandably, his audience finds it hard to take in such a sweeping modi-   7:17–19
fication of the law. Repeating the pattern of 4:10, 34, **when he got home** (literally, "went into the house"), **his disciples questioned him about the parable**. A parable can be a story or an enigmatic saying that calls for explanation (3:23; 13:28). Again there is a strong distinction between the crowds who flock around Jesus and the disciples who receive private instruction (4:10–11). But what sets apart a disciple is nothing other than a personal decision to follow Jesus and base one's life on his teaching. Before giving the explanation, Jesus admonishes the disciples for their dullness in these matters (see 4:13; 6:52). How is it that after all their time with him they have no more **understanding** than do the crowds?

Jesus restates his previous affirmation (v. 15) in terms that make its meaning clear. No foods, even those that are legally unclean (unkosher), can defile a person, since they merely enter the body and pass through the digestive system. In fact, nothing external can separate a person from God. The key word in Jesus' statement is **heart** (*kardia*), used three times in this passage (vv. 6, 19, 21). Biblically, the heart represents the inner depths of the person, the seat of decision where a person either responds to God or resists him. The heart is the source of emotions such as love, grief, anxiety, and joy, but in contrast to modern usage, it is also the source of thought, will, and conscience (see Jer 17:5–10; 1 Cor 4:5; 1 John 3:19–21). Jesus is declaring that the ceremonial distinction

---

10. The NAB, like most modern translations, omits v. 16, "Anyone who has ears to hear ought to hear," because it is missing from the most reliable ancient manuscripts.

between clean and unclean is incapable of bringing about purity of heart, the purity that God truly desires (see Matt 5:8).

In a parenthesis to his readers—to make sure they grasp the full significance of what has been said—Mark notes that Jesus thus **declared all foods clean** (literally, "cleansed all foods").[11] With this statement Jesus has implicitly set aside the entire Old Testament system of ritual purity, including the kosher laws that had created a strict distinction between foods that could and could not be eaten by God's people (Lev 11). Now it becomes clear that the ceremonial laws were a temporary and provisional arrangement, a divine expedient until their true purpose could be definitively realized. Ritual purity had value as a symbol pointing beyond itself to purity of heart, the true basis for covenant relationship with God. Now there is something new in place that can truly purify the heart! Because the former arrangement has fulfilled its purpose, it is now obsolete (see Rom 7:6; Heb 8:13). Although it took the early Church some time (and much controversy) to realize the full implications of this revolutionary change, it gradually did so with the help of the Holy Spirit (Acts 10; 15; Rom 14; Gal 2:11–16). The importance of the principle outlined here for the future of Christianity is incalculable. Because of it, Christianity would not become merely a branch of Judaism whose members are bound to keep all the prescriptions of the Torah; it would be the new and fully efficacious way for all human beings to enter into communion with the living God. The door is opened to the Gentiles.

7:20–23   Jesus now explains the second half of the statement in verse 15, which is the converse of the first half. From now on, the only uncleanness that should preoccupy people is that of sin: the evil dispositions and actions that originate from deep within the heart. **From within** the heart **come evil thoughts**—that is, the sinful intentions that separate a person from God. Jesus elaborates with a list of twelve sinful thoughts and deeds.[12] The first six terms are plural, indicating sinful acts. The second six are singular, indicating interior dispositions. **Envy** is literally the "evil eye," meaning to look with bitterness at the possessions or talents of another person. **Blasphemy** is usually translated "slander" and includes

11. Mark makes this editorial comment from the perspective of the early Church, which had come to increasing clarity about the full implications of Jesus' teaching. There is no evidence that Jesus' disciples immediately interpreted his teaching to mean that the kosher laws were no longer obligatory for Jews (see Acts 10:14). In fact, if Jesus himself had violated the kosher laws it would have given his enemies, who were watching him closely (Mark 3:2), ample grounds for condemnation. For the early Church the primary significance of Jesus' teaching was for Gentiles, who do not have to observe the prescriptions of the old covenant in order to enter into life in Christ (see Acts 15:28–29).

12. For similar lists see Wis 14:25–26; Rom 1:29–31; 1 Cor 6:9–10; Gal 5:19–21; 1 Tim 1:9–10; 2 Tim 3:2–5; 1 Pet 4:3.

all forms of abusive speech, such as gossip and insult. Jesus repeats his point for emphasis: **All these evils come from within and they defile**. Defilement is not ceremonial but moral; likewise, purity is a matter of the heart.

The Children's Bread (7:24–30)

24From that place he went off to the district of Tyre. He entered a house and wanted no one to know about it, but he could not escape notice. **25**Soon a woman whose daughter had an unclean spirit heard about him. She came and fell at his feet. **26**The woman was a Greek, a Syrophoenician by birth, and she begged him to drive the demon out of her daughter. **27**He said to her, "Let the children be fed first. For it is not right to take the food of the children and throw it to the dogs." **28**She replied and said to him, "Lord, even the dogs under the table eat the children's scraps." **29**Then he said to her, "For saying this, you may go. The demon has gone out of your daughter." **30**When the woman went home, she found the child lying in bed and the demon gone.

NT: Rom 3:29–30; 10:12; Eph 2:11–13. // Matt 15:21–28
Catechism: Jesus hears our prayer, 2616

It is not by chance that the dispute over ritual purity is immediately followed by two healings of Gentiles: the exorcism of a Syrophoenician child, and the healing of a deaf-mute (vv. 31–37). By placing these episodes here Mark hints at the far-reaching consequences of Jesus' "cleansing" of all foods (v. 19). The strict barrier that the ceremonial laws had created between Jews and Gentiles, which was part of God's plan in the old covenant, is now being removed by Jesus (see Eph 2:14). This barrier was most evident at table, since the precepts regarding kosher food and ritual purity meant that devout Jews could not share a meal with Gentiles (see Acts 10:28). The mention of "bread" (translated "food" in Mark 7:27) links this story with the multiplication of loaves (6:35–44), and anticipates the revolutionary table fellowship of the postresurrection Church, where Jew and Gentile would share bread at a single eucharistic table.

Jesus departs from the unspecified scene of the previous discussion (7:1–23) **7:24–27** and goes beyond the confines of Galilee **to the district of Tyre**. About forty miles northwest of the Sea of Galilee, Tyre was a predominantly Gentile city on the coast of present-day Lebanon. Jesus is making a deliberate turn to Gentile territory. He attempts to go there incognito, but without success (as in 1:45; 7:36). Some people have an innate talent for sniffing out the news—including this **woman**, desperate as she is with a demon-possessed **daughter**. She is a **Greek** by language and culture, a **Syrophoenician** by birth, and thus a Gentile in both religion and ethnic origin. Syrophoenicians were natives of the coastal region of the province of Syria, as distinct from the Phoenicians of north Africa. She cannot let the wonder-working rabbi from Nazareth, whose reputation has preceded him, pass through without seizing her opportunity. Her determination to seek him out indicates the depth of her love for her daughter. This healing, like many in the Gospels, takes place in response to the petition of a devoted parent (see Mark 5:22–43; 9:17–27; Luke 7:11–15). Her bold faith, like that of the woman with the hemorrhage (Mark 5:25–34), will draw from him the healing power she seeks.

She comes and falls **at his feet**, a gesture of homage (Acts 10:25), begging Jesus to **drive the demon out of her daughter**. But Jesus, unexpectedly, rebuffs her. **Let the children be fed first.** The children are the people of Israel, God's children (Exod 4:22; Hosea 2:1). **Dogs** (here literally, "puppies") was a pejorative term often used by Jews to refer to Gentiles. Here the point is that as household pets, dogs do not have the rights or privileges of the children. In the form of a parable, Jesus is asserting that the blessings of the kingdom must be given first to God's chosen people, to whom they had been promised (see Rom 9:4–5). But the qualifier "first" means that the time will come, after his passion and resurrection, when the Gentiles too will share in the full inheritance of God's children (Gal 3:26–29; Eph 3:6). The early Church followed this principle by preaching the gospel always to Jews first, before moving on to Gentiles (Acts 13:46; 18:6; Rom 1:16). By referring to his works of healing as "bread,"[13] Jesus indicates that there is a deeper symbolic meaning to the bread he has provided in the desert. As Shepherd-Messiah of his people, he provides the bread of a new life, which includes liberation from sin, from demonic oppression, and from all the forces of evil.

7:28   Despite Jesus' apparent harshness the woman is not put off in the least. Instead of taking offense, she quickly turns his reply to her advantage by retorting with a clever counterparable. She is the only person in Mark who addresses Jesus as **Lord**—the term by which the early Church addressed him in prayer (Acts 7:59; 9:10)—and it points to his true identity. Although lord (Greek *kyrie*) can be simply a title of respect ("sir"), it is also the term used in the †Septuagint in place of the holy name of God. Mark has already indirectly applied the title to Jesus in this exalted sense (Mark 1:3; 5:19–20).

---

13. The NAB unfortunately obscures the link with the multiplication of loaves by translating *artos* as "food" instead of its usual meaning, "bread."

The woman implicitly accepts Jesus' unflattering epithet, but points out that **dogs** too have their share of **scraps** from the family meal. She thereby acknowledges Jesus as the Giver of bread—the "one loaf" for Jew and Gentile (see 8:14)—and expresses her confidence that somehow the "dogs" will not be left out. Even though Jesus seemed to reject her request, he was in reality looking to evoke just such deep faith, the kind of faith that he finds it impossible to refuse (as in Mark 5:25–34; John 2:1–11). Indeed, soon after this incident he will feed Gentiles with not only crumbs but an abundance of bread (Mark 8:1–10)! Her faith has mysteriously opened the way.

Jesus' reply expresses his delight with her answer. One can imagine his smile **7:29–30** at this lady's chutzpah. Her indomitable faith has moved his heart to accelerate the plan: the "children's bread" is given ahead of schedule to a Gentile. Upon her return home the woman finds her **child** delivered from the demon. This exorcism is the only work of healing done at a distance in Mark, accenting the efficacy of the woman's faith. In fact, it is one of only two healings at a distance in the Gospels, the other being the cure of the centurion's servant (Matt 8:5–13; Luke 7:1–10; see John 4:46–54). Significantly, both involve Gentiles, and both demonstrate remarkable faith, in contrast to the tepid faith Jesus often finds among his own people. His ability to heal by a mere word someone who is not even present is a powerful message for the readers of the Gospel: to experience the Lord's power it is not necessary to have seen or touched him as he walked on earth before his resurrection. All that is needed is faith.

Reflection and Application (7:24–30)

In this striking incident the Syrophoenician woman turns out to be a model of Christian faith. She is not the last person who has come to Jesus with an urgent petition, only to encounter what seems to be a brick wall! But she is neither discouraged nor disheartened by the apparent setback. She simply perseveres in intrepid confidence. Somehow what she has heard about Jesus has given her a profound intuition that he cannot be indifferent to her plea. So she refuses to take no for an answer—and her boldness is rewarded. The clear lesson in this story is that the Lord does hear our prayers, and even his apparent refusals are meant to awaken in us a yet deeper faith, which opens us to receive the gift that he has for us. Few sayings of Jesus are recorded more often than his reassurance that what we ask in prayer with faith we will receive.[14]

14. Matt 7:7–11; 21:22; Mark 11:24; Luke 11:9–13; 18:1–8; John 14:13–14; 15:7, 16; 16:23–24, 26; 1 John 3:22; 5:14–15.

Opened Ears (7:31–37)

> ³¹Again he left the district of Tyre and went by way of Sidon to the Sea of Galilee, into the district of the Decapolis. ³²And people brought to him a deaf man who had a speech impediment and begged him to lay his hand on him. ³³He took him off by himself away from the crowd. He put his finger into the man's ears and, spitting, touched his tongue; ³⁴then he looked up to heaven and groaned, and said to him, "Ephphatha!" (that is, "Be opened!") ³⁵And [immediately] the man's ears were opened, his speech impediment was removed, and he spoke plainly. ³⁶He ordered them not to tell anyone. But the more he ordered them not to, the more they proclaimed it. ³⁷They were exceedingly astonished and they said, "He has done all things well. He makes the deaf hear and [the] mute speak."

OT: Exod 4:11; Isa 35:4–6; Wis 10:21
Catechism: Christ the physician, 1503–5; symbolic gestures, 1151–52

The second healing following the dispute over ritual purity takes place in the region of the Decapolis—another signal that the blessings of the kingdom are being extended to the Gentiles. The healing of the deaf-mute is one of the few episodes that only Mark records, and is perhaps the most graphically physical healing in all Scripture.

7:31 The description of Jesus' journey has led some commentators to conclude that Mark was geographically confused, since Sidon was twenty-two miles north of Tyre whereas the Decapolis lay far to the southeast (see map, p. 349). To say that he left **Tyre** and went by way of **Sidon** toward **the Decapolis** is a bit like saying "he left Washington and went by way of New York to Atlanta." But Mark's intent is probably to indicate that Jesus traveled in a wide circle, first north, then east and south. The whole journey takes place in Gentile territory, foreshadowing the international dimensions of the Church.

7:32 When Jesus arrives in the Decapolis he meets with a very different reception than on his first visit, when the people begged him to leave (5:17). Perhaps his way has been prepared by an unlikely evangelist: the liberated demoniac, who broadcast to the whole region what Jesus had done for him (5:20). Now the inhabitants recognize Jesus as a worker of mighty deeds who has compassion on the afflicted. So they bring to him **a deaf man**, begging him to **lay his hand** on him (as in 5:23). The rare word for **speech impediment** (*mogilalos*) appears only once elsewhere in Scripture, in the Greek translation of a prophecy of Isaiah: "Then will the eyes of the blind be opened, the ears of the deaf be cleared; Then will the lame leap like a stag, then the tongue of the dumb will

The Flesh as the Hinge of Salvation

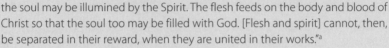

LIVING TRADITION

The importance of the flesh in God's plan of salvation was a continual source of wonder to early pagan converts to Christianity, especially those steeped in Greek philosophy, which had often disparaged the body. Tertullian, a third-century Father, wrote eloquently about how it is through our flesh that Christ mediates his grace in each of the sacraments: "The flesh is the hinge of salvation.... The flesh is washed so that the soul may be made clean. The flesh is anointed so that the soul may be consecrated. The flesh is signed so that the soul may be protected. The flesh is overshadowed by the laying on of hands so that the soul may be illumined by the Spirit. The flesh feeds on the body and blood of Christ so that the soul too may be filled with God. [Flesh and spirit] cannot, then, be separated in their reward, when they are united in their works."[a]

a. Tertullian, *The Resurrection of the Flesh* 8. See also Catechism, 1015.

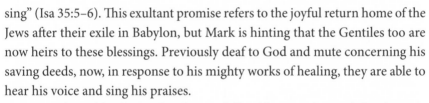

sing" (Isa 35:5–6). This exultant promise refers to the joyful return home of the Jews after their exile in Babylon, but Mark is hinting that the Gentiles too are now heirs to these blessings. Previously deaf to God and mute concerning his saving deeds, now, in response to his mighty works of healing, they are able to hear his voice and sing his praises.

Many of Jesus' healings take place in full public view (see 3:3), but here, in contrast, he takes the man **off by himself** (see also 8:23). This detail suggests that Jesus intuitively understands the unique needs of each person. For some people it is important to have a private encounter, away from the stares of **the crowd**, so that Jesus can minister to their needs one-on-one. Jesus performs the healing in no less than seven steps, as if speaking in sign language so the deaf man can follow what he is doing. After taking him aside, he puts **his finger into the man's ears**, spits, touches his **tongue**, looks up to heaven, groans, and says to him, **Ephphatha!** The spitting should be interpreted as Jesus' spitting on his own finger, then touching it to the man's tongue, so that both his impaired organs are healed by Jesus' direct touch. In the ancient world saliva was considered to have therapeutic qualities. Jesus' looking up to heaven is a gesture of prayer (see 6:41), expressing his total reliance on the Father. It is the only place in the Gospel where Jesus is said to groan (or "sigh," RSV, NRSV, JB, NJB), perhaps because of his grief over a person so ravaged by the effects of the fall. St. Paul uses a form of the same word to speak of the "inexpressible groanings" of the Spirit as he intercedes for us (Rom 8:26).

7:33–35

Some of Jesus' gestures may strike a modern reader as crudely physical. In fact, in every age, the Bible's profound respect for the body as a vehicle of divine grace has scandalized some who would prefer that God act on a purely spiritual plane. But this healing illustrates once again the sacramental quality of the body—its ability to be a visible sign and instrument of divine grace (see Mark 1:31, 41; 5:41; 6:5)—and the fact that Jesus' work of salvation involves the whole human being, soul and body.

Jesus completes the healing with a word of power: **Ephphatha! Be opened!** As in 5:41 Mark's preservation of the original word in †Aramaic shows how deeply this healing impressed itself on the memory of his disciples. Jesus' ministry to the man was unusually elaborate, but the healing is instantaneous and complete. His faculties are restored to the full functioning for which they were designed, and he is able to communicate freely with others.

7:36 But, oddly enough, Jesus now enjoins strict silence on the man who can now speak and on the witnesses—an instance of the "messianic secret" (see 1:44; 5:43). Why would Jesus not want people to spread the news? Probably because the focus would be on a spectacular outward feat, obscuring the real meaning of his messiahship. His miracles point to the truth of his messianic identity—but they are only part of the truth. The full truth of what it means to be Messiah will be revealed in the second part of the Gospel. But ironically, Jesus' injunction falls on deaf ears. The word **proclaimed** is the same used for Jesus' proclamation of the gospel in 1:14, and for the Church's later preaching of the good news (13:10). Even though their understanding is incomplete, the people of the Decapolis cannot contain their excitement about the marvelous deeds done by Jesus.

7:37 This healing, like others, is followed by exclamations of astonishment, but also by a mini confession of faith, alluding to Isa 35:5–6: **He has done all things well. He makes the deaf hear and [the] mute speak.** Once again Jesus has performed a role that Scripture ascribes to God alone: "Who gives one man speech and makes another deaf and dumb? Or who gives sight to one and makes another blind? Is it not I, the LORD?" (Exod 4:11; see Wis 10:21).

Reflection and Application (7:31–37)

Like all healings in the Gospels, the physical cure of the deaf and mute man is real, but also has a deeper spiritual significance. God designed human beings not only with the physical senses but also with marvelous spiritual capacities to see, hear, and relate to him. These interior faculties were disabled by original sin, causing a severe communication block between God and humanity. Jesus' healings of people who are deaf, blind, and lame is a sign of his restoration of humanity to the fullness of life and of communion with our Creator. Now by the grace of Christ we are able to hear God's voice in our hearts, sing his praises, and proclaim his mighty deeds (see Acts 2:11). "The glory of God is man fully alive" (St. Irenaeus).

Understanding the Bread II

Mark 8:1–26

The feeding of the four thousand in Gentile territory so closely parallels the feeding of the five thousand in Galilee (6:35–44) that some scholars hold that a single event was handed down in oral tradition in two different versions. Both miracles are set in a deserted place, where Jesus feeds a huge crowd with a small quantity of bread and fish, using gestures that clearly foreshadow the Eucharist. Both stress the disciples' lack of faith, and both end with abundant leftovers, the dismissal of the crowd, and a departure by boat. However, in other details the incidents are very different, and it is more likely that Mark narrated two distinct events so as to highlight their similarities. Each in its own way is a †prefigurement of the eucharistic meal (14:22) and the messianic banquet at the consummation of the kingdom.

The Feeding of the Four Thousand (8:1–10)

---

¹In those days when there again was a great crowd without anything to eat, he summoned the disciples and said, ²"My heart is moved with pity for the crowd, because they have been with me now for three days and have nothing to eat. ³If I send them away hungry to their homes, they will collapse on the way, and some of them have come a great distance." ⁴His disciples answered him, "Where can anyone get enough bread to satisfy them here in this deserted place?" ⁵Still he asked them, "How many loaves do you have?" "Seven," they replied. ⁶He ordered the crowd to sit down on

the ground. Then, taking the seven loaves he gave thanks, broke them, and gave them to his disciples to distribute, and they distributed them to the crowd. [7]They also had a few fish. He said the blessing over them and ordered them distributed also. [8]They ate and were satisfied. They picked up the fragments left over—seven baskets. [9]There were about four thousand people.

He dismissed them [10]and got into the boat with his disciples and came to the region of Dalmanutha.

OT: Deut 8:3; Ps 103:13; 145:15
NT: Mark 6:34–44. // Matt 15:32–39
Catechism: the miracles of the loaves, 1335

In contrast to the earlier miracle of the loaves, this time Jesus takes the initiative. He has continued his ministry of mercy in the Decapolis area, and so great is the people's attraction to him that they have remained with him **for three days and have nothing to eat**. Jesus is evidently satisfying a need deeper than physical hunger. Yet he also cares about the people's bodily needs. In the previous incident his compassion was occasioned by their being like sheep without a shepherd (6:34), a biblical image for God's people lacking sound leadership. Here it is their hunger that causes him to be **moved with pity**. As in 1:41 and 6:34 the verb denotes strong, gut-wrenching emotion. **8:1–2**

As if to test his disciples (see John 6:6), he presents the problem to them: **If I send them away hungry**, they will **collapse on the way**. The word for collapse (RSV "faint") is used elsewhere in the New Testament for losing heart or getting discouraged in the face of the struggles of the Christian life (Gal 6:9; Heb 12:3, 5). Jesus is challenging his disciples to stretch their faith, as a lesson for their future pastoral ministry: How will they respond when God's people faint for lack of spiritual nourishment, and they do not have the resources to feed them? Will their solution be to send the people away (as in Mark 6:36), or will they trust Jesus to provide, using whatever small amount they can give him? **8:3**

The disciples' skeptical response (echoing Moses' complaint in Num 11:13), seems strange in light of the miraculous feeding they have already witnessed. But many modern disciples of Jesus could attest how easy it is to forget the lessons of discipleship. Throughout the Bread Section Mark highlights the disciples' slowness to grasp the revelation of Jesus (Mark 6:52; 8:21)—not to disparage them, but to remind us, his readers, of the poverty of our own faith. Do we not yet understand that Jesus is the Bread, and that he is able to multiply whatever we put into his hands? **8:4**

8:5–7   Since the disciples do not yet grasp the point, Jesus gives them a hint to remind them of the earlier bread miracle: **How many loaves do you have?** This
time the answer is **seven**, barely enough for a lean meal for the Twelve. Again
Jesus orders the crowd to **sit down**, as if reclining for a banquet. Mark records
nearly the same sequence of actions as in 6:41, again with eucharistic overtones.
Instead of saying that Jesus "blessed" the loaves, Mark uses a synonym, **gave
thanks** (*eucharisteō*), the same word used for the blessing of the cup at the Last
Supper (14:23; see also Luke 22:19; 1 Cor 11:24). Once again the pattern is that
Jesus *takes* what little his disciples have to offer, blesses it, and *gives* it back to
them; in that very process the paltry amount mysteriously becomes more than
enough to satisfy the needs of all. Rather than handing out the loaves himself,
Jesus insists on the involvement of his disciples: he **gave them to his disciples
to distribute**. Because of its eucharistic significance, the primary focus is on
the bread; only afterward does Mark also mention the **blessing** and distribu-
tion of the **few fish**.

8:8–10   The people who were famished only moments before **ate and were satisfied**, as proven by the abundant leftover **fragments**. Mark carefully records the
numbers involved, hinting at their symbolic significance. In the first feast in the
desert Jesus had fed five thousand men with five loaves and two fish, ending up
with twelve baskets of leftovers; this time, in Gentile territory, he feeds **four thousand** with seven loaves and a few fish, ending up with **seven** baskets of leftovers.
The word for **baskets** is different; whereas in 6:43 Mark used a term denoting
wicker baskets typically used by Jews, here he uses the ordinary Greek word
for a (large) basket (see Acts 9:25). The numbers suggest a similar Jew–Gentile
contrast. Twelve signifies the twelve tribes of Israel; seven may be intended to
evoke the seven pagan nations that inhabited Canaan before Israel entered the
land (Deut 7:1; Acts 13:19). The number four alludes to the four directions of
the compass (see Rev 7:1); thus the four thousand fed by Jesus represent the
whole world, to whom the mission of the Church would be directed.

After dismissing the people, Jesus and the disciples cross to **the region of
Dalmanutha**, an unknown place mentioned only here in the Bible but presumably located on the western shore of the Sea of Galilee (see Matt 15:39).

The Demand for a Sign (8:11–13)

---

[11]The Pharisees came forward and began to argue with him, seeking
from him a sign from heaven to test him. [12]He sighed from the depth of
his spirit and said, "Why does this generation seek a sign? Amen, I say to

you, no sign will be given to this generation." [13]Then he left them, got into the boat again, and went off to the other shore.

OT: Exod 17:2; Num 14:11, 22; Deut 29:1–3; Ps 95:8–10
NT: // Matt 12:38–39; 16:1–4; Luke 11:16, 29; John 6:30
Catechism: unbelief, 673

The approach of the †Pharisees stands in stark contrast to the three previous   8:11
episodes—the exorcism of the Syrophoenician child, the healing of the deaf-mute, and the feeding of the four thousand—in which people approach Jesus to receive his love and compassion. The **Pharisees**, instead, come forward **to argue** and **to test him** by demanding **a sign from heaven**, that is, a validating miracle. Since Jesus has up to this point been performing one miracle after another, such a demand can be rooted only in stubborn perversity, the refusal to open their hearts to the testimony of his deeds of mercy.

The unwillingness to believe in spite of so many signs already given is a replay of the Israelites' rebellion in the desert. "The Lord said to Moses, 'How long will this people spurn me? How long will they refuse to believe in me, despite all the signs I have performed among them?'" (Num 14:11; see 14:22; Deut 29:1–3). The ancient Israelites had "quarreled" and "tested" the Lord by disbelieving him (Exod 17:2, 7). For the Pharisees, similarly, Jesus' abundant miracles, revealing God's love for humanity, are not enough. They are looking for some kind of cosmic phenomenon that would serve as infallible proof of his claims. But to make this demand is to presume they can impose their own criteria on how God should act. Even more, by seeking to "test" Jesus they play the role of Satan (see Mark 1:13): they are tempting Jesus to turn aside from his true messianic mission and instead win their esteem through a dazzling display of power.

Jesus sighs **from the depth of his spirit**, expressing his distress at their hardness   8:12–13
of heart (see 3:5). **This generation** again recalls the "evil generation" of Israelites who refused to trust God even after witnessing all that he had done in Egypt, and who were therefore denied entrance to the promised land (Deut 1:35; see Ps 95:8–10). Like them, Jesus' opponents are motivated not by a sincere desire for truth but by a refusal to relate to God on God's own terms. To insist on irrefutable evidence is really a demand for control, as if to say: "Force us to believe, so that we will not have to trust you or change our hearts." But faith that is compelled is not faith at all. Jesus' emphatic preface **Amen, I say to you** (see Mark 3:28) gives a special weight to what he is about to say: **No sign will be given to this generation**—that is, no sign that will satisfy their criteria for proof. His miracles

and deeds of mercy will invite faith, but not coerce it. For those who reject his offer, who choose to be "those outside" (see 4:11), he can only walk away.

This painful exchange marks the end of Jesus' ministry in Galilee. From now on his focus will be on training his disciples in preparation for the culminating events of his life, and he will return to Galilee only once, in secret (9:30).

Reflection and Application (8:11–13)

Demands for proof of religious claims are as strident today as they were among Jesus' contemporaries. Today there are a host of books, articles, and programs claiming to refute Christian beliefs simply by showing that they cannot be proven according to empirical scientific criteria. But such attempts reveal only a false and truncated view of reality—as if the only things that are real are those that can be visibly observed and measured. Pope Benedict comments, "There can be a thousand rational objections—not only in Jesus' generation, but throughout all generations, and today maybe more than ever. For we have developed a concept of reality that excludes reality's translucence to God. The only thing that counts is what can be experimentally proven. [But] God cannot be constrained into experimentation." Such demands for proof can be an excuse to avoid what God reveals of himself, because "knowledge of God always lays claim to the whole person."[1]

The Leaven of the Pharisees (8:14–21)

14They had forgotten to bring bread, and they had only one loaf with them in the boat. 15He enjoined them, "Watch out, guard against the leaven of the Pharisees and the leaven of Herod." 16They concluded among themselves that it was because they had no bread. 17When he became aware of this he said to them, "Why do you conclude that it is because you have no bread? Do you not yet understand or comprehend? Are your hearts hardened? 18Do you have eyes and not see, ears and not hear? And do you not remember, 19when I broke the five loaves for the five thousand, how many wicker baskets full of fragments you picked up?" They answered him, "Twelve." 20"When I broke the seven loaves for the four thousand, how many full baskets of fragments did you pick up?" They answered [him], "Seven." 21He said to them, "Do you still not understand?"

OT: Jer 5:21; Ezek 12:2
NT: 1 Cor 5:6–8; Gal 5:9. // Matt 16:5–12; Luke 12:1

1. Ratzinger, *Jesus of Nazareth*, 193–94.

The second discussion following the feeding of the four thousand again involves hardness of heart, this time on the part of the disciples. This passage brings to a climax the theme of the disciples' failure to understand the meaning of Jesus' words and actions, which has been growing steadily more pronounced (4:13, 40–41; 6:52; 7:18; 8:4). But whereas the Pharisees' hardness seems to be unyielding, that of the disciples is amenable to change. The very fact that they are continuing to follow Jesus and learn from him implies their willingness to let go of the inner resistance that hinders their understanding.

Mark begins by noting the seemingly irrelevant detail that the disciples had **forgotten to bring bread** and had only **one loaf** with them. On one level, this simply means that they have failed to replenish their food supplies. But the two miraculous feedings and ensuing discussions have prepared us to understand: What is the real "one loaf" (literally, "one bread") **with them in the boat?** It is Jesus! Mark clarifies in verse 16 that actually they have "no bread"—no earthly bread, that is. Bread will not be mentioned again in the Gospel until Jesus announces that the bread is his own body, to be given up for us on the cross (14:22).

8:14

But the disciples do not yet understand, so Jesus takes the opportunity for a teaching moment. He admonishes them with a mini parable: **guard against the leaven of the** †**Pharisees and of** †**Herod.** Leaven, or yeast, is used to make dough rise; a tiny amount is all that is needed to permeate the whole batch. Jesus is referring to a spiritual leaven—the hypocrisy, insincerity, and ill will that the Pharisees (3:6; 7:5–13; 8:11–13) and Herod and his supporters (3:6; 6:14–29) have shown toward him. This admonition shows that even his disciples are not immune to such faults. Elsewhere in the New Testament, leaven is an image for sinful attitudes that, left unchecked, have a corrupting influence on the whole Christian community (see 1 Cor 5:6–8; Gal 5:9). At the same time, this saying recalls the exodus. As Jews knew well, all leaven had to be cleared out of their homes during †Passover, commemorating their flight from Egypt in haste, with no time to let dough rise (Exod 12:14–20). Mark's first readers might have noticed an allusion to Jesus, the true Passover Lamb (see 1 Cor 5:7).

8:15

But all this goes over the heads of the disciples, who remain on an earthly level. With remarkable cluelessness, they conclude that Jesus is scolding them for having forgotten to bring **bread.** After twice seeing him bring overflowing abundance out of a few loaves and fish, they are still worried about where they will get their next meal. In a series of seven questions, Jesus reproves them for their spiritual blindness. The emphasis on **understand, comprehend, see, hear,** and **remember** accents the mental effort required to grasp the hidden meaning

8:16–18

of what they have witnessed. The most stinging question is in verse 17: **Are your hearts hardened?** Only in Mark (here and in 6:52) is hardness of heart attributed even to the disciples. Jesus echoes the prophetic indictment of Israel: **Do you have eyes and not see, ears and not hear?** (Jer 5:21; see Isa 6:9–10; 43:8; Ezek 12:2). Having seen so many wondrous acts of God on their behalf, Israel had failed to recognize what those deeds revealed about God himself. But although human beings are at fault for this spiritual blindness, ultimately only God can provide the solution. The breakthrough in understanding will come by a gift of God (see Deut 29:3), as will happen finally at Jesus' passion and resurrection.

8:19–21   The emphasis on the number of **wicker baskets full of fragments** left after the feeding miracles seems curious. What is the significance of these numbers? On one level they remind the disciples of Jesus' superabundant provision of nourishment for multitudes of people, a provision that will continue through the whole history of the Church. But symbolically they seem to refer to the nations who hear the gospel and are gathered into the Church: the **twelve** tribes of Israel and the **seven** nations representing the Gentiles, who once were excluded from God's people but now share in the "children's bread" (7:28; see Eph 2:11–13; 1 Pet 2:10). Together, both Jews and Gentiles will partake of the "one loaf" that is Jesus. This is the mystery that Jesus is urging his disciples to **understand**.

A Gradual Healing of Blindness (8:22–26)

> [22]When they arrived at Bethsaida, they brought to him a blind man and begged him to touch him. [23]He took the blind man by the hand and led him outside the village. Putting spittle on his eyes he laid his hands on him and asked, "Do you see anything?" [24]Looking up he replied, "I see people looking like trees and walking." [25]Then he laid hands on his eyes a second time and he saw clearly; his sight was restored and he could see everything distinctly. [26]Then he sent him home and said, "Do not even go into the village."

OT: Isa 41:13
NT: John 9:6; Rev 3:18
Catechism: symbolic gestures, 1151–52; Christ the physician, 1503–5; laying on hands, 699

This episode is unique among all the miracles recorded in the Gospels as the only healing that takes place in two stages. Mark strategically places this account here to conclude the second part of the Bread Section, just as he had concluded the first part with the healing of a deaf-mute man (7:31–37). There are close parallels between the two. Both take place outside Galilee and occur at the request of others; in both cases Jesus leads the disabled person away from town, uses spittle and the laying on of hands, and enjoins silence (implied in 8:26). These two unusual healings have a symbolic purpose: as real-life parables, they signify the coming to faith of the disciples, whom Jesus has just chided, "Do you have eyes and not see, ears and not hear?" (v. 18). The healings help to drive home the fact that only the Lord can overcome our spiritual blindness and deafness. The healing of the deaf man was followed by an enthusiastic but incomplete confession of faith in Jesus: "He has done all things well" (7:37). The healing of the blind man will be followed by a radical confession of faith that will mark the turning point of the Gospel (8:27–30).

Jesus and the disciples arrive at **Bethsaida**, a small fishing town just east of the mouth of the Jordan River—the destination they had earlier aimed at but did not reach (6:45). As often happens, the healing is initiated by friends or relatives who bring the afflicted person to Jesus (see 1:32; 2:3; 6:55; 7:32). Jesus first establishes a personal contact with the blind man by taking him **by the hand**, recalling the Old Testament theme that God himself leads his people by the hand (Isa 41:13; Jer 31:32). Like the healing of the deaf man, this cure involves a degree of physical contact that modern readers may find disconcerting. Putting **spittle on his eyes** (literally, "spitting into his eyes"), Jesus **laid his hands on him**. At times the mere word of Jesus is sufficient to heal; in other

8:22–25

Baptism as Enlightenment

LIVING TRADITION

From ancient times, the Church has associated the sacrament of baptism with the inner enlightenment symbolized by opening blind eyes. The Catechism (1216) quotes St. Gregory Nazianzen: "Baptism is God's most beautiful and magnificent gift. . . . We call it gift, grace, anointing, enlightenment, garment of immortality, bath of rebirth, seal, and most precious gift. It is called *gift* because it is conferred on those who bring nothing of their own; *grace* since it is given even to the guilty; *baptism* because sin is buried in the water; *anointing* for it is priestly and royal as are those who are anointed; *enlightenment* because it radiates light; *clothing* since it veils our shame; *bath* because it washes; and *seal* as it is our guard and the sign of God's Lordship."[a]

a. Gregory of Nazianzus, *Oration* 40.3–4.

cases his body is the instrument, reminding us that God is not embarrassed by the earthiness of the human body, and even delights to use it as a vehicle of his grace.

Jesus' question, **Do you see anything?** involves the man in the dynamics of his own recovery of sight. His reply bespeaks a partial recovery: he sees **people looking like trees.** The fact that he knows what trees look like indicates that he was not born blind but lost his sight due to illness or injury. Now his vision is beginning to be restored, but he still cannot distinguish objects clearly. The gradualness of his recovery symbolizes the slow and difficult process of opening the disciples' eyes to an understanding of Jesus and his mission. But Jesus will not leave the man with only a partial restoration. He lays on his **hands** again, and now the healing is complete. The verb for **see** (*emblepō*) could be translated "look intently" or "fix one's gaze upon," and suggests the penetrating gaze of faith into spiritual realities, which Jesus desires for his disciples.

8:26   Jesus sends the man **home**, now that he is able to walk on his own without guidance. The command not to **go into the village** seems to be an instance of Jesus' avoidance of the wrong kind of publicity. Although there will be further healings, his priorities now lie decisively with his journey toward Jerusalem and the training of the disciples. At the end of the journey there will be another healing of a blind man (10:46–52), this time instantaneous and complete. The two miracles of recovery of sight form a frame around the journey narrative, symbolizing the disciples' gradual growth in understanding. Their eyes are partly opened to see that Jesus is the Messiah (8:29), but their vision of him is still shadowy and obscure. They will need a further divine enlightenment to recognize that his messiahship is inextricably linked with the mystery of the cross.

On the Way of Discipleship I

Mark 8:27–9:29

Mark has already disclosed Jesus' identity for his readers at the very beginning of the Gospel (1:1). But now for the first time the disciples, in the person of Peter, display a clear recognition of who Jesus really is. Peter's confession of faith is the turning point in the Gospel. It is a breakthrough, a burst of light, symbolized by the healing of the blind man just recounted (8:22–26). The eyes of Peter's heart have finally been opened to see the import of all that Jesus has said and done so far. Yet as the subsequent narrative unfolds we will see that this confession is only the beginning. To grasp *that* Jesus is the Messiah is not the same as understanding what it means to be the Messiah. Now begins a period of intensive instruction in which Jesus will unveil the mystery of his vocation to be a *suffering Messiah* who will lay down his life for his people—and the disciples' vocation to follow in his footsteps.

The turning point is signified by a geographical turn. Up to this point, Jesus has been teaching and healing throughout Galilee and the surrounding areas. But now he begins a journey to Jerusalem that he knows will lead to the culminating events of his life. This part of the Gospel (8:27–10:52) is often called the travel narrative, and its great theme is the "way" (*hodos*), sometimes translated "journey" or "roadway" (8:27; 9:33–34; 10:17, 32, 46, 52). As they follow Jesus on the way to Jerusalem the disciples learn about the "way" of Christian discipleship, the "way of the Lord" announced at the beginning of the Gospel (1:2–3). Like the blind man of Bethsaida they are beginning to see, but not yet clearly. Three times along the way Jesus will prophesy his passion, with increasing candor and detail (8:31; 9:31; 10:33–34). Each prediction will be followed by an inept, bungling response on the part of the disciples (8:32; 9:34; 10:37), which in turn will become an occasion for further teaching on discipleship (8:34–38; 9:35–37; 10:42–45). These three instances provide a framework for the other teachings and narratives along the way. At the end of the travel narrative is another healing of a blind man (10:46–52), this time instantaneous and complete.

Who Do You Say That I Am? (8:27–30)

---

²⁷Now Jesus and his disciples set out for the villages of Caesarea Philippi. Along the way he asked his disciples, "Who do people say that I am?" ²⁸They said in reply, "John the Baptist, others Elijah, still others one of the prophets." ²⁹And he asked them, "But who do you say that I am?" Peter said to him in reply, "You are the Messiah." ³⁰Then he warned them not to tell anyone about him.

OT: Deut 18:15–18; Mal 3:23–24
NT: Mark 4:41; John 6:69. // Matt 16:13–20; Luke 9:18–21
Catechism: Jesus the Messiah, 436–40

8:27   Peter's confession serves as a hinge, marking the transition from the end of the Bread Section to the beginning of the travel narrative (8:31–10:52). After Jesus heals the blind man at Bethsaida, he and his disciples **set out** toward **Caesarea**

Caesarea Philippi

BIBLICAL BACKGROUND

Caesarea Philippi was a city built on an imposing cliff at the southern base of Mount Hermon, at the site of a spring that flowed out of a cave and formed one of the sources of the Jordan River. The site had long been a place of pagan worship, identified at one time with the Canaanite god Baal and later with the Greek nature god Pan. Herod the Great built a marble temple there in honor of Caesar Augustus, who was considered a god. Herod's son Philip, who ruled the region at the time of Jesus, enlarged the city and renamed it Caesarea in honor of the emperor, adding his own name to distinguish it from Caesarea on the Mediterranean coast.

Jesus and his disciples were near this city, probably among the settlements on the plain from where the rocky slopes of Hermon rose dramatically, when he asked them the question about his identity. Peter's confession of faith thus took place in a region that had been devoted to the veneration of false gods.

Philippi, about twenty-five miles to the north (in present-day Golan Heights). Jesus' travels take on the character of a purposeful journey as he directs his steps first north, then south toward Jerusalem. With the theme of **the way** (*hodos*), Mark is once again evoking the Old Testament as the backdrop that illuminates the meaning of Jesus' actions. God had led his people on "the way" out of Egypt into the promised land (Exod 13:21–22); later, during the Babylonian exile, Isaiah prophesied that God would prepare a "way" for his people to return home to Zion (Jerusalem) with great joy (Isa 35:8–10; 40:3–5; 62:10–12). Similarly the journey to Jerusalem is both a geographical and a spiritual journey in which the disciples learn that the way to sharing in Jesus' glory is by first following him on the way of the cross. For the early Church this theme of the Christian life as a journey, or pilgrimage, was so central that "the Way" became the first name for Christianity (Acts 9:2; 18:25–26).

As they walk along, Jesus takes the initiative in probing his disciples' thoughts concerning himself: **Who do people say that I am?** Often in the Gospel, Jesus' questions are a signal that he is about to give a new teaching (9:33; 12:24, 35). This first question, about the opinions of others, prepares for the more personal and weighty question of 8:29.

Their answer lists the same popular opinions already mentioned in connection with Herod (6:14–15). Some, like Herod, see Jesus as a reappearance of **John the Baptist,** though it is difficult to know how literally this was meant. Others see him as **Elijah,** who had been taken to heaven in a fiery chariot (2 Kings 2:11), and who according to Scripture would return to earth to usher in the messianic age (Mal 3:23–24; Sir 48:9–12). Still others identify him as **one of the prophets,** perhaps a specific prophet like Isaiah or Jeremiah, or simply a man who spoke for God. They do not go so far as to consider him *the* prophet promised by Moses, who would speak God's definitive word (Deut 18:15–18). People undoubtedly thought these views represented a very high opinion of Jesus. Yet it is striking that each assigns him a merely preparatory, auxiliary role. They envision him not as anything significant in himself, but merely as a new manifestation of an important figure from the past. There is no mention of any popular speculation that Jesus is the Messiah (as there had been of John; see Luke 3:15).

8:28

But who do you say that I am? This is the question at the heart of the Gospel, addressed not only to the disciples but to every reader. All that Mark has recounted so far has led up to this question. Jesus has appeared in Galilee as an authoritative teacher and miracle worker. He has spoken of himself as the bridegroom of God's people (2:19), Lord of the sabbath (2:28), physician (2:17),

8:29

and founder of a new Israel (3:14). His actions have prompted awe, amazement, and curiosity (1:27; 2:7; 4:41; 6:2). But he has also met with repeated resistance and misunderstanding on the part of the religious authorities (3:6), his family (3:21), his townspeople (6:3), and even his own disciples (8:14–21). Just as his teaching is in parables to "those outside" (4:11), so his actions are parables that both reveal and conceal the mystery of his identity. Everyone who encounters him must eventually wrestle with the question, Who is he? The form of the question is emphatic—it could be translated, "But *you*, who do you say that I am?"—suggesting that ultimately it must be answered from within the depths of each person's heart.

As on other occasions Peter acts as spokesman for the Twelve. His reply is equally emphatic: **You are the Messiah.** Mark's version of this confession is the most simple and stark (see Matt 16:16; Luke 9:20; John 6:69). For Christian readers already familiar with the gospel message, Peter's affirmation may seem like an obvious conclusion to draw from all that has occurred. But the rehearsal of popular opinions in 8:28 helps to convey that, in its real-life context, it represented a penetrating insight, an earth-shattering revelation that broke through the current notions of what the Messiah would be. Although Mark does not record Jesus' blessing in reply, "Blessed are you, Simon son of Jonah. For flesh and blood has not revealed this to you, but my heavenly Father" (Matt 16:17), the healing of the blind man (Mark 8:22–26) symbolically conveys that such an insight could come only by enlightenment from above.

What would †Messiah (Greek *Christos*, "anointed one")[1] have meant in the context of the time? In Israel's past, every king was an "anointed one," chosen and consecrated by God himself. But at the time of Jesus, Israel had no king, having been dominated by foreign rulers for most of the past six centuries. During that period, the Jews clung to God's promises of a future "anointed one," especially Nathan's prophecy that a descendant of David would reign on the throne of Israel forever (2 Sam 7:12–14). By the time of Jesus there were a variety of theories in circulation about this anointed one. Some held that he would be a Davidic warrior king who would expel the Romans and restore independence to Israel. Others envisioned a priestly Messiah descended from Aaron. Still others foresaw a superhuman figure who would usher in a new age of peace and prosperity. But none had described a Messiah like Jesus: a

---

1. The NAB usually translates *Christos* as Christ but here as Messiah (from the Hebrew *mashiah*, anointed) to make clear that Peter is recognizing Jesus as the fulfillment of the messianic hopes of Israel.

humble rabbi who walked among the villages of Galilee teaching, healing, and casting out demons.

For Peter to acknowledge Jesus as Messiah means, "You are the one through whom God will accomplish all that he promised!" Although Peter still has an imperfect understanding of what this means (like the blind man who was healed in part; 8:24), readers of the Gospel are meant to read "Messiah" with its full Christian content, which completely transcends all the Jewish expectations.[2] Peter represents all Christians, who are called to make his confession their own.

Jesus' response, surprisingly, is a stern injunction to silence. Why would he want them to keep this stunning revelation to themselves? In the ensuing conversation Mark will finally provide the key that explains the "messianic secret." Up to this point, the disciples do not yet comprehend the true nature of Jesus' messiahship. They cannot be allowed to fill its meaning with their own earthly dreams. Indeed, the misguided idea that he might take on a political role as leader of a messianic uprising (see John 6:15) could derail his whole mission as they approach Jerusalem.[3] The whole understanding of Messiah needed to be purged of its human, triumphalistic connotations before it could be proclaimed openly to the world. Jesus' mission had nothing to do with using political or military power to overthrow the enemies of Israel. It had everything to do with overthrowing the power of sin through the cross.

8:30

First Prophecy of the Passion (8:31–33)

---

[31]He began to teach them that the Son of Man must suffer greatly and be rejected by the elders, the chief priests, and the scribes, and be killed, and rise after three days. [32]He spoke this openly. Then Peter took him aside and began to rebuke him. [33]At this he turned around and, looking at his disciples, rebuked Peter and said, "Get behind me, Satan. You are thinking not as God does, but as human beings do."

OT: Isa 52:13–53:12; Dan 9:26
NT: 1 Cor 1:18–25. // Matt 16:21–23; Luke 9:22
Catechism: Christ's knowledge, 471–74; the paschal mystery, 571–73
Lectionary: 8:31–34: votive Mass of the Mystery of the Holy Cross

---

2. This content includes, for instance, Jesus' divine sonship (1:11; 9:7), his creation of a new Israel (3:14), his universal kingship (13:26–27; 14:62), his redemptive suffering and glorification by God (8:31, 38; 10:45), and his gift of eternal life (10:29–30).
3. See France, *Gospel of Mark*, 330.

8:31   Peter's confession is a high point, marking the transition from the first half of
the Gospel (all about the discovery of Jesus' identity) to the second half (all about
the mystery of his suffering and glory). But this dramatic climax is immediately
followed by a startling anticlimax. For there is now a sharp change of tone and
orientation. Leaving behind his method of teaching enigmatically in parables,
Jesus now speaks openly about what it means for him to be the Messiah and for
his followers to be identified with him: it means going to the cross. The rest of
the Gospel will be dominated by the theology of the cross and resurrection.

This first prophecy of the passion is a direct response to Peter's confession
of faith. Jesus **began to teach**, as if all his previous teaching were only leading
up to this point. Now that the disciples grasp his messianic *identity*, he can reveal what that implies for his *destiny*: his role is to suffer, die, and rise. Instead
of referring to himself as the Messiah, Jesus uses the title **the †Son of Man**, a
phrase that alludes to the paradox of his humiliation and his glory. Jesus will
use this phrase in the three major announcements of his passion and in the
three announcements of his coming in glory (8:38; 13:26; 14:62).

The Son of Man

BIBLICAL BACKGROUND

"Son of man" is the title Jesus characteristically uses to refer to himself,
especially when prophesying his passion and during the passion
narrative itself (fourteen times in Mark). It is found only on his lips in
the Gospels. On one level, "son of man" means simply "man." Jesus is
fully human; he is descended from Adam and thus shares in human
nature with all its fragility (see Ps 8:5). This sense was familiar to Jews
from the book of Ezekiel, where God frequently addresses the prophet
as "son of man."

But Mark's audience may also have recognized an allusion to the
prophet Daniel's vision of "one like a son of man, coming on the clouds of heaven"
(Dan 7:9–14). In this vision God is seated on his throne of judgment, and the "son
of man" is presented before him. This mysterious royal figure seems to represent
the people of Israel, the "holy ones of the Most High" who have suffered brutal
persecution. God will judge history in their favor and will vindicate them in the end
by bestowing on them everlasting "dominion, glory, and kingship" (Dan 7:16–27).
Jesus' use of this title for himself is an oblique hint that he will embody and sum
up in his own life the destiny of Israel. His own royal glory will be veiled in suffering
and humiliation, but this abasement is only the necessary prelude to his glorious
vindication by God, when his divine majesty will be fully revealed (Mark 13:26;
14:62).

There is a weight of meaning in the verb **must** (*dei* in Greek): Jesus *must* undergo these sufferings because it is the will of the Father (14:36), the plan that was established long ago and foretold in the Scriptures (9:12; 14:21, 27, 49; see Luke 24:26–27; Acts 2:23). This word will serve as a powerful reassurance to the disciples when the hour of Jesus' suffering arrives. Nothing of what will take place is a tragic mishap or a wrench in the works; it is exactly what was intended from the beginning.

Jesus will **suffer greatly** by being **rejected** by the three groups that made up the †Sanhedrin, the supreme religious authority of the Jewish people: **the elders, the chief priests, and the scribes.** Now it becomes clear that the rejection Jesus encountered in Galilee is only the prelude to the final events of his life. Early on he had prophesied in a cryptic manner that he would be "taken away" (Mark 2:20); now he says explicitly that this means a violent death. Underlying this prophecy is a rich tapestry of Old Testament passages, especially Isaiah's poems about a mysterious servant of the Lord who would suffer on behalf of God's people. Many of the psalms depict a just man who suffers greatly but puts his trust in the Lord (Ps 22; 55; 69; 88). Daniel had prophesied that an "anointed one" (messiah) would be "cut down" (Dan 9:26).

Jesus' mission would end not in horrific defeat but in glorious victory: **after three days** he would **rise.** The three days is based on the standard inclusive way of counting time, in which each appearance of daylight is counted as a day. Although the Old Testament nowhere speaks directly of the Messiah rising from the dead, Jesus is probably alluding to a prophecy of Hosea: "Come, let us return to the LORD. . . . He will revive us after two days; on the third day he will raise us up, to live in his presence" (Hosea 6:1–2). Hosea is speaking of Israel's hope that God would restore his people to the fullness of life after the devastation of conquest and exile. By applying this passage to himself, Jesus indicates that the whole destiny of Israel will be summed up in himself. God's people will rise again in a way that far transcends their hopes, by his first rising from the dead in the most literal sense.

Mark emphasizes that Jesus **spoke this openly,** reminding his readers of what an utterly foreign concept was this idea of a suffering Messiah. The reverberating shock caused by Jesus' words is shown in Peter's forceful response: he **took him aside and began to rebuke him.** This reaction can be interpreted properly only if we grasp how natural it would have been in its context. It took no genius to recognize that dark clouds had been forming over Jesus and his ministry. His actions had aroused the fury of the religious authorities, and now his identification as Messiah—the figure popularly expected to liberate Israel

8:32

and reestablish the Davidic dynasty—would be viewed as a dangerous threat by the Roman government. But surely, from Peter's point of view, God would not allow Jesus' powerful ministry of teaching and healing to be disrupted. The Messiah was going to conquer! It was simply unthinkable to any Jew of the time to think of "messiah" in conjunction with "suffering" or "death," despite the prophesies of Isa 53 and Dan 9:26. Perhaps Peter was also prompted by alarm over what such a violent outcome might mean for himself and the other disciples. Peter displays the presumption of a disciple who thinks he needs to correct his master.

8:33 Jesus' response is a warning of how perilous is the kind of misunderstanding of the gospel displayed by Peter. **He turned**, as if setting his face against a grievous temptation. **Looking at his disciples**, their faces still crestfallen in dismay over his words, Jesus must have drawn resolve from the thought of how far astray they could be led by Peter's false triumphalism. Peter had rebuked him, but now the Master rebukes Peter. The sharpest reprimand in the Gospel is reserved for the one chosen to lead the others and strengthen them in their faith (see Luke 22:32). **Get behind me** expresses Jesus' rejection of **Satan**, who was using the unwitting Peter as a mouthpiece. But at the same time it expresses his command to Peter to follow *behind him* as his disciple, not presume to lead him (the same phrase is translated "after me" in 8:34). Peter will be qualified

The Suffering Servant in Isaiah

BIBLICAL BACKGROUND

Among the Scripture passages that the Church has most cherished as prophecies of Christ's passion are four lyrical poems in the latter part of Isaiah, depicting a "servant of the Lord" whose heart is totally set on God's will (Isa 42:1–9; 49:1–7; 50:4–11; 52:13–53:12). These poems portray in increasing detail the servant's vocation to suffer vicariously for the sins of the people.

It is unclear to whom the prophet was originally referring in these poems (see Acts 8:34). Was he thinking of King Cyrus of Persia (Isa 45:1)? Or the people of Israel collectively (Isa 41:8–9)? Or perhaps the prophet himself, or his predecessor Jeremiah? Most likely, although he had some or all of these in mind, the prophet was also looking forward to the perfect servant whom God would send in the future (see 1 Pet 1:10–11).

Jesus revealed himself as the Suffering Servant (Mark 8:31; 10:45). The early Church recognized in the servant poems a prophecy of Jesus' passage from death to life, and plumbed them for an ever more profound understanding of the mystery of his passion (see Matt 12:15–21; Acts 8:32–35; 1 Cor 15:3).

to lead the others only if he is first a follower of Jesus. Although Satan in the New Testament refers to the prince of demons, its literal meaning in Hebrew is "adversary." In seeking to dissuade Jesus from the cross, Peter was making himself an opponent, an obstacle to the fulfillment of his mission. And to do that is to play the role of Satan: tempting Jesus to be a messiah other than that willed by God, a messiah of unbroken success and popularity (see Matt 4:3–10). Only a moment earlier Peter had spoken with supernatural insight into Jesus' identity (8:29); now he speaks out of his own flawed and worldly reasoning. It is a replay of the disciples' recurring lack of understanding due to their "hardness of heart" (Mark 4:13; 6:52; 7:18; 8:17–21).

Peter's recoil from the prospect of suffering is not surprising; it is thoroughly **human**, the same reaction almost any of Jesus' followers would have and often still have. But how striking it is that Jesus characterizes this merely human **thinking** as so wrong that it can be satanic—that is, it can become an *adversary* to Jesus' mission. The logical implication is that, for his followers, merely human thinking is no longer enough. According to human reasoning, the cross makes no sense—what good could come out of defeat, humiliation, and death? But God's thinking turns the values of this world upside down (see 1 Cor 1:18–25). Jesus' followers are called to undergo a conversion of mind, to take on a completely new, divine way of thinking (see Isa 55:8–9; Rom 12:2; Eph 4:23), the divine logic in which victory comes precisely by way of the cross.

The Cost of Discipleship (8:34–9:1)

[34]He summoned the crowd with his disciples and said to them, "Whoever wishes to come after me must deny himself, take up his cross, and follow me. [35]For whoever wishes to save his life will lose it, but whoever loses his life for my sake and that of the gospel will save it. [36]What profit is there for one to gain the whole world and forfeit his life? [37]What could one give in exchange for his life? [38]Whoever is ashamed of me and of my words in this faithless and sinful generation, the Son of Man will be ashamed of when he comes in his Father's glory with the holy angels."

[1]He also said to them, "Amen, I say to you, there are some standing here who will not taste death until they see that the kingdom of God has come in power."

OT: Job 2:4; Ps 49:8–10
NT: Matt 10:32–33, 38–39; John 12:25; Gal 5:24. // Matt 16:24–27; Luke 9:23–26; 12:8–9
Catechism: taking up the cross, 618, 1435, 1642, 1816, 2427; spiritual progress, 2012–16

Peter's blundering response to the first passion prediction becomes an occasion for Jesus to give a more general teaching (a pattern repeated in 9:35–37; 10:42–45). Here for the first time he speaks plainly—without parables—to the crowds as well as the disciples, outlining the radical demands of discipleship. Now that he has already spoken of the suffering he will undergo, he can explain how all who follow him must share in that suffering. The veil over the messianic secret is being removed.

8:34   Jesus summons **the crowd** because his invitation to discipleship is extended to all, and gives a teaching in the form of six sayings that describe what it really means to walk in his footsteps. The first saying is the strongest, and sums up the rest. **Whoever wishes** indicates that to be a Christian is not something that happens by default or by cultural heritage: it is a personal decision that must be made with utmost sincerity and resolve—and with at least a partial grasp of the implications (see Luke 14:28). The conditions that Jesus is about to outline apply not only to some of his followers but to all without exception. To **follow** Jesus is a key term for discipleship. The same Greek verb (*akoloutheō*) is at the beginning and end of the sentence, so the gist of the sentence is: "Whoever wishes to follow me must deny himself and take up his cross—*that* is the way to follow me." Jesus is saying, in effect, "Don't imagine that to follow me is merely to come along as a passive spectator to healings, miracles, and wise teachings." To follow Jesus means to go where he goes, and as he has just made clear (8:31), his destination is the cross.

Crucifixion: The Ultimate Punishment   BIBLICAL BACKGROUND

It is difficult for Jesus' modern-day followers to re-create the sense of horror that his reference to a cross must have evoked. Crucifixion was the cruelest and most degrading form of capital punishment known to the ancient world, a means of execution reserved for slaves, rebels, and violent criminals, and always carried out in public so as to serve as a powerful deterrent. According to the Roman statesman Cicero, it was the "extreme and ultimate punishment of slaves," "the cruelest and most disgusting penalty."[a] Josephus, a first-century Jewish historian, called it "the most wretched of deaths."[b] The condemned person was forced to carry the crossbeam to the site of execution, where it would be fastened to the upright beam. Then the victim would be either nailed or tied to the cross and left to die, which sometimes occurred only after days of torment.

a. *Against Verres* 2.5.169, 165.
b. *Jewish War* 7.203.

To **deny** (or "renounce," JB, NJB) was a legal term signifying a complete disownment. It is easy to brush over Jesus' reference to *self*-denial—saying no to oneself—without fully appreciating what a radical notion it is. Most people recognize the value of occasional acts of moderation or self-restraint. But as the next phrase makes clear, Jesus is referring to a total shift of the center of gravity in one's life, a reckless abandonment to him that entails the letting go of all one's own attachments and agendas, even one's hold on life itself (see John 21:18–19).

Jesus' reference to taking up one's **cross** would have evoked the fearsome image of a death march. These words had a concrete meaning for Mark's first readers, some of whose fellow Christians had been burned at the stake, thrown to the wild beasts, or crucified under the brutal persecution of the Emperor Nero. Jesus does not call his disciples to tread this path alone, but *following* him. Discipleship is a continuous contact with the Master who leads the way at every step.

The second saying begins to supply the logic underlying the first. Jesus' call **8:35** to radical self-denial is not mere fatalism, a grim resignation to harsh fate. Nor is he saying that suffering and death should be accepted as good in themselves. Rather, the Christian paradox is that death is the way to the fullness of life. The Greek word for **life**, *psychē*, can also be translated "soul" or "self." On one level Jesus is warning of the temptation to deny him under threat of persecution (see 8:38), a very real temptation for the early Christians in Mark's audience. But to wish to **save** one's **life** means more than merely avoiding physical death. It means being so ruled by the human instinct for self-protection and self-promotion that all other values have lesser priority. Such attachment to self will lead only to corruption of the self, and ultimately to eternal death.

The positive side of the equation is that **whoever loses his life** for the sake of Jesus and the gospel **will save it**. The only way to preserve oneself—to attain the ultimate fulfillment for which we are created—is to be willing to give oneself away. With the phrase **for my sake**, the absoluteness of Jesus' claim appears for the first time. Jesus is asking more than any general ever asked of his soldiers or any religious leader ever asked of his adherents. He is not merely demanding a willingness to die for a great cause; he is calling for an unconditional, personal allegiance to himself. Whoever loses his life is to do so *for the sake of Jesus and his good news*. No greater motive is necessary or possible. But this is the very thing that Jesus will do for us: he will give his life (*psychē*) as a ransom for many (10:45).

In the third and fourth sayings Jesus uses language drawn from commerce— **8:36–37** **profit, gain, forfeit, exchange**—to show that his claim, though paradoxical, is also eminently reasonable. The two synonymous questions highlight the un-speakably great value of the *psychē* or self that we are to give up. We are called to give it up precisely because it has such great worth! When weighed on the scale against any competing values, there is simply no comparison. Any earthly gain (whether physical survival, wealth, power, pleasure, or ego-promotion of any kind) is totally useless to someone whose very self has been forfeited in the process—that is, whose capacity for eternal life has been lost. The second question alludes to Ps 49:7–9: "Truly no man can ransom himself, or give to God the price of his life, for the ransom of his life is costly, and can never suffice, that he should continue to live on for ever, and never see the Pit" (RSV). Jesus is calling his followers to accept a sensible tradeoff: to accept small short-term losses in exchange for a very great long-term gain.

8:38   The fifth saying explains the motive that someone could have for turning away from the gospel: concern for one's reputation and the fear of human disap-proval. This saying too reflects the situation of the early Church, when Chris-tians, besides being subject to violent persecution, were mercilessly ridiculed for being the followers of a crucified carpenter from Galilee. Jesus solemnly warns against the temptation to dilute the gospel out of accommodation to the world. The word translated **faithless** is literally "adulterous," and recalls the biblical denunciations of the infidelities of Israel (Deut 32:5; Isa 1:4; Jer 3:20; Hosea 2:4). The divine Bridegroom has come (Mark 2:19), but he has not met with a wholly faithful and welcoming bride. Jesus again refers to himself as the †**Son of Man** (see 8:31), this time with a clear reference to the glorious vision in Dan 7, where "one like a son of man" is presented to God and given everlasting honor and dominion. It is the first time in the Gospel that Jesus speaks directly of his **Father**, and the first reference to his coming in **glory** at the end of time (see 13:26–27; 14:62). With this saying, earthly life is suddenly put in a new perspective. All that happens to us is relativized. Both the pleasures and the hardships of this life, real as they are, are infinitely outweighed by the momentous consequences of our decisions that will appear in the life to come.

9:1   The final saying is a word of comfort to those who remain loyal to Jesus despite the cost. From the beginning of his ministry Jesus has proclaimed that the **kingdom of God** is "at hand" (1:15). But now he says that some of his listen-ers will see that it **has come in power** before they **taste death**. This saying has presented a puzzle to interpreters. Was Jesus referring to his coming in glory at the end of history (as in 8:38), and was he therefore mistaken about the timing? Or was he referring to the Transfiguration, which would occur only six days later (9:2)? If not, to what was he referring? The meaning must be sought in the context, in which he is teaching about his coming passion and the radical demands of discipleship (8:31–38). What will validate the truth of his teachings and enable his disciples to experience the reality of the kingdom even in the midst of their trials? His passion and resurrection from the dead (8:31)! It is the crucified and risen Jesus, revealing God's triumphant power over sin and death, whom **some standing here** would **see** (either by sight or by faith) and recognize as the coming of the kingdom.[4] Jesus is not implying that some of his listeners would be dead by the time his resurrection occurred, only that not all would "see" it. Probably also in view is the preaching of the gospel throughout the Roman Empire and the growth of the Church. By the time Mark wrote his Gospel, the presence of the kingdom was being powerfully manifested in the Church. Signs and wonders had been done by the apostles in Jesus' name and tens of thousands had come to faith in the risen Lord (see Acts 4:4; 5:12; 21:20; Rom 15:19). Even though eyes of faith were still needed to recognize the kingdom, these events provided a powerful validation for those who followed Jesus and a foreshadowing of the ultimate coming of the kingdom at the end of history (Mark 8:38). An anticipatory sign of this fulfillment occurs in the Transfiguration, which immediately follows this prophecy.

Reflection and Application (8:34–9:1)

These sayings of Jesus would have hit home for Christians in first-century Rome, for some of whom "taking up the cross" became a cruel reality during Nero's persecution. But what about those times and places where there is little direct persecution of the Church? It is easy to forget that the self-denial and readiness to suffer that Jesus describes are part of the normal Christian life—in fact, the only way to the inner transformation that prepares us to enter into his glory. There are kinds of persecution more subtle than that of ancient Rome but no less a threat to Christian discipleship. How often are Christians pressured to tailor their words and behavior so as to win approval and avoid derision from the world? How often are they tempted to soft-pedal the gospel in order to conform to the political correctness of the age? The danger of refashioning Christianity into something more safe and comfortable is summed up in Jesus' challenge to Peter: "You are thinking not as God does, but as human beings do."

These sayings help account for the tremendous importance the Church has always placed on not merely believing privately in one's heart but confessing one's faith publicly (see Rom 10:10). To be a disciple of Jesus means to stand up

---

4. See Moloney, *Gospel of Mark*, 175–77.

The Cost of Discipleship

LIVING TRADITION

Dietrich Bonhoeffer, a German Lutheran pastor executed by the Nazis, wrote eloquently about the cost of discipleship: "Cheap grace is grace without discipleship, grace without the cross, grace without Jesus Christ, living and incarnate. Costly grace is the treasure hidden in the field; for the sake of it a man will gladly go and sell all that he has. It is the pearl of great price to buy which the merchant will sell all his goods. It is the kingly rule of Christ, for whose sake a man will pluck out the eye which causes him to stumble. . . . Such grace is *costly* because it calls us to follow, and it is *grace* because it calls us to follow *Jesus Christ*. It is costly because it costs a man his life, and it is grace because it gives a man the only true life. It is costly because it condemns sin, and grace because it justifies the sinner. Above all, it is *costly* because it cost God the life of his Son. . . . Above all, it is *grace* because God did not reckon his Son too dear a price to pay for our life."[a]

a. Dietrich Bonhoeffer, *The Cost of Discipleship*, trans. R. H. Fuller (New York: Macmillan, 1963), 47–48. Italics in the original.

and be counted. Over the last two millennia, tens of thousands of martyrs have borne eloquent witness to the priceless treasure of knowing Christ, preferring to shed their blood rather than betray him. And their witness has helped draw countless others to faith. The famous axiom of Tertullian holds true: "The blood of martyrs is the seed of Christians."[5]

The Transfiguration (9:2–8)

²After six days Jesus took Peter, James, and John and led them up a high mountain apart by themselves. And he was transfigured before them, ³and his clothes became dazzling white, such as no fuller on earth could bleach them. ⁴Then Elijah appeared to them along with Moses, and they were conversing with Jesus. ⁵Then Peter said to Jesus in reply, "Rabbi, it is good that we are here! Let us make three tents: one for you, one for Moses, and one for Elijah." ⁶He hardly knew what to say, they were so terrified. ⁷Then a cloud came, casting a shadow over them; then from the cloud came a voice, "This is my beloved Son. Listen to him." ⁸Suddenly, looking around, they no longer saw anyone but Jesus alone with them.

5. *Apology* 50.13.

OT: Exod 24:15–16; 1 Kings 8:10–12
NT: Mark 1:10–11; 2 Pet 1:16–18. // Matt 17:1–8; Luke 9:28–36
Catechism: the Transfiguration, 554–56
Lectionary: Second Sunday of Lent (Year B); Transfiguration of the Lord (Year B)

The Transfiguration is the opening event in the second half of Mark's Gospel, a revelatory event like Jesus' baptism that sheds its radiant light on the whole journey to the cross that is to follow. Coming right after the announcement of the passion, it is a visible anticipation—a prophecy—of what Jesus has just revealed about his resurrection and future glory. For a brief moment the veil of ordinariness is lifted and the three privileged disciples see Jesus as he really is, his human nature suffused with his divine glory. **9:2–3**

After six days is one of the most precise time references in the Gospel. This event, burned into the memory of the three apostles (see 2 Pet 1:16–18), took place when they were still reeling from Jesus' words about his passion (Mark 8:27–9:1). There is also an allusion to the †theophany on Mount Sinai, where the cloud of God's presence covered the mountain for six days before God spoke to Moses (Exod 24:16–17). Jesus brings only the most intimate circle of his disciples, **Peter, James, and John**, those who were to have prominent roles in the early Church (Acts 3–4; 12:2) and would most need to be strengthened in faith to lead the others on the arduous road ahead. He leads them **up a high mountain,** the "Sinai" of the new covenant, where God's glory is revealed not in the thunder, lightning, smoke, and fire of the exodus (Exod 19:16; 24:17) but in the transfigured face of Jesus. The mount of the Transfiguration has traditionally been identified with Tabor, a majestic hill in Galilee, but it could also have been Hermon, a much higher mountain rising to the northeast of Caesarea Philippi, where Jesus and the disciples had just been traveling (Mark 8:27). Often in the Gospel a mountain is the setting for revelation and for key events in the life of Jesus (3:13; 13:3; 14:26).

Jesus **was transfigured before them**, his humanity radiating his majesty as Son of God, the glory that will be fully and permanently revealed at his †second coming (8:38; 13:26).[6] Even **his clothes became dazzling white**. Often in Scripture clothing is a visible expression of the person; white clothing signifies the holiness that can come only from God.[7] Only Mark adds the homely detail that **no fuller** (launderer) **on earth** could achieve such brightness. This event is a visible confirmation of what Jesus had just said

---

6. Paul uses the same verb, *metamorphoō*, to describe the Christian's gradual transformation into Christ, even in this life: "All of us, gazing with unveiled face on the glory of the Lord, are being trans-figured into his image from glory to glory" (2 Cor 3:18, author's translation; see Rom 12:2).
7. Ps 51:9; Dan 7:9; Mark 16:5; Rev 3:4–5; 7:14.

concerning his "Father's glory" (8:38). Since Scripture foretells that in the age to come the righteous will shine with God's glory (Dan 12:3; Wis 3:7; Matt 13:43), Jesus' Transfiguration is also a foreshadowing of resurrected humanity.

9:4   The transfigured Jesus is accompanied by two great figures of the old covenant, whom the three disciples recognize as **Elijah**, the wonder-working prophet, and **Moses**, the great lawgiver. Elijah had ascended to heaven in a whirlwind (2 Kings 2:11), and although Moses had died (Deut 34:5–6), Jewish traditions held that he too was taken up to heaven.[8] Both Moses (Exod 19:3) and Elijah (1 Kings 19:8–12) had encountered God on the "high mountain" of Sinai (also called Horeb) and both had suffered for their fidelity to him. Together they signify the totality of the Old Testament—the Law and the Prophets (Luke 16:16; 24:27)—bearing witness to Jesus.

9:5–6   Peter's impulsive response bespeaks his overwhelming awe and elation at this experience of heavenly glory. †**Rabbi** (literally, "my great one") is a Jewish title of respect for those in authority. Understandably, Peter desires to prolong this mountaintop experience, so he enthusiastically proposes to **make three tents**. Peter may have in mind the autumn Feast of Tabernacles, when the Jews camped out in small shelters made of interwoven branches to celebrate the harvest and commemorate the forty years in the desert (Lev 23:39–43). But his enthusiasm is misplaced; he wishes to capture this moment of theophany, and has not yet grasped what Jesus has told them: his glory will come only by way of the cross. Nor does Peter yet realize the full dignity of the one he so recently identified as the Messiah (Mark 8:29) but now puts on a level with **Moses** and **Elijah**. Peter's confusion is partly because they were **terrified**—the typical human reaction to a theophany (see Gen 28:16–17; Exod 20:18; Luke 2:9).

9:7   **Then a cloud came**. For the people of Israel during the exodus, a cloud was the visible sign of God's presence, the manifestation of his glory (Exod 19:9, 16). The same verb for **casting a shadow** was used for the cloud that "over-shadowed" the tent of meeting to signify that God had made his dwelling there (Exod 40:34 LXX). The implication is that Jesus, and his disciples along with him, is the new tabernacle of God's presence, his permanent dwelling place among his people (see John 2:21).

The Transfiguration, like Jesus' baptism (Mark 1:11), is a Trinitarian event, with the Holy Spirit's presence now symbolized by the cloud rather than a dove. Just as at the baptism, the heavenly Father gives audible testimony to his

---

8. See the apocryphal *Assumption of Moses*, dating from the first century AD.

beloved Son. At the baptism God had addressed Jesus himself; now he speaks to the disciples about Jesus, revealing a status that far exceeds that of Moses and Elijah. This testimony to Jesus (here and at his baptism) is the only word the Father is recorded as saying in the Gospels, since Jesus is the fullness of all that he has to say to humanity. The command to **Listen to him** recalls Moses' promise that God would one day raise up "a prophet like me . . . from among your own kinsmen; to him you shall listen" (Deut 18:15). The disciples are to listen to everything Jesus has to say, but especially, in the context of the conversation that has just transpired (Mark 8:31–38), his prophecy about his messianic suffering and its implications for them. They have been shown a glimpse of the road far ahead: if they listen carefully and obey his commands all the way to the cross, their destiny will be joined to his, and they too will one day be transfigured with divine glory.

At the pinnacle of this experience the disciples **suddenly** find themselves   **9:8** with **Jesus alone**. Moses and Elijah have already accomplished their tasks, but Jesus must now complete the Father's plan by going to the cross alone. His own life and mission will be the fulfillment that transcends all that took place in the Old Testament.

The Cloud of God's Presence

BIBLICAL BACKGROUND

A cloud had profound significance for the people of Israel as the means by which God visibly manifested his presence and protection during their desert wanderings. "The LORD preceded them, in the daytime by means of a column of cloud to show them the way, and at night by means of a column of fire to give them light" (Exod 13:21; see 24:15–16). A cloud symbolizes God's mystery, since it reveals his presence while at the same time veiling him. When the Israelites had finished constructing the tent of meeting, "the cloud settled down upon it and the glory of the LORD filled the Dwelling" to signify that the Lord had chosen it as his dwelling place (Exod 40:34–38). The same phenomenon is described at Solomon's dedication of the temple (1 Kings 8:10–11). Later Jewish literature uses the term *Shekinah* for this radiant manifestation of God's presence.

The cloud came to be seen as a sign of the Holy Spirit (see Isa 63:14), who "overshadowed" Mary at the annunciation (Luke 1:35) and who dwells in the hearts of believers (Rom 8:9–11). At the Transfiguration the cloud reveals that God's new and eternal dwelling place, where heaven meets earth, is Jesus himself, and by implication, all those who are joined to him.

The Coming of Elijah (9:9–13)

⁹As they were coming down from the mountain, he charged them not to relate what they had seen to anyone, except when the Son of Man had risen from the dead. ¹⁰So they kept the matter to themselves, questioning what rising from the dead meant. ¹¹Then they asked him, "Why do the scribes say that Elijah must come first?" ¹²He told them, "Elijah will indeed come first and restore all things, yet how is it written regarding the Son of Man that he must suffer greatly and be treated with contempt? ¹³But I tell you that Elijah has come and they did to him whatever they pleased, as it is written of him."

OT: 1 Kings 19:1–2; 2 Kings 2:11; Sir 48:10; Mal 3:23–24
NT: Mark 6:17–29; Acts 10:37. // Matt 17:9–13
Catechism: John the Baptist, 717–20

9:9–10   Jesus and his disciples cannot remain indefinitely basking in heavenly glory, but must come **down from the mountain** and continue on their journey toward another mountain: the hill of Golgotha. On the way Jesus charges them **not to relate** their experience to anyone until he has **risen from the dead**. The glorious transformation of his human nature, foreshadowed in the Transfiguration, cannot take place apart from his humiliation on the cross, nor can it be understood properly until the passion has taken place. He can become the exalted, risen ⁺**Son of Man** only by first being a dead man. Then his glory will be openly proclaimed to all. But this mystery eludes the understanding of the three disciples, who question among themselves **what rising from the dead meant**. Why would the Messiah have to die? Daniel had prophesied a resurrection of all the dead at the end of the age (Dan 12:2, 13); was Jesus talking about the end of the age? Or would he simply be taken up to heaven like Moses and Elijah?

9:11–12   The disciples try to grapple with this puzzle by raising a related question about **Elijah**. According to the prophet Malachi, the arrival of "the day of the Lord" would be signaled by the reappearance of Elijah, who would "turn the hearts of the fathers to their children, and the hearts of the children to their fathers" (Mal 3:23–24; see Sir 48:9–12). The gist of the disciples' question is: If the end of the age has come, where is Elijah? Jesus affirms the truth of this tradition: **Elijah will indeed come first and restore all things**, referring to Elijah's mission of preparing the people through ⁺repentance and the healing of family relationships broken by sin. Jesus then adds an unexpected counterquestion, indicating that not only Elijah's appearance but also the sufferings of the Messiah were foretold in Scripture. He is not quoting any one passage directly, but alluding to a whole array of passages that foreshadow his passion, especially the Suffering Servant poems of Isaiah: "He was spurned and avoided by men, a man of suffering, accustomed to infirmity, One of those from whom men hide their faces, spurned, and we held him in no esteem" (Isa 53:3).

Jesus then explains: **Elijah has come,** in the person of John the Baptist   9:13
(1:2–6). But John's identity, like that of Jesus, is hidden from most people until after the resurrection. No biblical passage explicitly states that the returning Elijah would suffer at the hands of others. But Jesus is teaching his disciples to interpret Scripture figuratively (see Luke 24:25–27), to recognize how Old Testament persons and events foreshadow the way God would accomplish his future purposes. Like Elijah, who was harassed by Queen Jezebel and King Ahab (1 Kings 19:1–2, 10), John was persecuted by a wicked woman and a cowardly king (Mark 6:14–29). Jesus' statement reassures the disciples that John's violent death did not disqualify him from fulfilling the role of Elijah. Indeed, it was fitting that the forerunner of the Son of Man would prefigure in his own life the suffering of the Son of Man. John is also a model for persecuted Christians, to whom ruthless rulers will do "whatever they please," but through whom God will bring about his victory.

Everything Is Possible to One Who Has Faith (9:14–29)

¹⁴When they came to the disciples, they saw a large crowd around them and scribes arguing with them. ¹⁵Immediately on seeing him, the whole crowd was utterly amazed. They ran up to him and greeted him. ¹⁶He asked them, "What are you arguing about with them?" ¹⁷Someone from the crowd answered him, "Teacher, I have brought to you my son possessed by a mute spirit. ¹⁸Wherever it seizes him, it throws him down; he foams at the mouth, grinds his teeth, and becomes rigid. I asked your disciples to drive it out, but they were unable to do so." ¹⁹He said to them in reply, "O faithless generation, how long will I be with you? How long will I endure you? Bring him to me." ²⁰They brought the boy to him. And when he saw him, the spirit immediately threw the boy into convulsions. As he fell to the ground, he began to roll around and foam at the mouth. ²¹Then he questioned his father, "How long has this been happening to him?" He replied, "Since childhood. ²²It has often thrown him into fire and into water to kill him. But if you can do anything, have compassion on us and help us." ²³Jesus said to him, "'If you can!' Everything is possible to one who has faith." ²⁴Then the boy's father cried out, "I do believe, help my unbelief!" ²⁵Jesus, on seeing a crowd rapidly gathering, rebuked the unclean

spirit and said to it, "Mute and deaf spirit, I command you: come out of him and never enter him again!" ²⁶Shouting and throwing the boy into convulsions, it came out. He became like a corpse, which caused many to say, "He is dead!" ²⁷But Jesus took him by the hand, raised him, and he stood up. ²⁸When he entered the house, his disciples asked him in private, "Why could we not drive it out?" ²⁹He said to them, "This kind can only come out through prayer."

NT: // Matt 17:14–20; Luke 9:37–43
Catechism: prayer with faith, 2609–11; exorcisms, 550, 1673

Just as the Father's affirmation of Jesus at his baptism was immediately followed by a confrontation with evil—the temptation in the desert (1:9–13)—so the Father's affirmation of Jesus at the Transfiguration is followed by a confrontation with evil in this exorcism. It is the last exorcism in Mark, and it symbolically reveals the ultimate aim of Jesus' deliverance of humanity from evil: resurrection from the dead.

9:14–16   As Jesus and his three companions rejoin the rest of the **disciples**, they find them embroiled in an argument with †**scribes** in the midst of a **crowd**. Scribes have previously questioned and accused Jesus regarding his exorcisms (3:22); they are probably doing the same with his disciples. Mark does not tell us why the crowd was **utterly amazed** as soon as they caught sight of Jesus, but he may be implying that after the Transfiguration, something of the splendor of his divine glory lingers on his face (as with Moses; see Exod 34:29). Mark will use the same verb to describe the women's amazement at seeing the angel who announces Jesus' resurrection (Mark 16:5). As if irresistibly drawn to him, the crowd runs toward Jesus and greets him. Jesus' question is probably addressed to the disciples: **What are you arguing about with them?**

9:17–18   A man from the crowd speaks up to explain what has transpired. He had brought to Jesus his son who was **possessed by a mute spirit**—that is, a spirit that both makes the boy incapable of speaking and is speechless itself (unlike other evil spirits in the Gospel, this one makes no attempt to blurt out Jesus' identity; see 1:24, 34; 5:7). The boy's symptoms resemble those of epilepsy: he is "seized" and "thrown down," **foams at the mouth, grinds his teeth, and becomes rigid**. This is not an indication that epilepsy is the result of demonic possession, but that demonic possession can sometimes be manifested in physical symptoms (see 1:26; 9:25; Luke 13:11). In the absence of Jesus, the man rightly expected Jesus' power to be exercised by the disciples, since they had been delegated his authority over evil spirits (Mark 6:7). But although the disciples have had success in exorcisms before (6:13), in this particularly stubborn case they find themselves **unable to do so.**

Jesus' reply expresses his anguish of heart over the persistent incomprehen-   **9:19** sion and unbelief of those around him. **O faithless generation, how long will I be with you?** He had voiced a similar indictment in 8:38, where the Greek phrase is "adulterous and sinful." Here the word is literally "faithless," lacking in faith even though they have witnessed so many signs of God's presence and grace in Jesus (see Num 14:11; John 12:37; Heb 3:10). Although this reproach is aimed most directly at his disciples, it applies to his contemporaries in general and to all humanity, often stubborn and unbelieving in the face of God's mercy. The disciples, with whom Jesus has spent so much time, are still practically indistinguishable from the unbelieving crowd. Jesus' words hint at the fact that his time with them is running short, and the sufferings he will soon endure are the result of unbelief.

His command, **Bring him to me**, is in the plural, indicating that it is addressed to the disciples. The man had brought his son "to Jesus," meaning to his disciples (v. 17); the disciples in turn are to bring the boy directly to Jesus—the proper pattern for their future ministry of healing.

The sight of Jesus seems to embolden the evil spirit, and the boy's symptoms   **9:20–22** suddenly worsen: he falls and begins to **roll around and foam at the mouth.** But it is empty bluster, and perhaps an attempt to dampen the fragile faith of the bystanders. Jesus' authority over evil remains invincible. But before taking action, he questions the father regarding the duration of the symptoms. The father reports that the symptoms have occurred **since childhood**, establishing the boy's innocence in regard to the evil that has taken hold of his body. The seizures seem to be evidence of a malevolent intent to destroy his son, since the boy is driven toward suicidal actions. The father ends his explanation with a cry of anguish, expressing his total identification with his son's suffering: **if you can do anything, have compassion on us and help us.**

The keynote to the story is Jesus' reply: **"If you can!" Everything is pos-**   **9:23–24** **sible to one who has faith.** The man expressed a cautious, tentative hope that perhaps Jesus might be able to help somehow; Jesus responds with a resounding call to confident trust. "If Jesus can" is never in question! There is no limit to his power; the only limitation is the barrier created by unbelief (see 6:5–6). Jesus will later express the same affirmation in a different form: "All things are possible for God" (10:27; see Jer 32:17). But here the accent is on the human capacity to open the door to God's mighty works through the boldness of faith. In the man's response we hear him stretching his faith to its limits: **I do believe, help my unbelief!** The very fact that he asks Jesus to cure his unbelief already shows a dramatically deepened faith: he understands that this rabbi standing before him is capable of reaching into his heart and transforming him.

9:25–27   Even though a crowd is already present (v. 14), here Mark notes a **crowd** is **rapidly gathering**, perhaps to emphasize the spectacle caused by the outbreak of the boy's violent symptoms. Having no wish to provide public entertainment at the expense of an afflicted boy, Jesus rebukes the **mute and deaf spirit**. Because the affliction was recurrent, in this case he bids the demon not only to **come out** but to **never enter him again**. The spirit departs in a final show of contempt, **shouting and throwing the boy into convulsions**. With this detail Mark portrays the heightening of demonic resistance to Jesus, who has been taking ground from Satan's kingdom step by step since the beginning of the Gospel. But once again the tantrums are mere bluster. The spirit, powerless before the Lord's command, departs in defeat.

The exorcised boy lies pale and motionless, apparently destroyed by the trauma of the ordeal. The bystanders assume **he is dead**; faith is still sorely lacking among the people. But in a gesture that recalls earlier healings (1:31; 5:41), Jesus took the boy by the hand, **raised him**, and he **stood up**. These are the two primary verbs used for the resurrection of Jesus, both in Mark and in the proclamation of the early Church (16:6, 9, 14; Acts 3:15; 10:41). Here they symbolically affirm that the dethronement of Satan in human beings is always a reversal of death and a restoration to life. Yet this victory will come at the cost of Jesus' own surrender to death.

9:28–29   As soon as they return to a **private** setting, the disciples ask Jesus for further explanation (as in 4:10; 7:17), puzzled over their failure. They have cast out demons before (6:13), and it makes no sense that their methods did not work this time. Jesus' reply suggests that they have lost sight of the need to depend completely on God and have imperceptibly taken on an attitude of self-reliance, as if exorcism were a mere formula. **This kind can only come out through prayer.**[9] Their efforts will never be under their own control (see v. 19). All their ministry of healing and deliverance will bear fruit only through a reliance on God as they bring all needs to the feet of Jesus in prayer. It is a salutary lesson in humility in preparation for their ministry in the Church.

9. Some ancient manuscripts add "and fasting," perhaps because of the early Christians' view, rooted in Jewish piety, that prayer is inseparable from self-denial as expressed in fasting (see Luke 2:37; Acts 13:2–3).

Reflection and Application (9:14–29)

Although the Church grants the faculty of performing exorcisms only to priests granted permission by their bishop, this passage provides some important lessons for all Christians who minister to others through prayer. Some wise steps to take in praying with a person for healing or the relief of any difficulty are the following: Ask a question or two to ascertain the nature of the problem (v. 21); invite the person to an act of faith in Jesus (v. 23); bring the person "to Jesus" (v. 19) through prayer (v. 29), combined with fasting when possible; and persevere with expectant faith even in the face of seeming failure (v. 26). This kind of simple but faith-filled prayer has enabled many to experience the living presence and power of Jesus in their lives, whether they are healed in body or in spirit.

On the Way of Discipleship II

Mark 9:30–50

Peter's confession of faith at Caesarea Philippi had marked a turning point, the beginning of Jesus' journey toward his passion. In this section Jesus continues along "the way" with his disciples, an image of the Christian life for all who would later follow him. As we will see, the disciples do not yet understand that the way of the Messiah is the *via dolorosa*, the way of the cross. They are expecting the Messiah-King to enter his capital city, take up his throne, and begin his glorious reign. They have not yet truly "seen" and "heard" (8:18) Jesus' call to deny oneself, take up the cross, and follow him (8:34).

Jesus' second prophecy of his passion, like the first, will be followed by a blundering response on the part of his disciples (9:34), which becomes an occasion for further teaching. This time Jesus expounds on three deep-rooted tendencies of fallen human nature: the craving for power (9:33–50), pleasure (10:1–16), and possessions (10:17–31), and shows how they must be countered with the lifestyle of the gospel: humble service, lifelong fidelity in marriage and family, and detachment from earthly goods.[1]

Second Prophecy of the Passion (9:30–32)

³⁰They left from there and began a journey through Galilee, but he did not wish anyone to know about it. ³¹He was teaching his disciples and

1. See John Michael McDermott, "Didn't Jesus Know He Was God? Mk. 10:17–22," *Irish Theological Quarterly* 73 (2008): 307–33.

telling them, "The Son of Man is to be handed over to men and they will kill him, and three days after his death he will rise." [32]But they did not understand the saying, and they were afraid to question him.

OT: Isa 53:12
NT: Rom 4:25; 8:32. // Matt 17:22–23; Luke 9:44–45
Catechism: Jesus' journey to Jerusalem, 557–58

Setting out from the mount of the Transfiguration (9:2–8), Jesus and his disciples make their way **through Galilee** toward Jerusalem. The action is markedly different from Jesus' Galilean ministry earlier in the Gospel. Instead of teaching multitudes by the sea or being mobbed by crowds bringing the needy and afflicted, Jesus is privately instructing his disciples in the final and most intensive part of their formation. For now, he does **not wish anyone to know** about his travels so that his disciples' attention can be entirely focused on what he has to teach them about the ordeal that lies ahead.

9:30

He **was teaching** and **telling** them: the verbs indicate a continuous process of teaching rather than a single statement. It is the second formal announcement of the passion (see 8:31; 10:32–34 for the first and third). Now Jesus begins to hint at the divine drama underlying the mystery of the cross: **The Son of Man is to be handed over to men**. The Greek verb for hand over (*paradidōmi*) was a key word in the early Church's understanding of the passion, expressing the whole process by which Jesus was rejected and given over to death by those he loved:[2] Judas hands him over to the Jewish leaders (14:10), who hand him over to Pilate (15:1), who hands him over to be crucified (15:15). This theme evokes Isaiah's prophecy of the Suffering Servant, who "surrendered himself" (*paradidōmi*) to death (Isa 53:12 LXX). Jesus was not a helpless victim of forces beyond his control; he *handed himself over* in loving obedience to the Father's plan. But the greatest mystery is that it is the Father himself who sent Jesus (v. 37) and thus originated all this handing over: God "did not spare his own Son but handed him over for us all" (Rom 8:32). The human handing over of Jesus out of sin, betrayal, and hardness of heart becomes the instrument of the Father's handing over of his Son in love for the redemption of the world. Jesus is †Son of Man in that he has fully identified himself with humanity and shares our nature with all its frailty. Yet he is "handed over to men," as if from the side of God, to be subject to all the concentrated violence of human rebellion against God.

9:31

---

2. The theme is not always recognizable in translation, since *paradidōmi* is translated "arrest" (1:14; 14:44), "hand over" (9:31; 10:33; 13:9, etc.), or "betray" (3:19; 14:18, 21) in different contexts.

Jesus' forewarnings of the passion never end on a note of gloom, since his suffering is only the necessary prelude to a glorious triumph: **Three days after his death he will rise**. The verbs "be handed over" and "be killed" are in the passive, indicating actions to which Jesus is subjected, but "rise" has an active meaning: Jesus will take up the divine power and sovereign control of his own destiny that he had temporarily laid down.

9:32   This time Peter and the disciples voice no protest (see 8:32), but remain in stunned silence. **They did not understand the saying.** Jesus' words were simple enough at face value. Readers might wonder, what part of "be killed" is hard to understand? With the hindsight of two thousand years of Christian catechesis we have to strive to appreciate how utterly shocking, counterintuitive, and worldview-shattering was this idea of a suffering Messiah. It simply did not fit into any of the preconceived categories of Jesus' contemporaries. Perhaps we can glimpse a fraction of their bafflement by observing our own reaction to a heavy cross in our life. Surely *this* can't be part of God's plan! How could any good ever come of it? It is no wonder that the disciples were **afraid** to probe Jesus any further. Was he speaking metaphorically, or could he possibly be referring to a violent death in the literal sense? They are terrified that their worst fears might be confirmed. Jesus patiently persists in his instruction, recognizing that it takes time for human minds to conform themselves to the utter otherness of divine logic.

Who Is the Greatest? (9:33–37)

---

[33]They came to Capernaum and, once inside the house, he began to ask them, "What were you arguing about on the way?" [34]But they remained silent. They had been discussing among themselves on the way who was the greatest. [35]Then he sat down, called the Twelve, and said to them, "If anyone wishes to be first, he shall be the last of all and the servant of all." [36]Taking a child he placed it in their midst, and putting his arms around it he said to them, [37]"Whoever receives one child such as this in my name, receives me; and whoever receives me, receives not me but the one who sent me."

OT: Isa 29:19; Zeph 2:3
NT: Phil 2:3–4; 1 Pet 5:3. // Matt 18:1–5; Luke 9:46–48
Catechism: authority as service, 876, 2235; love for children, 1825
Lectionary: Common of Pastors

9:33   Jesus and the disciples come to **Capernaum** for the last time, arriving at **the house** of Peter and Andrew, which Jesus has adopted as his own (1:29; 2:1).

In private once again, Jesus takes the occasion to question his disciples about their discussion on the road. **On the way**, mentioned twice, recalls Mark's theme of Christian discipleship, prominent throughout the travel narrative (8:31–10:52).

The disciples are **silent** with embarrassment, since **they had been discussing   9:34 ... who was the greatest**. This is the second time that Jesus' prophecy of the passion has been followed by a completely inappropriate response (see 8:32). Having just heard Jesus speak of his willing acceptance of rejection and death, they are suddenly preoccupied with jealous competition for privilege and prestige. No conversation could have been more contrary to what he was trying to impart to them. Yet Mark, once again, does not display the disciples' failures so his readers can marvel at their ineptitude. Rather, it is to bring us face-to-face with our human tendencies to seek our own glory in competition with others, which hinder us from yielding ourselves to God's marvelous plan.

Jesus sits, the customary posture for a teacher in the ancient world (see 4:1),   9:35 and calls **the Twelve** around him for a further lesson on discipleship. For those appointed to leadership in the community Jesus is founding (3:13–15), there is all the more need to preclude a false idea of authority. **If anyone wishes to be first, he shall be the last of all and the servant of all.** To be first means to have priority over others, as for instance the "leading men of Galilee" (literally, the "firsts of Galilee" in 6:21) had more influence, prestige, and power than ordinary folk. Jesus does not condemn the innate desires for grandeur in the human heart. But he turns human thinking on its head: the only way to fulfill these desires, paradoxically, is to put oneself last in priority. And this is not merely a pious thought; it must be expressed in concrete actions, by becoming a servant (*diakonos*) of all. This was a radically unconventional idea in the ancient world, where humility and meekness were viewed not as virtues but as signs of weakness. Those in authority should expect to be served and showered with honors. No one in their right mind would aspire to be a servant. The early Church's embrace of this new ethic was part of what made Christianity so novel and attractive to many in the ancient world. The same principle is expressed by St. Paul to the believers at Philippi: "Do nothing out of selfishness or out of vainglory; rather, humbly regard others as more important than yourselves" (Phil 2:3–4; see 1 Pet 5:3).

In prophetic style, Jesus follows the pronouncement with a symbolic action: 9:36 he puts **his arms around** a **child**. The connection with his previous statement (v. 35) would be natural to his listeners, since the word for child (both in †Aramaic and in Greek) can also mean servant. Jesus is continuing to overturn their worldview and system of values. In ancient society, children were viewed as nonpersons who had no legal rights or status of their own. Already in the Old Testament God had revealed his special love for the lowly, who are often overlooked or oppressed by the powerful (Deut 10:18; Ps 146:9; Isa 29:19). With his gesture Jesus shows human affection for this child (see Mark 10:13–16), and at the same time teaches his disciples to have a whole new esteem for and responsibility toward those who seem the most helpless or inconsequential.

9:37   Jesus explains his gesture: **Whoever receives one child such as this in my name, receives me.** To receive a little one is to accept, lovingly serve, and care for those who most need it and cannot repay it. To receive "in Jesus' name" is to welcome such a person for the sake of Jesus and in deference to him. This implies that Jesus identifies with those who are most insignificant in the eyes of the world—so much so that he himself is mysteriously present wherever they are welcomed. Moreover, to receive them is to receive **the one who sent me.** A principle recognized in the ancient world, as today, is that an emissary should be accorded the same respect and dignity due to the authority who sent him. Jesus is making an astounding claim: our treatment of the lowly, the "nobodies" of the world, is the measure of our treatment of God himself. The reference to the Father as "the one who sent me" alludes to Jesus' incarnation, using the same verb "send" (*apostellō*) from which "apostle" is derived. Jesus is the apostle of the Father. Thus all that his apostles are and do is an extension of his own apostleship, the mission on which he has been sent into the world.

Another Exorcist (9:38–41)

> [38]John said to him, "Teacher, we saw someone driving out demons in your name, and we tried to prevent him because he does not follow us." [39]Jesus replied, "Do not prevent him. There is no one who performs a mighty deed in my name who can at the same time speak ill of me. [40]For whoever is not against us is for us. [41]Anyone who gives you a cup of water to drink because you belong to Christ, amen, I say to you, will surely not lose his reward.

OT: Num 11:24–29
NT: Matt 12:30; Acts 19:13–16; Phil 1:15–18. // Matt 10:42; Luke 9:49–50

9:38   This episode is linked to the previous one by the idea of someone acting in Jesus' **name** (see v. 37). The apostle John complains about a fellow who has been spotted **driving out demons** in Jesus' name even though he does not belong to the band of disciples (see Luke 9:54 for a similar instance of intolerance). It is interesting that John says **follow us** rather than "follow you." Apparently his criterion for legitimate ministry is acting under the disciples' authority. Perhaps he does not yet fully recognize that Jesus himself is the only source of their power.[3] His protest echoes the objection of Joshua, who grumbled to Moses that Eldad and Medad were not in the gathering of those to whom Moses imparted his spirit, yet they too received the gift of prophecy (Num 11:24–29). Moses' reply could be paraphrased for this occasion: "Are you jealous for my sake? Would that all the people of the LORD drove out demons! Would that the LORD might bestow his Spirit on them all!" Indeed, at the end of the Gospel, the risen Lord will announce that those who believe in him will drive out demons in his name (Mark 16:17).

One might wonder why, in this instance, the unnamed exorcist is successful, whereas the book of Acts recounts an episode where those who tried to drive out demons in Jesus' name were thoroughly defeated and humiliated (Acts 19:13–16). In light of Mark 16:17 the most likely reason is that here the unknown exorcist is acting with an authentic faith in Jesus, whereas the seven brothers in Acts 19 were using his name as if it were a magic formula (see also Matt 7:22–23).

Jesus' reply directs his disciples to take an expansive rather than a restrictive   9:39–40
approach toward others who are acting in his name: **Do not prevent him.** There is no place for exclusivism among those who invoke the name of Jesus. Paul illustrates a similar principle in Phil 1:15–18: "Some preach Christ from envy and rivalry. . . . What difference does it make, as long as in every way, whether in pretense or in truth, Christ is being proclaimed? And in that I rejoice." The disciples should not presume to restrict the invocation of Jesus' name, because no one who **performs a mighty deed** in his name **can at the same time speak ill** of him. There were plenty of people who did speak ill of him, and Jesus will take all the friends he can get! To do a work of healing or deliverance in his name is to honor him, and is not compatible with being his adversary.[4] For **whoever is not against us is for us.** Jesus is directing the disciples to take a stance of openness toward those who are not within the formal bounds of the Christian community, and not to consider them foes. But the converse is stated in Matt 12:30: "Whoever is not with me is against me." In the end there is no neutral ground in relation to Jesus: sooner or later everyone chooses (consciously or unconsciously) either to be on his side or to oppose him.

3. Donahue and Harrington, *Mark*, 286.
4. This is not to imply that someone doing ministry in Jesus' name cannot *become* his adversary (see Matt 7:22–23).

9:41   With the solemn formula **amen, I say to you**, Jesus emphasizes God's generosity toward all and the great value of simple, humble acts of service. No good
deed will be overlooked, whether done by someone inside or outside the Church.
Even the smallest act of kindness toward a disciple because of his association
with Christ will be rewarded by God. **Reward** does not mean compensation
that is earned but a generous gift freely given by God in response to a good
deed. Mark words this saying so as to highlight its relevance for his audience:
because you belong to Christ is similar to Paul's description of Christians as
those who are "of Christ" (1 Cor 1:12; Gal 3:29).

Reflection and Application (9:38–41)

This passage is applicable to evangelization today, in which Christians
often find themselves in a situation of disunity and competition that hinders
the spread of the gospel. Since Vatican Council II the Church has encouraged
Catholics to collaborate with Christians of different traditions, even in missionary work when possible, without ignoring the real doctrinal differences
that exist. "Other Churches and ecclesial Communities which draw people
to faith in Christ the Savior and to baptism in the name of the Father, Son
and Holy Spirit draw them into the real though imperfect communion that
exists between them and the Catholic Church. Catholics . . . should be careful to respect the lively faith of other Churches and ecclesial Communities
which preach the Gospel, and rejoice in the grace of God that is at work
among them."[5]

Temptations to Sin (9:42–48)

[42]"Whoever causes one of these little ones who believe [in me] to sin, it
would be better for him if a great millstone were put around his neck and
he were thrown into the sea. [43]If your hand causes you to sin, cut it off. It
is better for you to enter into life maimed than with two hands to go into
Gehenna, into the unquenchable fire. [[44]] [45]And if your foot causes you to
sin, cut it off. It is better for you to enter into life crippled than with two
feet to be thrown into Gehenna. [[46]] [47]And if your eye causes you to sin,
pluck it out. Better for you to enter into the kingdom of God with one eye

5. Pontifical Council for Promoting Christian Unity, *Directory for the Application of Principles and Norms on Ecumenism* (1993), 206. See also Pope Paul VI, *Evangelii nuntiandi*, 77; John Paul II, *Ut Unum Sint*, 15.

than with two eyes to be thrown into Gehenna, [48]where 'their worm does not die, and the fire is not quenched.'

OT: Deut 30:19–20; 2 Macc 7; Isa 66:24
NT: Rom 14:13–15. // Matt 18:6–9; Luke 17:1–2
Catechism: scandal, 2284–87; temptation, 2846–49; hell, 1033–37

To preclude any risk of the previous saying being misunderstood Mark in-   **9:42**
serts here a second group of sayings, quoted by Matthew and Luke in different
contexts (Matt 18:6–9; Luke 17:1–2). Whereas verses 38–41 accented the need
for broadmindedness regarding the good deeds of others, the present passage shows how seriously Jesus takes sin. If God graciously rewards little acts
of kindness, he also severely punishes acts of evil, especially those that lead
little ones astray. "Little ones" is synonymous with "child" in 9:36–37, and
here too it refers more broadly to those who are weak or vulnerable. The verb
translated as **causes . . . to sin** (*skandalizō*) is literally to "lay an obstacle" that
causes someone to stumble. Scandal can be caused either deliberately or by
irresponsible negligence, especially by speech or conduct that shakes the faith
of others and so leads them into sin. Paul wrote at length on the obligation to

Fig. 8. Ancient millstone found at Capernaum.

Church Teaching on Scandal

The Catechism teaches, "Scandal is an attitude or behavior which leads another to do evil. The person who gives scandal becomes his neighbor's tempter. He damages virtue and integrity; he may even draw his brother into spiritual death. Scandal is a grave offense if by deed or omission another is deliberately led into a grave offense.

"Scandal takes on a particular gravity by reason of the authority of those who cause it or the weakness of those who are scandalized" (2284–85).

moderate one's behavior so as not to lead weaker Christians into acting against their consciences (Rom 14:1–15:6; 1 Cor 8:1–13).

Jesus could hardly have stated more strongly the gravity of sins that harm the weak. Drowning was among the punishments reserved for God's enemies (Exod 14:28; Neh 9:11; Zech 9:4; Rev 18:21). A **great millstone** is literally a "donkey millstone," the kind so heavy it had to be turned by a donkey, in contrast to a smaller one turned by women (see Matt 24:41). One might picture a giant stone collar around a person's **neck** that would make him quickly plummet to the bottom of **the sea**. Such a person suffers the fate that is destined for sin itself: God "will cast into the depths of the sea all our sins" (Mic 7:19).

9:43   The next three sayings consider the effect of scandal not on others but on oneself. Jesus uses graphic imagery, in typical Jewish style (see Deut 10:16), to convey the eternal consequences of our choices for good or evil. These parallel sayings emphasize the absolute value of life in the world to come relative to life

The Fires of Gehenna

Jesus' listeners might have shuddered at the mention of Gehenna (in Hebrew, the Valley of the Son of Hinnom), a steep ravine southwest of Jerusalem where idolatrous Israelites had sacrificed their own children to the pagan god Moloch (Jer 7:31; 19:5–6). Under the reforms of King Josiah, this vile site was desecrated (2 Kings 23:10) and later became a garbage dump, full of maggot-ridden carcasses and burning refuse. In Jewish extrabiblical literature, Gehenna became an image of the future punishments of the damned,[a] and Jesus uses it in this sense.

a. See *4 Ezra* 7.36; *1 Enoch* 27.2.

Church Teaching on Hell

LIVING TRADITION

"The teaching of the Church affirms the existence of hell and its eternity. Immediately after death the souls of those who die in a state of mortal sin descend into hell, where they suffer the punishments of hell, 'eternal fire.' The chief punishment of hell is eternal separation from God, in whom alone man can possess the life and happiness for which he was created and for which he longs" (Catechism, 1035).

"God predestines no one to go to hell" (1037).

in this world—reinforcing Jesus' earlier words about forfeiting one's life (Mark 8:36–37). **If your hand causes you to sin** (*skandalizō*), **cut it off**. Obviously, in the literal sense it is not a body part that causes sin but the human will. Jesus is not advocating physical self-mutilation but ruthless action against all our sinful drives, temptations, and attachments—even the ones that seem to be an inseparable part of ourselves. No earthly good or pleasure is too costly to give up, in view of gaining eternal life. **Enter into life** is parallel to "enter into the kingdom of God" in 9:47, referring to the heavenly life to come, which begins even in this life. Far better to lose a limb and gain eternal life than to **go into Gehenna** with limbs intact. The **unquenchable fire** echoes Isaiah's warning about the fate of God's enemies: "Their worm shall not die, nor their fire be extinguished; and they shall be abhorrent to all mankind" (Isa 66:24; see Jdt 16:17).[6]

Verse 45 repeats the same thought. The idea of a hand or **foot** being cut off for the sake of eternal life brings to mind the heroic mother and seven brothers who endured torture and dismemberment rather than disobey God's law (2 Macc 7). Jesus intensifies the pronouncement by speaking of being **thrown into Gehenna**.

9:45–48

The final saying (9:47) again contrasts the two possible destinies resulting from God's final judgment. Jesus' whole preaching has centered on **the kingdom of God** (1:15); now he reveals that the kingdom is something we will enter into fully only at the final judgment. A more radical self-denial could hardly be imagined than amputating one's limb or plucking out one's **eye**. Yet just as a surgeon would do so to save a life, so we are called to cut off the sinful enticements that imperil our eternal destiny. But no one need worry that they might remain

---

6. The NAB, like most modern translations, omits vv. 44 and 46 (which are identical to v. 48) because they are missing from the most reliable ancient manuscripts of the Gospel.

forever maimed, crippled, or one-eyed; the resurrected body will be glorious and liberated from all the brokenness of earthly existence (1 Cor 15:42–44; Phil 3:21). The final verse again quotes Isa 66:24, describing in figurative language the unbearable torment of eternal separation from God.

Reflection and Application (9:42–48)

Jesus' teaching on the two possible destinations of human life after death—heaven or hell, the eternal joy of union with God or the eternal misery of separation from him—has been constantly reaffirmed throughout Church tradition. Yet it is often brushed over or treated with outright skepticism by Christians today. Many of those who teach or catechize seem reluctant to comment on this most crucial perspective within which to live our lives. Some may be struggling with the question of how a good God could send someone to hell. But the truth conveyed in Jesus' teaching is that we choose our own destiny. With every decision and action over the course of a lifetime we orient ourselves either to heaven or to hell, and at the moment of death we embrace what has truly become our choice. C. S. Lewis expresses it well: "There are only two kinds of people in the end: those who say to God, 'Thy will be done,' and those to whom God says, in the end, 'Thy will be done.' All that are in Hell, choose it. Without that self-choice there could be no Hell."[7] But God never ceases to hold out his unfathomable mercy, even at the very moment when a person steps over the threshold into eternity.

Jesus' warnings can also help to arouse in us a healthy hatred of sin, especially the sin toward which we are most inclined. Recognizing the seriousness of our responsibility to others can lead us to zeal for avoiding speech, attitudes, or conduct that could cause others to stumble. Recently at a large dinner party I was edified to notice that the hosts quietly avoided serving alcohol, aware that one of their guests was struggling with alcohol addiction. Similarly, I have observed people making sacrifices to avoid employment in a field that brings temptation to others.

Salt Sayings (9:49–50)

---

[49]"Everyone will be salted with fire. [50]Salt is good, but if salt becomes insipid, with what will you restore its flavor? Keep salt in yourselves and you will have peace with one another."

---

7. C. S. Lewis, *The Great Divorce* (New York: Macmillan, 1946), 72–73. Italics in the original.

OT: Exod 30:35; Job 6:6; Ezek 43:24
NT: // Matt 5:13; Luke 14:34–35

The three sayings on salt seem to be only loosely connected with the fore-   9:49
going passage (by the mention of fire) and with one another (by the mention
of salt). Mark portrays Jesus teaching in typical rabbinic style, linking apparently disparate points through word association so as to invite his listeners
to thoughtful reflection. Upon consideration, the sayings are not so disparate
as appears at first. **Everyone will be salted with fire.** What could Jesus mean
by this cryptic proverb? The meaning hinges on the purpose of salt, which is
used both to preserve and to season. In the Old Testament, temple sacrifices
had to be offered with salt (Ezek 43:24; see Exod 30:35), and the Israelites are
warned not to insult God with offerings that lack "the salt of the covenant
of your God" (Lev 2:13)—that is, offerings that are mere perfunctory ritual,
devoid of genuine zeal for God and his covenant. Jesus is speaking of salt as
a necessary quality in his disciples, the quality that keeps their spiritual life
keen and vibrant. Perhaps "fervor" would best capture the meaning. In verse 48
he spoke of the fires of eternal torment, but here he balances the point by
indicating that not all fire is bad. Even his disciples should expect to endure
some "fire" in this life that will "salt" them. The fire of persecution and other
kinds of suffering has a salutary, purifying effect, as in the refining of precious
metals (see Mal 3:2–3).

The second saying is similar to those recorded in Matt 5:13 and Luke 14:34–35.   9:50
Here Jesus refers to the possibility that **salt** can become so diluted that it loses
its **flavor** (see Job 6:6). Salt is what seasons everything else; if even salt becomes
tasteless, what is left to season *it*? Jesus is cautioning his disciples against falling
into a bland, insipid spirituality that has no power to attract others. They are the
salt of the earth (see Matt 5:13); if even *they* become mediocre in their Christian
life, what is left for the world? In the context of the whole discussion (9:33–50)
such spiritual blandness results primarily from a reluctance to embrace Jesus'
call to humility and radical self-denial.

The final saying rounds up the whole section that began with the disciples'
quarrel (9:33) by reminding them that the way to **have peace with one another**
is to **keep salt** in themselves. Peace in biblical thought (*shalom*) means not
merely the absence of conflict, but the presence of all that is meant to be in a
relationship: the fullness of communion. The idea is similar to Paul's injunction:
"Let your speech always be gracious, seasoned with salt" (Col 4:6). The disciples'
conversations with one another and with outsiders (see 9:38) must be marked
by the fervent love for Christ that leads to humility. It is their spiritual intensity,

kept alive through a profound conformity to Jesus in his self-emptying love, that will bring them into unity with one another.

Reflection and Application (9:49–50)

Besides its seasoning and preservative qualities, salt has another effect: it makes people thirsty. Jesus is exhorting his disciples to maintain that spiritual vitality that will make others thirst for the living water that he gives, the Holy Spirit (see John 4:14; 7:37–39). And in placing these sayings at the end of Jesus' instructions on humility and self-renunciation, Mark indicates that what can make the salt tasteless is the creeping attachment to self, the desire for human recognition, and the compromise with sin to which we can so easily succumb. Those who have had the privilege of being with a truly humble person—for instance, Mother Teresa of Calcutta—can testify to the indefinable lifting of one's spirit, the deeper thirst for holiness, that arises simply from being in his or her presence. St. Seraphim of Sarov, a Russian saint, expressed a similar idea: "Acquire the Spirit of peace and thousands around you will be saved."

The Gospel in Daily Life

Mark 10:1–31

The first half of chapter 10 is a kind of interlude in the travel narrative, continuing the series of teachings that follow the second passion prediction and spelling out some of the practical implications of Christian discipleship. Jesus has already spoken of the radical demands of being his disciple (8:34–38; 9:35, 43–39). But what does that entail for ordinary life—for those called to marry, raise children, run a business, or own an estate?

God's Plan for Marriage (10:1–12)

¹He set out from there and went into the district of Judea [and] across the Jordan. Again crowds gathered around him and, as was his custom, he again taught them. ²The Pharisees approached and asked, "Is it lawful for a husband to divorce his wife?" They were testing him. ³He said to them in reply, "What did Moses command you?" ⁴They replied, "Moses permitted him to write a bill of divorce and dismiss her." ⁵But Jesus told them, "Because of the hardness of your hearts he wrote you this commandment. ⁶But from the beginning of creation, 'God made them male and female. ⁷For this reason a man shall leave his father and mother [and be joined to his wife], ⁸and the two shall become one flesh.' So they are no longer two but one flesh. ⁹Therefore what God has joined together, no human being must separate." ¹⁰In the house the disciples again questioned him about this. ¹¹He said to them, "Whoever divorces his wife and marries another

commits adultery against her; [12]and if she divorces her husband and marries another, she commits adultery."

OT: Gen 1:27; 2:24; Deut 24:1–4; Mal 2:14–16
NT: Eph 5:21–33. // Matt 19:1–12; Luke 16:18
Catechism: marriage and fidelity, 1601–17, 1638–54, 2360–2400
Lectionary: 10:6–9: Sacrament of Marriage

10:1   Here Mark indicates a new stage in Jesus' itinerary. From Capernaum (9:33), he proceeds for the first time since his baptism (1:9) to the heart of Jewish territory, **the district of Judea** (see map, p. 349). Jesus will not set foot again in Galilee until his resurrection from the dead (16:7). The region **across the Jordan** from Judea was Perea, part of the territory ruled by Herod Antipas. Jesus' reputation had long preceded him into these regions (see 3:7–8). Although in his recent travels he had focused on private instruction for the disciples, now he resumes his public teaching for the **crowds**.

10:2   As had often occurred in Galilee, [†]**Pharisees** approach Jesus with a question designed to ensnare him: **Is it lawful for a husband to divorce his wife?** Divorce was widely accepted in Jewish society of the time, despite the biblical assertion that God hates divorce (Mal 2:16). There was some controversy among Pharisees over what constituted sufficient grounds for divorce, but here the question is whether divorce is permissible at all. Why would they ask this, knowing that the law of Moses did permit divorce (Deut 24:1–4)? We can surmise that Jesus had already given a teaching on the matter that apparently conflicted with the concession in the law, and the Pharisees **were testing him** in order to expose what they considered his unorthodox views.

10:3–4   In rabbinic fashion, Jesus responds with a counterquestion, putting the ball back in their court: **What did Moses command you?** In fact, Moses gave no command about divorce. The only mention of divorce in the [†]Torah is in Deut 24:1–4, which takes for granted the possibility that a husband could dismiss his wife by writing her a bill of divorce. A **bill of divorce** was a man's relinquishment of legal claims on his wife, freeing her from any obligations to him and allowing her to marry someone else. This provision afforded some legal protection to a woman whose husband repudiated her, in a society where it was unthinkable for a woman to live on her own. The purpose of the bill of divorce was not to authorize divorce, but merely to limit its consequences for the woman. There was no corresponding legal right for a woman to divorce her husband.

10:5   Jesus then explains the reason for the legislation in Deut 24:1–4: **because of the hardness of your hearts**. That is, Moses had made provision for a divorced wife on account of the hard-heartedness that led men to dissolve their marriages.

Israel is often chastised in the Old Testament for being hard-hearted or, the synonym, stiff-necked (Deut 10:16; 2 Kings 17:14; Ps 95:8; Isa 63:17). Hardness of heart, literally *sklērokardia*, sclerosis of the heart, is a stubborn refusal to yield to God and his ways. It is the willful blindness to truth for which Jesus has chided the Pharisees and even his disciples (Mark 3:5; 6:52; 8:17).

Now Jesus comes to the heart of the matter, the real "commandment" he   **10:6–8** wishes to draw attention to, which is given not in the fifth book of Moses, Deuteronomy, but in the first, Genesis. He quotes two passages from the story of creation, referring to humanity prior to the sin of Adam and Eve. The first, Gen 1:27, recounts God's creation of human beings in his image on the sixth day: **God made them male and female.** The second, Gen 2:24, describes the covenant bond of love between husband and wife, expressed in sexual union: **a man shall leave his father and mother [and be joined to his wife], and the two shall become one flesh.**[1] In biblical thought flesh is not merely the physical body but the whole human being as present in the visible world. For a husband and wife to become "one flesh" is the bodily expression of a personal union at the deepest level of their being. Jesus links these two scriptures to indicate that the communion of love between a husband and wife is a sign pointing to God's ultimate purpose in creating humanity in his image.

With these statements, Jesus brings the discussion—and the whole understanding of marriage itself—to a new level. By the very fact of referring to humanity before the fall, Jesus is implying that from now on, God's original intention is the true standard for marriage and other human relationships. He is saying, in effect, that the concession in Deuteronomy no longer applies because humanity is no longer captive to sin, hardness of heart, and the resultant family breakdown. Now there is a new reality at hand—the kingdom of God—with a new power to live and experience what God intended from the beginning. As Jesus has already suggested (Mark 8:31–9:1), this new possibility will come about through his paschal mystery.

Jesus concludes with his own solemn injunction: **what God has joined to-**   **10:9** **gether, no human being must separate.** He thereby confirms what Genesis already implied: the union of husband and wife is no mere human convention but a bond made by God himself (see Mal 2:14–16). No human being is authorized to dissolve that bond once it has been made.[2]

---

1. The Hebrew text of Gen 2:24 uses the word for flesh: "and they become one flesh." The NAB translates the phrase as "one body."

2. Jesus' prohibition of divorce is unconditional here and in Luke 16:19 (see also 1 Cor 7:10–11). Although the parallel passages in Matthew contain an exception clause (Matt 5:32; 19:9), this clause seems to refer to cases where no valid marriage has occurred in the first place. The Church interprets

10:10–12   It is no wonder that the disciples, as often happens, find it difficult to digest the radical change Jesus has just instituted (see Matt 19:10). On his own authority Jesus has just taken away a concession given in the law of Moses. Why would he set this stricter standard? Surely it is not to make life more difficult for his followers. Rather, it is because through his cross and resurrection he is now giving them a new power to live according to God's original plan for human love. They can no longer settle for less. Once again, in a private indoor setting, the disciples ask Jesus to explain himself (see Mark 4:10; 7:17; 9:28). For Mark's first readers, **in the house** probably called to mind the Church, which gathered in homes just as the first disciples had often gathered around Jesus in a house (1:29; 2:15; 7:24; 9:33). Jesus unpacks the implications of his teaching by declaring that remarriage after divorce is not permissible. **Whoever divorces his wife and marries another commits adultery against her**. This statement is radical in two ways. First, it affirms the indissolubility of marriage, a teaching that is as challenging and countercultural today as it was then. Second, it recognizes adultery as an offense that can be committed against a wife. Jewish law and custom had viewed adultery as an offense against a man, whose wife was considered in some sense his property (see Exod 20:17). Jesus acknowledges the total equality of man and woman, and the *mutual* belonging of husband and wife in marriage. The final statement reflects the situation in the Roman world where women had a legal right to divorce, and affirms that women are equally responsible for upholding the permanence of the marriage bond.

With this pronouncement on marriage, Jesus brings his teachings on suffering, self-denial, humility, and service into the most intimate sphere of human life.[3] It is in the daily challenges of family relationships, in the struggle to live out God's design for human love—especially in lifelong fidelity to another fallen and imperfect person—that "taking up the cross" (Mark 8:34) has its most concrete application. But equally it is here that those who obey Jesus' new law will be able to experience the coming of the kingdom with power (9:1).

Reflection and Application (10:1–12)

Today it is nearly impossible to read this passage, and its parallels in Matthew and Luke, without calling to mind Pope John Paul the Great and his profound reflections on human love in the divine plan, known as the theology of the

---

Jesus' prohibition as absolute, and in faithfulness to his teaching has constantly upheld the indissolubility of marriage (see Catechism, 2382–86; Code of Canon Law, canon 1141).

3. Moloney, *Mark*, 196.

body.[4] As the pope explains, in this passage Jesus recalls "the beginning" to show that it is only by rediscovering God's original plan that we can find the answer to our longing for relationships of lasting, authentic love. God gave us a symbolic key to that plan by creating us in his image as "male and female"—that is, with bodily differences that are designed for union. The one-flesh union of man and woman in marriage is a sign pointing to God's own mystery and our call to communion with him. Only in the New Testament is the mystery fully revealed: God himself is a communion of persons, an eternal exchange of love, and he has destined us to share in that exchange (Catechism, 221).

Blessing of the Children (10:13–16)

[13]And people were bringing children to him that he might touch them, but the disciples rebuked them. [14]When Jesus saw this he became indignant and said to them, "Let the children come to me; do not prevent them, for the kingdom of God belongs to such as these. [15]Amen, I say to you, whoever does not accept the kingdom of God like a child will not enter it." [16]Then he embraced them and blessed them, placing his hands on them.

OT: Gen 48:14–16; Ps 115:14–15
NT: Mark 9:36–37; Acts 2:39; 1 Pet 2:2. // Matt 18:3; 19:13–15; Luke 18:15–17
Catechism: becoming a child, 526, 2785; the gift of children, 2373–79; laying on of hands, 699
Lectionary: Common of Pastors; Infant Baptism; Christian Initiation Apart from the Easter Vigil

This pronouncement about children immediately follows one about marriage—not accidentally, since Mark is grouping together teachings on the implications of discipleship for ordinary life. **People**, probably both mothers and fathers, **were bringing children to** Jesus, not only for healing but simply **that he might touch them**. The blessing of children through the laying on of hands was an ancient Israelite practice, usually done by the child's father (Gen 27:30; 48:14–16). Not surprisingly, parents wanted their children to be blessed by the renowned miracle-working rabbi from Nazareth. But those approaching Jesus often have to overcome obstacles (Mark 2:4; 7:27; 10:48). Here it is the reprimand of **the disciples**, who perhaps with good intentions are trying to protect Jesus from what they deem a nuisance. In their view, Jesus has more important things to do than attend to children, who had no status in the culture of the

10:13

---

4. See John Paul II, *Men and Women He Created Them: A Theology of the Body*, trans. Michael Waldstein (Boston: Pauline, 2006). For a brief introduction, see Mary Healy, *Men and Women Are from Eden: A Study Guide to John Paul II's Theology of the Body* (Cincinnati: Servant, 2005).

time. Once again they have fumbled, completely forgetting his teaching that to receive a child is to receive him (9:36–37).

10:14–15   This is the only instance in the Gospels where Jesus becomes **indignant**, a term indicating outrage at an offense—in this case the disciples' attempt to hinder little ones from coming to him. Jesus states in the strongest possible terms his desire that **children** be granted access to him. He then gives an explanation that must have taken his disciples aback. The **kingdom of God** has been the whole subject of his preaching and ministry (1:15; 4:11; 9:1). It sums up everything to which the disciples aspire—and now he says it **belongs** to these little people whom they were just shooing away? Once again Jesus is overturning their whole scale of values. To explain further, he makes a solemn pronouncement: **whoever does not accept the kingdom of God like a child will not enter it**. All are called to be "children" in relation to the kingdom. What is it about children that makes them such apt recipients of the kingdom? Children have no accomplishments with which to earn God's favor, no status that makes them worthy. In their dependency they exemplify the only disposition that makes entrance into the kingdom possible: simply to *receive* it as a pure, unmerited gift (see Matt 5:3).

10:16   Jesus shows the children even more care and affection than their parents sought: he **embraced** and **blessed them, placing his hands on them**. It is the second time he has shown the warmth of his love for children (see 9:36). In so doing he reveals the disposition of God toward all his sons and daughters, his desire to bless them and enfold them in his embrace. Jesus' action is a parable

---

St. Thérèse on Receiving the Kingdom like a Child

LIVING TRADITION

What does it mean to be a child before God? "It is to recognize our nothingness, to expect everything from God as a little child expects everything from its father; it is to be disquieted about nothing, and not to be set on gaining our living. . . . To be little is not attributing to oneself the virtues that one practices, believing oneself capable of anything, but to recognize that God places this treasure in the hands of his little child to be used when necessary; but it remains always God's treasure. Finally, it is not to become discouraged over one's faults, for children fail often, but they are too little to hurt themselves very much."[a]

a. *St. Thérèse of Lisieux: Her Last Conversations*, trans. John Clarke (Washington: ICS, 1977), 138–39.

in gesture, complementing his earlier parables of the kingdom (4:1–33): to receive the kingdom is as simple, trusting, and humble an action as receiving the embrace of Jesus. Indeed, to enter the kingdom is nothing other than to enter into a relationship with Jesus.

Reflection and Application (10:13–16)

Jesus' command to let the children come to him, along with the references in Acts to the baptism of entire households (Acts 16:15, 33; 18:8), formed part of the ancient Church's rationale for the practice of infant baptism. Origen (ca. 185–254), and later St. Augustine (354–430), regarded infant baptism as a tradition received from the apostles.[5] St. Irenaeus considered it a matter of course that the baptized should include "infants and small children."[6] Several Fathers, including Basil, Gregory of Nyssa, Ambrose, John Chrysostom, Jerome, and Augustine, vigorously reacted against the postponement of baptism, which they viewed as parental negligence, and begged parents not to delay the sacrament since it is necessary for salvation.

The Man with Many Possessions (10:17–22)

[17]As he was setting out on a journey, a man ran up, knelt down before him, and asked him, "Good teacher, what must I do to inherit eternal life?" [18]Jesus answered him, "Why do you call me good? No one is good but God alone. [19]You know the commandments: 'You shall not kill; you shall not commit adultery; you shall not steal; you shall not bear false witness; you shall not defraud; honor your father and your mother.'" [20]He replied and said to him, "Teacher, all of these I have observed from my youth." [21]Jesus, looking at him, loved him and said to him, "You are lacking in one thing. Go, sell what you have, and give to [the] poor and you will have treasure in heaven; then come, follow me." [22]At that statement his face fell, and he went away sad, for he had many possessions.

OT: Exod 20:12–17; Tob 4:7–11; Sir 29:8–12
NT: Acts 2:45. // Matt 19:16–22; Luke 18:18–23
Catechism: Jesus and the commandments, 2052–55; eternal life, 1020–29; giving to the poor, 2443–49
Lectionary: 10:17–30: Common of Pastors

5. Origen, *Commentarii in Romanos* 5.9; Augustine, *On Genesis Literally Interpreted*, 10.23.39.
6. *Against Heresies* 2.22.4.

10:17   As if on cue, a man approaches who exemplifies the opposite of what Jesus has just described: a pursuit of eternal life on the basis of one's own efforts. This episode begins a section of teachings on what is given up for the sake of the kingdom (10:17–31), reinforcing Jesus' earlier lesson that the kingdom is a gift given those who acknowledge their neediness (10:15; see Eph 2:8; 2 Tim 1:9).

The mention of a **journey** (*hodos*), or "way," is a subtle reminder that Jesus is proceeding toward Jerusalem (Mark 10:1, 32), where he will face the sufferings that are at the heart of his messianic mission. There is an unusual zeal and earnestness to the fellow who runs up and kneels before him, acknowledging Jesus' competence to answer the question burning on his heart. To kneel is a gesture of petition and of profound homage (Ps 22:30; 95:6). He addresses Jesus with a title of respect: **Good teacher, what must I do to inherit eternal life?** His question is one form of the ultimate question on every person's heart, even when it is unacknowledged: "What is the meaning of life? What is my ultimate aim, and how do I attain it?" It is another way of asking, "How do I enter the kingdom of God?" (see 10:15). The concept of "eternal life" was a relatively late development in the Old Testament, which increasingly recognized the reality of life after death (see Dan 12:2; 2 Macc 7:9). It would be natural for a Jew like this man to assume that observance of the law was the way to eternal life. But the very fact that he asks suggests that he is dissatisfied with the traditional answer. He senses that there must be something more to it.

10:18   Jesus' initial response is puzzling and has occasioned much speculation. **Why do you call me good? No one is good but God alone.** But the mistake is to assume that Jesus is repudiating the attribute of good for himself. He is not denying that he is good; rather, he is inviting the man to reflect more deeply on what he has just said (see 10:3; 12:35; John 2:4 for similar examples). On what basis does he call Jesus good? Is it because he is a wise teacher and powerful miracle worker? Because he treats everyone with kindness? Or is there a more profound basis for Jesus' goodness? Does the man recognize that ultimately, God alone is good, and that what he perceives in Jesus is not merely unusual human qualities but that infinite goodness that belongs to God alone? Jesus gently directs the man's gaze toward the answer to his heart's longing.

10:19–20   As if to probe the man's dissatisfaction, Jesus rehearses the part of the answer he already knows. The clear teaching of the Old Testament is that one who obeys God's law will live (Deut 30:15–16; Ezek 33:14–15). Jesus lists some of the ten **commandments** (Exod 20:1–17; Deut 5:6–21), adding **you shall not defraud** (see Deut 24:14). To honor one's **father** and **mother** was linked in a special way with the promise of long life (Exod 20:12; Deut 5:16; Sir 3:6). Each of the commandments listed by Jesus concerns conduct toward fellow human beings (the second tablet of the †Decalogue). But what about the first three commandments (the first tablet), which concern conduct toward God? As will be seen below, Jesus has not neglected them.

The man is a faithfully observant Jew who has been well catechized, and without boasting he states simply, **Teacher, all of these I have observed from my youth.** From his youth probably means from age twelve, when a Jewish boy formally assumed the yoke of the commandments. The Jewish belief was that it was not impossible to keep all the commandments (Sir 15:15; Phil 3:6), and Jesus does not dispute the man's claim.[7]

The key to the story is found in the next statement: **Jesus, looking at him,** **loved him.** It is the only time in the Gospel that Jesus is said to have looked with love on an individual. But the verb, *agapaō* (from which derives the noun *agapē*), is at the heart of the early Church's message concerning Jesus' mission: "God so loved the world that he gave his only Son" (John 3:16); "Christ loved us and handed himself over for us" (Eph 5:2). It is this gaze of divine love that would have captivated the man's heart and moved him to surrender all his earthly attachments—if he had seen it. But sadly, preoccupied with his own thoughts, he seems not to have noticed Jesus' gaze.

10:21

Jesus puts his finger on the source of the man's dissatisfaction. Despite his fidelity to the law, he lacks the **one thing** necessary (see Luke 10:42). Why does Jesus tell him to **sell** all that he owns? Perhaps because the man was bound by his possessions and attached to the independence they made possible. They were the earthly treasure that was hindering him from freely receiving the heavenly treasure that was being offered to him. Jesus wishes to set the man free to follow the true longing of his heart without reserve. And the relinquishment of his possessions is not to be an abstract, isolated act: he is to place himself in solidarity with the **poor** by giving the proceeds to them. The Old Testament already recognized that to give alms to the needy is to store up **treasure** in the sight of God (Tob 4:7–11; Sir 29:8–12). Jesus is asking this man to become as dependent on God's providence as children, to whom he has just said the kingdom belongs (10:14). He then offers the same invitation he gave his disciples earlier (Mark 1:17; 2:14): **Come, follow me.** Here is where the first tablet of the Decalogue comes in: it is in giving one's life unconditionally to Jesus that the covenant obligation to love God is lived out. Jesus is in the place of God.[8]

7. This is not to deny that, in the most profound sense of righteousness, "none is righteous, no, not one" (Rom 3:10 RSV; see Ps 14:3; 53:3).

8. See McDermott, "Didn't Jesus Know?" 319.

10:22   Tragically, the man cannot bring himself to pay such a high price, even for the "eternal life" that he so passionately seeks. The word for **possessions** can also be translated "properties" or "estates." Evidently the man finds his security and comfort in earthly wealth and he is not willing to embrace the self-denial that leads to true wealth. It is a sobering conclusion to the story, the first time that Jesus' invitation to discipleship has been directly refused.

Reflection and Application (10:17–22)

Is Jesus' directive to the rich man a requirement for all who wish to inherit eternal life? Other passages in the Gospel indicate that Jesus did not ask all his disciples to sell their possessions (see 1 Tim 6:17–19). Peter apparently keeps his house and boat, at least for a time (Mark 1:29; John 21:3); the women of Galilee continued to have access to their material resources (Mark 15:41), as did Joseph of Arimathea (15:43). Thus his call to this man was in some way tailored to the man himself. But as the following passage will show, total detachment from one's possessions is demanded of every disciple. The Church recognizes an especially great model of discipleship in those who voluntarily commit themselves to a life of poverty in response to God's call (Catechism, 2103).

The Danger of Riches (10:23–27)

---

²³Jesus looked around and said to his disciples, "How hard it is for those who have wealth to enter the kingdom of God!" ²⁴The disciples were amazed at his words. So Jesus again said to them in reply, "Children, how hard it is to enter the kingdom of God! ²⁵It is easier for a camel to pass through [the] eye of [a] needle than for one who is rich to enter the kingdom of God." ²⁶They were exceedingly astonished and said among themselves, "Then who can be saved?" ²⁷Jesus looked at them and said, "For human beings it is impossible, but not for God. All things are possible for God."

OT: Deut 32:15; Ps 49; Hosea 12:9
NT: // Matt 19:23–26; Luke 18:24–27
Catechism: detachment from riches, 2544–47, 2728; all things possible for God, 1058
Lectionary: 10:24b–30: Mass for the Consecration of Virgins and Religious Profession

10:23   Jesus takes the occasion of the rich man's departure to instruct his disciples about the dangerous snare that earthly prosperity can be. He **looked around** as if searching the hearts of his listeners. **How hard it is!** It is a sober warning against the spiritual complacency that can result from material **wealth.** Those whose earthly needs and desires are well satisfied can all too easily become comfortable and self-reliant, avoiding the total surrender to God demanded by the gospel—not to mention the risk of becoming self-indulgent, arrogant, and inconsiderate of the poor. The great temptation is to trust in one's status, wealth, and abilities as a substitute for trust in God alone.

The disciples' amazement is a measure of how radical Jesus' pronouncement **10:24-26** was. In the Old Testament, before an understanding of life after death had fully developed, wealth was considered a mark of God's favor (Deut 28:1-14; Ps 25:12-13; Sir 11:21-22). Yet there are also many warnings of the danger of riches (Deut 32:15; Ps 49; 52:9; Prov 11:28). Despite all of Jesus' previous teaching on the cost of discipleship (8:34-37), the disciples still regard the prosperous as those who have first claim on the kingdom. But since wealth and power generate false security, they are utterly useless as a means of access to the kingdom; they serve only to block the way.

Jesus replies in a tone of affection, addressing them as **children,** perhaps a gentle reminder of his earlier words about receiving the kingdom like a child (10:15). He repeats his statement in even stronger terms, this time including not only the rich but all: **how hard it is to enter the kingdom of God!** He drives home the point with a picturesque comparison. A **camel** was the largest beast familiar to first-century Jews; the **eye of a needle** was the smallest aperture imaginable. Jesus intends to conjure an absurd and even comical image in their minds. At these words his disciples' jaws drop. No interpretation of his statement is adequate unless it takes into account their stunned reaction: they were **exceedingly astonished.** If even those most favored find it that hard to enter the kingdom, what hope is there for anyone else? One can imagine them whispering in dismay to one another, **Then who can be saved?** "Being saved" (see 8:35) is a synonym for "entering the kingdom" or obtaining "eternal life," accenting the fact that one is saved *from* eternal death or separation from God.

Once again Jesus focuses his gaze on them, seeking to gain the full attention **10:27** of their hearts. His final pronouncement forestalls any discouragement resulting from what he has just said, and reveals the key to the whole discourse: **All things are possible for God.** The kingdom of God, which Jesus has been announcing from the beginning of his public ministry (1:15), is something utterly beyond human achievement. It cannot be earned, it cannot be claimed as a right, it does not come as a reward for good behavior. It depends solely on the goodness of God, who freely offers it as a gift. So great is this gift that it must be recognized as God

Not Owners but Stewards

According to Catholic social teaching, our material goods are entrusted to us by God not for our own personal advantage but for the privilege of using them for the good of others. "The ownership of any property makes its holder a steward of Providence, with the task of making it fruitful and communicating its benefits to others, first of all his family. Goods of production—material or immaterial—such as land, factories, practical or artistic skills, oblige their possessors to employ them in ways that will benefit the greatest number. Those who hold goods for use and consumption should use them with moderation, reserving the better part for guests, for the sick and the poor" (Catechism, 2404–5).

accomplishing the **impossible**, *for me*. The exultant proclamation that nothing is beyond God's capability recalls Jesus' encouragement to the man with the possessed boy (9:23), and God's reassurance to Sarah that she would bear a child at age ninety (Gen 17:17; 18:14). Mary too proclaimed, "The Mighty One has done great things for me. . . . The hungry he has filled with good things; the rich he has sent away empty" (Luke 1:49, 53). Although Jesus does not say so explicitly here, his death and resurrection are the means by which God does the impossible, bestowing the kingdom on those who would otherwise be utterly bereft of it.

Reflection and Application (10:23–27)

In this teaching on the danger of riches, Jesus does not denounce wealth as evil in itself. In fact, it is remarkable how many of his sayings and parables indirectly affirm the values of ownership, business, trade, and investment.[9] Rather, it is the *attachment* to wealth that is spiritually perilous (Matt 6:24; 1 Tim 6:10; Heb 13:5). For those of us who live in the wealthiest civilization in the history of humanity, it is all too easy to breeze over Jesus' words. "Others might be attached to money, but I'm just trying to pay the bills." His exclamation, "How hard it is!" is a sobering warning of how difficult it is to have money or possessions and yet not be attached to them.

Many Catholics today are rediscovering the benefit of the biblical practice of tithing—giving 10 percent or more of one's income to the poor, to missions,

9. Matt 20:1–15; 25:14–29; Luke 16:1–12; 19:12–27; John 4:36.

and to the Church. In the Old Testament, giving a tithe of the harvest was a way of expressing awareness that what one has comes from God and belongs ultimately to him (Deut 14:22). The New Testament does not explicitly teach tithing, but if anything summons Christians to an even more generous use of their financial resources. Although 10 percent is a good rule of thumb, some people's financial circumstances allow them to "tithe"—that is, contribute regularly— only a smaller amount. Others are in a position to give more. Some singles I know donate 15–20 percent of their gross income; a widow who receives her husband's retirement pension is happy to be able to give away 30 percent. A tithing program in the diocese of Wichita, Kansas, has enabled parishes to sustain schools, serve the poor, and bring spiritual renewal to many people who have discovered the joy of giving generously of their time, talent, and treasure.

The Rewards of Discipleship (10:28–31)

²⁸Peter began to say to him, "We have given up everything and followed you." ²⁹Jesus said, "Amen, I say to you, there is no one who has given up house or brothers or sisters or mother or father or children or lands for my sake and for the sake of the gospel ³⁰who will not receive a hundred times more now in this present age: houses and brothers and sisters and mothers and children and lands, with persecutions, and eternal life in the age to come. ³¹But many that are first will be last, and [the] last will be first."

OT: Gen 12:1–3
NT: Matt 20:16; Luke 22:28–30; Phil 3:7–8. // Matt 19:27–30; Luke 18:28–30
Catechism: the evangelical counsels, 915–18
Lectionary: Mass for Vocations to Holy Orders or Religious Life

Jesus' declaration prompts a reply from Peter as spokesman for the disciples: **10:28**
We have given up everything and followed you. Peter speaks truly (see 1:18, 20; 2:14), though perhaps with a hint of boasting.[10] In contrast to the rich man of 10:22, the disciples have been willing to leave behind not only their possessions but their whole former life for the sake of following Jesus. The Greek verb for "give up" (*aphiēmi*) can also mean "release" or "let go." Exteriorly they have indeed left all behind, yet their squabbling for positions of honor (9:34; 10:40)

10. Peter's claim does not necessarily imply that he has sold all his possessions and donated the proceeds to the poor (see 1:29; John 21:3). But he has nevertheless given up the lifestyle in which he freely enjoyed them in order to travel on mission with Jesus.

and their aversion to the prospect of suffering (8:32) show that they have not yet interiorly abandoned all to Jesus.

10:29   Jesus does not rebut Peter's claim. Instead, he makes a great promise, addressed to all who make earthly sacrifices to follow him. The list of possible sacrifices, **house or brothers or sisters or mother or father or children or lands,** affirms the radical nature of the Christian life. Jesus' claim on a person far outweighs the value of home, relatives, or property. On one level, these terms reflect the unusual lifestyle of those called to travel around preaching the gospel, dependent on the hospitality of others (6:8–9). But more broadly, they refer to the detachment that is required of all Christ's disciples. These words reflect the experience of the early Christians, many of whom turned their properties over to the Church for the care of the needy (Acts 2:45; 4:32–37), and some of whom may have been disowned by their families because of their allegiance to Christ. The motivation for doing so is the same as that for losing one's life (Mark 8:35): **For my sake and for the sake of the gospel.** Only Mark (here and in 8:35) includes "and for the sake of the gospel" (see Matt 10:39; Luke 9:24), accenting the priceless value of the good news for which so many had suffered.

10:30   But the promise is of a hundredfold recompense, like the seed bearing abundant fruit (4:8, 20), not only **in the age to come** but even **in this present age.** Those who give up all for Jesus will not be left lonely and isolated: they will experience the warmth of hospitality in which fellow believers and even unbelievers will welcome them into their homes (Acts 16:15; 28:2, 7; 2 Cor 8:1–4). As Jesus indicated earlier (3:34–35), they will become members of his own family. They will experience deep bonds of brotherhood and sisterhood with other members of "the family of the faith" (Gal 6:10; see Rom 16:13), which will more than compensate for their loss of blood relatives. Significantly, "fathers" is absent from the list (as in Mark 3:35), since God himself is the Father of the new family of Jesus (see 11:25; Matt 23:9).

Perhaps there is a touch of wry humor in the inclusion of **persecutions** in the list of rewards, which is only in Mark. Jesus does not want his followers to lose a sense of realism: it is not so much a question of *whether* as of *how* his followers will be persecuted. If not by official state repression, it might be by mockery and social ostracism, or by obstacles and trials thrown our way by the powers of darkness. But all that is not worthy of comparison with the **eternal life** that we will gain in the end—the life the rich man so yearned for (10:17), and that corresponds to the longing of every human heart. Jesus has now given the full answer to the question with which the rich man had approached him.

Mark concludes the discourse with a saying found in different contexts in   **10:31** Matthew (20:16; see 19:30) and Luke (13:30). It describes a great reversal that will take place at the end of history when Jesus comes in glory. Many of those who in "this present age" were regarded as successful, important, honored, and powerful (like the "firsts" of Galilee in Mark 6:21) will be revealed as the poorest in what truly counts. Many of those who are downtrodden, overlooked, weak, and insignificant in the eyes of the world will be revealed as the preeminent ones in the kingdom.

On the Way of Discipleship III

Mark 10:32–52

In this section Jesus formally prophesies his death and resurrection for the third and last time. It is the most solemn and detailed of his passion predictions, almost a synopsis of what is soon to occur. Like the first two (8:31; 9:31) it is immediately followed by an inept response on the part of his disciples (10:37), which becomes an opportunity for Jesus to give further instruction on discipleship (10:42–45). He is continuing to open his disciples' eyes to the mystery of his messianic vocation and their call to follow in his footsteps.

Third Prophecy of the Passion (10:32–34)

---

³²They were on the way, going up to Jerusalem, and Jesus went ahead of them. They were amazed, and those who followed were afraid. Taking the Twelve aside again, he began to tell them what was going to happen to him. ³³"Behold, we are going up to Jerusalem, and the Son of Man will be handed over to the chief priests and the scribes, and they will condemn him to death and hand him over to the Gentiles ³⁴who will mock him, spit upon him, scourge him, and put him to death, but after three days he will rise."

OT: Isa 53:12
NT: John 11:16; Acts 2:23; 13:27; Rom 8:32. // Matt 20:17–19; Luke 18:31–34
Catechism: Jesus' journey to Jerusalem, 557–58

With the refrain characteristic of the journey narrative, **on the way**, Mark   10:32–34
reminds us that this episode, and the teaching that follows, is all about "the way"
of the Christian life. Now he explicitly notes that they were **going up to Jerusalem**, to the suffering and death that Jesus knew awaited him there. Whether
one is traveling north or south, in Jewish idiom one always goes "up" to Jerusalem
(Ezra 7:13; Zech 14:17), the holy hill where God's dwelling place on earth, the
temple, was located. It is likely that Jesus went to Jerusalem many times in his life
(see Luke 2:22, 41; John 2:13; 5:1; 7:10), but Mark mentions only this one time
to highlight its significance as the time he went there to fulfill his destiny as the
suffering Messiah. That **Jesus went ahead of them** indicates his firm resolve, his
determination to embrace the will of the Father. One can imagine his disciples
dragging their feet a little, having a foreboding feeling about what lay ahead.

Mark leaves much unsaid in this cryptic passage. He gives no indication
why Jesus' companions are **amazed** as they walk along the road. Are **those
who followed** his disciples, or others? And why were they **afraid**? Earlier, the
crowds had been "utterly amazed" when they encountered Jesus descending
from the mount of the Transfiguration (Mark 9:15). Here too Mark seems to
hint that there is an awe-inspiring quality to Jesus' countenance, expressing at
once both authority and humility. It may also be that they were amazed that
Jesus would dare to go to Jerusalem, knowing he had powerful enemies there
(3:22; 7:1, 5).

Far from dismissing their fears, Jesus calls aside **the Twelve** to forewarn them
once again about his passion, this time giving more precise details. He again
uses the key verb "hand over" (*paradidōmi*), which on a human level expresses
the treachery of Judas and the religious authorities, but on a theological level
expresses God's loving, redemptive purpose in handing over his Son to sinful
humanity (see 9:31; Rom 8:32). This is the first time Jesus indicates that he will be
handed over by his own people **to the Gentiles**, a particularly painful rejection
for a Jew to experience. He foretells the details of his suffering, all of which are
fulfilled to the letter in the Gospel (Mark 15:15, 19–20, 37; 16:6). The last phrase
puts everything in proper context: Jesus' passion will end in a glorious victory
over death itself. His own destiny is the model for that of his disciples, in which
"persecutions" are part of the necessary way to "eternal life" (see 10:30).

Seeking the Glory Seats (10:35–45)

---

³⁵Then James and John, the sons of Zebedee, came to him and said to
him, "Teacher, we want you to do for us whatever we ask of you." ³⁶He

211

replied, "What do you wish [me] to do for you?" [37]They answered him, "Grant that in your glory we may sit one at your right and the other at your left." [38]Jesus said to them, "You do not know what you are asking. Can you drink the cup that I drink or be baptized with the baptism with which I am baptized?" [39]They said to him, "We can." Jesus said to them, "The cup that I drink, you will drink, and with the baptism with which I am baptized, you will be baptized; [40]but to sit at my right or at my left is not mine to give but is for those for whom it has been prepared." [41]When the ten heard this, they became indignant at James and John. [42]Jesus summoned them and said to them, "You know that those who are recognized as rulers over the Gentiles lord it over them, and their great ones make their authority over them felt. [43]But it shall not be so among you. Rather, whoever wishes to be great among you will be your servant; [44]whoever wishes to be first among you will be the slave of all. [45]For the Son of Man did not come to be served but to serve and to give his life as a ransom for many."

OT: 1 Kings 22:19; Isa 51:17–22
NT: Luke 12:50; Acts 12:2; Rom 6:4; Col 2:12; 1 Tim 2:6. // Matt 20:20–28; Luke 22:25–27
Catechism: Jesus' sacrifice, 599–618, 1225; authority as service, 876, 2235

10:35–37   **James and John,** two of Jesus' earliest and closest disciples (1:19–20; 5:37; 9:2), could hardly have chosen a more tactless moment for their request. Perhaps they were dreaming so much about their future prominence that they were completely oblivious to his words about imminent suffering and death. Their approach is designed to get Jesus to agree to their request before they say what it is. The "sons of thunder" (3:17) may be counting on their special status among the Twelve to expect such an open-ended grant. Jesus does not accept this tactic, but asks what they have in mind. The two brothers are seeking to secure for themselves the top posts in the Messiah's future government. To sit at a ruler's **right** or **left** hand was a sign of power and prestige (1 Kings 2:19; 22:19; Ps 110:1). Although Jesus had spoken earlier of his coming "in his Father's glory with the holy angels" (Mark 8:38), James and John probably still had only a foggy idea of what his "glory" meant. What they do know is that they want first rights to a share in that glory, before the others get in on it.

10:38   Jesus does not reproach them for their boldness. Instead he lays out what appears to be a condition. In the Old Testament, a **cup** is a metaphor for what God has in store for someone, whether a cup of blessing (Ps 16:5; 23:5; 116:13) or, more frequently, the cup of his wrath (Ps 75:9; Isa 51:17–22; Jer 49:12; Ezek 23:31–34). Jesus has the latter in mind, since "drinking the cup" symbolizes his accepting the full brunt of God's judgment on sin (Mark 14:36; see John 18:11). He is asking whether the disciples are willing to be united with him in his redemptive suffering (see Col 1:24). Yet the other meaning is also in the background, since through the eucharistic cup of his blood (Mark 14:23–24), his passion becomes the source of salvation to all who receive it.

The idea of **baptism** (immersion in water) as a metaphor for the passion occurs in a different context in Luke 12:50, where Jesus cries out, "There is a baptism with which I must be baptized, and how great is my anguish until it is accomplished!" Immersion in water is a biblical image for overwhelming calamity (Ps 42:8; 88:17–18; Isa 43:2). Jesus' own baptism in the Jordan (Mark 1:9) was a prefigurement of his death, and the early Church understood Christian baptism as a union with Christ in his death (Rom 6:4; Col 2:12) by which believers die to their old self and begin a new life in him. To share in Christ's sufferings was considered a privilege and a joy (Matt 5:11–12; Acts 5:41; Col 1:24; 1 Pet 4:12–13).

Jesus' reply thus alludes to the two foundational sacraments of the new covenant—baptism (see Mark 16:16) and the Eucharist (see 14:23-24)—pointing toward the way in which all his followers can be made worthy to share in his future glory.

The two brothers reply eagerly, and perhaps glibly, **We can.** They do not yet realize what they are asserting. Only on Golgotha will the deep irony of their request become clear: those at the right and left hand of the Messiah-King are the two thieves crucified with him (15:27). Yet Jesus takes their willingness seriously: they will indeed drink his cup, and be plunged into his baptism. For James, this promise will be fulfilled literally in his martyrdom not many years later (Acts 12:2). Suffering is the unavoidable doorway to glory, for Jesus' disciples as for himself (see Luke 24:26). Yet to assign the seating at his **right** or **left** in glory is the Father's prerogative alone. `10:39–40`

Understandably, the other ten disciples are **indignant**, perhaps because they too want to be VIPs in the kingdom and are annoyed that others have upstaged them. Jesus patiently takes the occasion for another lesson in discipleship, explaining in different terms what he has said before (9:35; 10:15). In the ancient world, as today, authority is naturally assumed to entail perks and benefits for those who wield it, and the powerful often enjoy throwing their weight around. But Jesus' command is stark: **It shall not be so among you.** His disciples are to display a radical and countercultural attitude toward leadership. There is no place for self-promotion, rivalry, or domineering conduct among them. Jesus does not deny that there will be offices of authority in the community he is establishing, `10:41–44`

Jesus Died for All

LIVING TRADITION

The Catechism teaches: Jesus "affirms that he came 'to give his life as a ransom for many'; this last term is not restrictive, but contrasts the whole of humanity with the unique person of the redeemer who hands himself over to save us. The Church, following the apostles, teaches that Christ died for all men without exception. 'There is not, never has been, and never will be a single human being for whom Christ did not suffer'" (605, quoting the Council of Quiercy).

the Church. Nor does he reject the aspiration to greatness that lies deep in the human heart. Rather, he reveals that the only way to greatness, paradoxically, is by imitating him in his humble, self-emptying love. The whole mentality on which Church leadership is exercised must be that of service (*diakonia*), acting entirely for the benefit of others, putting oneself at their disposal, caring for their humblest needs (see John 13:14; Phil 2:3–4). A **slave** can be called on to perform the most menial tasks, such as washing feet or waiting at table. To be a "slave of all" is an incredibly tall order. St. Paul often characterizes his own apostleship as being a slave of those to whom he ministered (1 Cor 9:19; 2 Cor 4:5).

10:45   The passage concludes with one of the most important sayings in the Gospel, summing up the purpose of Jesus' messianic mission: **For the Son of Man did not come to be served but to serve and to give his life as a ransom for many.** Jesus' own coming into the world (see 1:38; 2:17) was not for the sake of any advantage to himself, but only to serve his heavenly Father and all men and women. Here he explains that this service entails giving up his life as a ransom. The idea of a ransom expresses a price that is paid on someone's behalf; for instance, to free a slave (Lev 25:51) or to save someone whose life is in jeopardy (Exod 21:30). God is often said in the Old Testament to have ransomed his people from slavery in Egypt or exile in Babylon (Deut 7:8; Isa 35:10), and the Jewish hope was that God would definitively ransom his people from sin and death (Ps 130:7; Isa 59:20; Hosea 13:14; Luke 24:21). The Old Testament never clarifies how God could be said to "pay a price" for his people; only in the passion of his Son does the price become clear. "For" many can mean both "in place of" and "on behalf of" many. Though we have nothing to give in exchange for our life (Mark 8:37), Jesus can give his own life, a gift of infinite value, in exchange for us. "Many" is not intended to exclude some, as if Jesus did not die for all (Christ "gave himself as ransom for all"; 1 Tim 2:6); it is a Hebrew way of expressing a vast multitude. The saying alludes to the Suffering Servant in Isaiah (Isa 52:13–53:12), who "gives his life" as an offering for sin—that is, a sacrifice that atones for sin—on behalf of "many." St. Paul further developed this insight into the meaning of Jesus' passion (Rom 3:24; 1 Cor 7:23; Gal 3:13; 1 Tim 2:6), which became a crucial part of the Church's theology of redemption.

Reflection and Application (10:35–45)

This episode, in which Jesus extends to his disciples the privilege of drinking the cup he will drink, is part of the foundation for the Church's teaching on redemptive suffering (Catechism, 618). St. Paul experienced to a profound degree this reality of sharing in Christ's passion, and reflected on it theologically in his letters. As ambassadors of Christ, Paul wrote, he and his coworkers "are constantly being given up to death for the sake of Jesus, so that the life of Jesus may be manifested in our mortal flesh" (2 Cor 4:11; see Gal 6:17). Paul could even say, "In my flesh I am filling up what is lacking in the afflictions of Christ on behalf of his body, which is the church" (Col 1:24). Our bodies, by being joined to the body of Christ, can be transformed into instruments of redemptive grace. Our sufferings, willingly united with his, become in a mysterious but real way the means of grace for others. This principle was given eloquent expression by a contemporary martyr, Fr. Andrea Santoro, an Italian priest who was assassinated in Turkey in 2006. Shortly before he died, Fr. Santoro wrote, "I am here to dwell among these people and enable Jesus to do so by lending him my flesh. . . . One becomes capable of salvation only by offering one's own flesh. The evil in the world must be borne and the pain shared, assimilating it into one's own flesh as did Jesus."[1]

The Healing of Blind Bartimaeus (10:46–52)

[46]They came to Jericho. And as he was leaving Jericho with his disciples and a sizable crowd, Bartimaeus, a blind man, the son of Timaeus, sat by the roadside begging. [47]On hearing that it was Jesus of Nazareth, he began to cry out and say, "Jesus, son of David, have pity on me." [48]And many rebuked him, telling him to be silent. But he kept calling out all the more, "Son of David, have pity on me." [49]Jesus stopped and said, "Call him." So they called the blind man, saying to him, "Take courage; get up, he

1. See Pope Benedict XVI, Homily, April 13, 2006.

is calling you." ⁵⁰He threw aside his cloak, sprang up, and came to Jesus. ⁵¹Jesus said to him in reply, "What do you want me to do for you?" The blind man replied to him, "Master, I want to see." ⁵²Jesus told him, "Go your way; your faith has saved you." Immediately he received his sight and followed him on the way.

OT: Isa 29:18; 35:5
NT: Matt 9:27–31; Eph 1:18. // Matt 20:29–34; Luke 18:35–43
Catechism: Jesus hears our prayer, 2616; signs of the kingdom, 547–50
Lectionary: Anointing of the Sick

The beginning of the journey toward Jerusalem was preceded by the gradual healing of a blind man at Bethsaida (8:22–26). Now at the end of the journey, just before the entrance into Jerusalem, is another healing of a blind man—this time instantaneous and complete. Mark has framed the journey in this way to symbolize that it has been all about the healing of the disciples' spiritual blindness. Although Jesus has been teaching them all along "the way," at this point their vision is still only partial; they do not yet grasp who Jesus is and what it means to follow him. Only after the resurrection will their eyes be fully opened.

10:46   Jesus and his companions arrive at **Jericho**, an ancient city fifteen miles northeast of Jerusalem, the site of Israel's first conquest in the holy land (Josh 6). After passing through the city, they are accompanied by a **sizable crowd**, probably including both Jesus' followers and pilgrims heading toward Jerusalem for the feast of Passover (Mark 14:1). Every year all Jews in Palestine who were able would travel to the holy city to celebrate Passover (see Luke 2:41), commemorating the exodus from Egypt. **Bartimaeus** (Aramaic for **son of Timaeus**),

The Oldest City in the World

BIBLICAL BACKGROUND

Jericho, at 850 feet below sea level, has the distinction of being both the lowest and the oldest continuously inhabited city in the world. It was built at the site of a freshwater spring in the Jordan River valley, a few miles north of the Dead Sea. Archaeologists have unearthed there the remains of settlements dating back to 8000 BC. Jericho is most famous for being the Israelites' first conquest in the promised land nearly seven thousand years later. The book of Joshua recounts how the Israelites, led by Joshua, conquered the city by God's power after a seven-day liturgical march in which the Ark of the Covenant was carried around the city in procession with horns blowing and finally a jubilant shout (Josh 6).

The Jesus Prayer

LIVING TRADITION

As the Catechism points out (2616), the urgent plea of the blind man, "Jesus, son of David, have pity on me," is renewed in the traditional prayer known as the Jesus Prayer: "Lord Jesus Christ, Son of God, have mercy on me, a sinner!" This prayer, prayed unceasingly throughout the day, sometimes in rhythm with breathing, is especially cherished in Eastern Christian spirituality.

a **blind** beggar, is strategically located at the **roadside** where he can beg for alms from passing pilgrims. In contrast to the festive crowds walking along, he sits, emphasizing his social isolation as a disabled person.

Sensing something unusual, Bartimaeus inquires and is told that **Jesus of**   **10:47**
Nazareth is passing by. He has evidently heard enough about this miracle-working rabbi to stir his faith. Bartimaeus is the only recipient of healing in Mark to address **Jesus** by name. This is also the first time in the Gospel that the title **son of David** has been applied to Jesus.[2] The title literally means a descendant of David (see Matt 1:20), but for the Jews it had much greater meaning as the heir of God's promises, the Messiah-King who would restore the Davidic monarchy and rule over Israel forever (2 Sam 7:12–16; 1 Chron 17:11–15; Ps 89:21–38; Jer 23:5–6). Moreover, one of the promises associated with the coming of the messiah was the opening of the eyes of the blind (see Isa 29:18; 35:5; Luke 4:18). **Have pity on me** is a plea often lifted to God in the Psalms (Ps 6:3; 25:16; 51:3; 86:16). Blind Bartimaeus already sees much more than those around him.

Yet as often happens (2:4; 7:27; 10:13) there are impediments in the way of   **10:48**
coming to Jesus: **many rebuked him, telling him to be silent.** Perhaps there is a quiet solemnity to Jesus' procession out of Jericho, and the blind man seems to be making an unseemly commotion. But it is a callous reaction, given Jesus' many works of healing. Those following Jesus have not yet learned to bring people *to* him instead of sending them away (see 6:36). But Bartimaeus is undaunted by this public reprimand. Like the Syrophoenician woman (7:25–29), his determination is only toughened in the face of an obstacle. And Jesus cannot

---

2. Elsewhere the New Testament affirms Jesus' literal descent from the line of David (Matt 1:1; Acts 3:20, 34; Rom 1:3; 2 Tim 2:8), which for the early Church was an extremely important part of the credentials of the gospel.

refuse such bold, exuberant faith, even when it interrupts his messianic journey. He is totally accessible: "Everyone who calls on the name of the LORD will be saved" (Joel 3:5; Acts 2:21). It is the first time that Jesus allows a public acclamation of his messianic identity. Up to this point it has been a secret (Mark 8:30), but now that the fulfillment of his mission as suffering Messiah is near, the time has come when it can be openly revealed. "Nothing is secret except to come to light" (4:22).

10:49–50   Instead of calling the man himself, Jesus asks those around him to reverse their previous stance: **Call him.** Ironically, they now reassure the blind man, **Take courage; get up, he is calling you**—as if Bartimaeus were the one needing encouragement. His response is a model of enthusiastic and decisive faith: he **sprang up, and came to Jesus.** To cast off **his cloak** symbolizes his leaving behind his former life, as Christians are called to put off the old nature at baptism and throughout their life (Rom 13:12; Eph 4:22; Col 3:8–9; Heb 12:1).

10:51–52   Jesus asks the same thing he had just asked James and John (10:36), challenging Bartimaeus to express his faith in concrete form. Unlike the sons of Zebedee, Bartimaeus does not ask for any special honor for himself, but only the restoration to wholeness that is part of God's messianic promise. Jesus replies as he had to the hemorrhaging woman (5:34), **Go your way; your faith has saved you.** The man's faith is his absolute confidence in God's power to do the "impossible" through Jesus (10:27). The Greek verb *sōzō*, meaning both "heal" and "save," calls to mind the eternal salvation of which Jesus has been speaking along the way (8:35; 10:26, 30).

Bartimaeus is healed physically, but even more, the eyes of his heart are enlightened (see Eph 1:18)—an image of what happens to every Christian at baptism. He demonstrates the perfect response to being healed: he follows Jesus **on the way** of discipleship (Mark 10:52), the way through Jesus' passion and death to the resurrection and eternal life. Bartimaeus is the only recipient of healing whose name is recorded by Mark, suggesting that he became a disciple and was known in the early Church.

The Lord Comes to His Temple

Mark 11:1–26

Jesus' arrival in Jerusalem marks the beginning of passion week, the final days of his life in which he will fulfill his destiny as suffering and glorified Messiah. Everything in the Gospel has been leading up to these climactic events, to which Mark devotes over a third of his narrative. It begins with Jesus' entrance into the Holy City and the temple as her humble king. But how will Jerusalem receive her Messiah?

The King Enters His City (11:1–11)

¹When they drew near to Jerusalem, to Bethphage and Bethany at the Mount of Olives, he sent two of his disciples ²and said to them, "Go into the village opposite you, and immediately on entering it, you will find a colt tethered on which no one has ever sat. Untie it and bring it here. ³If anyone should say to you, 'Why are you doing this?' reply, 'The Master has need of it and will send it back here at once.'" ⁴So they went off and found a colt tethered at a gate outside on the street, and they untied it. ⁵Some of the bystanders said to them, "What are you doing, untying the colt?" ⁶They answered them just as Jesus had told them to, and they permitted them to do it. ⁷So they brought the colt to Jesus and put their cloaks over it. And he sat on it. ⁸Many people spread their cloaks on the road, and others spread leafy branches that they had cut from the fields. ⁹Those preceding him as well as those following kept crying out:

"Hosanna!
Blessed is he who comes in the name of the Lord!

¹⁰**Blessed is the kingdom of our father David that is to come! Hosanna in the highest!"**

¹¹**He entered Jerusalem and went into the temple area. He looked around at everything and, since it was already late, went out to Bethany with the Twelve.**

OT: 1 Kings 1:32–34; 1 Macc 13:51; Ps 118:25–26; Zech 9:9
NT: // Matt 21:1–11; Luke 19:28–40; John 12:12–16
Catechism: Jesus' messianic entrance, 559–60
Lectionary: Palm Sunday Procession (Year B)

11:1–2   Jesus has come to the last stage of his journey, the resolute journey to the cross that began when he first announced his coming passion (8:27–31). Although he most likely visited **Jerusalem** many times in his life to celebrate the Jewish feasts (see Luke 2:22, 41; John 2:13; 5:1; 7:10), Mark mentions only this one visit: it is the Messiah-King's entrance into the Holy City. **Bethany** and **Bethphage** were the last villages on the road from Jericho (Mark 10:46), located on the **Mount of Olives** just east of Jerusalem. Zechariah had prophesied that the Mount of Olives would be the site where God's kingship over the whole earth would be revealed in the last days (Zech 14:4–9)—a prophecy that was about to be fulfilled, but in a hidden manner.

Jesus had refused popular acclaim as Messiah (Mark 8:30; see John 6:15), but now he takes the initiative in preparing for his messianic entry into the

Fig. 9. Scale model of the Herodian temple.

Jerusalem, the Holy City

BIBLICAL BACKGROUND

Jerusalem—"the city of our God; the holy mountain, fairest of heights, the joy of all the earth, . . . the city of the great king" (Ps 48:2–4)—was identified in Jewish tradition as the site of Mount Moriah, where Abraham had been willing to offer his son Isaac in sacrifice (Gen 22:2; 2 Chron 3:1), a prefigurement of the ultimate sacrifice of the Beloved Son (Rom 8:32). Jerusalem was also identified as the Salem of the mysterious priest-king Melchizedek, who offered bread and wine (Gen 14:18), foreshadowing the Eucharist.

King David conquered the city in about 1000 BC and chose it as his capital. One of the great moments in Israel's history was when David brought the Ark of the Covenant into the city in procession, with music, sacrifices, and dancing for joy before the Lord (2 Sam 6:12–19). His son Solomon built the magnificent temple to house the Ark, and the Holy City became the center of religious life for the Israelites and the place of God's special favor.

After the Jews' exile and return from Babylon, the city and temple were rebuilt, but without attaining their former glory. Through the prophets God promised a new and glorious Jerusalem, a place of overflowing joy and center of worship for the entire world (see Isa 2:2–3; 60:1–22; Zeph 3:14–17; Hag 2:7–9).

At the time of Jesus, the temple had been renovated and Jerusalem was near the pinnacle of her earthly splendor. On each of the three great Jewish feasts—Passover, Weeks (Pentecost), and Booths—the city was flooded with pilgrims, more than tripling its normal population of about 40,000. Yet as Jesus' words and prophetic gestures make clear, the Holy City was marred by corruption and religious hypocrisy. His warning of a great devastation (Mark 13:1–30) was tragically fulfilled when Jerusalem was leveled to the ground by Roman legions in AD 70.

city. The elaborate preparations point to the deeply symbolic significance of what he is about to do. He sends **two of his disciples** to carry out the task, as he had sent them out in pairs previously (Mark 6:7) and will do again for the Passover meal (14:13). The **village opposite** is probably Bethphage, less than a mile from the city. There a **colt** (a young donkey) is tethered, on whom **no one has ever sat**—recalling Old Testament stipulations that an animal devoted to a sacred purpose must be one that has not been put to any ordinary use (Num 19:2; Deut 21:3; 1 Sam 6:7). The **tethered** colt evokes Gen 49:10–11, Jacob's prophecy of a king to come from the tribe of Judah (see Matt 2:6), another clue to the messianic significance of Jesus' action.

Jesus instructs his disciples how to answer if anyone should challenge them. The word for **Master** is literally "the Lord" (*ho Kyrios*), the term used in the

11:3–6

†Septuagint for the sacred name of God. It is the only time in Mark that Jesus explicitly refers to himself as the Lord, pointing to his divine identity, though he does so implicitly at times.[1] The disciples find things just as he had said (see 14:16). Jesus' precise instructions and foreknowledge of what would happen seem to indicate that he had made some prearrangements with the colt's owner. The implication is that he has faithful followers in many places, who consider themselves and their possessions to be wholly at his disposal. On a symbolic level he is exercising the kingly right to requisition an animal for his service. But more importantly, these details serve as a reminder that Jesus is fully aware of the destiny that will meet him in Jerusalem, and that every detail takes place according to the plan of God (see Acts 2:23).

11:7   Why did Jesus choose to ride a **colt**, when most pilgrims would enter the city on foot? It was a prophetic gesture, fulfilling the messianic prophecy of Zechariah: "Rejoice heartily, O daughter Zion, shout for joy, O daughter Jerusalem! See, your king shall come to you; a just savior is he, meek, and riding on an ass, on a colt, the foal of an ass" (Zech 9:9). The lowly animal shows that he, the King of glory (see Ps 24:7–10), comes in humility and peace, not as a warrior-king mounted on a stallion to lead a rebellion against Rome. It is also reminiscent of the royal procession of Solomon, the son of David, who rode a mule into the city at his coronation (1 Kings 1:32–34). Jesus knew what he was about, even if those around him did not yet realize its significance.

11:8–9   Jesus' triumphal entry takes place among thousands of pilgrims arriving in the Holy City for the feast of Passover (14:1). There is a sense of excitement and elation, as the crowd around him shouts for joy and spontaneously shows him signs of honor. To spread **cloaks on the road** was a gesture of homage before a newly crowned king (see 2 Kings 9:13). Mark's description evokes an occasion some two centuries earlier, when Simon Maccabeus and his followers entered the city after their successful revolt "with shouts of jubilation, waving of palm branches . . . and the singing of hymns and canticles, because a great enemy of Israel had been destroyed" (1 Macc 13:51). The crowd chants from Ps 118:25–26: **Hosanna! Blessed is he who comes in the name of the Lord!** This psalm, originally a royal song of thanksgiving for a military victory, was one of the great hymns sung by pilgrims processing into the temple for a festival. Jesus will later apply it specifically to his coming passion and resurrection (Mark 12:10–11). Hosanna is a Hebrew word that originally meant "Save us!" but in liturgical usage had become a shout of praise or acclamation, much like "Hallelujah!" The blessing on "he who

---

1. See 2:28; 5:19–20; 12:35–37; 13:35. Mark attributes the title to him in 1:3; 16:19–20.

Biblical Acclamations in the Liturgy

LIVING TRADITION

The acclamations with which the crowds greeted Jesus are among the many biblical phrases that have become part of the eucharistic liturgy. "Hosanna in the highest!" and "Blessed is he who comes in the name of the Lord!" are joined with the angelic chorus, "Holy, holy, holy is the Lord God almighty" (Rev 4:8; see Isa 6:3) as the people's acclamation introducing the eucharistic prayer. These phrases are now understood in their fullest meaning: God's people jubilantly welcome our Messiah-King, Jesus, who is truly present on the altar, and who comes in the name of the Lord to save us and establish God's kingdom.

comes in the name of the Lord" was a customary greeting, but also has a deeper significance: Jesus comes in God's name as his faithful representative, who will perfectly accomplish his will.

The cry, **Blessed is the kingdom of our father David that is to come!** expresses messianic hope, but without directly acknowledging Jesus as Messiah. The people's enthusiasm is genuine, but they do not seem to recognize that the time of fulfillment has already arrived (1:15), and that the kingdom has come in the person of Jesus himself, the "son of David" (10:47). Nor do they realize

11:10

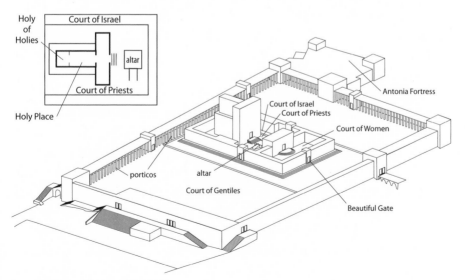

Fig. 10. Diagram of the Herodian Temple

The Temple

For the Jews, the holiest place on earth, where God had chosen to make his dwelling, was the Jerusalem temple. Solomon constructed the magnificent edifice with quarried stones and cedars brought by ship from Lebanon (1 Kings 6), completing it in about 950 BC, and it stood as the center of Jewish worship until it was destroyed by the Babylonians in 587 BC. It was soon rebuilt, and just before the birth of Jesus, King Herod the Great began a grandiose temple renovation project. He decorated the sanctuary's white marble façade with gold that gleamed in the sun, and expanded the platform on which the building stood to a massive thirty-five acres. This was the temple Jesus knew.

Temple worship took place in the open air. Only priests entered the sanctuary itself, which was relatively small. Within the sanctuary was the Holy Place, where incense was offered, and the inner chamber set off by a curtain, the Holy of Holies. The sanctuary was surrounded by a series of outdoor courts, each with strict rules of access. Immediately in front of it was the Court of Priests, accessible only to priests and Levites, in which stood the great altar of sacrifice. Smoke from the daily burning sacrifices was visible for miles around. Beyond it was the Court of Israel, which only ritually pure Jewish men could enter. Next was the Court of Women; prominent inscriptions warned Gentiles not to enter on pain of death. Finally, the largest part of the temple plaza was the Court of Gentiles, a vast rectangular area enclosed with stately colonnades, interspersed with nine gates. Typically it was crowded with Jews and Gentile converts to Judaism from all over Palestine and the Roman Empire. At the time of Jesus it was also full of merchants, animal stalls, and currency exchanges.

that his kingship will be exercised not in a political restoration of the Davidic monarchy, but on the cross.

11:11   The royal entrance that began so exuberantly ends on a quieter note. The crowd seems to have dispersed by the time Jesus enters **the temple area**. He comes as the Lord of the temple, who looks around the holy dwelling with his searching gaze to see whether its true purposes are being fulfilled. The prophet Malachi had foretold such a coming of the Lord, marked by a purifying judgment: "And suddenly there will come to the temple the Lord whom you seek. . . . But who will endure the day of his coming? And who can stand when he appears? For he is like the refiner's fire" (Mal 3:1–2).

Since it is late in the day, Jesus and the Twelve leave the city and return to their lodgings (or campsite) in **Bethany**.

The Fruitless Fig Tree (11:12–14)

[12]The next day as they were leaving Bethany he was hungry. [13]Seeing from a distance a fig tree in leaf, he went over to see if he could find anything on it. When he reached it he found nothing but leaves; it was not the time for figs. [14]And he said to it in reply, "May no one ever eat of your fruit again!" And his disciples heard it.

OT: Hosea 9:10; Mic 7:1
NT: Luke 13:6–9. // Matt 21:18–19

The episode of the fig tree (vv. 11–14 and 20–26) at first seems very perplexing. Is Jesus' reaction to the tree simply an outburst of temper? Like his triumphal entry on the previous day, both the fig tree incident and the cleansing of the temple inserted in the middle of it (vv. 15–19) are real-life parables, symbolic actions that must be pondered to discover their hidden meaning.

Jesus and his disciples leave their lodgings in **Bethany** to enter the Holy City once again. It is the only occasion in Mark where Jesus is said to be **hungry**. Seeing **a fig tree in leaf**, he walks over to see if it could satisfy his hunger—only to find it fruitless. But there is something odd about this action, to which Mark alerts us by noting that **it was not the time for figs**. It is the time of Passover, in April, and Jesus, like any native of Palestine, would know that ripe figs do not appear until June. Why, then, is he looking for fruit? The meaning of his action comes to light only when considered against the Old Testament background. In the prophets, Israel is often symbolized by figs or a fig tree (Jer 24:1–8; 29:17; Hosea 9:10; Joel 1:7). Jesus' search for ripe figs recalls God's desire to find in Israel the fruit of righteousness and covenant fidelity, and his grief at not finding it: "Alas! . . . There is no cluster to eat, no early fig that I crave" (Mic 7:1). The withering of a fig tree is a symbol of God's judgment against Israel and the temple for the idolatry and injustices perpetrated there (Joel 1:7–12; see Jer 8:13; Hosea 2:14). Moreover, in Mark, fruitfulness is an image for responding to Jesus in faith (see Mark 4:1–20; 12:1–12). The tree's lack of fruit thus signifies the absence of faith and prayer that Jesus finds in the temple (11:17–18). Now, at the time of visitation by her Messiah and Lord (Luke 19:44), the temple and its leadership are devoid of the spiritual fruit that God desires. Jesus' pronouncement upon the tree, **May no one ever eat of your fruit again!** is a prophetic signal that Israel's temple worship and sacrifices, with all their earthly splendor, are drawing to an end. That **his disciples heard** Jesus' saying prepares us for the resumption of the story in 11:20.

11:12–14

The Cleansing of the Temple (11:15–19)

15They came to Jerusalem, and on entering the temple area he began to drive out those selling and buying there. He overturned the tables of the money changers and the seats of those who were selling doves. 16He did not permit anyone to carry anything through the temple area. 17Then he taught them saying, "Is it not written:

'My house shall be called a house of prayer for all peoples'?
But you have made it a den of thieves.'"

18The chief priests and the scribes came to hear of it and were seeking a way to put him to death, yet they feared him because the whole crowd was astonished at his teaching. 19When evening came, they went out of the city.

OT: Ps 69:10; Jer 7:1–15; Zech 14:21
NT: // Matt 21:12–17; Luke 19:45–48; John 2:13–17
Catechism: Jesus and the temple, 583–86; the temple, 2580

11:15–16   On the previous evening, Jesus had "looked around at everything" in the temple (v. 11) as if to assess its spiritual condition. Now he takes vehement action against the commercialism and rank corruption he has found. Commercial activity connected with the temple was necessary, since pilgrims had to purchase the unblemished animals or birds that they would offer in sacrifice. A lamb or goat brought from the flock at home, perhaps hundreds of miles away, would not necessarily be in shape to pass inspection by the time it arrived in the city. There were several markets for sacrificial animals on the Mount of Olives. But the temple authorities had also allowed trading *within* the temple precincts, in the vast Court of the Gentiles. Since all adult Jewish men had to pay an annual temple tax (see Matt 17:24), **money changers** had also been conveniently set up to exchange pilgrims' Greek or Roman coins for the shekels in which the tax had to be paid. Other merchants were **selling doves**, required for ritual purifications of women after childbirth or of those healed of disease who could not afford lambs (Lev 12:8; 14:21–22; Luke 2:22–24). The temple area had become a marketplace, a noisy hubbub of business. Instead of the temple sanctifying the city, the city was profaning the temple.

Jesus is appalled at this flagrant desecration of a place consecrated to the worship of the living God. His actions bespeak burning indignation and zeal for the holiness of God's house (see John 2:17; Ps 69:10). He overturns the **tables** and **seats** of the merchants, putting a halt to the trading activity. Moreover, he forbids people to **carry anything** (literally, "any vessel") **through the temple**

Fig. 11. Stone found on the site of the temple, with Greek inscription forbidding Gentiles to enter the inner courts, on pain of death.

area, as if they could use the sacred precincts as a thoroughfare.[2] One can imagine the stunned surprise of those whose trade has been disrupted. For anyone paying attention, Jesus' actions signal the arrival of "that day" prophesied by Zechariah, when the Lord would gather all nations to worship him in Jerusalem, and "there shall no longer be any merchant in the house of the Lord of hosts" (Zech 14:21). Moreover, Jesus is exercising a royal prerogative: the reformer kings of Judah, Hezekiah and Josiah, had "cleaned house" in the temple in their own day (2 Chron 29; 34).

Jesus explains the meaning of this prophetic gesture—his third since arriving at **11:17** Jerusalem—by quoting two scriptures, first from Isaiah: **My house shall be called a house of prayer for all peoples**. Only Mark includes "for all peoples" (that is, for all Gentiles),[3] a phrase that would have special meaning for his mostly Gentile readers. In the context of this scripture God had promised to bring the Gentiles "to my holy mountain, and make them joyful in my house of prayer" (Isa 56:6–7 RSV). The temple was to be a place of reverence and awe before the Lord, the air filled with psalms of praise or teaching on God's word (Neh 8:1–8; Ps 27:4; 48:10;

---

2. Many interpreters regard "vessel" (*skeuos*) as referring specifically to the implements needed for sacrifices and offerings. If so, Jesus is not only disrupting business traffic but (temporarily) bringing the normal liturgical activities of the temple to a halt. However, there is no direct mention of a disruption of the sacrificial cult, which surely would have been brought up at Jesus' trial before the Sanhedrin. In the absence of confirming evidence, a more plausible interpretation is that Jesus' target was the improper and corrupt commercial activity in the temple precincts.

3. The Greek word *ethnē* can be translated "peoples," "nations," or "Gentiles."

100:4). But the market activity had effectively prevented the temple courts from being a place of prayer where Gentiles could enter into God's presence. Israel was faltering in its mission to lead the whole world in the worship of †YHWH (see Ps 105:1; Isa 2:2–3; Jer 3:17), a mission that would, however, paradoxically be fulfilled through the death of Israel's Messiah (see Mark 15:39).

Jesus continues with a quote from Jeremiah: **But you have made it a den of thieves.** Jeremiah had denounced those who thought they could get away with greed and dishonesty by taking refuge in ceremonial piety (Jer 7:9–11). The prophet warned that just as God had allowed his earlier shrine at Shiloh to be destroyed, so he would do with the temple in Jerusalem unless his people mended their ways. Jeremiah's dire warning came to pass in 587 BC, and a replay of that calamity would occur within forty years of Jesus' words.

11:18–19   Jesus' actions may have affected only a portion of the vast temple courts, but their symbolic import as a challenge to the temple authorities—and a threat to their lucrative sources of income—did not go unnoticed. The temple authorities controlled all commerce, donations, and taxes connected with the temple, enriching themselves with the profits. Archaeological excavations near the temple mount have uncovered the remains of palatial mansions that belonged to the ruling priestly families. It is no surprise that, hearing of what Jesus had done, the authorities **were seeking a way to put him to death**. For now they do nothing for fear of popular reprisals. Mark does not tell us the content of Jesus' **teaching**, but perhaps it was about the holiness of God's house and the new temple "not made with hands" that he was about to establish (see 14:58).

Reflection and Application (11:15–19)

Jesus' gesture of disrupting the temple commerce is a prophetic warning of the far greater disruption that he foretells (13:2). As the following episode will show, it also prepares the way for understanding the new and greater temple of the new covenant, the temple "not made with hands" (14:58) that is his own body (John 2:21; Heb 9:11). Thus Jesus' cleansing of the temple also has significance for the Church, the body of Christ. Christians today can ask: Are we consumed with the zeal for God's house that motivated Jesus (John 2:17)? If we consider the "temple" of our own parish or community, do we find it polluted with what does not belong there—with self-serving leadership, factions, gossip, sexual immorality, commercialization, or lack of charity toward those outside one's socioethnic group? Are we bringing the Church into the world, or the world into the Church? Surely the stewards of the ancient temple are not the only ones guilty of compromising the holiness of God's house. The book of Revelation (2–3) depicts Christ coming to judge local churches, threatening to remove the lampstand of those that do not repent and bear good fruit. The point is not for us to judge others—which would only compound the problem—but to repent for our own part, "to weep and mourn" (Joel 1:13–14), interceding that God's living temple would be restored to holiness.

On another level, St. Paul affirms that not only the Church but also our individual bodies are temples of the Holy Spirit (1 Cor 6:19–20). If we consider our own heart, is it sometimes more like a marketplace than a temple? Is it cluttered with worldly pursuits, busyness, lust, or selfish preoccupations? If so, we can pray that Jesus would cleanse this temple too and make it a house of prayer.

The Withered Fig Tree (11:20–26)

²⁰**Early in the morning, as they were walking along, they saw the fig tree withered to its roots. ²¹Peter remembered and said to him, "Rabbi, look! The fig tree that you cursed has withered." ²²Jesus said to them in reply, "Have faith in God. ²³Amen, I say to you, whoever says to this mountain, 'Be lifted up and thrown into the sea,' and does not doubt in his heart but believes that what he says will happen, it shall be done for him. ²⁴Therefore I tell you, all that you ask for in prayer, believe that you will receive it and it shall be yours. ²⁵When you stand to pray, forgive anyone against whom you have a grievance, so that your heavenly Father may in turn forgive you your transgressions." [²⁶]**

OT: Ezek 17:24; Hosea 2:14; Joel 1:7–12
NT: Matt 6:14–15; 17:20; Luke 17:5–6; 1 John 5:14–15. // Matt 21:20–22
Catechism: boldness in prayer, 2609–11, 2734–41; forgiveness, 2842–45

Mark helps us understand the withering of the fig tree in light of the cleansing of the temple by weaving together the two incidents. Jesus' pronouncement on the tree symbolizes God's judgment on the temple and its stewards for their spiritual barrenness, a barrenness that consists fundamentally in their refusal to heed Jesus, the Lord of the temple. Like the tree, the temple will come to an end: "There will not be one stone left upon another" (13:2).

Noticing **the fig tree withered to its roots**, Peter marvels at the effect of Jesus'   **11:20–21**
pronouncement the previous day (v. 14). The tree is not only fruitless, but completely dead. Another, more fruitful tree must take its place. Perhaps in the background is Ezekiel's vision of the new temple, from which flowed a river with trees along its banks, bearing fruit all year round (Ezek 47:1–12; see Mark 11:13).

The Tree of Life

LIVING TRADITION

The early Church came to understand the cross on which Christ died as the tree of life (see Gen 2:9), bearing the fruit of conversion and holiness all year long (see Ezek 47:1–12; 1 Pet 2:24; Rev 22:2). A troparion (antiphon) sung in Orthodox churches on Holy Cross Sunday proclaims: "Today the ranks of angels dance with gladness at the veneration of Thy Cross. For through the Cross, Christ, Thou hast shattered the hosts of devils and saved mankind. The Church has been revealed as a second Paradise, having within it, like the first Paradise of old, a tree of life, Thy Cross, O Lord. By touching it we share in immortality."[a]

a. From *The Lenten Triodion*, trans. Mother Mary and Kallistos Ware (London: Faber and Faber, 1978), 341.

11:22   Jesus responds with a call to **faith**, followed by a short teaching on faith, prayer, and forgiveness. *Faith* is the right human response to God's *faithfulness*: a complete trust and reliance on him, including the confident expectation that he will hear and respond to our prayers.[4] Without it, prayers are empty words. The disciples must trust that their prayers will be heard and that their prophetic utterances, like that of Jesus, will actually be carried out. The context suggests that Jesus is also encouraging the disciples, who are undoubtedly shaken by his prophetic judgment of the temple and the omen of the withered fig tree, not to lose confidence in God's sovereignty over events. God has the solution to the tragedy of the barren temple, symbolized by the withered tree. He can even "make the withered tree bloom" (Ezek 17:24).

11:23   Jesus continues with a solemn promise, found in different contexts in Matthew (17:20) and Luke (17:6). **This mountain** could refer to the Mount of Olives or, more likely, to the temple mount that looms before them as they walk into the city. The Old Testament often has the image of mountains being leveled to make way for the establishment of God's reign (Isa 40:4; Bar 5:7; Zech 14:10). What could be more impossible than a mountain being **lifted up and thrown into the sea**? But Jesus has already assured his disciples that "all things are possible for God" (10:27). The image of a mountain moving is not an invitation to test God by asking for spectacular phenomena (see 8:12). Rather, it expresses the limitless power of prayer rooted in unconditional faith: before it all obstacles to God's plan are removed, even the seemingly impossible.

4. See Mark 2:5; 4:40; 5:34–36; 9:23–24; 10:52.

The third saying puts the same principle in more general terms. The men-   **11:24**
tion of **prayer** recalls Jesus' earlier words about the temple being a "house of
prayer" (11:17) and thus hints that the replacement for the defunct temple will
be the community of disciples gathered around Jesus in faith and prayer.[5] Jesus'
"house," the Church, is the new house of prayer for all peoples (see John 4:21,
23). Jesus' disciples are to pray with the utter confidence of children who know
their Father hears even before they ask (see Isa 65:24; Matt 6:8; 1 John 3:22;
5:14–15). The Greek reads literally, "believe that you *have received* it."

Finally, Jesus mentions a condition for efficacious prayer, the same recorded   **11:25**
in Matthew after the Our Father (Matt 6:14).[6] Standing was the primary traditional posture of prayer for Jews and Christians (1 Kings 8:22; Ps 134:1).
Jesus had earlier spoken of God as his own Father (Mark 8:38), but now he
includes his disciples in that filial relationship. The basis for our confidence in
God in prayer is that he is our loving **Father**, who cares for all our needs and
listens to us as to his own beloved children. But unforgiveness is an obstacle
that blocks us both from receiving God's forgiveness and from drawing near
to him in prayer. By the hidden laws of the spiritual life, we are not able to
open ourselves to God's boundless mercy unless we release others from their
infinitely smaller debts to us, as the parable of the unmerciful servant illustrates (Matt 18:21–35).

Reflection and Application (11:20–26)

These words on faith and prayer present a challenge to every believer. Did
Jesus really mean what he said? If so, why have our fervent prayers sometimes
apparently gone unanswered? The answer lies in understanding "believe" in the
biblical sense in which Jesus used it. To believe is not to work up a subjective
feeling of certitude that our prayers will be answered. Rather, it is to enter into
a personal, trusting relationship with God so that our prayers become aligned
with the true good that he desires for us. Elsewhere this promise includes the
qualification that our prayers must be in Jesus' name (John 14:13) or "according to his will" (1 John 5:14), and not with a divided heart (James 4:3–5). Jesus
himself is the model for prayer that is always answered because of his total surrender to the Father's will (see John 8:29; 11:42). The more we are united with
him the more his desires and priorities become our own, and the more we will

5. See Moloney, *Mark*, 227–28.
6. The NAB, like most translations, does not include v. 26 because it is not found in the most reliable ancient manuscripts.

see how God answers them. This is the kind of faith Jesus is referring to, not a "faith" that views God as a kind of cosmic vending machine ready to carry out our every request. "Do not be troubled if you do not immediately receive from God what you ask him; for he desires to do something even greater for you, while you cling to him in prayer."[7]

---

7. Evagrius Ponticus, *De oratione* 34; see Catechism, 2737.

The Authority of the Son

Mark 11:27–12:44

Early in his public ministry Jesus' healings had sparked a series of controversies with the religious authorities revolving around the issue of his authority (2:1–3:6). Now there is a new round of conflicts, focused even more sharply on the question of his authority (11:27–12:44). With his prophetic gesture of cleansing the temple (11:15–17), Jesus had pronounced judgment on the very center of Jewish religious life and provoked its rulers. Now they demand an account from him: by what authority has he dared to judge the temple and its leadership? This question prompts a series of discussions within the temple itself, all taking place within a single day (11:27–13:1). Just as the earlier conflicts occasion a revelation of Jesus' identity, so the present conflicts further unveil his identity and the true source of his authority.

By What Authority? (11:27–33)

²⁷They returned once more to Jerusalem. As he was walking in the temple area, the chief priests, the scribes, and the elders approached him ²⁸and said to him, "By what authority are you doing these things? Or who gave you this authority to do them?" ²⁹Jesus said to them, "I shall ask you one question. Answer me, and I will tell you by what authority I do these things. ³⁰Was John's baptism of heavenly or of human origin? Answer me." ³¹They discussed this among themselves and said, "If we say, 'Of heavenly origin,' he will say, '[Then] why did you not believe him?' ³²But shall we say, 'Of human origin'?"—they feared the crowd, for they all thought John really was a prophet. ³³So they said to Jesus in reply, "We do not know."

> Then Jesus said to them, "Neither shall I tell you by what authority I do these things."

OT: Mic 6:3
NT: // Matt 21:23–27; Luke 20:1–8
Catechism: Jesus and Israel, 574–94

11:27   It is now the third time since their arrival that Jesus and his disciples enter the Holy City. As he is walking among the temple porticos, perhaps teaching as he walked, he is approached by a delegation of the three groups that made up the †Sanhedrin (15:1): **the chief priests, the scribes, and the elders**. These are the three groups that Jesus had prophesied would reject and kill him (8:31). For the first time they openly confront him, challenging him about his recent provocative actions—his triumphal entry into the city (11:7–10) and especially his prophetic demonstration in the temple (11:15–17). Since Mark has already noted their determination that Jesus must die (11:18), the reader is alerted that their intentions are hostile.

11:28–32   Their twofold question brings to a climax the theme of Jesus' **authority**. Their point is to force Jesus to admit that they, the temple leadership, have not authorized his actions. But for readers of the Gospel, Mark has already provided the answer: Jesus is the beloved Son sent by the Father (1:11; 9:7, 37), and as such he has *in himself* authority over all Israel and its religious institutions (see 2:28). He is the "lord of the house" (13:35)—that is, the temple. The question is full of hidden irony: the stewards of the temple, whose authority is only delegated, are demanding that the Lord of the temple answer to them for his actions. Jesus responds, in typical rabbinic fashion, with a counterquestion. His repeated demand, **Answer me**, reverses the inquiry: now it is the Lord who is calling the stewards to account. His words echo the divine exclamation in Micah: "O my people, what have I done to you, or how have I wearied you? Answer me!" (Mic 6:3). Micah's prophecy is in a strikingly similar context: an indictment of the greed and corrupt trading practices that have desecrated the temple, and a threat of divine punishment (Mic 6:1–16).

Jesus' insistence that those challenging him answer his question is not merely a debate tactic. He is seeking to expose the hardness of heart that prevents them from asking their question sincerely and from being open to the true answer. Their inquiry concerned human authority, but Jesus raises the issue to the level of divine authority, linking his own ministry with that of John the Baptist. Now his opponents are faced with a dilemma. On the one hand, if they answer that **John's baptism** was **of heavenly origin**, then they will be forced to admit that they have opposed God by refusing to **believe** John. And since John had spoken of his own ministry as a preparation for that of Jesus, the "mightier one" (Mark 1:7), they will have to acknowledge that Jesus too was divinely attested. If, on the other hand, they claim that John's baptism was merely **of human origin,** they have reason to fear the wrath of the crowds, since all revered John as a †**prophet**—and now also a martyr (6:21–27).

Their self-serving calculations bring to light the real motives underlying their inquiry: not an honest search for truth but an adamant determination to maintain the status quo and preserve their grip on power. Their refusal to face squarely the question of whether John—and Jesus—are from God is exposed in their evasive answer, **We do not know.** Jesus has hinted that his authority is from God but he knows that to say so directly will only give them an excuse for further malice. Yet in his very next words he will in fact proceed to answer their questions—only in a veiled manner, for those who "have ears to hear" (see 4:9, 23).

11:33

The Parable of the Rejected Son (12:1–9)

¹He began to speak to them in parables. "A man planted a vineyard, put a hedge around it, dug a wine press, and built a tower. Then he leased it to tenant farmers and left on a journey. ²At the proper time he sent a servant to the tenants to obtain from them some of the produce of the vineyard. ³But they seized him, beat him, and sent him away empty-handed. ⁴Again he sent them another servant. And that one they beat over the head and treated shamefully. ⁵He sent yet another whom they killed. So, too, many others; some they beat, others they killed. ⁶He had one other to send, a beloved son. He sent him to them last of all, thinking, 'They will respect my son.' ⁷But those tenants said to one another, 'This is the heir. Come, let us kill him, and the inheritance will be ours.' ⁸So they seized him and killed him, and threw him out of the vineyard. ⁹What [then] will the owner of the vineyard do? He will come, put the tenants to death, and give the vineyard to others.

OT: Gen 37:20; Ps 80:9–12; Isa 5:1–7
NT: Mark 1:11; 9:7. // Matt 21:33–42; Luke 20:9–16
Catechism: Church as God's vineyard, 755; Jesus the only Son of God, 441–45
Lectionary: 12:1–12: votive Mass of the Mystery of the Holy Cross

Challenged by the temple authorities, Jesus begins to speak to them **in parables,** his way of addressing "those outside" (4:11). He tells a story about a vineyard (12:1–9), followed by a quotation from Ps 118 that helps to explain its meaning (vv. 10–11). Like many of Jesus' parables, this one describes a typical agricultural scene in his native Galilee. For Jesus' listeners, this vineyard parable

12:1–2

would bring to mind Isaiah's "song of the vineyard," an allegory about God's dealings with unfaithful Israel (Isa 5:1–2, 7).[1]

But Jesus' version takes a new turn: this vineyard owner **leased it to tenant farmers and left on a journey**. The tenants signify the leaders of Israel, to whom God had entrusted his vineyard. At **the proper time**—each harvest beginning with the fifth year after planting, according to the Mosaic law (Lev 19:23–25)—the owner sends a servant to obtain his share of **the produce** (literally, the fruits). Fruit is often used in Scripture to signify the results of good or evil conduct (Isa 3:10; Jer 6:19; Matt 7:16–20). God desires to obtain from his people the fruit of justice, piety, and good deeds (Hosea 10:12; John 15:2; Gal 5:22).

12:3–5   But the tenants' reaction is shocking: instead of paying the agreed-upon share, they seize the servant, **beat him**, and send him away **empty-handed**. Such brazen defiance could hardly be expected to go unpunished. Yet when the landlord tries again to collect his profits the violence continues and even escalates. In the ancient world, to treat someone **shamefully** could be more offensive even than physical assault (see 2 Sam 10:4–5). The third emissary is **killed**, and a succession of others are likewise beaten or killed.

In real life, for a landlord to keep sending emissaries in the face of such vicious maltreatment would be folly. But by now Jesus' listeners grasp that he is speaking of God's persistent sending of the prophets to call his people back to himself.[2] Like the vineyard owner's servants, God's prophets were repeatedly ignored (2 Kings 17:13–14; Jer 7:25–26; 25:4), mistreated (2 Chron 36:15–16), and killed (1 Kings 19:10; Neh 9:26; Luke 13:34). Micaiah, for example, was imprisoned on bread and water (1 Kings 22:27), Jeremiah was scourged and put in the stocks (Jer 20:2), Zechariah was stoned in the temple courts (2 Chron 24:20–22), and Isaiah was sawn in two.[3]

12:6   At this point in the parable, the landlord does something inexplicable: instead of servants he sends his own **beloved son**. In the Old Testament, "beloved son" signifies "only son," and is always used in reference to an only son who is destined to die.[4] Mark has already identified Jesus as God's "beloved Son" at his baptism (1:11) and Transfiguration (9:7). Here Jesus himself claims this title in a veiled way and implicitly answers the question of 11:28: he acts with the authority of the beloved Son and heir, who has come to claim the produce of

---

1. The vineyard is a common biblical image for Israel: see Ps 80:9–17; Isa 27:2–6; Jer 2:21; 12:10; Ezek 19:10–14; Hosea 10:1.
2. "Servants" (*douloi*, in the Septuagint translation) is often used in the Old Testament to refer to the prophets: see 2 Kings 9:7; Ezra 9:11; Amos 3:7; Zech 1:6.
3. See the apocryphal *Ascension of Isaiah* 5.1–14; see also Heb 11:37.
4. See Gen 22:2; Jer 6:26; Amos 8:10; Zech 12:10. The feminine form is used this way for an only daughter who is destined to die: Judg 11:34; see also Tob 3:10.

God's vineyard. The word for **last of all**, *eschaton*, is a subtle reminder that the coming of Jesus signifies the fullness of time (see 1:15), the time of the definitive accomplishment of God's plan.

But how could the vineyard owner think the tenants would respect his son after all they had done to his servants? Jesus is deliberately highlighting the apparent foolishness of the landlord to help his listeners understand the reckless love of the Father, who continually holds out mercy to his people even in the face of their arrogant defiance. Though his people had rejected a host of prophets, God sent them his only Son, desiring that he be shown honor and respect but knowing full well that he would be treated even worse than the rest. Far from respecting the son, **those tenants** conspire to murder him and usurp the vineyard. Their reasoning reflects inheritance law at the time, which provided that in the absence of an **heir** land could be regarded as "ownerless property" and lawfully possessed by the first claimant.[5] **Come, let us kill him** is an exact echo of the scheming of the sons of Jacob when they plot their brother Joseph's death (Gen 37:20). Like them, the religious leaders are plotting against Jesus, their own brother Jew (Mark 3:6; 11:18). The parable thus depicts Jesus as true heir of the vineyard of Israel, and the leaders of Israel as the usurpers who have abused their stewardship and seized the vineyard for their own greed. The tenants in the parable end by killing the owner's son and throwing him **out of the vineyard**. The vileness of their behavior extends even to denying him a proper burial.

12:7–8

In conclusion Jesus asks his listeners a rhetorical question and immediately provides the answer. **What will the owner of the vineyard do?** The Greek reads literally, "the lord of the vineyard," obviously alluding to the Lord, the God of Israel. God's longsuffering patience gives way to severity toward the tenants who had shown such flagrant contempt for his will. It is significant that God does not punish the **vineyard** itself (Israel), but its corrupt leadership. He will turn his vineyard over to new managers who will care for it properly—that is, the apostles, leaders of the new Israel that Jesus is establishing (see 3:14; Luke 22:29–30).

12:9

The Parable of the Rejected Stone (12:10–12)

> [10] Have you not read this scripture passage:
>
> 'The stone that the builders rejected
>   has become the cornerstone;
> [11]by the Lord has this been done,
>   and it is wonderful in our eyes'?"

5. See Lane, *Mark*, 418–19.

¹²They were seeking to arrest him, but they feared the crowd, for they realized that he had addressed the parable to them. So they left him and went away.

OT: Ps 118:22–23
NT: Acts 4:11; 1 Pet 2:7. // Matt 21:42–46; Luke 20:17–19
Catechism: the Church as God's building, 756, 797–98

Jesus concludes with a rhetorical question quoting Ps 118:22–23, a kind of mini parable. With this quotation he moves from the agricultural to the architectural in portraying his rejection by Israel's leaders. These verses are among those most often quoted by the early Church in interpreting Jesus' passion (Matt 21:44; Luke 20:17; Acts 4:11; 1 Pet 2:7). Psalm 118 was a pilgrimage psalm sung by worshippers entering the temple (Ps 118:19–29). Indeed, it is the very psalm sung at Jesus' own procession to the temple (Mark 11:9–10). Thus the building referred to is not just any edifice, but the holy dwelling place of God, the very setting in which the whole discussion is taking place (11:27; 13:1).

12:10–11 The word for **rejected** is the same word Jesus had used in his first passion prediction (8:31). He himself is the rejected son (12:7) and rejected **stone** (12:10), cast off by the leaders of Israel but ultimately vindicated by God. Like the wicked tenants and the shortsighted builders, the religious leaders have made a drastic mistake in rejecting him. Yet God will use their error to do something marvelous. He will raise up Jesus to be the **cornerstone** of a new building, a temple "not made with hands" (see 14:58). It is the first hint in the Gospel that the earthly temple in Jerusalem will be replaced by a new temple built by God himself, the temple of the risen Lord and all those who are joined to him (see 1 Cor 3:9; Eph 2:20–21; 1 Pet 2:5).

12:12 Jesus' listeners—the chief priests, scribes, and elders (11:27)—have no trouble grasping that **he had addressed the parable** (the combined parable of the wicked tenants and the shortsighted builders) **to them**. Yet they refuse to accept its underlying message by acknowledging their sin and turning to God in †repentance. Instead they proceed to fulfill the parable by **seeking to arrest** Jesus. Temporarily stymied by fear of the **crowd**, they leave to await a more opportune moment for doing away with him.

Caesar and God (12:13–17)

---

¹³They sent some Pharisees and Herodians to him to ensnare him in
his speech. ¹⁴They came and said to him, "Teacher, we know that you are a

truthful man and that you are not concerned with anyone's opinion. You do not regard a person's status but teach the way of God in accordance with the truth. Is it lawful to pay the census tax to Caesar or not? Should we pay or should we not pay?" [15]Knowing their hypocrisy he said to them, "Why are you testing me? Bring me a denarius to look at." [16]They brought one to him and he said to them, "Whose image and inscription is this?" They replied to him, "Caesar's." [17]So Jesus said to them, "Repay to Caesar what belongs to Caesar and to God what belongs to God." They were utterly amazed at him.

OT: Gen 1:27; Ps 95:9; Jer 18:18
NT: Rom 13:1–7. // Matt 22:15–22; Luke 20:20–26
Catechism: authorities in civil society, 2234–46

The religious authorities mentioned above (11:27) now send others to try to **ensnare** Jesus **in his speech**. This begins a series of three questions posed to Jesus by representative groups of Israel's leadership: Pharisees and Herodians (12:13–14), Sadducees (12:18–23), and scribes (12:28). The first question, on the payment of taxes to Rome, employs a clever tactic: the **Pharisees and Herodians** came from opposite ends of the political spectrum, and would have had contrary opinions on the imperial tax. The Pharisees, as members of a reform movement advocating Jewish separatism and strict religious observance, abhorred the presence of a pagan occupying power in Israel. The Herodians, as supporters of Herod Antipas, had a stake in cooperating with Rome and maintaining the

12:13

The Roman Tax

BIBLICAL
BACKGROUND

The census tax was an imperial tribute imposed on Judea beginning in AD 6, when Rome deposed the client king, Herod Archelaus, and installed a Roman governor in his place. At that time a census was taken to establish a list of those obligated to pay the tax. There was also a tax on agricultural produce and many other indirect taxes. The census tax was an onerous burden to the Jews and a galling symbol of their subjugation to Rome, and was so bitterly opposed that it had sparked a revolt led by Judas the Galilean in AD 6 (Acts 5:37). The revolt was quickly crushed but helped inspire Jewish nationalism, eventually giving rise to the Zealot movement that spearheaded the climactic revolt and war of AD 66–70.

As a Galilean, Jesus was not obliged to pay the tax, which applied only to provinces under direct Roman rule.

status quo. Despite their usual hostility to each other these two groups were united enough in their opposition to Jesus to join forces against him, as occurred earlier (3:6). They approach Jesus as if he were a political candidate, seeking to back him into a corner where any answer he gives will arouse the wrath of one constituency or another. If he supports paying the tax he will be discredited in the eyes of the common people, who resent the Roman occupation. He will then lose the popular support that has made the religious leaders afraid to arrest him (see 11:18). But if he opposes the tax he can be denounced to the government as a rebel.

12:14   They preface their question with a generous dose of flattery, designed to prevent Jesus from evading the issue and perhaps to convince the bystanders of their good intentions. They address him as a **Teacher** who is **truthful**, who does not pander to human **opinion** or tailor his words depending on his listeners' **status**. In a final redundant compliment they gush that he teaches **the way of God**. All that they say is true, but it is said disingenuously. Their own actions belie their words, since they do not accept Jesus' teachings, nor do they admit the truth of what he says, nor are they willing to follow "the way of God" that he teaches. Their very flattery and their inflammatory question presuppose that he will indeed be swayed by human opinion.

The query is designed to trap Jesus in an inescapable dilemma. **Lawful** refers to God's law, specifically the first commandment (Exod 20:2–6). For faithful Jews the coin used for paying the **census tax** represented a gross affront to God's sovereignty, because of both its graven image of †**Caesar** and the blasphemous title attributed to him (see below).

12:15–16   Jesus sees through their disingenuous attempt at flattery and perceives the **hypocrisy** motivating their question. Hypocrisy (from the Greek word for stage actor) is a pretense or outward show that hides a person's real intentions (see 7:6). He summons his questioners to examine their motives: **Why are you testing me?** Testing the Lord was a sin for which the Israelites were often chastised (Num 14:22; Deut 6:16; Ps 95:8–9). In fact, by testing Jesus (Greek *peirazō*) the Pharisees and Herodians are playing the role of Satan, who had tempted Jesus (*peirazō*) in an effort to derail his messianic mission (Mark 1:13).

In traditional prophetic fashion, Jesus uses a visual aid to illustrate what he is about to say (see Jer 19:1–10; 27:2; Ezek 4). The **denarius** was a silver Roman coin equivalent to the daily wage for a laborer. Stamped on it was the image of the emperor, who at the time was Tiberius, and the inscription: "Tiberius Caesar Augustus, son of the divine Augustus." On the reverse side was the title "High Priest" (*Pontifex Maximus*), claiming that the emperor was the supreme

Joe Geranio

Fig. 12. Denarius from the reign of Tiberius Caesar.

mediator between human beings and the gods. Tiberius's claim of divinity was a way of promoting the emperor worship that was widespread in Roman civic religion, but was an abomination to Jews. Jesus' questioners bring him a denarius, revealing that they were carrying the idolatrous coin within the temple precincts. He forces them into their own dilemma by asking a counterquestion: **Whose image and inscription is this?** In reply, they admit that the portrait and legend on the coin are **Caesar's**. By using Caesar's coins, they are implicitly recognizing his authority as emperor.

Jesus' reply eludes the trap set for him and raises the whole discussion above the realm of politics. The common understanding of the time was that coins were the property of the ruler who issued them. By referring to the coin as **what belongs to Caesar** Jesus implicitly affirms a state's right to exact tribute. Paying taxes to support the government is not in itself a compromise of religious integrity. Jesus thereby distances himself from Jewish nationalists who refused to pay tribute to the Roman government. But **what belongs to God** is what

12:17

The Roman Emperor

Tiberius Caesar reigned from AD 14 to 37 over an empire that stretched from France in the northwest to Syria in the east, including all the lands bordering on the Mediterranean Sea. Rome had originally been ruled by a senate of noblemen, but by the first century BC power had become consolidated in the hands of a single emperor. The family name Caesar, inherited from Julius Caesar, became an imperial title. During the first century AD the Caesars increasingly claimed divine status and encouraged emperor worship. The empire was approaching the zenith of its economic and military power, while beginning a downward moral and political spiral that would end with the dissolution of its entire western portion in the fifth century.

The Jews had been subject to Roman rule since 63 BC, when Palestine was conquered by the Roman general Pompey. The idolatrous claims of the Roman emperors and their usurpation of Jewish national sovereignty were continuing sources of outrage to the Jews.

bears *his* image—that is, every human being, including Caesar! Jesus' listeners recognize that he is alluding to Gen 1:27: "God created man in his image." The state may lay claim to a paltry piece of metal, but God lays claim to our whole being—mind, heart, soul, and strength (see v. 30). Our obligation to the state, which is limited, is subsumed under our obligation to God, which is absolute. Jesus is implicitly warning his listeners, Do not give to Caesar (to the state, to society, or to any human institution) what belongs to God alone and to his Son: your absolute, unconditional allegiance and devotion (Mark 8:34–38).

It is no wonder that Jesus' listeners, recognizing the wisdom of this answer, are **utterly amazed at him**. Once again his opponents are reduced to silence. This is the last time the Pharisees and the Herodians appear in the Gospel.

Reflection and Application (12:13–17)

The principle Jesus enunciates here forms part of the basis of Catholic teaching on the relationship of Church and state. Other New Testament writings elaborate on Jesus' principle, affirming both our duty to respect civil authority (Rom 13:1–7; 1 Tim 2:1–6; Titus 3:1–2; 1 Pet 2:13–17) and our overriding allegiance to God wherever civil authority oversteps its bounds or imposes laws contrary to the moral law (Acts 5:29; Rev 13:1–18). The Catechism articulates this balanced understanding. "Those subject to authority should regard those in authority as representatives of God" (2238); "Submission to authority and co-responsibility for the common good make it morally obligatory to pay taxes, to exercise the right to vote, and to defend one's country" (2240). However, "The citizen is obliged in conscience not to follow the directives of civil authorities when they are contrary to the demands of the moral order, to the fundamental rights of persons or the teachings of the Gospel" (2242).

Whose Wife Will She Be? (12:18–27)

> [18]Some Sadducees, who say there is no resurrection, came to him and put this question to him, [19]saying, "Teacher, Moses wrote for us, 'If someone's brother dies, leaving a wife but no child, his brother must take the wife and raise up descendants for his brother.' [20]Now there were seven brothers. The first married a woman and died, leaving no descendants. [21]So the second married her and died, leaving no descendants, and the third likewise. [22]And the seven left no descendants. Last of all the woman

also died. ²³At the resurrection [when they arise] whose wife will she be? For all seven had been married to her." ²⁴Jesus said to them, "Are you not misled because you do not know the scriptures or the power of God? ²⁵When they rise from the dead, they neither marry nor are given in marriage, but they are like the angels in heaven. ²⁶As for the dead being raised, have you not read in the Book of Moses, in the passage about the bush, how God told him, 'I am the God of Abraham, [the] God of Isaac, and [the] God of Jacob'? ²⁷He is not God of the dead but of the living. You are greatly misled."

OT: Exod 3:6; Deut 25:5–6
NT: 1 Cor 15:35–55. // Matt 22:23–33; Luke 20:27–40
Catechism: Christ's resurrection and ours, 992–1004; marriage as passing away, 1619

Like the Pharisees and Herodians above (12:13), the †**Sadducees** approach   **12:18**
Jesus with a loaded question, attempting to force him into an untenable position. As Mark informs his readers, the Sadducees rejected belief in the **resurrection**, holding that the soul perishes along with the body at death. Their question is designed to prove that belief in the resurrection leads to absurdity.

The question is posed as a hypothetical case, based on a command of **Moses**   **12:19–23**
that is sometimes called the levirate law of marriage (from Latin *levir*, brother-in-law). According to this law, if a man's brother died leaving a widow but no child, the man was obligated to marry his brother's widow to "continue the line of the deceased brother, that his name may not be blotted out from Israel" (Deut 25:5–6). In the Sadducees' fictional scenario, each of **seven brothers**

The Sadducees

BIBLICAL BACKGROUND

The Sadducees were an elite and powerful party within Judaism, consisting of the priestly aristocracy, their families, and supporters. Their name may come either from the priest Zadok at the time of David (2 Sam 8:17; 15:24), or from the Hebrew word for righteous (*tsaddiq*), or both. They had more lenient religious views than the Pharisees, accepting only the Torah (not the Prophets or Psalms) as sacred Scripture, and rejecting traditions that had arisen more recently in Judaism, such as belief in angels, spirits, and the resurrection from the dead (see Acts 23:6–10). The Sadducees maintained their privileged status by cooperating with the Roman government, and had much less popular appeal than the Pharisees.

marries the same woman in succession only to die **leaving no descendants**. This case is curiously similar to the story described in the book of Tobit, which the Sadducees did not accept as Scripture (Tob 3:8). Finally the woman also dies. This leads them to the question that they hope will stump Jesus: **whose wife will she be?** The question presupposes that one woman cannot be married to several men at once. The Sadducees evidently feel that they have presented an insoluble dilemma, disproving the resurrection.

12:24   Jesus' reply asserts in no uncertain terms that the Sadducees are wrong. He attributes their error to ignorance on two counts: they understand neither **the scriptures** nor **the power of God.** He then elaborates on these points in reverse order.

12:25   First, the Sadducees do not understand "the power of God" because they fail to recognize that God is able not only to restore the dead to life but to give them a completely new and transformed existence. Jesus exposes the Sadducees' faulty premise: that the resurrected life will be simply a continuation of earthly life, a mere resuscitation of corpses. On the contrary, it will differ unimaginably from life as we know it now: those who rise from the dead **neither marry nor are given in marriage**. Jesus uses the active and passive forms of the verb "to marry," used for men and women respectively, implying that resurrected human beings will still be male or female. But sexual differentiation will no longer be linked to marriage or childbearing, since earthly marriage will have fulfilled its purpose. Rather, risen human beings are **like the angels in heaven**. This does not imply they are disembodied spirits, but that they have a glorious and eternal existence like the angels. With this answer Jesus affirms several points denied by the Sadducees: life after death, bodily resurrection, and the existence of angels.

12:26–27   Second, the Sadducees do not understand "the scriptures." It is not that they are unfamiliar with the Scriptures—some of them may have memorized the †Torah—but they do not understand the God who is revealed in the Scriptures. They have entirely missed the point of God's words to Moses at the burning bush (Exod 3:6, 15–16). What they fail to grasp is that for God to be the **God** *of someone*, that person must be in relationship with God, and therefore alive. For **he is not God of the dead but of the living.** God cannot claim to be the God of Abraham, Isaac, and Jacob unless he is their protector and defender—which includes saving them from death in its most profound sense of eternal separation from himself. Moreover, because human beings are embodied, salvation from death is impossible apart from the body. In biblical thought, the body is not just a component of the person, it *is* the person insofar as the person is present in the visible world. Ultimately, to be alive is to be alive as a whole person, body and soul. Jesus' manner of reasoning is profound, and very different from the logic we are used to. His argument is based on the absolute commitment, the unimaginable love and care, to which God has obliged himself in choosing to be our God.

By repeating, **You are greatly misled**, Jesus forcefully emphasizes how foolish and mistaken is the view that the human body is a mere appendage to the soul, destined to be discarded at death.

Reflection and Application (12:18–27)

Every Sunday, Catholics and many other Christians profess our faith in "the resurrection of the body" as we recite the creed. Yet how many are fully aware of this truth and all that it implies? Paul, whose teaching on this topic was rooted in his own encounter with the risen Lord on the road to Damascus, explains that our resurrected bodies will be radiant with divine glory (see Rom 8:18–23; 1 Cor 15:42–44). No longer will there be any sickness, pain, or disability. John affirms that we shall be like God, "for we shall see him as he is" (1 John 3:2). We will share in the very life of God, the eternal exchange of love within the Holy Trinity (see 2 Pet 1:4).

This passage on the resurrection is an important counterpart and balance to the earlier passage on the permanence of marriage (Mark 10:2–12). There Jesus established that marriage, as part of God's plan "from the beginning," is a sacred bond that no one is authorized to break. Here he reveals that marriage is a reality of the present age that is passing away (which is not to deny that a unique relationship may remain in heaven between those who were spouses on earth). Earthly marriage, as good as it is, will give way to something far greater: a union with God and all the saints that will infinitely surpass the earthly one-flesh union of husband and wife.

In Catholic tradition, the vocation to consecrated celibacy is especially valued as a sign reminding us of this ultimate destiny (Catechism, 1619; see 1 Cor 7:29–31). Like earthly marriage, consecration to Christ in a vow of lifelong celibacy is the expression of a total and exclusive gift of self. A consecrated woman is "married" to Christ, and a consecrated man is "married" to the Church, in a union that is a source of joy and of abundant spiritual fruitfulness. Those who have the charism of celibacy for the kingdom are signs of the life to which we are all called for eternity.

The Great Commandment (12:28–34)

28One of the scribes, when he came forward and heard them disputing and saw how well he had answered them, asked him, "Which is the first of all the commandments?" 29Jesus replied, "The first is this: 'Hear, O Israel! The Lord our God is Lord alone! 30You shall love the Lord your God with all your heart, with all your soul, with all your mind, and with all your strength.' 31The second is this: 'You shall love your neighbor as yourself.' There is no other commandment greater than these." 32The scribe said to him, "Well said, teacher. You are right in saying, 'He is One and there is no other than he.' 33And 'to love him with all your heart, with all your understanding, with all your strength, and to love your neighbor as yourself' is worth more than all burnt offerings and sacrifices." 34And when Jesus saw that [he] answered with understanding, he said to him, "You are not far from the kingdom of God." And no one dared to ask him any more questions.

OT: Lev 19:18; Deut 6:4–5
NT: 1 John 4:11, 20–21. // Matt 22:34–40; Luke 10:25–28
Catechism: the two great commandments, 201–2, 2055, 2196
Lectionary: Infant Baptism

12:28   This conversation with **one of the scribes** is very different in tone from the preceding disputes. Unlike the Pharisees and Herodians (12:13–14), the Sadducees (12:18–23), and other scribes (3:22; 7:1), this man approaches Jesus in sincerity and good will. As a professional scholar of the Mosaic law, he had observed and wondered at the astuteness of Jesus' response regarding the resurrection (12:24–27). So he seeks his wisdom on another live issue that was debated among scholars of the day. The †Torah was full of **commandments**—613 of them, according to later rabbinic tradition—and it was common in scribal discussions to look for the one general statement or overriding principle that would summarize and ground them all.

12:29–30   Jesus responds by quoting Deut 6:4–5, the great Israelite confession of faith known as the Shema (Hebrew for "hear"): **Hear, O Israel! The Lord our God is Lord alone!** By the time of Jesus, this statement was understood to mean that †YHWH is not only the one God of the Jews but the one and only God of the whole universe. In a world of polytheism, the Jews were the only people to have been granted this earth-shattering insight: there is but one God, who has created all things and who holds all things in existence by his goodness and power. His claim on us is therefore total, calling for a total response at every level of our being. To **love** God is to have a profound reverence and affection for him, to give ourselves over to him and desire to please him above all else. Jesus is spelling out what he had said earlier about repaying to God what belongs to him (12:17).

Jesus uses four terms that, taken together, signify not distinct faculties or parts of the human being but different ways of referring to the whole person. The **heart** (*kardia*) is the inner depths of a person, the wellspring from which all our decisions and actions flow (see 7:19). The **soul** (*psychē*) is our whole self as a living being, that which Jesus said we must be willing to give up for his sake (8:35) and which he will give up for our sake (10:45). Jesus adds another term, **mind**, to emphasize that even our thoughts and reasoning must be animated by love for God. The last phrase, **with all your strength**, emphasizes that love for God is not a sentiment that arises spontaneously, but a commitment that calls for every ounce of our energy. How can such love without measure be possible? Only by our first knowing and experiencing God's love for us (Rom 5:5, 8; 1 John 4:11).

The second part of Jesus' response quotes Lev 19:18: **You shall love your neighbor as yourself.** Jesus is the first one known to have explicitly combined these two commandments. But they are the foundations underlying the first three and last seven commandments of the †Decalogue respectively (Exod 20:2–11, 12–17). His implication is that they are inseparable: our love for God is concretized and expressed in our love for fellow human beings (see 1 John 4:11, 20–21). To love others "as yourself" means to make their well-being as high a

12:31

The Great Shema

BIBLICAL
BACKGROUND

The Shema was and still is the central prayer and confession of faith for Jews. Its full form includes three biblical passages: Deut 6:4–9; 11:13–21; and Num 15:37–41. In fidelity to Deut 6:7 devout Jews recite the Shema every morning and evening. Jewish homes usually have a mezuzah, a little box containing the Shema inscribed on parchment, affixed to the doorpost (see Deut 6:9). Orthodox Jewish men (and sometimes women) wear tefillin (or phylacteries), leather boxes containing the Shema, on their head and hand during prayer (Deut 6:8).

Jesus' emphatic affirmation of the Shema shows that he did not come to reject or overturn Judaism, but to fulfill it. The New Testament never views the proclamation of Christ's divinity as contrary to the Old Testament revelation that God is one. Rather it is a disclosure of God's innermost mystery as a communion of Persons. "We do not confess three Gods, but one God in three persons" (Catechism, 253).

Loving God and Neighbor

A seventh-century Father comments, "Neither of these two kinds of love is expressed with full maturity without the other, because God cannot be loved apart from our neighbor, nor our neighbor apart from God. Hence as many times as Peter was asked by our Lord if he loved him, and attested his love, the Lord added at the end of each inquiry, 'Feed my sheep,' or 'feed my lambs' (John 21:15–17), as if he were clearly saying: 'There is only one adequate confirmation of whole-hearted love of God—laboring steadily for the needy in your midst, exercising continuing care of them.'"[a]

a. Bede, *Exposition on the Gospel of Mark* 2.22, in Oden and Hall, *Mark*, 165.

priority as your own (see Phil 2:3–4)—a very demanding standard. Although in its original context "neighbor" meant one's fellow Israelite, elsewhere Jesus makes clear that our love must extend to every person without limit (Matt 5:43–44; Luke 10:29–37), since the one God is God of all.

Jesus concludes: **There is no other commandment greater than these.** The rest of the law merely spells out how to love God and neighbor. To fulfill this

Burnt Offerings and Sacrifices

The Old Testament gives instructions for several different kinds of sacrifice, including the whole burnt offering or holocaust, in which an animal was entirely consumed on the altar (Lev 1:3–17). In the time of Jesus, when the temple was still standing, Jewish worship was centered on the system of animal sacrifices. The Old Testament affirmed the supreme importance of obedience and love over ceremonial offerings.[a] But even so, for the scribe conversing with Jesus in the temple and surrounded by members of the priestly hierarchy (12:18), to state that loving God is worth more than all the temple sacrifices is a bold statement. Little did he realize that the entire sacrificial system was about to be replaced by the all-sufficient sacrifice of Jesus, the Lamb of God (John 1:29), which simultaneously fulfills both the commandment of love and the old covenant sacrifices. Like the temple holocausts, Jesus would be entirely consumed in his self-offering. Yet the value of his sacrifice is infinitely greater than the temple holocausts because of the fire of love for God with which it was offered. Jesus' perfect sacrifice becomes the source and model for the love of Christians (Rom 12:1–2; Eph 5:2).

a. See Ps 40:7–9; Prov 21:3; Hosea 6:6; Amos 5:21–24; Mic 6:6–8.

twofold commandment perfectly would be to fulfill the entire law (see Rom 13:8–10; James 2:8).

Recognizing the wisdom of Jesus' answer **the scribe** voices his approval, adding a common biblical affirmation of the uniqueness of God (see Deut 4:39; 1 Kings 8:60; Isa 46:9). The scribe then elaborates: to love God with one's whole being and love others **is worth more than all burnt offerings and sacrifices.**
12:32–33

Jesus in turn praises the scribe's insight. But his reply is two-edged. The scribe's understanding of what God truly desires shows that he is **not far from the kingdom**, the presence and reign of God that has been the object of Jesus' whole mission (see 1:15). But he is not yet *in* the kingdom. Jesus has both affirmed the scribe and challenged him to go further. It is not surprising that **no one dared to ask him any more questions.**
12:34

David's Son and Lord (12:35–37)

[35]As Jesus was teaching in the temple area he said, "How do the scribes claim that the Messiah is the son of David? [36]David himself, inspired by the holy Spirit, said:

'The Lord said to my lord,
  "Sit at my right hand
    until I place your enemies under your feet."'

[37]David himself calls him 'lord'; so how is he his son?" [The] great crowd heard this with delight.

OT: Ps 89:21–38; 110:1; Jer 23:5–6
NT: Matt 1:6–23; Luke 1:30–33; John 7:42; Rom 1:3–4. // Matt 22:41–46; Luke 20:41–44
Catechism: Jesus' lordship, 446–51; Son of David, 437–39

Up to this point, Jesus has been challenged and questioned from all sides (11:27–12:34), but now his opponents have run out of questions—or courage (12:34)—with which to confront him. From this point on, Jesus takes the initiative. He raises a provocative question: **How do the scribes claim that the Messiah is the son of David?** Like his earlier reply to the rich man (10:18), this is meant to be taken as a genuine question, not a denial.[6] Jesus is not denying that the Messiah is the son of David, the very title that Bartimaeus proclaimed and
12:35–37

6. The NAB makes the question sound more like an implicit denial by translating the Greek verb *legō* as "claim" (compare RSV, NIV "say"; JB, NJB "maintain"). The question could be rendered: "What do the scribes mean when they say that the Messiah is the son of David?"

Jesus implicitly accepted during his messianic journey to Jerusalem (10:47–48). Rather, he is inviting his listeners to reflect more deeply on what Scripture reveals about the Messiah, the promised son of David. Drawing from Psalm 110, a psalm attributed to King David, Jesus raises an apparent dilemma. But first he emphasizes the authority of this psalm by noting that in composing it David was **inspired by the holy Spirit** (literally, "in the holy Spirit"). The implication is that the psalm—and by extension, all Scripture—is ultimately attributable to the Spirit of God, and therefore has divine authority (see 2 Sam 23:2; Acts 1:16). Jesus thereby affirms the doctrine of biblical inspiration (see 2 Tim 3:16; 2 Pet 1:20–21).

Psalm 110 in its original context was an enthronement psalm, sung at the coronation ceremonies for the kings of Judah. In it the new king is promised royal dominion and victory over his enemies. The psalmist addresses the king as **my lord** (Hebrew *adoni*), a title of honor (1 Sam 26:19; 1 Kings 1:37). **The Lord** refers to God himself.[7] God invites the king to sit at his **right hand**, the position of highest honor (see Mark 10:37), until his enemies are utterly defeated. By the time of Jesus, when the monarchy had long ceased to exist, Psalm 110 was viewed as a prophecy of the Messiah, the promised royal descendant of David who would revive the monarchy and restore sovereignty to Israel. But how, Jesus asks, can the Messiah be David's son if **David himself calls him "lord"**? In ancient culture, it would be unthinkable for a father to address his son or descendant as "lord." Jesus is challenging his listeners: What are the implications of the fact that David reveres the Messiah as someone superior to himself? What does this psalm reveal about the majesty of the Messiah? Is he merely an earthly monarch, descended from the line of David, or is he something much greater? Could he even be Lord in the same sense in which †YHWH himself is "the Lord"? Elsewhere the Gospels indicate that Jesus is "greater than Solomon" (Matt 12:42), "greater than Jacob" (John 4:12), "greater than Abraham" (John 8:53); here Jesus hints that he is greater than David.

In interpreting this passage it is beside the point to question whether David himself actually composed Psalm 110 or whether it comes from a later time. The ancient Jews had a broader view of authorship than we do today, and many of the psalms were ascribed to David, who summed up in himself the praises of Israel. In their worship all Israel joined David in addressing the Messiah as "my lord." Jesus is pointing to the mystery of the incarnation, foreshadowed in

---

7. The Hebrew text says YHWH; out of reverence for God's holy name a Jew praying the psalm would substitute *Adonai* (the Lord).

the Psalms: the Messiah is the son of David, who is born of God's people yet in a mysterious way also far transcends them in dignity.

The **great crowd heard this with delight**, for Jesus had broken open the meaning of the Scriptures for them. For the early Church, Psalm 110 was one of the most important Old Testament prophecies of Christ, fulfilled in its deepest meaning at his resurrection when he won victory over his enemies—sin, Satan, and death—and was enthroned at the Father's right hand.[8]

The Danger of Honors (12:38–40)

[38]In the course of his teaching he said, "Beware of the scribes, who like to go around in long robes and accept greetings in the marketplaces, [39]seats of honor in synagogues, and places of honor at banquets. [40]They devour the houses of widows and, as a pretext, recite lengthy prayers. They will receive a very severe condemnation."

OT: Isa 10:1–2
NT: Mark 10:42–45. // Matt 23:5–7; Luke 20:45–47
Catechism: judgment day, 678–79; greed, 2536

As Jesus continues **teaching** in the temple courts he now takes direct aim   12:38–39
at the scribes, who have been among his fiercest opponents. Earlier he had warned his disciples to "beware of the leaven of the Pharisees" (8:15 RSV); now he tells his listeners, **Beware of the scribes** (using the same Greek verb, *blepō*). His point is not for people to stay away from the scribes, one of whom he has just praised (12:34), but to take care to avoid *conduct* like theirs. Such conduct—the opposite of what Jesus enjoins on Christian leaders (9:35; 10:15, 42–44)—will be severely condemned.

As professional lawyer-theologians, †scribes were among the most eminent members of Jewish society. Their word was considered to have weighty authority. They wore distinctive long linen **robes** as a mark of status, and were greeted with great deference by ordinary folk in the **marketplaces**. All were expected to rise respectfully as a scribe passed by.[9] The **seats of honor in synagogues** were reserved for them, on a bench directly in front of the ark containing the sacred scrolls. Jesus has just spoken of the real seat of honor, the seat destined for the Messiah at God's right hand (12:36). At

---

8. See Mark 14:62; 16:19; Acts 2:34–35; Rom 8:34; 1 Cor 15:25; Eph 1:20; Col 3:1; Heb 1:3, 13; 8:1; 10:12.
9. See the Talmud, *b. Qiddushin* 33a.

banquets too the scribes were given the **places of honor**, since the presence of a distinguished scholar would be considered an ornament to the feast. Jesus warns of the danger of relishing and actively inviting these tokens of human esteem.

12:40   Even worse, the scribes have used their privileged status to exploit others. Since scribes were forbidden to receive payment for teaching, they depended on private donations for their living. To subsidize a scribe was considered a meritorious act of piety. That the scribes **devour the houses of widows** could refer to their mismanaging widows' estates, or sponging off their hospitality, or charging excessive legal fees, or other ways of fleecing them.[10] Such financial abuse recalls Jesus' denunciation of the temple as a "den of thieves" (11:17). Widows were among the most vulnerable members of society because of their limited possibilities for income, and therefore among those most deserving of care and support (Deut 24:17, 21; Isa 1:17; James 1:27). The Old Testament often condemns the exploitation of widows (Isa 10:1–2; Jer 7:6; Ezek 22:7). In an empty show of piety, and perhaps as a cover for their fraudulent activity, the scribes **recite lengthy prayers**. The problem is not that the prayers are lengthy per se but that they are aimed at human beings rather than at God. Like the hypocrites Jesus denounces in Matt 6:2, the scribes "have received their reward" in paltry human praise and forfeited a true and eternal reward from God. Instead they will receive **a very severe condemnation** (or "judgment"). Jesus' sternest words are for those who abuse religion for personal gain or human praise and who thereby cause the weak to stumble (see Mark 9:42; 11:17; Luke 16:15).

Reflection and Application (12:38–40)

Hearing this stern admonition, one might wonder how it applies to the marks of status and prestige that accompany positions of prominence today, both in the Church and in the world—distinctive dress, respectful greetings, places of honor at religious and civil functions. Jesus' warning is similar to his pronouncement on wealth in 10:23–25. He does not say that signs of esteem are necessarily wrong in themselves, but that they are *spiritually dangerous*. It is all too easy to begin to enjoy them, to consider oneself entitled to them, to subtly encourage them and seek them, and even to use them to take advantage of others. In that case one has ceased serving God and begun to serve oneself.

10. France, *Mark*, 491–92.

The Widow's Offering (12:41–44)

[41]He sat down opposite the treasury and observed how the crowd put money into the treasury. Many rich people put in large sums. [42]A poor widow also came and put in two small coins worth a few cents. [43]Calling his disciples to himself, he said to them, "Amen, I say to you, this poor widow put in more than all the other contributors to the treasury. [44]For they have all contributed from their surplus wealth, but she, from her poverty, has contributed all she had, her whole livelihood."

OT: Ps 68:6; Isa 29:19; Zeph 2:3
NT: Luke 6:20; James 2:5. // Luke 21:1–4
Catechism: love for the poor, 2443–49; giving to the Church, 1351, 2043

After denouncing the counterfeit piety of the scribes who "devour the houses   **12:41** of widows" (v. 40), Jesus now shows his disciples an example of true piety, on the part of a widow. The **treasury** probably refers to thirteen trumpet-shaped donation chests that stood in the temple precincts, each labeled for its different purpose.[11] Jesus observes **how the crowd put money** (literally, "copper") into them. All money was metal coinage, and the **large sums** donated by the **rich** would have clanked handsomely as they were thrown into the chests. The effect would be similar to the ostentation of the scribes described above (12:38–40).

The **poor widow** who comes along is an example of the *anawim* (lowly ones)   **12:42** often mentioned in the Old Testament, the poor and afflicted who find their joy in God alone (Isa 29:19; 61:1; Zeph 2:3). Widows had no inheritance rights in ancient Israel, and usually had to rely on their children, male relatives, or charity for survival. Though often oppressed by the powerful, they are promised protection and vindication by God (Ps 68:6; 72:4; Jer 49:11). Jesus observes how this widow donates to the house of God **two small coins** (*lepta*), the smallest Jewish coins in circulation, each worth one four-hundredth of a shekel. Mark explains for his Roman readers that two *lepta* are equivalent to one *quadrans*, the smallest Roman coin (translated as **a few cents**). That the widow gave *two* suggests that she did not spare even what she could justifiably have kept for herself. The rich had drawn attention to themselves with their noisy donations, but Jesus' attention is drawn to this lowly widow.

Jesus calls **his disciples to himself**—Mark's signal that important instruction   **12:43–44** is about to take place—and makes a solemn declaration: **this poor widow put**

11. See the Mishnah, *Sheqalim* 6.5.

in more than all the other contributors. One can imagine the disciples' jaws dropping, as they had when Jesus declared the danger of riches (10:25–26). Had not the wealthy contributed far more toward the adornment and maintenance of the temple? Was not this woman's donation practically worthless, so insignificant as to be beneath mentioning? Jesus explains: God measures the gifts given him on a basis totally different from human calculations. He looks at the inner motives of the heart (see 1 Sam 16:7; Luke 16:15). The others had **contributed from their surplus**,[12] but this woman contributed **from her poverty**. The others were content to give God some of their overflow, having provided sufficiently for themselves—and impress other people to boot. But this destitute woman had given God what she could not afford, **all she had, her whole livelihood**. She had given not out of her surplus but out of her *substance*. Her gift meant that she would have to rely on God even to provide her next meal. Such reckless generosity parallels the self-emptying generosity of God himself, who did not hold back from us even his beloved Son (12:6). She is an exemplar of "the poor" who are blessed by God (see Matt 5:6; Luke 6:20) because their whole treasure is not in earthly possessions but in God. These words of praise for an impoverished widow are the last words spoken by the Lord in the temple of the old covenant.

Some commentators have raised the question whether Jesus' words should be interpreted more as a lament for the temple authorities' exploitation of the poor than as a praise of the widow's generosity. In the very next passage Jesus will prophesy the temple's doom (Mark 13:2). Does he disapprove of the woman contributing her meager life savings to a lost cause? Is he implying that the money would have been better spent on her own needs than on a religious edifice? These interpretations miss the point. The woman's plight does reflect the unscrupulous greed and callous disregard for the poor of which the temple authorities were guilty (see 11:17). But Jesus' focus is on her, not on them. He implicitly equates her gift to the house of God with a gift to God himself, a gift that outweighs all the others and causes him to marvel.

Reflection and Application (12:41–44)

Jesus' comments on the destitute widow are an example of the divine logic that overturns human ways of thinking. Who looked like pillars of the temple that day? Surely it was the well-to-do who helped make possible the splendid

---

12. The NAB adds the word "wealth," but the context suggests that Jesus is not speaking only of the wealthy, but of "all" the contributors other than the poor widow.

adornment of Herod's renovated temple. But it was different in the eyes of Jesus. Who contributes most to the flourishing of the Church today? Perhaps it is those who are overlooked and insignificant in human terms. This point brings to mind the story of the third-century martyr St. Lawrence, who was archdeacon of Rome and distributor of the Church's alms. In 258, by decree of the emperor, the pope and six deacons were beheaded, leaving Lawrence the ranking Church official in Rome. The city prefect summoned Lawrence and demanded that he hand over the treasures of the Church. Lawrence responded that the Church was indeed very rich, and asked for a little time to gather its treasures. He then went all over the city seeking out the poor and infirm. On the third day, he gathered together a great crowd of orphans, widows, and people who were lame, blind, maimed, or suffering various diseases, and invited the prefect to come and see "the wondrous riches of our God." The prefect was furious; in a rage he ordered Lawrence to be put to death on a gridiron over a slow fire. Lawrence is honored as one of the great martyrs of the early Church.

The Beginning of the End

Mark 13:1–37

Chapter 13 is one of the most difficult passages to interpret in Mark—and in the entire New Testament. It is often called the †eschatological or end-times discourse because Jesus here speaks of the "last things" (Greek *eschata*).[1] But what events or time period precisely is meant? Is it the events surrounding the destruction of Jerusalem that would occur just a few decades later? If so, what are we to make of the cosmic upheavals and glorious coming of the Son of Man in verses 24–27? Or is it referring to the end of the world? Then what are we to make of the statement that "this generation will not pass away until all these things have taken place" (v. 30)? Did Mark, or Jesus, mistakenly assume that Jesus' coming in glory would take place within a few short years?

These and other thorny interpretive questions have led some commentators to dismiss the discourse as an awkward fusion of sayings of Jesus with various elements from Jewish and early Christian sources. But this approach overlooks clues that Mark himself gives as to the exceptional importance of this discourse and its strategic role in the Gospel. First, it is the longest discourse in the Gospel, a kind of farewell discourse in which Jesus gives his final words of instruction and consolation for his disciples prior to his departure (as in John 14–16). Second, it is placed in a key position between Jesus' prophetic judgment on the temple (chaps. 11–12) and the passion narrative (chaps. 14–15). Finally, the discourse is framed by two episodes in which women offer generous gifts at great personal cost, one for the temple (12:41–44), the other for Jesus (14:3–9),

---

1. Although the term *eschata* does not appear in Mark 13, there are references to the "end" (*telos*) in vv. 7 and 13.

confirming the link between the earthly temple and the new temple "not made with hands" that God is establishing in Jesus (see 14:58).[2]

Part of the key to interpreting the discourse properly is to read it in light of its biblical background, since Jesus' words are brimming over with echoes and allusions to the prophets, especially Daniel. Moreover, Jesus speaks in the †typological manner of the prophets: that is, he sees God acting in history according to a pattern by which earlier events point forward to and help disclose the meaning of later events.[3] He thus weaves together images referring to the end of the temple and the old covenant worship with images referring to the end of his life and, finally, the end of human history. The discourse must be read with a kind of telescopic vision, focusing now on the near events lying within a generation, now on the far events to come at an unknown time. The former are the prelude, sign, and interpretative key to the latter.

The Doomed Temple (13:1–4)

---

[1]As he was making his way out of the temple area one of his disciples said to him, "Look, teacher, what stones and what buildings!" [2]Jesus said to him, "Do you see these great buildings? There will not be one stone left upon another that will not be thrown down."

[3]As he was sitting on the Mount of Olives opposite the temple area, Peter, James, John, and Andrew asked him privately, [4]"Tell us, when will this happen, and what sign will there be when all these things are about to come to an end?"

OT: 1 Kings 9:6–8; Jer 26:18; Dan 9:26; Mic 3:9–12
NT: // Matt 24:1–3; Luke 21:5–7
Catechism: Jesus and the temple, 583–86

Having delivered his prophetic indictment of the temple and its authorities **13:1** (11:11–12:44), Jesus leaves the **temple area** for the last time. The Lord has come to his temple (Mal 3:1) and has found its leadership corrupt, hard-hearted, and spiritually bankrupt. But **his disciples** are not yet aware of the import of this divine visitation. As they exit the precincts, one of them takes occasion to marvel at the grandeur of the edifice. The second temple, built in 516 BC and

---

2. See Timothy C. Gray, *The Temple in the Gospel of Mark: A Study in Its Narrative Role* (Tübingen: Mohr Siebeck, 2008), 100–102.

3. The Jews' return from exile in Babylon, for example, is a new exodus (Isa 41:17–20; 43:16–17); the Messiah would be a new David (Isa 9:5–6); God would make a new covenant (Jer 31:31). The prophets continually present God's past salvific deeds as the prototype and pattern for his future acts.

Jesus' Love for the Temple

LIVING TRADITION

The Catechism observes, "Jesus venerated the Temple by going up to it for the Jewish feasts of pilgrimage, and with a jealous love he loved this dwelling of God among men. The Temple prefigures his own mystery. When he announces its destruction, it is as a manifestation of his own execution and of the entry into a new age in the history of salvation, when his Body would be the definitive Temple" (593).

later renovated by Herod the Great, was indeed a spectacular feat of ancient architecture (see sidebar on p. 224). Its façade of white marble was adorned with dazzling gold. The retaining walls of the massive temple plaza rested on blocks of limestone so huge that archeologists are still unable to explain how they were moved into place. Some of them measure over forty feet in length and weigh over five hundred tons (the largest stone of the Egyptian pyramids, in comparison, weighs eleven tons). The eastern wall of the platform towered more than three hundred feet in height. Jewish pilgrims and converts from all over the empire were in awe at the sight. Few things on earth looked more permanent and indestructible than the temple.

13:2   Jesus' reply must have come as a shock: **There will not be one stone left upon another**.[4] This grim prophecy expresses in plain words what was already implied by the withered fig tree (11:20). Jesus is echoing the Old Testament prophecies of doom pronounced over the first temple before it was destroyed in 587 BC. Then too the temple's demise was the divine punishment for the corruption of its leadership (Mic 3:9–12; see 1 Kings 9:6–8; Jer 26:18). Centuries later, after the temple had been rebuilt, the prophet Daniel foretold that it would again be destroyed—and that this would happen at the time when "an anointed" (messiah) would be cut down (Dan 9:26).

13:3   The end times discourse takes place on the **Mount of Olives** as Jesus and his disciples gaze west across the Kidron Valley at the magnificent temple, a mere five hundred yards away. This setting evokes Ezekiel's prophecy that "the glory of the LORD," his holy presence, would depart from the temple and come

---

4. Some scholars hold that this is a prophecy after the fact (*ex eventu*), which the early Christians projected back onto the lips of Jesus. But there is no solid evidence to support this theory. Even for those skeptical of prophecy, Jesus' word stands within the long tradition of biblical warnings of future calamities, including the destruction of the temple. Moreover, the discourse lacks details about the actual event, such as the demolition by fire, which the early Christians could easily have included.

to rest on the Mount of Olives (Ezek 11:23). The Mount of Olives is also the site of God's victory over his enemies on the last day, according to Zechariah (Zech 14:4).

Only Jesus' closest disciples, the four fishermen who have been with him the 13:4 longest (see 1:16–20), are privy to this discourse. In response to Jesus' prophecy, they ask him a twofold question. They recognize that the ruin of the temple would not be an isolated event but part of a series of events (**these things**) signaling the end of the present age of history. The verb for **come to an end** could also be translated "fulfilled" (JB, NIV) or "accomplished" (RSV, NRSV).

The Birth Pangs (13:5–8)

---

[5]Jesus began to say to them, "See that no one deceives you. [6]Many will come in my name saying, 'I am he,' and they will deceive many. [7]When you hear of wars and reports of wars do not be alarmed; such things must happen, but it will not yet be the end. [8]Nation will rise against nation and kingdom against kingdom. There will be earthquakes from place to place and there will be famines. These are the beginnings of the labor pains.

OT: Isa 19:2; 29:6; Jer 51:45–47; Ezek 5:12
NT: John 16:21. // Matt 24:4–8; Luke 21:8–11

Jesus begins by responding to the disciples' second question, regarding the 13:5 signs of the end; he will take up the first question, "When?" in verse 28. He gives a series of warnings about what to expect in the difficult times ahead. The verb **see** (*blepō*)—elsewhere translated "watch out" (8:15) or "beware" (12:38)—is the keyword of this discourse (repeated in vv. 9, 23, 33), just as "hear" was the keyword of the "Sermon on the Sea" (4:1–34). The disciples are to be constantly alert to the signs of the times around them and on guard against being deceived.

Jesus begins to elaborate on his prophecy by foretelling a threefold series of 13:6 tribulations. First, **many will come in my name**, that is, deceivers will come invoking the authority of Jesus for their false teaching. They will seek to draw attention to themselves rather than to him, **saying, "I am he,"** which could mean, "I am Jesus," or in a more general sense, "I am the one you should follow and give your unconditional allegiance to." Later in the discourse Jesus will speak more specifically of messianic pretenders and false prophets (v. 22). The warning that they will **deceive many** highlights the need for vigilance and careful discernment of those who claim to speak or act in the name of Jesus.

13:7–8   Second, there will be **wars and reports of wars**. In Jewish †apocalyptic literature wars and strife were a standard part of descriptions of end-time events.[5] For the early Christians it would have been natural to conclude that the disastrous Jewish revolt against Rome, which began in AD 66, was a signal that the end had come. But Jesus' words are both a reassurance and a warning not to anticipate the end prematurely. That such things **must happen** is a word of consolation: everything will take place according to God's sovereign plan, so there is no reason for panic or dismay. Jesus had used the same word "must" (*dei*) when prophesying his own suffering and death (8:31).

Finally, there will be calamities such as **earthquakes** and **famines** in various places. A severe famine did occur in Palestine in AD 46–48 (Acts 11:28); an earthquake destroyed Laodicea in 60; a volcano severely damaged Pompeii in lava in 62. Such natural disasters were often foretold by the prophets as manifestations of God's judgment (Isa 29:6; Jer 11:22; Ezek 5:12; 38:19–20). Again, it would be natural to take these frightening events as signs that the end has come. But Jesus gives a different rule of interpretation: they are only **the beginnings of the labor pains**. In the Old Testament, birth pangs were a common image for the sufferings of God's people, especially the sufferings that precede the coming of the messiah (Jer 30:5–9; Mic 5:2–4). This image suggests that, like the pains of a woman in labor, the severe trials preceding the end will come in successive waves, each more distressing than the last, but ultimately leading to a joy that far surpasses the pain. They are but the prelude to a new life that is not yet seen (see John 16:21).[6]

The Coming Persecution (13:9–13)

[9]"Watch out for yourselves. They will hand you over to the courts. You will be beaten in synagogues. You will be arraigned before governors and kings because of me, as a witness before them. [10]But the gospel must first be preached to all nations. [11]When they lead you away and hand you over, do not worry beforehand about what you are to say. But say whatever will be given to you at that hour. For it will not be you who are speaking but the holy Spirit. [12]Brother will hand over brother to death, and the father his child; children will rise up against parents and have them put to death.

5. See Dan 2:36–45; 9:26; 11:40; and the extrabiblical *4 Ezra* 13.31–32. Similar prophecies occur in Isa 19:2; Jer 51:45–47.
6. Brant Pitre, *Jesus, the Tribulation, and the End of the Exile* (Tübingen: Mohr Siebeck; Grand Rapids: Baker Academic, 2005), 231.

¹³**You will be hated by all because of my name. But the one who perseveres to the end will be saved.**

OT: Mic 7:6–7
NT: John 15:26–27. // Matt 10:17–22; 24:9–14; Luke 12:11–12; 21:12–19
Catechism: keeping watch, 2612, 2849; persecution of the Church, 675–77, 1816

Jesus now speaks more specifically of the trials his own followers will endure. **13:9–10**
He repeats the warning of verse 5: **Watch out for yourselves.** Jesus' disciples must be aware that part of their role in this world is to be as defendants on trial because of their faithfulness to the gospel. Their sufferings are described in terms that directly parallel Jesus' passion. Like Jesus, they will be "handed over" (see 9:31; 10:33; 14:41) and suffer persecution by both religious authorities (**courts** and **synagogues**) and civil authorities (**governors** and **kings**). The courts (literally, sanhedrins) were local Jewish tribunals that had authority to punish offenders, for instance by beatings or scourgings. Paul himself inflicted such punishments before his conversion, and endured them afterward (Acts 26:11; 2 Cor 11:24–25). The secular authorities could include Roman provincial rulers such as Felix and Festus, before whom Paul was **arraigned** (Acts 23–25), and Roman client kings such as Herod Agrippa I, who violently persecuted the Church (Acts 12:1–4).

But in God's providence, such ordeals will be the very means by which Christians will bear **witness** (*martyrion*) to Christ and cause **the gospel** to be spread throughout the world. This is precisely what occurred in the early Church (see Acts 8:1–5; 20:24; Phil 1:12–14), fulfilling the Old Testament promise that "the nations" would come to faith in the God of Israel (Isa 56:3–8; 66:18–23). It is not only by their words of proclamation but by their sufferings that Christians make Jesus known and present in the world (see 2 Cor 4:8–11). By saying that the gospel **must first be preached to all nations** (or "all Gentiles"), Jesus suggests that God's plan will not be complete until the full number of the Gentiles is gathered in (see Rom 11:25). He does not say that all will *accept* the gospel, but that the gospel must be preached in all lands. Mark has already anticipated the Church's mission to the Gentiles by recounting Jesus' ministry in pagan territory. But now for the first time there is a clear indication that the Church's mission is universal. Until that mission is complete the end is not yet at hand.

In undergoing tribulations, Jesus' followers are to be serene and confident be- **13:11**
cause it is not they who have to defend themselves but the **holy Spirit**[7]—the same

---

7. The NAB does not capitalize "holy," presumably to indicate that Holy Spirit was not yet a fixed title for the Third Person of the Trinity.

You Will Be Hated by All

BIBLICAL BACKGROUND

The intense hostility to Christians described in Mark 13:13 is exemplified in an account by Tacitus, a Roman historian. Tacitus reports that the Emperor Nero attempted to shift blame off himself and onto Christians for the great fire of Rome in AD 64: "Nero fastened the guilt and inflicted the most exquisite tortures on a class hated for their abominations, called Christians by the populace. Christus, from whom the name had its origin, suffered the extreme penalty during the reign of Tiberius at the hands of one of our procurators, Pontius Pilate, and a most mischievous superstition, thus checked for the moment, again broke out not only in Judea, the first source of the evil, but even in Rome, where all things hideous and shameful from every part of the world find their centre and become popular. Accordingly, an arrest was first made of all who pleaded guilty; then, upon their information, an immense multitude was convicted, not so much of the crime of firing the city, as of hatred against mankind. Mockery of every sort was added to their deaths. Covered with the skins of beasts, they were torn by dogs and perished, or were nailed to crosses, or were doomed to the flames and burnt, to serve as a nightly illumination, when daylight had expired. Nero offered his gardens for the spectacle, and was exhibiting a show in the circus. . . . Hence, even for criminals who deserved extreme and exemplary punishment, there arose a feeling of compassion; for it was not, as it seemed, for the public good, but to glut one man's cruelty, that they were being destroyed."[a]

a. Tacitus, *Annals* 15.44, trans. Alfred John Church and William Jackson Brodribb (New York: Random House, 1942).

Spirit who inspired the biblical authors (12:36). The Gospel of John expresses a similar promise: the Holy Spirit is the Paraclete—advocate, counselor, defense attorney—who will strengthen Christians when they are under pressure from the world (John 15:26; 16:8). This is Mark's only mention of the Spirit's role in the life of Jesus' disciples, and it is a prophetic role—the Spirit himself will speak through the mouth of Christians on trial. By referring to **that hour** Mark again associates the tribulations the disciples will undergo with Jesus' own passion (see Mark 14:35, 37, 41); their suffering is a participation in his. The disciples are not to **worry beforehand** about what to say, since God will give them the right words at the right time. This was a consoling promise for the early Christians, for whom the prospect of a public trial could be terrifying, especially for those who were simple, uneducated peasants or slaves (see Acts 4:13; 1 Cor 1:26).

13:12   Far more painful than any government persecution would be betrayal by one's own family members. For the third time Jesus speaks of his followers

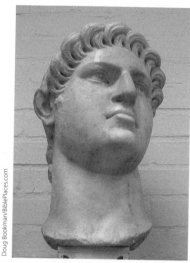
Fig. 13. Caesar Nero

being "handed over" as he will be handed over, that is, betrayed. **Brother** could refer to either a fellow Christian or a blood relative. Hostility to the gospel or fear of persecution will override even the most intimate of bonds, as people **hand over** to **death** their own siblings, **children**, or **parents**. Jesus' words echo a prophecy of Micah, which affirms God's faithfulness in the midst of such family strife (Mic 7:6–7; see Matt 10:35). As Jesus himself suffered misunderstanding and estrangement from his family (Mark 3:21), so his disciples will from theirs. During the first major persecution of the Church, under the Emperor Nero in AD 64, some Christians did succumb to threats or torture and became informants, leading to the arrest and death of others.

Jesus' followers cannot expect to be admired and applauded by the world (see John 15:18–19). On the contrary, the disciples will be **hated by all** and persecuted because of their identification with Jesus. The abuse heaped on them is really intended for him (see 1 Pet 4:12–14).[8] Because their suffering is a participation in his, they too can have confidence that their vindication by God is at hand. Mark's first readers could take courage from Jesus' example and the promise that whoever **perseveres to the end will be saved.**

13:13

Reflection and Application (13:9–13)

Jesus' promise that Christians would be "given what to say" in the hour of trial has been fulfilled quite literally on many occasions, even in our own times. One example is Nijolė Sadūnaitė, a Lithuanian arrested in 1974 for distributing clandestine Catholic literature. As the young woman stood trial, without legal representation, before men skilled in interrogation techniques, her defense so stung them that they blanched and hung their heads in shame. Among her words of testimony were the following: "This is the happiest day of my life. . . . I have been accorded the enviable task, the honorable fate, not only to struggle for human rights, but also to be sentenced for them. My sentence will become triumph! My only regret is that I have been given so little opportunity to work

8. Lane, *Mark*, 464.

on behalf of man. I will joyfully go into slavery for others and I agree to die so that others may live. Today, as I approach the Eternal Truth, Jesus Christ, I remember His fourth beatitude: 'Blessed are they who thirst for justice, for they shall be satisfied.' . . . I would like to request the court to free from prisons, labor camps, and psychiatric hospitals all of those who fought for human rights and justice."[9] After this Spirit-inspired testimony, Sadūnaitė was sentenced to three years in a strict-regime Soviet labor camp and three years of exile. Her example is an encouragement to all Christians to ask the Spirit for boldness and clarity whenever we are called to give witness in unfriendly settings.

The Desolating Abomination (13:14–27)

[14]"When you see the desolating abomination standing where he should not (let the reader understand), then those in Judea must flee to the mountains, [15][and] a person on a housetop must not go down or enter to get anything out of his house, [16]and a person in a field must not return to get his cloak. [17]Woe to pregnant women and nursing mothers in those days. [18]Pray that this does not happen in winter. [19]For those times will have tribulation such as has not been since the beginning of God's creation until now, nor ever will be. [20]If the Lord had not shortened those days, no one would be saved; but for the sake of the elect whom he chose, he did shorten the days. [21]If anyone says to you then, 'Look, here is the Messiah! Look, there he is!' do not believe it. [22]False messiahs and false prophets will arise and will perform signs and wonders in order to mislead, if that were possible, the elect. [23]Be watchful! I have told it all to you beforehand.

> [24]"But in those days after that tribulation
>   the sun will be darkened,
>   and the moon will not give its light,
>   [25]and the stars will be falling from the sky,
>   and the powers in the heavens will be shaken.

[26]And then they will see 'the Son of Man coming in the clouds' with great power and glory, [27]and then he will send out the angels and gather [his] elect from the four winds, from the end of the earth to the end of the sky.

OT: 1 Macc 1:54–59; Isa 13:9–10; Dan 7:13–14; 9:27; 12:1; Joel 3
NT: 1 Thess 4:16–17; 2 Pet 2:1; 1 John 4:1. // Matt 24:15–31; Luke 17:23; 21:20–28
Catechism: the great tribulation, 675–77, 2642; Christ's coming in glory, 668–82

9. Nijolė Sadūnaitė, *A Radiance in the Gulag*, trans. Casimir Pugevicius and Marian Skabeikis (Manassas, VA: Trinity Communications, 1987), 58–60.

This part of the discourse is Jesus' most explicit and dramatic prophecy of future tribulation. It is no longer merely the beginning but the climax of the "labor pains" (v. 8). Jesus is using biblical imagery associated with divine judgment on the last day, "the day of the Lord." He is referring to the calamities that will accompany the destruction of the temple (v. 2), which will be the end of *a* world, the world of the old covenant with its old order of worship. But indirectly these disasters are portrayed as a foreshadowing of the final tribulations that will occur at the end of history.

The **desolating abomination** is an expression from Daniel (9:27; 11:31; 12:11), **13:14** where it alludes to the terrible sacrilege committed by the Syrian ruler Antiochus IV Epiphanes in 167 BC.[10] After plundering Jerusalem, this infamous tyrant erected an idol of the Greek god Zeus on the altar of sacrifice in the temple (see 1 Macc 1:31, 54–59). A *desolating* abomination is one so egregious that it leads to the utter destruction of the temple and city, turning it into a desolate wasteland. Here that tragic event of the past is viewed as a foreshadowing of the final desecration of the temple[11] that will lead to its destruction by the pagan armies of Rome (see Matt 24:15; Luke 21:20). **Standing where he should not**[12] is precisely in the temple sanctuary, the holy place where the living God is worshipped. The masculine "he" suggests that this evil will be carried out by an individual, perhaps a military general, who is a kind of anti-Messiah figure (see 2 Thess 2:3–4).

Let the reader understand is probably intended as part of Jesus' discourse, calling his disciples to pay close attention to hidden clues in the book of Daniel (see Matt 24:15).[13] According to Daniel, both the sacrilege and the ensuing destruction, although carried out by wicked men, are a consequence of the sins of God's people (see Dan 9:24). But God allows these disasters so that his people can be "refined, purified, and tested" (Dan 12:10). Jesus is hinting that the appearance of a horrendous sacrilege will signal the onset of a most devastating period of tribulation by which God's people will be severely tried.

10. Daniel's oracle cannot be *fully* explained in reference to the sacrilege of 167 BC, because it refers to the total destruction of the temple and city, which did not occur at that time.

11. It is not known precisely to which first-century event the desolating abomination could refer. Scholars have proposed the following: (1) The Emperor Caligula's attempt to erect a massive statue of himself in the temple in AD 40; however, his orders were never carried out. (2) The Zealots' takeover of the temple as their military headquarters and the appointment of their own high priest in AD 67, leading to numerous murders among Jewish factions within the temple. (3) The Roman general Titus's entry into the ruined temple amid idolatrous acclamations in AD 70; however, this occurred too late for people to carry out Jesus' warning to flee. The second possibility seems to be the most plausible.

12. Compare RSV, NRSV, JB, NJB, "set up where it ought not to be." The NAB correctly translates the masculine participle using "he."

13. Other commentators hold that this phrase is *Mark's* aside to readers of his Gospel. For arguments for the reference to Daniel, see Pitre, *Jesus, the Tribulation, and the End of the Exile*, 309–13.

13:15–16   Jesus then instructs his disciples how to conduct themselves when they see these ominous words fulfilled. They should avoid every temptation to wait out the conflict or to defend the city in a misguided hope of military success, since the outcome of utter destruction is inevitable. Like people fleeing a burning building, they must leave behind all their possessions and evacuate as quickly as possible. These instructions echo the Old Testament theme of flight from a city doomed to destruction, as Lot and his wife fled Sodom (Gen 19:15–17; see 1 Macc 2:28; Jer 6:1–25). According to the ancient Church historian Eusebius, Christians in Judea did in fact follow this advice closely during the war of AD 66–70. When the Roman armies surrounded Jerusalem they fled across the Jordan to the region of Pella, thereby escaping the slaughter.[14]

13:17–18   The announcement of **woe to pregnant women and nursing mothers** is an expression of grief at the fact that, as often happens in times of war and tragedy, the brunt of suffering will be borne by women and children. The calamities of **those days** will affect not only the wicked but also the innocent (as in Jer 16:3; Hosea 14:1). For this reason, the disciples are to **pray that this does not happen in winter**, when such suffering would be greatest. The very fact that they are enjoined to pray implies that their prayers can have a real effect in limiting the severity of the tribulation.

13:19–20   Jesus again draws on the book of Daniel, characterizing the final tribulation as worse than any human suffering before or since (Dan 12:1; see Jer 30:7; Ezek 5:9). However grievous the ordeals of war, natural disasters, persecution, and family strife mentioned above (13:7–13), they will not compare to the suffering of **those times**. It will be so dreadful that if God had not cut short his timetable, **no one** would survive. "No one" is literally "no flesh," echoing a refrain in the story of the great flood (Gen 6:12–13, 17, 19 RSV).

Yet in the midst of this dire forecast there is an assurance of God's mercy. The **elect** is a central biblical theme, referring to those God has sovereignly chosen as his own apart from anything they deserve—first Israel (Deut 10:15), and now the Church (John 15:16; 1 Pet 2:9). Jesus' disciples are this chosen remnant for whose sake God has already determined to make the period of calamity shorter than the wicked deserve.

13:21   Part of the tribulation will be the confusion caused by impostors making false messianic claims. Jesus instructs his disciples in no uncertain terms not to **believe** such claims. The principle is simple: If you have to rely on someone else's purported sighting of the **Messiah**, it is not the Messiah. As Jesus will

14. Eusebius, *Ecclesiastical History* 3.5.3.

shortly make clear, his true coming will be absolutely unmistakable (v. 26). The experience of the early Church, as of the Church today, bears out the need for this warning (see 2 Thess 2:1–3).

Not only false alarms but imposters, **false messiahs and false prophets** (lit-   **13:22–23**
erally, pseudo-Christs and pseudoprophets) **will arise**. They will even perform **signs and wonders** to validate their claims. But as the Old Testament already made clear, signs and wonders can be counterfeited and are not to be taken in themselves as divine credentials (Exod 7:11–12; Deut 13:2–4; see 2 Thess 2:9; Rev 13:13–14). Jesus chided those who would make their faith in him dependent on signs and wonders (Mark 8:11–13; John 4:48). The tribulation will be a time of testing (see Deut 12:1–3), in which the temptation to follow such wonder-working impostors will be great. Jesus' urgent call to vigilance underlines the real possibility that even **the elect** can be deluded if they are not on their guard. Several messianic pretenders did in fact appear in the volatile atmosphere of first-century Palestine (see Acts 5:35–39).[15] False prophets have been a perennial problem in both Israel (Deut 18:20–22; Jer 29:8–9; Acts 13:6) and the Church (Matt 7:15; 2 Pet 2:1; 1 John 4:1). Jesus again exhorts his listeners, **Be watchful!** Through his discourse to the four disciples (13:3), he has provided his followers in every age with the information needed to endure the difficult times ahead.

Finally, Jesus comes to the climactic event that will occur after the **tribula-**   **13:24–25**
tion already mentioned but **in those days**, that is, in the same period of unparalleled distress that follows the desolating abomination (see vv. 17, 19–20). Using biblical imagery Jesus describes cosmic upheavals: the **sun** and **moon** will be darkened, **stars** will fall, and the heavenly powers **will be shaken**. In the prophets such heavenly disturbances symbolize the earth-shattering impact of God's judgment upon a rebellious city or empire.[16] But what do they signify here?

On one level, Jesus is giving a symbolic portrayal of the fall of Jerusalem and the temple. For the Jews the temple was a microcosm of the universe. Images of the stars and constellations were embroidered on the temple veils; the seven lights of the menorah represented the sun, the moon, and the five known planets. The temple was the center of the universe, the meeting point of heaven and earth. Thus its destruction would be a cataclysm of cosmic proportions.[17]

---

15. See also Josephus, *Antiquities* 17.261–85; 20.167–72.

16. See Isa 13:9–13; Ezek 32:7; Joel 2:10–11; 3:3–4; Amos 8:9.

17. The symbolic language does not preclude the possibility of literal cosmic portents, which the ancients interpreted as signs of a cataclysmic event in human history. Josephus describes a number of such portents preceding the fall of Jerusalem (*Jewish War* 6.288–300).

The Disaster of AD 70

BIBLICAL BACKGROUND

The Jewish War of AD 66–70, culminating in the destruction of the temple and Holy City, was one of the most devastating calamities in world history. To crush the Jewish revolt that had begun in 66 the Roman armies under Titus besieged Jerusalem. During the five-month siege a terrible famine raged in the city. Corpses were stacked like cordwood in the streets, and mothers ate their own children to preserve their strength. The Jewish armies were hopelessly divided into factions, killing one another. Because some Jews had swallowed gold coins, others disemboweled members of rival factions, looking for money. Anyone caught by the Romans was crucified, until thousands of crucified bodies encircled the city so the defenders could watch their agony.

After breaching the walls the Roman legions ransacked and burned the city. Many were burned alive. Infants were thrown to their deaths from the city walls. The Romans used fire to undermine the foundations of the temple walls, then tumbled the huge stones into a heap of rubble. The temple burned on the ninth of the Hebrew month of Av (late August), the same date as the destruction of the first temple, according to Jewish tradition. All that remains today is part of the walls that supported the temple mount, including what is called the Western Wall. Hundreds of thousands of Jews perished in the slaughter; thousands more were sold into slavery. Of the few who survived, nearly all were dispersed outside Palestine.

In this sense Jesus' words were fulfilled in AD 70, when the Roman legions under Titus reduced the temple to charred rubble and permanently ended the old covenant sacrifices.

But Mark hints at other levels of meaning. Jesus' words were also fulfilled in part at his crucifixion, when the sun was darkened at midday (15:33).[18] Mark has already suggested that the temple prefigures the mystery of Jesus himself, the new and definitive dwelling place of God among his people (see on 9:7; 12:10–11). Jesus' bodily death portends the destruction of the earthly temple, bringing the transition from the former age to the new and final age of salvation history.

Ultimately the imagery of heavenly chaos—a kind of undoing of God's work of creation (see Gen 1:14–18)—points to the end of the world (see 2 Pet 3:10; Rev 21:1). For Mark these various levels of meaning are closely interconnected. The end time tribulations begin in Jesus' own passion, which signals the end

18. Peter's Pentecost speech (Acts 2:17–21) apparently interprets this imagery in the same way, that is, in reference to Jesus' passion and the turn of the ages that it brings about.

Fig. 14. Panel from the Arch of Titus in Rome, depicting Roman soldiers triumphantly carrying off the spoils of the temple after the conquest of Jerusalem in AD 70.

of the age of the old covenant and ultimately the end of the universe that will follow the final upheavals at the close of history.

The shattering events described so far are the necessary prelude to God's ultimate victory. †**Son of Man** is the term Jesus characteristically uses to refer to himself, evoking Daniel's prophecy of "one like a son of man" who comes into God's presence on the **clouds** and is given everlasting dominion and **glory** (Dan 7:13–14). Jesus has already invoked this prophecy (Mark 8:38–9:1) and will explicitly apply it to himself in his trial before the Sanhedrin (14:62). Again Mark telescopes near and far events to show that they are inextricably linked. On one level the **coming** of the Son of Man is Jesus' ascension and enthronement as king at the Father's right hand (16:19; Acts 1:9), manifested in the Church and visible to the eyes of faith (see Heb 2:9). Ultimately it is his coming at the end of time, when evil will be vanquished once and for all and Jesus will be seen by all in his full power and glory, the glory that was revealed to three disciples at his Transfiguration (Mark 9:2–3). **13:26**

God's **elect**, as in verses 20 and 22, are his chosen remnant, those who have remained faithful to him through the period of great distress—both the distress of the generation following Jesus and the tribulations of the whole age of the Church, culminating at the end of history. In the Old Testament, the **four winds** designate the four points of the compass, the distant places to which the people of Israel were scattered in exile but from which God promised to bring them back (Ezek 37:9, 21; see Deut 30:3–4; Isa 11:12). Jesus is speaking **13:27**

269

of the fulfillment of this long-standing hope of Israel: the end of the exile, when the dispersed people of God would be regathered from among the nations and live under the reign of God and his Messiah. The word for †**angels** (*angeloi*) also means "messengers," and on one level Jesus is referring to his apostles, who will bring the message of the gospel to the ends of the earth, gathering in the new people of God. But he is also referring to the angels who will gather the righteous into God's kingdom at the end of time (see Matt 13:30, 38–43). **From the end of the earth to the end of the sky** embraces all creation. The worldwide proclamation of the gospel, leading to faith in Christ and ultimately to eternal life, is the true and final restoration of Israel.

Reading the Fig Leaves (13:28–31)

> [28]"Learn a lesson from the fig tree. When its branch becomes tender and sprouts leaves, you know that summer is near. [29]In the same way, when you see these things happening, know that he is near, at the gates. [30]Amen, I say to you, this generation will not pass away until all these things have taken place. [31]Heaven and earth will pass away, but my words will not pass away.

OT: Isa 40:8; 51:6
NT: Mark 8:38; 9:1; Rev 22:12, 20. // Matt 24:32–36; Luke 21:29–33
Catechism: Christ's coming in glory, 673–74; Christ's human knowledge, 471–74

13:28–29 Jesus now returns to the first question asked him in verse 4—"When will this happen?"—but enigmatically. **Learn a lesson** (literally, "learn the parable") **from the fig tree**. This recalls the real-life parable of the withered fig tree (11:20), a symbol of the barren and doomed temple. Most trees in Palestine are evergreens, but the fig has an annual cycle of growing leaves and bearing fruit, marking the seasons of the year. It **sprouts leaves** in April, around the time of Passover—just at the time Jesus is giving this discourse (see 11:13)—and is a sure sign that **summer**, or harvest time, is around the corner.[19] Jesus advises his disciples to read the signs of the times; when they see the events he has just described begin to take place, they should be aware that the end is close at hand. **He is near** could also be translated "it is near," and thus could refer to the destruction of the temple about which the disciples had questioned him (13:2–4). But it could also allude to Jesus' coming in glory (13:26), since **at the**

19. Summer (*theros*) is the time of harvest (*therismos*) in Palestine. The harvest is a common biblical image for eschatological judgment (see Isa 34:4–5; Joel 4:13–18; Matt 13:30, 39; Rev 14:15).

gates looks forward to his words about the disciples as "gatekeepers" waiting for their master to return (13:34).

With his formula of solemn assurance, **Amen, I say to you,** Jesus declares   13:30
that **this generation will not pass away until all these things have taken place.**
In traditional Jewish reckoning, a generation was forty years. And indeed, the events in the foreground of Jesus' discourse—the fall of the earthly temple and the cataclysmic transition from the former age to the new—did take place within forty years of his prophecy. Jesus is repeating his promise that the kingdom of God would come with power within the lifetime of his contemporaries (9:1).

Jesus reaffirms the utter trustworthiness of what he has said with an allusion   13:31
to Isa 40:8 and 51:6. Jesus identifies his own **words**, including the words of prophecy he has just uttered, with the word of God. His word is more enduring and reliable than the created universe itself. By speaking of the created universe "passing away" Jesus again links the tribulations he has just spoken about with the end of all things.

But was Jesus mistaken in placing these distinct events in such close proximity? Was he wrong to assume that the ruin of Jerusalem meant that his return in glory was imminent? The idea that Jesus, and much of the New Testament, erred in assuming that the second coming would happen soon has influenced much modern biblical interpretation. But this view fails to take into account the symbolic and figural way in which Jesus and the early Church interpreted history, in which past and future events both shed light on and are understood in light of Jesus and his paschal mystery. Jesus is not asserting that the end of history will come immediately, but rather that his passion, and with it the transition from the old covenant to the new, is the beginning of the end, the entrance into the final stage of God's plan that will culminate in a new heaven and a new earth. In that sense his coming in glory is "imminent" from the day of his ascension on (see Rev 22:20).

Be on the Watch (13:32–37)

[32]"But of that day or hour, no one knows, neither the angels in heaven, nor the Son, but only the Father. [33]Be watchful! Be alert! You do not know when the time will come. [34]It is like a man traveling abroad. He leaves home and places his servants in charge, each with his work, and orders the gatekeeper to be on the watch. [35]Watch, therefore; you do not know when the lord of the house is coming, whether in the evening, or at midnight, or

at cockcrow, or in the morning. ³⁶May he not come suddenly and find you sleeping. ³⁷What I say to you, I say to all: 'Watch!'"

OT: Lam 2:19; Ezek 3:17; Hab 2:1
NT: Matt 24:42–51; Luke 12:35–40; 21:34–36
Catechism: keeping watch, 2612, 2849; Christ's coming in glory, 668–82
Lectionary: First Sunday of Advent (Year B)

13:32   At this point there is a transition in the discourse. So far the events surrounding the fall of Jerusalem have been in the foreground of Jesus' words with the end of history in the background; now the end of history comes into the foreground. After declaring that the events described above would happen within a generation (v. 30) Jesus now says that **of that day or hour, no one knows.** What does "that day" refer to? The most direct meaning is the last day, the day of judgment foretold in the Old Testament (Amos 8:3–14; Zech 12:3–14; see Matt 24:36–42). But "that day" is also the day of Jesus' passion (Mark 2:20). Likewise, the "hour" is the time of the unexpected coming of the Son of Man as judge (13:26–27, 35; see Matt 24:50) but also the hour of the suffering of Jesus (Mark 14:35, 41) and of his disciples (13:11). Mark has again overlaid near and far events to reveal their close interconnection. The passion of Jesus is the beginning of the end of history. Just as the hour of Jesus' passion points to the future suffering of those who follow him, so the end of the temple and of old covenant worship points to the end of the world.

That moment, the culmination of salvation history, remains the Father's secret—it is known to **no one, neither the angels in heaven, nor the Son.** This list, in ascending order, places the Son above both angels and human beings. Yet as man, he too had to live in obedient and watchful faith, trusting in the Father's plan.

13:33   **Be watchful!** is the refrain that has been repeated throughout the discourse (vv. 5, 9, 23). This time Jesus adds, **Be alert!** (or "stay awake!"), as he will again urge the disciples during his agony in the garden (14:34). The fact that the disciples **do not know when the time will come** means that they are to live in a state of constant watchfulness. Although Jesus has not given them the exact timetable that they may have wanted, he has given them the clues that will enable them to be sufficiently prepared. God withholds the timetable because what he desires is not calculation but vigilance.

13:34–37   The parable of the **traveling** landlord, which is only in Mark (though variations are found in Matt 24:45–51; Luke 12:35–40), drives home this point. The man **places his servants in charge** (literally, gives his slaves authority). This scenario clearly points to Jesus and the Church.[20] Jesus has already delegated authority to his apostles (Mark 6:7; 10:42–44); now he speaks of his departure, when they will exercise his authority over the community he has founded. **Each** has been entrusted with **his work**, a unique service or ministry to carry out within the household of faith. The **gatekeeper**, referring to Peter who has greatest responsibility for vigilance (see 14:37; Luke 12:41–42), has an especially important duty: to perceive the master's return in time to prepare a suitable welcome.

Be on the watch (*grēgoreō*) is another verb that means to stay awake and be on the lookout, part of the duty of prophets (Lam 2:19; Ezek 3:17; Hab 2:1). Again Jesus emphasizes that they **do not know** when he is coming. **Lord** (Greek *kyrios*) refers to Jesus in his lordship over the **house** of God—both the temple of the old covenant and the Church of the new covenant. He may appear at any of the four divisions of the night, in Roman reckoning. Jesus is speaking of his sudden and unexpected coming at the end of time, when he will judge his disciples for how they have exercised their authority in the Church. But Mark also links this warning to Jesus' passion by structuring the passion narrative precisely in terms of these four night watches: **evening** (Mark 14:17), **midnight** (implied in 14:32–65), **cockcrow** (14:72), and **morning** (15:1). Jesus warns that he may **come suddenly** and find them **sleeping**—which is just what will happen during his agony in Gethsemane (14:37–41). To be asleep signifies spiritual torpor and self-indulgence (Rom 11:8; 1 Thess 5:6–8); to be awake is to be alive in faith (Rom 13:11; Eph 5:14). The trial in Gethsemane is the beginning of the trial that will last throughout the whole age of the Church, in which Jesus' followers are called to be constantly alert and attentive to the presence of their Lord.

The final verse affirms that his warning is directed not only at the four who are privy to this discourse (13:3), but to all his disciples for all time: **Watch!** There is no room for complacency in the Christian life.

---

20. The Church is often referred to as a house or household in the New Testament: Gal 6:10; Eph 2:19; 1 Tim 3:15; 2 Tim 2:20–21; 1 Pet 4:17.

The Hour of Decision

Mark 14:1–31

With the passion narrative (chaps. 14–15) Mark reaches the climax of his Gospel. He has prepared his readers for the events that are about to unfold, first by recounting the increasing hostility of the leaders of Israel toward Jesus, and Jesus' own prophecies of his passion (8:31; 9:31; 10:33–34). Chapter 11 recounted Jesus' messianic entry into Jerusalem and his cleansing of the temple, actions that directly precipitate his arrest and execution. Chapter 12 established the basis of Jesus' authority to carry out these actions: he is the beloved Son sent by the Father to gather the fruit of Israel. Finally, the end times discourse in chapter 13 provided an interpretive key to the passion by showing that it marks the transition from the former age to the new and definitive stage of salvation history, the stage that will be consummated at Jesus' coming in glory at the end of time.

In the passion narrative the four Gospels come closest to one another in their wording and chronology, showing the importance the early Church placed on the details of Jesus' sufferings. Mark, like the other three Evangelists, interprets the passion in light of the Old Testament, especially Isaiah's Suffering Servant poems and the psalms of the suffering just man. Without glossing over the agony of the passion, Mark suffuses his whole account with the light of the resurrection. All that he writes is meant to lead his readers to understand the deeper significance of this mystery: Who is this man who died on a cross under †Pontius Pilate? And what does his death have to do with me?

The Plot to Kill Jesus (14:1–2)

---

¹The Passover and the Feast of Unleavened Bread were to take place in two days' time. So the chief priests and the scribes were seeking a way to

arrest him by treachery and put him to death. ²They said, "Not during the
festival, for fear that there may be a riot among the people."

OT: Ps 31:13; 64:2; Jer 20:10
NT: Mark 11:18; 12:12. // Matt 26:1–5; Luke 22:1–2
Catechism: divisions among Jewish authorities concerning Jesus, 595–97
Lectionary: 14:1–15:47: Palm Sunday (Year B)

It is the third day of Jesus' visit to Jerusalem, the day that runs from Tuesday   14:1
evening to Wednesday evening of holy week. Mark notes the time precisely,
since the chronology of Jesus' passion was a matter of great importance for the
early Church. The combined feast of **Passover** and **Unleavened Bread** was the

---

The Passover and the Feast of Unleavened Bread

BIBLICAL BACKGROUND

The Passover is the great feast commemorating God's deliverance of
Israel from slavery in Egypt. The institution of the feast is recounted in
Exod 12, where God instructed Moses as to how the people should
annually celebrate his mighty act of redemption. Passover began
in the afternoon of the fourteenth of Nisan, when the lambs were
slaughtered in the temple. After sunset the lambs would be eaten
in the ceremonial Passover meal, the Seder. The Feast of Unleavened
Bread began with Passover and continued for a full week (like an
octave in the Christian liturgical calendar), during which the Israelites allowed no
trace of yeast in their homes.

The Passover (or Pasch) was meant not only to commemorate but to relive the
events of the exodus, making them present anew to each generation. The paschal
lamb recalled the slaughtered lambs whose blood the Israelites had put on their
doorposts, saving them from the angel of death (Exod 12:6–13). Unleavened
bread recalled the haste with which they departed from Egypt (Exod 12:15, 39);
bitter herbs evoked the bitterness of their bondage. When the temple was built,
the Passover became a pilgrimage feast: devout Jews traveled to Jerusalem each
year to celebrate it, since it was in the temple that the lambs were sacrificed. The
Passover was also a feast of hope for future liberation, recalling God's promise of
a new and greater exodus (Isa 52).

For the New Testament, Jesus' suffering, death, and resurrection is his Passover
or paschal mystery, the event that brings to fulfillment all that was prefigured in
the Passover. By curious coincidence, the Greek rendering of the Hebrew word for
Passover (*pascha*) is very similar to the Greek verb for suffer (*paschō*), highlighting
the link between the Passover and the passion.

greatest holy day of the old covenant, commemorating the exodus. Jesus' passion was to be the fulfillment of this event, God's definitive deliverance of his people from slavery to sin and death.

The **chief priests and the scribes**, along with the elders, were the religious authorities whom Jesus had prophesied would "hand him over" and condemn him to death (8:31; 10:33), and who have long been plotting his demise (3:6; 11:18; 12:12). Now they seek to put their plans into action. But they wish to do so **by treachery** so as to avoid an inflammatory confrontation with Jesus' supporters. It is a replay of the scheming of Israel's leaders of old against the prophet Jeremiah (Jer 18:18–20; 20:10). Treachery, or "deceit," was one of those evils that Jesus had said defile a person from within (Mark 7:21–23).

14:2   Ironically, the Passover is the one time when the religious authorities do *not* want to take action against Jesus, for fear of out-of-control popular reactions. **During the festival** the city's population swelled to three times its usual size and Jewish nationalism was at fever pitch. Yet at the Last Supper Jesus will deliberately associate this feast with the culmination and most profound meaning of his mission. The fact that he did die during the feast, despite the religious leaders' calculations, highlights the fact that everything took place according to the precise plan and timetable of God.

The Anointing at Bethany (14:3–9)

> ³When he was in Bethany reclining at table in the house of Simon the leper, a woman came with an alabaster jar of perfumed oil, costly genuine spikenard. She broke the alabaster jar and poured it on his head. ⁴There were some who were indignant. "Why has there been this waste of perfumed oil? ⁵It could have been sold for more than three hundred days' wages and the money given to the poor." They were infuriated with her. ⁶Jesus said, "Let her alone. Why do you make trouble for her? She has done a good thing for me. ⁷The poor you will always have with you, and whenever you wish you can do good to them, but you will not always have me. ⁸She has done what she could. She has anticipated anointing my body for burial. ⁹Amen, I say to you, wherever the gospel is proclaimed to the whole world, what she has done will be told in memory of her."

OT: 1 Sam 10:1; 16:13; Ps 23:5; Song 1:12
NT: // Matt 26:6–13; John 12:1–8
Catechism: serving the poor in Jesus, 2449

In stark contrast to the malicious scheming of the chief priests and scribes (14:1–2) is the tender gesture of the anonymous woman recounted here. In his typical †sandwich technique, Mark frames this story between the account of the treachery of the religious authorities (vv. 1–2) and the treachery of Judas (vv. 10–11), accenting two diametrically opposed responses to Jesus. Those from whom we might naturally expect the most—the religious leaders and the specially chosen friends of Jesus—turn out to be the perpetrators of the worst evil. The woman, in contrast, represents the exemplary response of a disciple.

The anointing takes place in **Bethany**, where Jesus and his disciples are lodging during their stay in Jerusalem (11:11). **Simon the leper** may have been someone healed by Jesus and known by name to the early Church. That they were **reclining at table** suggests a formal banquet, and recalls the earlier scenes of Jesus' table fellowship: his supper with sinners (2:15) and messianic banquets in the desert (6:35–44; 8:1–10). In the midst of the meal a woman comes onto the scene **with an alabaster jar of perfumed oil**. Mark does not tell us who the woman is (though John identifies her as Mary, the sister of Martha and Lazarus; John 12:2–3). Nard, an aromatic oil made from a root native to India, appears in the Song of Songs as the bride's perfume for the banquet of the king (Song 1:12).[1] Such a treasure might have been a family heirloom. Completely unconcerned about expense or decorum, the woman breaks the **alabaster jar** and pours the perfumed oil on the head of Jesus. Her boldness in doing so, risking the indignation of host and guests, stands out against the stealth of the chief priests and scribes (14:1). The word for break is literally "shatter"; the woman gives up any possibility of reusing the flask or saving some of its contents.

14:3

What did she mean by this gesture? On one level, it was her way of giving Jesus the very best she had. To anoint someone's head with oil was a gracious and hospitable gesture (see Ps 23:5; Luke 7:46). This woman must have experienced Jesus' healing, forgiveness, or unconditional love, and wanted to express her love in return. But for Jews steeped in the Old Testament, to anoint the head with oil also has another unmistakable significance: it is the way to crown a king (1 Sam 10:1; 16:13) and to ordain a priest (Exod 29:7). This woman's gesture is a symbolic recognition of Jesus the messianic king and high priest! Although she may have been only vaguely aware of the significance of her act, Jesus recognized and affirmed it. It is the only time in the Gospel that he is literally *anointed* (the meaning of "messiah"), and it takes place just days before he completes his messianic mission.

---

1. The NAB translates the same Greek term *nardos* as "spikenard" here but simply "nard" in Song 1:12; 4:14; John 12:3.

14:4–5   But some of the banqueters, perhaps including the disciples (see Matt 26:8), are **indignant** at what they consider a breach of propriety and a **waste** of valuable resources. Mark notes the vehemence of their reaction by adding **they were infuriated with her**, which could also be translated "they snorted at her," "they rebuked her harshly" (NIV), or "they scolded her" (NRSV). On the surface their complaint may seem logical. Jesus, in the tradition of the Old Testament, had taught and modeled the importance of generosity to **the poor** (Mark 10:21; see Luke 14:13; 16:19–31). It was customary to give alms on feast days, and the Passover was near. But like the disciples on many occasions, the woman's critics are oblivious to the true significance of what is happening (Mark 6:49, 52; 8:17; 10:13). "Waste" implies giving more than is due for something of little value. But how could anything given to the Messiah be a waste? The woman, with deep intuition, had recognized the primacy of devotion to Jesus over all other works of charity. With her gesture she proclaimed that Jesus is worthy of *all*, worthy of her whole life being poured out.

14:6–7   Jesus, in response, commends the woman and reproaches the grumbling men. They have no authorization to judge her according to their worldly reasoning. **She has done a good thing** (literally, a beautiful thing) **for me**—that is, she has shown Jesus the honor and devotion of which he is worthy. Jesus alludes to a teaching of Moses (Deut 15:11): **The poor you will always have with you**. This statement is in no way an excuse to ignore the plight of the poor. Jesus, like Moses, affirms that the perpetual presence of the poor, far from being a reason for complacency, is a constant reminder of our obligation to **do good to them**. God's plan for human life is that no one be in need (Deut 15:4), but he wills to involve us in carrying out that plan. But Jesus now reveals what the critics have missed: **you will not always have me**. Like his earlier words about the bridegroom being taken away (Mark 2:20), it is a veiled prophecy of his passion.

14:8   Jesus then interprets the woman's action: **She has done what she could.** Like the impoverished widow (12:44), she gave everything she had to give, holding nothing back. Where others were moderate, balanced, and measured in their response to Jesus, this woman was extravagant: she poured out on him what was most precious to her. Moreover, her **anointing** was a prophetic gesture, anticipating his death. Because Jesus would die like a common criminal, his body would not be properly anointed for **burial**. In fact, the passion account ends with women going to anoint his body (16:1)—but only this woman succeeds, because she has done it *beforehand*. On a deeper level, she has prepared Jesus for his burial by affirming the unspeakable value of the life he was about to pour out. Whereas Peter had tried to hinder Jesus from his messianic vocation (8:32), this woman prophetically affirms and opens the way for it. She is the first person in Mark, other than Jesus himself, to have an intuition into the meaning of his passion.

Jesus concludes his praise of the woman with a solemn pledge. The assurance that the good news would be **proclaimed to the whole world** is a pointer to his ultimate triumph. Like many exemplary characters in the Gospel the woman remains anonymous, perhaps because Mark invites every reader to identify with her. But her gesture will be remembered and always linked with what Jesus himself did. As an act exemplifying the Church's response to Jesus' passion, it will **be told** as an essential part of the proclamation of the **gospel**. Indeed, it will lead many others to do what she did: to recklessly "waste" all that is most precious on Jesus.

14:9

The anointing at Bethany parallels the widow's offering (12:41–44), forming a frame around the discourse of chapter 13.[2] The two stories are closely connected. Both women give generous gifts at great sacrifice, despite the monetary difference (a penny versus three hundred days' wages). In each case Jesus alone recognizes the value of the gift. He praises both women, beginning with his solemn "Amen" formula—the only times in the Gospel where Jesus gives praise to a person. And both cases offer a contrast with evil men: the scribes who devour widows' houses (12:40) and the scribes who plot Jesus' death (14:1). Each woman's gift foreshadows the death of Jesus, the widow by giving "her whole living" (literally, "her whole life") as Jesus was about to do, the other woman by anointing him for his burial.

Immediately after this episode, Jesus will again recline at table, and there will be another ritual action that is a symbolic anticipation of his death: the institution of the Eucharist. There too is a reference to Jesus' body and a solemn pronouncement, "Amen, I say to you." Mark has placed these two actions in close proximity so that they shed light on each other. The woman's gesture anticipates what Jesus himself will do: she breaks and pours out her greatest treasure on him, as he would break and pour out his life for all humanity.

The Plotting of Judas (14:10–11)

[10]Then Judas Iscariot, one of the Twelve, went off to the chief priests to hand him over to them. [11]When they heard him they were pleased and

2. Gray, *Temple*, 100.

promised to pay him money. Then he looked for an opportunity to hand him over.

OT: Ps 55:13–15
NT: // Matt 26:14–16; Luke 22:3–6
Catechism: all sinners as authors of Christ's passion, 597–98, 1851

14:10   An act of lavish love is followed by one of cold, calculating treachery. Judas Iscariot takes the initiative in going **to the chief priests** to betray Jesus. Judas had undoubtedly been present during Jesus' confrontations with the religious leaders (11:15–18; 12:1–12), and knew that they wanted him dead. **Hand over** (*paradidōmi*) is a key word in the passion narrative, expressing the successive betrayals that Jesus had said he would undergo (9:31; 10:33): Judas, a disciple, hands him over to the Jewish leaders; the Jewish leaders hand him over to a pagan ruler (15:1); the pagan ruler hands him over to be crucified (15:15). This chain of events symbolizes the complicity of all human beings in the rejection and crucifixion of the Son of God. Mark accents the painfulness of the betrayal by repeatedly noting that Judas was **one of the Twelve** (14:10, 20, 43), one of those chosen by Jesus for special intimacy with him and a share in his authority (3:14–15).

Mark is remarkably reticent about Judas' motives. But it is noteworthy that Judas makes his move immediately after the anointing at Bethany. It may be that he finally realized that Jesus was not going to buy into the earthly program of action on which he had pinned his hopes, whether a violent uprising against the Romans or radical social reform. Jesus' values were of an entirely different order. Perhaps Judas could not accept Jesus' approval of the woman's costly gesture—and what it implied about who he considered himself to be.

14:11   Not surprisingly, the chief priests are **pleased** with Judas's offer. They have been hampered so far by Jesus' popularity with the crowds (11:18; 12:12; 14:2), but Judas could provide them with an opportunity to arrest Jesus quietly in a private setting. In Mark's account Judas does not ask for **money** but is offered it.

Passover Preparations (14:12–16)

---

¹²On the first day of the Feast of Unleavened Bread, when they sacrificed the Passover lamb, his disciples said to him, "Where do you want us to go and prepare for you to eat the Passover?" ¹³He sent two of his disciples and said to them, "Go into the city and a man will meet you, carrying

a jar of water. Follow him. [14]Wherever he enters, say to the master of the house, 'The Teacher says, "Where is my guest room where I may eat the Passover with my disciples?"' [15]Then he will show you a large upper room furnished and ready. Make the preparations for us there." [16]The disciples then went off, entered the city, and found it just as he had told them; and they prepared the Passover.

OT: Exod 12:6; Lev 23:5
NT: 1 Cor 5:7. // Matt 26:17–19; Luke 22:7–13
Catechism: Christians and Jews both celebrate the Passover, 1096
Lectionary: 14:12–16, 22–26: Corpus Christi (Year B); Blessing of a Chalice and Paten

Mark's careful reference to the Passover is not merely a chronological but   14:12–15
also a theological signal. Jesus chose the setting of the great feast, commemorating the exodus from Egypt, for the culmination of his mission. He is the true paschal lamb that is about to be sacrificed (see John 1:29), and the unleavened bread about to be given (14:22). In him the Passover of Israel is fulfilled and revealed in its deepest meaning.

The combined feast of Passover and **Unleavened Bread** began with the late-evening Passover meal. In preparation for the feast, that afternoon each family's **Passover lamb** would be brought to the temple.[3] After passing inspection, the lamb was **sacrificed** and its blood sprinkled on the altar. It was then returned to the family to be roasted. Jesus' **disciples** take the initiative in placing themselves at his service for preparing the meal. According to Jewish law, the Passover meal had to be eaten within the Holy City (see Deut 16:5–6). Jesus' precise instructions show that he had already made arrangements, just as he did for his entrance into Jerusalem (11:1–6). As he always does when sending his disciples on a mission (6:7; 11:1), Jesus sends **two** of them together.

Jesus' instructions seem to indicate a prearranged signal. Ordinarily, carrying water jugs was a woman's task. Apparently Jesus has arranged for this man to be waiting for the disciples, and when they see him they need not say anything but simply **follow him**. These precautions were probably designed to elude the religious leaders who were constantly on the lookout for a chance to arrest Jesus (14:1). He would not fall into their hands until the proper time had come. As in 11:3 Jesus has hidden friends who place their resources entirely at his disposal. Moreover, his exact foreknowledge shows that he is in full control of his destiny as he approaches the passion, freely embracing the Father's will. The disciples

---

3. Mark refers to these events as taking place on the same day (perhaps for the benefit of his Gentile readers), although in Jewish reckoning the Passover meal was technically the day *after* the lambs were slaughtered (see Lev 23:5–6), since the day begins at sunset.

The Upper Room

BIBLICAL
BACKGROUND

According to ancient tradition, the upper room or cenacle was on Mount Zion, a hillock on the southern end of Jerusalem's western hill (Zion is sometimes used poetically to refer to the whole city). This room, whose owner was evidently a follower of Jesus, was probably also the place where the 120 disciples waited in prayer after Jesus' ascension, and where the Holy Spirit was poured out on Pentecost (Acts 1:13; 2:1). It may have been in the house of Mark himself, which was a gathering place for the early Church (Acts 12:12). An ancient Jewish Christian synagogue was built on the site. Today a medieval church stands there; just beneath the "upper room" is the site venerated as the tomb of King David.

will be shown **a large upper room**, probably with carpets or couches on which the guests would recline as they ate.

14:16   Upon following these instructions, they find everything exactly as Jesus had described and undertake the traditional "preparations" for the Passover meal: the roasted lamb, unleavened bread, bitter herbs, and other ceremonial items.

Prophecy of Betrayal (14:17–21)

> **[17]When it was evening, he came with the Twelve. [18]And as they reclined at table and were eating, Jesus said, "Amen, I say to you, one of you will betray me, one who is eating with me." [19]They began to be distressed and to say to him, one by one, "Surely it is not I?" [20]He said to them, "One of the Twelve, the one who dips with me into the dish. [21]For the Son of Man indeed goes, as it is written of him, but woe to that man by whom the Son of Man is betrayed. It would be better for that man if he had never been born."**

OT: Ps 41:10–11; 55:13–15; Sir 37:2
NT: 1 Cor 11:28. // Matt 26:20–25; Luke 22:21–23; John 13:21–30
Catechism: the Last Supper, 610–11

14:17–18   In the biblical world, the greatest expression of communion among friends is to share a meal (Gen 26:30; 31:54; 1 Sam 9:24). Table fellowship is even the sign of the covenant relationship between God and man (Exod 24:11; Deut 12:7). On the night before his passion, Jesus desires to enjoy this intimate communion with **the Twelve**, his closest disciples. Yet in this very setting, he speaks of a horrendous break in communion: **one of you will betray me**. This prediction alludes to Ps 41:10 (see Sir 37:2): "Even the friend who had my trust, who shared my table, has scorned me." In ancient culture, there was no greater breach of loyalty than to turn against someone whose hospitality you have enjoyed and whose **table** you have shared. The psalmist expresses anguish at this experience, but also confidence that he would be vindicated by God. The very next line reads: "But you, LORD, have mercy and raise me up" (Ps 41:11).

Jesus does not identify who it is who will betray him. There may be two rea- **14:19–20**
sons for this. First, his announcement is a sobering admonition for the other disciples, causing each of them to search their hearts and discern whether there is any bitter root inside (see Heb 12:15) that could eventually lead them to such a heinous act. It is as if they need an examination of conscience to be prepared to receive the unfathomable gift he is about to give them (14:22–25; see 1 Cor 11:28). **Distressed** at his words, they ask him one by one, **Surely it is not I?** Each disciple must humbly recognize the evil of which he is capable if left to his own devices. Jesus accents the pain of the betrayal by reaffirming that the betrayer will be **one of the Twelve** dipping into the **dish** with him, perhaps the dish into which herbs were dipped during the Passover ceremony. This statement (unlike that of John 13:26) does not identify the traitor, since several or all of the disciples may have been using the same dish. The other disciples seem to have had no suspicions about Judas, but Jesus sees into the heart (see Mark 2:8).

Second, Jesus' announcement gives Judas a chance to repent and abandon **14:21**
his evil plans without anyone having to know. He appeals to Judas by warning him in advance of the dreadful consequences of his act. This scene depicts the mysterious interaction of God's sovereign will and human freedom. Jesus, the **Son of Man**, is the suffering Messiah whose vocation to die has been foreordained by God and prophesied in the Scriptures (especially in Isa 52:13–53:12). But that does not excuse Judas of responsibility for the sinful role he played in the process. God's plan anticipates human freewill decisions, but does not cause them. Jesus' statement is a solemn warning, expressing grief at the bitter fate the betrayer is bringing on himself.

The Institution of the Eucharist (14:22–25)

---

²²While they were eating, he took bread, said the blessing, broke it, and gave it to them, and said, "Take it; this is my body." ²³Then he took a cup, gave thanks, and gave it to them, and they all drank from it. ²⁴He said

to them, "This is my blood of the covenant, which will be shed for many. ²⁵Amen, I say to you, I shall not drink again the fruit of the vine until the day when I drink it new in the kingdom of God."

OT: Exod 12:13; 24:3–8; Isa 53:11–12; Jer 31:31–32
NT: John 6:51–58; 13:1–17; Rev 19:9. // Matt 26:26–29; Luke 22:15–20; 1 Cor 11:23–27
Catechism: the Last Supper, 610–11; institution of the Eucharist, 1337–44; Eucharist as pledge of glory to come, 1402–5

Mark's whole account of the public ministry has illumined and prepared readers for what Jesus is about to do. The disciples had shared many meals with Jesus. They had learned that he overturns social and legal barriers, that he is the messianic Shepherd who feeds God's people, and that he is able to provide more than enough to satisfy all. They had learned that he would "give his life as a ransom for many" (10:45) and be raised from the dead. Although they had not understood "about the loaves" (6:52; 8:17–21), and will still not fully understand until after the resurrection, now the mystery is being unveiled: Jesus himself is the bread, broken and given for many.

14:22   To understand Mark's succinct account, it is important to read it in light of its setting as a Passover supper (see vv. 12–16). A Passover supper would include the traditional elements: a blessing by the head of the household, the ceremonial foods and wine, the retelling of the story of the exodus, and the singing of hymns. Jesus' initial actions are typical of the host at a Jewish banquet, and are identical to what he had done in the two miracles of the loaves (6:41; 8:6): **he took bread, said the blessing, broke it, and gave it to them**. The customary blessing was a prayer of thanksgiving to God for having provided for his people. The sharing of one loaf was a sign of the fellowship the banqueters were enjoying. Mark implies that even Judas is included in this fellowship, since he has said nothing about his departure.

According to custom the host at Passover interprets each of the ceremonial foods by relating them to the exodus. But Jesus' interpretation goes far beyond the Passover and brings the meal to an entirely new level: **Take it; this is my body**. With these simple words, the Last Supper becomes a prophecy in gesture, anticipating and interpreting the passion that was to occur the next day. Jesus identifies the broken bread with his own body about to be broken on the cross. In Hebrew thought, "body" is not merely the flesh but the whole person as a physical being. Jesus is revealing that his death will be a gift of *himself* to them (see 10:45). By asking them to "take," that is, to eat the bread that is his body, he is inviting them to receive this gift of himself into the depth of their being.

The Eucharist, Sacrament of Unity

The Fathers of the Church often spoke of the unifying power of the Eucharist, an efficacious power going far beyond the symbolic value of a loaf shared by friends. St. John Chrysostom writes, "For what is the bread? It is the body of Christ. And what do those who receive it become? The Body of Christ—not many bodies but one body. For as bread is completely one, though made up of many grains of wheat, and these, albeit unseen, remain nonetheless present, in such a way that their difference is not apparent since they have been made a perfect whole, so too are we mutually joined to one another and together united with Christ."[a]

St. Augustine explains that Holy Communion is both a gift and a task. "'The Body of Christ,' you are told, and you answer 'Amen.' Be members then of the Body of Christ so that your Amen may be true! Why is this mystery accomplished with bread? . . . Consider that the bread is not made of one grain, but of many. During the time of exorcism [before baptism], you were, so to say, in the mill. When you were baptized you were wetted with water. Then the Holy Spirit came into you like the fire that bakes the dough. Be then what you see and receive what you are."[b]

a. *Homilies on First Corinthians* 24.2, cited in John Paul II, *Ecclesia de Eucharistia*, 23.
b. *Sermon* 272.

There is no mention of the central element in a Passover supper: the lamb. It was the blood of sacrificed lambs that saved the Israelites from death (Exod 12:13). But Jesus' words reveal that he himself is the paschal Lamb whose blood will save the many from death. Just as the Passover was not complete without eating the paschal lamb, Jesus' sacrifice is complete only when his disciples consume his body and blood. By inviting them to share the one bread that is his body, Jesus is drawing them into a union with himself and one another that is far deeper than any earthly table fellowship.

Then he took a cup. Jesus invites his disciples to drink from the cup before giving its explanation. The verb for **give thanks** (*eucharisteō*) is the origin of the Church's name for the sacrament commemorating the Last Supper, the Eucharist. Like a shared loaf, wine from a shared cup was a sign of fellowship. Wine is also a symbol of joy, festivity, and abundance (Ps 4:8; Isa 62:9), and of divine life (Mark 2:22; John 2:3, 9). But Mark also suggests another level of meaning: the cup that Jesus will drink is his passion, the full force of God's judgment on sin, which he willingly accepts (Mark 14:36; see Isa 51:17;

14:23

Jer 25:16–18). As Jesus already indicated to James and John, for the disciples drink from *his* cup (Mark 10:38) means to participate in his atoning sacrifice, both to share in his sufferings willingly and to receive their benefit: restored communion with God.

14:24   Jesus' interpretation of his gift of the cup again transcends and fulfills the Passover: **This is my blood of the covenant**. For the Jews, it was forbidden—unthinkable—to drink blood (Gen 9:4; Deut 12:16). The Old Testament teaches that blood is sacred because it is the seat of life: "the life of all flesh is in its blood" (Lev 17:14 JB). For the same reason, it is blood that makes atonement for sin (Lev 17:11), since nothing could be offered to God more valuable than the blood of a living creature. But how could Jesus ask his disciples to do what was forbidden in the law? To drink the blood of animals would be demeaning. But to drink the blood of the Son of God is to be elevated to a share in his own divine life.

The "blood of the covenant" was the phrase used at the moment when God established his †covenant with Israel at Sinai at the climax of the exodus (Exod 24:1–8). Nearly all ancient covenants were sealed with blood, since a covenant was the forging of a kinship bond and kinship is constituted by blood. The Sinai covenant was ratified by the blood of sacrificed bulls sprinkled on the altar, representing God, and on the people. That covenant too was consummated in a sacred meal (Exod 24:9–11). Jesus' declaration that now *his* blood is the blood of the covenant means that the covenant is now being definitively renewed, just as Jeremiah had prophesied (Jer 31:31–32). Now there is kinship bond between God and his people that can never be broken.

That Jesus' blood **will be shed** or poured out signifies a violent death. The verb is actually in the present tense ("is shed") because Jesus' words are not merely a prophecy but a window into the inner reality of his passion. His supreme gift of self, offered on the cross, is now made available to all. That it will be shed **for many** means that Jesus' death is more than a martyrdom; it is an efficacious sacrifice, providing the total forgiveness of sin that was only foreshadowed in the animal sacrifices of the old covenant. "For many" also recalls Isaiah's prophecy of the servant who through his suffering would "justify many" and "take away the sins of many" (Isa 53:11–12). "Many" does not mean a limited number, but is a Semitic way of expressing a vast multitude: Jesus "died for all" (2 Cor 5:14).

14:25   Jesus concludes with a solemn vow, assuring the disciples that his bitter passion will end in the joy of the resurrection. Wine is a symbol of the messianic banquet prophesied in the Old Testament (Isa 25:6; 55:1). Jesus is implying that his joy will not be complete until his disciples—both present and future—are united with him in the final and glorious banquet in heaven (see Luke 13:29; Rev 19:9). Thus the Church has always understood the eucharistic meal as not only a making present of the past (the passion) but also a foretaste of the future (the full coming of God's **kingdom**).

At the time Mark wrote his Gospel, the Eucharist was already the center of the early Church's worship. Mark's first audience would have read his account in light of their own celebrations of "the breaking of the bread" (Acts 2:42), "the Lord's supper" (1 Cor 11:20). Although Mark does not record Jesus' injunction to "Do this in memory of me" (Luke 22:19; 1 Cor 11:24–25), the liturgy was already a living fulfillment of that word.[4]

Reflection and Application (14:22–25)

Jesus' words over the bread and cup reveal that his death on the cross is an atoning sacrifice, fulfilling the Passover and all the sacrifices of the old covenant. He himself is both the sacrifice and the high priest who offers it (Heb 2:17; 4:14). At the same time, according to Luke and Paul, Jesus transforms his last supper into a memorial that will make his sacrifice present in the Church until the end of time (Luke 22:19; 1 Cor 11:24–25). He instructs his apostles to continue to offer his once-for-all sacrifice and distribute it to the people of God as he had to them. Catholic tradition thus recognizes the Last Supper as the moment when Jesus ordains his apostles as priests of the new covenant, who share in a unique way in his ministry as high priest (Catechism, 1380).

Prophecy of Denial (14:26–31)

²⁶Then, after singing a hymn, they went out to the Mount of Olives.

²⁷Then Jesus said to them, "All of you will have your faith shaken, for it is written:

> 'I will strike the shepherd,
>   and the sheep will be dispersed.'

²⁸But after I have been raised up, I shall go before you to Galilee." ²⁹Peter said to him, "Even though all should have their faith shaken, mine will not be." ³⁰Then Jesus said to him, "Amen, I say to you, this very night before

---

4. Harrington, *Mark*, 218.

the cock crows twice you will deny me three times." ³¹But he vehemently replied, "Even though I should have to die with you, I will not deny you." And they all spoke similarly.

OT: Zech 13:7
NT: John 16:32; 2 Tim 4:16. // Matt 26:30–35; Luke 22:31–34; John 13:36–38
Catechism: perseverance as a gift, 162

14:26–27   The Passover meal traditionally concludes with **singing a hymn** (or hymns) of praise, especially Psalms 113–118, known as the Hallel Psalms. After the supper, Jesus and his disciples cross the Kidron Valley to the **Mount of Olives**, the same setting where he gave the end times discourse (13:3–37). Just as he had prophesied the failure of one disciple (14:18), now he prophesies the failure of all: you will **have your faith shaken** (*skandalizomai*), literally, "stumble" or "fall away." Jesus quotes the prophet Zechariah to explain this disturbing forecast (Zech 13:7). In this passage, after declaring that the **sheep** (God's people) would be scattered, Zechariah goes on to show how God would turn the disaster to good. A remnant would be left, whom God would refine like gold and silver. Humbled by their trials, they would live in true covenant fidelity: "They shall call upon my name, and I will hear them. I will say, 'They are my people,' and they shall say, 'The LORD is my God'" (Zech 13:9). Jesus identifies himself as the Shepherd-Messiah who will be struck down, and whose followers would scatter in fear and confusion. As he had warned in the parable of the seeds, some who eagerly embraced his words would quickly "fall away" in the face of trials (Mark 4:16–17). By giving this prophecy, Jesus is reassuring the disciples in advance that even their failure will be incorporated into God's saving plan.

14:28   Jesus does not end his prophecy on a note of gloom but announces the resurrection. He will regather his scattered flock, since to **go before** them is to lead them as a Shepherd. It is an assurance that forgiveness and restoration are available to all those who desert or deny Jesus under persecution, as some of Mark's first readers may have done. Jesus' mission will end where it began, in **Galilee**, and there he will commission the disciples to continue his work of salvation by bringing the gospel to the ends of the earth (16:15).

14:29–30   But Jesus' warning is lost on Peter, who brashly asserts that his own **faith** will not be **shaken**, evidently confident that his own fortitude exceeds that of the other disciples. Peter's deep loyalty and love for Jesus is not yet matched by sober self-knowledge and humility. Jesus responds with another solemn warning: **you will deny me three times.** To deny Jesus is to disown or repudiate him, the antithesis of discipleship, which entails denying *oneself* (8:34). Jesus had warned earlier that some would be ashamed of him (8:38), that is, afraid or embarrassed to be associated with him. Peter will be singled out not for exemplary conduct but for failure.

As has happened before (8:32; see John 13:8), Peter does not hesitate to con- **14:31** tradict his Lord. His strident self-assurance sets the tone for the other disciples, who **similarly** declare their readiness **to die with** Jesus. Like many of Jesus' later followers they will have to undergo a painful trial to be purified of their self-deception and learn that their faithfulness to him is a pure gift of grace. But even though they do not yet know what they are saying (as in Mark 10:39), Jesus delights in and will eventually fulfill their as-yet-immature desire to give their lives in fidelity to him.

Betrayal and Condemnation

Mark 14:32-72

Up to this point Jesus has spoken of his coming passion with calm serenity. But something new happens in his prayer at Gethsemane: here Jesus' human frailty and vulnerability are fully exposed. Mark gives us a window into the heart of Jesus and his human struggle to surrender to the will of the Father. It is a crucial phase in the passion narrative: the moment of decision in which Jesus, fully aware of the cost, embraces the Father's will for his agonizing death. From this point on, Mark will show the relentless progress of the passion, as the suffering Messiah endures rejection and abandonment by his disciples, by the leaders of his people, and by all humanity (represented by Pilate and the crowd).

The Agony in Gethsemane (14:32–42)

---

³²Then they came to a place named Gethsemane, and he said to his disciples, "Sit here while I pray." ³³He took with him Peter, James, and John, and began to be troubled and distressed. ³⁴Then he said to them, "My soul is sorrowful even to death. Remain here and keep watch." ³⁵He advanced a little and fell to the ground and prayed that if it were possible the hour might pass by him; ³⁶he said, "Abba, Father, all things are possible to you. Take this cup away from me, but not what I will but what you will." ³⁷When he returned he found them asleep. He said to Peter, "Simon, are you asleep? Could you not keep watch for one hour? ³⁸Watch and pray that you may not undergo the test. The spirit is willing but the flesh is weak." ³⁹Withdrawing again, he prayed, saying the same thing. ⁴⁰Then he

returned once more and found them asleep, for they could not keep their eyes open and did not know what to answer him. [41]He returned a third time and said to them, "Are you still sleeping and taking your rest? It is enough. The hour has come. Behold, the Son of Man is to be handed over to sinners. [42]Get up, let us go. See, my betrayer is at hand."

OT: Ps 55:5–6; 88:4; 116:3
NT: Col 4:2; Heb 5:7–9. // Matt 26:36–46; Luke 22:39–46; John 12:27
Catechism: agony in Gethsemane, 612; Christ's human will, 475
Lectionary: votive Mass of the Mystery of the Holy Cross

Gethsemane (Hebrew for "oil press") was a garden (see John 18:1) on the   14:32–34
western slope of the Mount of Olives, the same setting where Jesus had given his end times discourse (Mark 13:3–37). Arriving there after the Last Supper, Jesus asks his disciples to wait while he prays. This is the third time Mark has shown Jesus at prayer (see 1:35; 6:46), each time at a key moment for defining the nature of his mission. On the previous occasions he prayed in solitude, but now he brings with him his closest companions, **Peter, James, and John.** These three have witnessed his divine glory in the raising of the daughter of Jairus (5:37) and the Transfiguration (9:2); now they will see his human fragility. Significantly, all three have pledged to share in Jesus' sufferings (10:39; 14:31).

Jesus begins to be **troubled and distressed.** The Greek verbs are forceful and could be translated "alarmed, distraught, and in anguish." Jesus' distress recalls the psalms of lament in which an innocent man cries out to God: "My heart pounds within me; death's terrors fall upon me. Fear and trembling overwhelm me; shuddering sweeps over me" (Ps 55:5–6; see 88:4; 116:3). Jesus makes his own, and fulfills, the prayer of Israel. His sorrow is so intense as to even threaten his life (see Ps 31:10–11; 42:6, 12). In his moment of agony in the face of impending death Jesus seeks the human solace and support of his friends. He asks them to **keep watch**, that is, stay awake, be spiritually alert, and pay attention—the same admonition he gave them in the end times discourse (Mark 13:34–37). It is the disposition needed in a time of testing.

Jesus advances away from the presence of his companions. In his supreme   14:35
moment of decision he is alone with the Father. So great is his inner torment that he collapses **to the ground.** In the ancient world it was customary to pray out loud; by recording this prayer, Mark gives his readers a privileged glimpse into the relationship between the Son and the Father. Jesus' prayer is an acknowledgment that the entire passion is in the Father's control, and a plea that, if **possible**, the Father might somehow rearrange his plan to spare his Son such horrendous suffering.

14:36   Only Mark records Jesus using the Aramaic word **Abba,** the word used to address one's father ("Dad"). Although the Old Testament sometimes refers to God as the Father (*Ab*) of Israel (Deut 32:6; Ps 103:13; Jer 31:9), there is no evidence for anyone prior to Jesus addressing God with this word of daring intimacy. Abba appears elsewhere in the New Testament only in Rom 8:15 and Gal 4:6, where Paul declares that through the Spirit Jesus has now brought *us* into his own filial relationship with the Father. Translated as **Father,** it is the same word that begins the Lord's Prayer (Matt 6:9). With this term of affection Mark accents the fact that Jesus' obedience is no mere resignation but an act of unbounded trust, commitment, and love for his Father.

Jesus affirms, as he has previously said to his disciples (Mark 10:27), that **all things are possible to** God. He pleads, **Take this cup away from me.** The cup, like the hour (14:35), signifies the passion, and evokes the Old Testament image of the cup of devastation that will fall on the wicked in punishment for their sin (Ps 75:9; Isa 51:17; Ezek 23:33). At the Last Supper Jesus spoke of the cup of his "blood of the covenant, which will be shed for many" (Mark 14:24), indicating that his sufferings will be transformed into a source of immeasurable blessing. Jesus, aware of his saving role in God's plan, nevertheless recoils in trembling and horror from his approaching death. The temptation that had been present throughout his ministry (see 1:13; 8:11, 32)—to be a Messiah other than that willed by the Father—reaches its climax. But precisely in this culmination of his anguish he surrenders unconditionally to the Father, reversing the whole history of human rebellion: **not what I will but what you will.**

14:37   Returning to the disciples Jesus finds them **asleep,** the antithesis of the vigilance he had asked of them (v. 34). On a natural level they are overcome by the lateness of the hour and perhaps the distress of witnessing Jesus' ordeal. But spiritually they are oblivious to the †eschatological drama that is unfolding and thus are unable to respond properly. Jesus addresses Peter as the leader: **Could you not keep watch for one hour?** That Jesus has been praying for an hour suggests that his prayer was not instantaneous but a prolonged struggle to confirm that the way of the cross really was what the Father was asking of him, and to bring his human will into perfect submission to the Father.

14:38   His command, **Watch and pray that you may not undergo the test** (*peirasmos*), echoes the sixth petition of the Lord's Prayer: "Lead us not into temptation (*peirasmos*)." The disciples are to pray that God would protect them from a trial greater than their human weakness can bear, like the trial that is about to come upon them at Jesus' arrest. This last admonition of Jesus is also addressed to his future disciples, to be constantly on guard against the temptations that could cause them to "fall away" (v. 27) and to overcome them by prayer (see Col 4:2; Heb 4:16). **The spirit is willing but the flesh is weak.** In the New Testament the flesh often signifies the weakness of human nature, which easily inclines toward sin; the spirit is our aspiration toward God and capacity to relate to him. As Paul emphasized, we are caught in perpetual conflict between the two (Rom 8:12–14; Gal 5:19–24). The disciples desire to be faithful to Jesus (14:31), but their flesh is liable to fall into cowardice, complacency, or selfishness. Jesus' word of warning is also a word of encouragement, implying that his victory is the prototype for all Christians in their struggle against the flesh. "Because he himself was tested through what he suffered, he is able to help those who are being tested" (Heb 2:18).

Three times the scene is repeated, highlighting its importance for the future Church. Each time Jesus withdraws to wrestle in prayer and returns to the disciples only to find them fast **asleep**. Three times he had commanded them to watch (vv. 34, 37, 38); their threefold failure, like Peter's threefold denial (vv. 66–72), will humble them and convince them of their need to rely on God through prayer. It is a crucial part of their formation as future leaders of the Church. Mark notes that they **did not know what to answer him**, just as had happened at the Transfiguration (9:6).
14:39–40

Upon returning the third time, Jesus declares, **It is enough.** The Greek term could also be translated, "It is settled," meaning that the threshold has been fully crossed, the decision has been made. The rest of the passion narrative will be an unfolding of the implications of Jesus' resolve. **The hour has come**: the hour of Jesus' passion and of the culmination of the Father's plan of salvation. On a human level, Jesus is **handed over** by Judas. But in God's unfathomable plan God has handed over his only Son to **sinners** out of love for them (Rom 8:32), and Jesus has freely handed himself over with the same love (Gal 2:20; Eph 5:2). Jesus now speaks with serenity and resolve: **Get up, let us go.** He does not wait passively but goes forward to meet those who will unknowingly carry out the Father's plan.
14:41–42

Reflection and Application (14:32–42)

Readers of this passage have sometimes questioned: why would the Son of God collapse in anguish when so many heroes, such as Christian martyrs and even the pagan philosopher Socrates, have gone to their deaths calm and composed? In the context of the New Testament, what Jesus experiences in Gethsemane is not merely the dread of suffering but the full weight of human sin and its consequence of alienation from God: the "cup" of wrath (see Isa 51:17). The Christian gospel is far from the Stoic or Buddhist ideal of cool, emotionless detachment from the drama of human suffering. Jesus enters into the depths of the human condition to transform it from within. In Gethsemane we begin to see that God willed the entire passion process so as to bring about the most perfect act of love conceivable from a human heart. The cross would have no value if Jesus had not freely willed it. It is not Jesus' death in itself that God desired, since God has "no pleasure in the death of anyone" (Ezek 18:32). Rather, what redeems humanity is the fire of divine love enkindled in the human heart of Jesus, the love that bound him to the cross (see John 14:31; Eph 5:2).

Betrayal and Arrest (14:43–52)

[43]Then, while he was still speaking, Judas, one of the Twelve, arrived, accompanied by a crowd with swords and clubs who had come from the chief priests, the scribes, and the elders. [44]His betrayer had arranged a signal with them, saying, "The man I shall kiss is the one; arrest him and lead him away securely." [45]He came and immediately went over to him and said, "Rabbi." And he kissed him. [46]At this they laid hands on him and arrested him. [47]One of the bystanders drew his sword, struck the high priest's servant, and cut off his ear. [48]Jesus said to them in reply, "Have you come out as against a robber, with swords and clubs, to seize me? [49]Day after day I was with you teaching in the temple area, yet you did not arrest me; but that the scriptures may be fulfilled." [50]And they all left him and fled. [51]Now a young man followed him wearing nothing but a linen cloth about his body. They seized him, [52]but he left the cloth behind and ran off naked.

OT: Ps 38:12; 88:9; Jer 37:13–16
NT: // Matt 26:47–56; Luke 22:47–53; John 18:2–12
Catechism: sin and Christ's passion, 1851

14:43   Once Jesus has affirmed his resolve, the "hour" designated by the Father for the passion (v. 41) arrives without delay. Up to now Jesus has acted with sovereign authority: he has taught, healed, and performed great symbolic gestures. But from this point on there is a fundamental change: rather than acting, Jesus is *acted on*. He seems to have a wholly passive role in the action that unfolds. Yet the reader of the Gospel knows that it is precisely in that way, in his submission to the Father's plan, that his most powerful work is being accomplished.

Mark does not say whether it was during the Last Supper that **Judas** had slipped away for his rendezvous with Jesus' enemies (see John 13:30), or later while the other disciples were asleep in Gethsemane. But he has carried out his plan as an informant who had inside knowledge of where Jesus might be found and arrested without a commotion (14:10–11). Mark again describes Judas as **one of the Twelve** (see vv. 10, 20) to highlight the enormity of the betrayal. He arrives accompanied by an armed **crowd**, probably consisting of the temple police and others hired by **the chief priests, the scribes, and the elders**. These three groups, which together made up the †Sanhedrin, have issued the warrant for Jesus' arrest and are the driving force in the events of the passion.

14:44–46

The description of Judas's actions suggests a chilling deliberateness: he wants to ensure that there is no mishap in the arrest and that Jesus is led away **securely**. He evidently has no comprehension of Jesus' resolve to fulfill the Father's plan. Judas had **arranged a signal**; apparently those in the arresting party would not know Jesus by sight. A **kiss** on the cheek, a typical greeting of affection and respect (Luke 7:45; Rom 16:16; 1 Pet 5:14), is the means Judas has cynically chosen to expose his master to utter contempt. Judas approaches Jesus **immediately**—without hesitation—and salutes him with both a kiss and the respectful greeting, †**Rabbi**. Since Jesus offers no resistance, he is immediately **arrested**. He who often laid his hands on the sick for healing (Mark 5:23; 6:5; 7:32; 8:23) now has **hands** laid on him in violence.

14:47–48

In an impulsive, misguided attempt to rescue Jesus, **one of the bystanders** draws **his sword** and cuts off the ear of the **high priest's servant**. Mark does not give the impression that the assailant was a disciple (though John tells us it was Peter, John 18:10), perhaps to conceal his identity. Jesus reproves the crowd for their violent methods. The word for **robber** could also be translated bandit or revolutionary. Jesus had condemned the temple for being a "den of robbers" (Mark 11:17 RSV); now the temple authorities treat the Lord of the temple as if he himself were a robber. A real robber, Barabbas, will be released instead of Jesus (15:15), and Jesus will be crucified between two robbers (15:27), the culmination of his solidarity with sinners that is part of the divine plan.

14:49

Jesus continues his protest against this show of force that misrepresents him as an armed and dangerous criminal. Yet his ordeal fulfills **the scriptures**—that is, it recapitulates the suffering of all God's faithful people, and especially of the many biblical figures who suffered for their fidelity to the Lord. Jeremiah, for instance, like Jesus was arrested for faithfully carrying out his commission from God (Jer 37:13–16).

14:50   Jesus' prophecy of abandonment by his closest companions (v. 27) is now fulfilled: **they all left him and fled**. The apostles are those called to "be with him" (3:14); now in his darkest hour they forsake him. It is the last time we encounter Jesus' disciples—apart from the women disciples (15:41)—until after the resurrection. The agonizing experience of desertion by friends in time of trouble is often described in the Psalms. "To all my foes I am a thing of scorn, to my neighbors, a dreaded sight, a horror to my friends" (Ps 31:12); "Friends and companions shun my pain; my neighbors stand far off" (Ps 38:12; see 88:9).

14:51–52   The account of the arrest ends with a curious incident found only in Mark. Who is this **young man**, and why is he wearing only a **linen cloth** on a chilly night in April (see v. 54)? One traditional suggestion is that the man is Mark himself, in whose house Jesus may have celebrated the Last Supper (see sidebar p. 282). Linen was a fabric of the wealthy, and the absence of an undergarment suggests that the youth may have dressed quickly to follow Jesus to Gethsemane. Perhaps he was there in the shadows, listening to Jesus' prayer of anguish. Although "all" flee after the arrest, the young man *follows* Jesus, the action characteristic of a disciple. But when **seized** he too gives way to fear. Nakedness is a sign of misery and shame (see James 2:15; Rev 3:18), and the young man's desertion is all the more poignant in that he prefers to run away **naked** than to follow Jesus all the way to his passion. This episode is a real-life parable illustrating the failure of the disciples. There may also be an allusion to Amos's prophecy of the fearful judgment to fall on the day of the Lord: "the most stouthearted of warriors shall flee naked on that day, says the LORD" (Amos 2:16). No one can bear the divine wrath that is crashing in on Jesus. He goes to his passion totally alone.

Another "young man," clothed in a white robe, will appear at the empty tomb (Mark 16:5) and announce the resurrection to the women. Perhaps it is symbolic of this unknown disciple's restoration to dignity and faithful discipleship.[1]

Trial before the Sanhedrin (14:53–65)

> ⁵³They led Jesus away to the high priest, and all the chief priests and the elders and the scribes came together. ⁵⁴Peter followed him at a distance into the high priest's courtyard and was seated with the guards, warming himself at the fire. ⁵⁵The chief priests and the entire Sanhedrin kept trying to obtain testimony against Jesus in order to put him to death, but they found none. ⁵⁶Many gave false witness against him, but their testimony

1. See Moloney, *Mark*, 299–300.

did not agree. [57]Some took the stand and testified falsely against him, alleging, [58]"We heard him say, 'I will destroy this temple made with hands and within three days I will build another not made with hands.'" [59]Even so their testimony did not agree. [60]The high priest rose before the assembly and questioned Jesus, saying, "Have you no answer? What are these men testifying against you?" [61]But he was silent and answered nothing. Again the high priest asked him and said to him, "Are you the Messiah, the son of the Blessed One?" [62]Then Jesus answered, "I am;

> and 'you will see the Son of Man
> seated at the right hand of the Power
> and coming with the clouds of heaven.'"

[63]At that the high priest tore his garments and said, "What further need have we of witnesses? [64]You have heard the blasphemy. What do you think?" They all condemned him as deserving to die. [65]Some began to spit on him. They blindfolded him and struck him and said to him, "Prophesy!" And the guards greeted him with blows.

OT: Ps 35:11–12; 110:1; Isa 50:6; 53:7; Dan 7:13–14
NT: John 2:19–21. // Matt 26:57–68; Luke 22:54–55, 63–71; John 18:12–16, 19–23
Catechism: Jesus' divine sonship, 441–45; Jesus at God's right hand, 659–64; Jesus and the temple, 583–86
Lectionary: votive Mass of the Mystery of the Holy Cross

Mark's familiar insertion technique is at work again, with Jesus' trial before the †Sanhedrin placed in the middle of the story of Peter's denial (vv. 54 and 66–72). Peter, who will crumble under pressure, stands in sharp contrast with Jesus, who stands firm in his witness to the truth, even at the cost of his life.[2]

After his arrest, Jesus is led to the house of the **high priest**, who at the time **14:53** was Caiaphas. There the Sanhedrin is hastily convened. The highly irregular assembly—at night, and away from their official meeting place inside the temple precincts—is for the sake of secrecy, in view of Jesus' popularity with the people (11:18; 12:12).

Meanwhile **Peter** follows the arresting party surreptitiously **into the high** **14:54** **priest's courtyard**. His following **at a distance** is symbolic of his discipleship: he desires to be loyal, yet is still hesitant and safely "distant" from Jesus. Peter has not yet understood or accepted God's plan for a suffering Messiah (see 8:31–32). Twice Mark mentions Peter's **warming himself at the fire** (14:54 and 67), pro-

---

2. France, *Mark*, 598.

The Sanhedrin and the High Priest

BIBLICAL
BACKGROUND

The Sanhedrin (Greek for "sitting together") was the ruling council of the Jews, whose main role was to enforce Jewish law and customs. Rome usually gave its subject peoples some freedom to manage their own affairs but reserved for itself the power of capital punishment. The Sanhedrin had seventy members, including chief priests, scribes, and elders (15:1), presided over by the high priest. The high priest was a political appointee and was the highest-ranking Jewish authority in the land. Religiously, he alone had the privilege of entering the Holy of Holies in the temple once a year, on the Day of Atonement. Politically, he was held accountable to Rome for maintaining public order and ensuring the payment of tribute, and he could be deposed at will. Financially, he oversaw the temple and all its commerce, the hub of Jerusalem's economy. Under the Romans, the average term of office for the high priest was four years. Caiaphas's unusually long tenure (AD 18–36) testifies to his adeptness at collaborating with Rome.

Peter and John (Acts 4:5–21), Stephen (Acts 6:12–15), and Paul (Acts 22:30–23:10) would all stand trial before the Sanhedrin as Jesus did.

viding for his own comfort while his Lord faces the hostile machinations of the Sanhedrin. Once again Mark is remarkably honest about Peter's failings.

14:55 The trial is rigged from the start, since the chief priests, scribes, and elders have already decided that Jesus must die (3:6; 11:18; 14:1). But as many a corrupt government has done before and since, they seek at least an appearance of legal propriety to justify their action. Like the suffering just man of the Psalms, Jesus is surrounded by false witnesses who seek to do him in: "Malicious witnesses come forward, accuse me of things I do not know. They repay me evil for good and I am all alone" (Ps 35:11–12; see Ps 27:12). The Sanhedrin finds no lack of people willing to swear falsely, in violation of the eighth commandment (Exod 20:16; see Mark 10:19). In Jewish law at least two witnesses were necessary for any criminal prosecution (Deut 19:15), especially where the death penalty was involved (Num 35:30; Deut 17:6). But the Sanhedrin is unable to produce even two whose **testimony** agrees.

14:56–59 By twice noting that **their testimony did not agree** (vv. 56 and 59), Mark draws special attention to the accusation in between: that Jesus threatened to **destroy this temple made with hands** and **build another not made with hands**. Had Jesus really said this? He did prophesy that the temple would be destroyed (13:2), and he hinted that God would raise up a new temple, of which he himself would be the cornerstone (12:10–11). He also spoke of his own resurrection after **three days** (8:31; 9:31; 10:34). Taken together, these are veiled references to the replacement of the earthly temple with the Church, the true "house of prayer for all peoples" (11:17). But nowhere did Jesus remotely suggest that he himself would destroy the Jerusalem temple. Every lie is built on a partial truth, and the false witnesses have twisted his words.

The fact that this charge is the main accusation against Jesus, repeated in mockery as he hangs on the cross (15:29),[3] indicates its crucial importance in the unfolding drama. Underlying it are several layers of irony. Jesus was perceived as a dangerous threat to the temple establishment. Indeed, he had pronounced divine judgment on the temple authorities for their greed and corruption, and had driven out the merchants (11:15–17; 12:38–40). He had told a parable implying that he was God's beloved Son and the temple authorities were murderous tenants from whom God's vineyard would be taken away (12:1–9). In fact, the destruction of the earthly temple *is* imminent, and it will be a greater cataclysm than the Sanhedrin can imagine: it will bring a permanent end to the old covenant worship with its rituals and sacrifices. But though the disaster is a punishment decreed by God (see Dan 9:26), it will be carried out by Roman legions. God allows the consequences of sin to take their toll only so that he can bring about a greater good. Jesus will indeed raise up a new temple "not made with hands," the living temple where God will be worshipped in Spirit and in truth (see John 4:23). Mark here hints at what John and Paul develop explicitly: that the earthly temple comes to an end only to be replaced by the greater temple that God had intended all along: the temple of the Body of Christ (see John 2:19–21; 4:21–24; Eph 2:19–22).

Seeking to ensnare Jesus in his own speech, as the Pharisees and Herodians have attempted previously (12:13), the high priest rises to demand: **Have you no answer?** Jesus knows that to rebut the trumped up charges would be futile. His silence evokes the Suffering Servant in Isaiah, who "though he was harshly treated . . . submitted and opened not his mouth; Like a lamb led to the slaughter or a sheep before the shearers, he was silent and opened not his mouth" (Isa 53:7).   **14:60–61**

The high priest takes a more direct approach: **Are you the Messiah, the son of the Blessed One?** These are the two titles Mark directly attributed to Jesus at the very beginning of the Gospel (1:1). The †Messiah was the promised descendant of David who, it was hoped, would restore sovereignty to Israel and bring peace to the world. The "Blessed One" is an indirect reference to God.

---

3. The same charge reappears at the trial of Stephen (Acts 6:14).

Although Israel's kings were sometimes called "son of God" (2 Sam 7:12–14; Ps 2:7), it was not a typical title in Jewish messianic expectation. Caiaphas may have in mind Jesus' provocative parable of the vineyard (Mark 12:1–9).

14:62   Jesus' response is the first and only time in the Gospel where he directly affirms his messianic identity and divine sonship. In fact, it is the most direct and explicit claim to divine sonship ascribed to Jesus in any of the Gospels.[4] Moreover, Jesus may be alluding to his own divinity, since **I am** (*egō eimi*) is the Greek equivalent of the divine name, †YHWH (see Exod 3:14). When Peter had acknowledged him as Messiah, Jesus had commanded strict silence (Mark 8:30). But now it is finally the hour for his full revelation, because there is no longer any danger of his messiahship being misunderstood. His true messianic vocation—to lay down his life as a ransom for many (10:45)—is about to be fulfilled.

Jesus continues with a prophecy, combining two scriptures he has invoked previously (12:36; 13:26) to point to his exaltation by the Father. Psalm 110:1 speaks of the Messiah's enthronement at the **right hand** of God; Dan 7:9–14 speaks of a "son of man" coming before God's throne with the **clouds of heaven** and being given dominion, glory, and a kingdom. Jesus interprets this vision to refer to his coming in judgment at the end of the age (see Mark 8:38; 13:26–27). The members of the Sanhedrin who now see before them only a helpless prisoner will see Jesus in the fullness of his divine majesty. They who now stand in unjust judgment over him will instead be judged by him. Jesus knows that this answer will clinch the death sentence. Yet this is according to God's plan, because it is precisely through his cross and resurrection that he will be established in his sovereign majesty at God's right hand.

14:63–64   In response to Jesus' self-revelation the **high priest** tears **his garments**, a customary sign of grief or distress (Gen 37:34; 2 Sam 1:11; 2 Kings 19:1).[5] Here it serves as a theatrical gesture of dismay. In reality Jesus' response was just the kind of self-incrimination the high priest was looking for. There is no more need for witnesses. All that is needed is the Sanhedrin's approval for the verdict. The charge of **blasphemy** could be leveled not only for the misuse of God's name but for any claim to prerogatives that belong to God alone (see Mark 2:7). In the eyes of the high priest, Jesus' claim to be Messiah and Son of God, enthroned with divine authority, is a sacrilege and an insult to God. The biblical punishment for blasphemy was death by stoning (Lev 24:16). Not surprisingly, the Sanhedrin concurs.

---

4. In Matthew (26:64) and Luke (22:70), Jesus answers more enigmatically: "You have said so" or "You say that I am." Of Jesus' claims in the Gospel of John, 10:34–36 is indirect and 5:17 and 10:30 are implicit. John 8:58 is a claim of divinity not referring to sonship; John 17:5 is in the form of a prayer.

5. He apparently ignores the law that forbids a high priest to rend his garments (Lev 21:10).

His Insults Remove Our Shame

LIVING
TRADITION

In what is probably the earliest complete commentary on Mark, an ancient Christian writer comments on the suffering and death of Jesus: "This was so that by his guilt he might remove our guilt; that by the blindfold on his face, he might take the blindfold from our hearts; that by receiving the spits, he might wash the face of our soul; that by the blows by which he was struck on the head, he might heal the head of the human race, which is Adam; that by the blows by which he was slapped, his greatest praise might applaud by means of our hands and lips . . . that by his cross he might eliminate our torment; that by his death, he might put to death our death. . . . The insults he received remove our shame. His bonds made us free. By the crown of thorns on his head, we have obtained the diadem of the kingdom. By his wounds we have been healed. By his burial we resurrect. By his descent into hell we ascend into heaven."[a]

a. See Cahill, *First Commentary on Mark*, 112.

Once the death sentence has been rendered, there is no longer anything to **14:65** prevent physical abuse of Jesus. Mark implies that those who **began to spit on** Jesus are some of the members of the Sanhedrin. Spitting was an act of contempt in the ancient world (Deut 25:9; Job 30:10) as it is today. In mockery of Jesus' claim to prophesy his future exaltation, they blindfold and begin to strike him, demanding that he **prophesy** and identify the one who delivered the blow (see Matt 26:68). Ironically, the very fact that Jesus is suffering mockery is a fulfillment of his prophecy (Mark 10:34). Moreover, his prophecy of Peter's denial (14:30) is being fulfilled that very moment in the courtyard below (14:66–72). The guards holding Jesus join in the abuse, greeting him **with blows**. The scene evokes Isaiah's third Suffering Servant poem: "I gave my back to those who beat me, my cheeks to those who plucked my beard; My face I did not shield from buffets and spitting" (Isa 50:6).

Reflection and Application (14:53–65)

An ancient and venerable practice among Christians is to meditate on the passion of our Lord as it is narrated for us in the Gospels. But many find this practice difficult, or wonder what is its purpose. Isn't it morbid to focus on the details of Jesus' sufferings? No, it cannot be so, because he is alive, risen from the dead! To meditate on his passion is to begin to be illumined by the fire of divine love that radiates from the heart of Jesus through every moment of his sufferings, to begin to experience that in his passion he loved *me* and gave himself *for me* (Gal 2:20). It is also to begin to recognize the life-changing power that is present in every detail. Some of the best ways to do so are to pray the sorrowful mysteries of the rosary, to pray the Stations of the Cross, or to read slowly through the passion account in one of the Gospels or an Old Testament passage such as Isa 53 or Ps 22.

Peter's Denial (14:66–72)

> **⁶⁶While Peter was below in the courtyard, one of the high priest's maids came along. ⁶⁷Seeing Peter warming himself, she looked intently at him and said, "You too were with the Nazarene, Jesus." ⁶⁸But he denied it saying, "I neither know nor understand what you are talking about." So he went out into the outer court. [Then the cock crowed.] ⁶⁹The maid saw him and began again to say to the bystanders, "This man is one of them." ⁷⁰Once again he denied it. A little later the bystanders said to Peter once more, "Surely you are one of them; for you too are a Galilean." ⁷¹He began to curse and to swear, "I do not know this man about whom you are talking." ⁷²And immediately a cock crowed a second time. Then Peter remembered the word that Jesus had said to him, "Before the cock crows twice you will deny me three times." He broke down and wept.**

OT: Jer 31:19; Ezek 16:63
NT: // Matt 26:69–75; Luke 22:56–62; John 18:17–18, 25–27

14:66–67   After the account of the trial before the Sanhedrin (vv. 53–65), Mark resumes the story of Peter's denial. Peter has shown some courage in following the arresting party all the way into the high priest's **courtyard**, below the room where the Sanhedrin is assembled. But he is doing his best to lie low and not be noticed. Again Mark notes that Peter is **warming himself** at the fire, underscoring his concern for his own comfort and safety. A servant girl, seeing Peter in the firelight, recognizes him as a disciple. The **Nazarene** or "of Nazareth" was a common way of identifying Jesus (see 10:47; 16:6; Acts 2:22). Ironically, to be **with Jesus** is the very first task of a disciple (Mark 3:14), an association that Peter now refuses.

14:68–69   In contrast to Jesus, who has just affirmed the truth before an assembly of the powerful (v. 62), Peter denies the truth when confronted by a woman of

Why Peter Fell into Sin

LIVING TRADITION

St. John Chrysostom comments, "The reason God's plan permitted Peter to sin was because he was to be entrusted with the whole people of God, and sinlessness added to his severity might have made him unforgiving toward his brothers and sisters. He fell into sin so that, remembering his own fault and the Lord's forgiveness, he also might forgive others out of love for them. This was God's providential dispensation. He to whom the Church was to be entrusted, he, the pillar of the churches, the harbor of faith, was allowed to sin; Peter, the teacher of the world, was permitted to sin, so that having been forgiven himself he would be merciful to others."[a]

a. From *Tradition, Day by Day: Readings from Church Writers*, ed. John E. Rotelle (Villanova, PA: Augustinian Press, 1994), 240.

no status or authority. Nervous about being identified, he edges farther away **into the outer court**. When the maid persists in her allegation, Peter disavows any association with his Lord. The verb **denied** is in a form indicating repeated denials. Jesus had taught that a disciple is one who "denies himself" to follow Jesus (8:34); Peter now does the opposite.

Soon other bystanders corroborate the maid's accusation. Peter's speech has given him away, since Galileans spoke with a provincial accent (see Matt 26:73). In panic, he reiterates his denial in the strongest possible terms. To **curse** means to call down God's wrath on oneself if one is lying. More appallingly, it could even imply that Peter is invoking curses on Jesus, as Christians would later be pressured to do under threat of death. To **swear** is to confirm his denial with an oath. Peter cannot bring himself even to mention the name of Jesus: **I do not know this man about whom you are talking.** His denial has progressed from evasion (v. 68) to outright repudiation (v. 70) to perjury (v. 71). But there is an ironic truth in his denial: he does not yet truly know Jesus.[6]

14:70–71

The third watch of the night, between midnight and 3:00 AM, was called cock-crow because of the predictable crowing of roosters. The sound suddenly brings Peter to his senses, and he remembers Jesus' prophecy of his denial (v. 30) and his own rash boast (v. 31). Shattered with the realization of what he has done, Peter leaves the scene weeping tears of grief and remorse (see 2 Cor 7:10).

14:72

What is remarkable about the Gospel account of Peter's ignominious behavior in the hour of trial is that there could be only one source for this account: Peter

6. Martin, *Mark*, 412.

himself. Neither Peter nor his protégé, Mark, show the slightest inclination to whitewash the reputation of the first leader of the Church. The story thus serves as both a warning and a source of profound encouragement to later disciples tempted to fall away. If even Peter's resolve could break down under pressure, so could theirs. They too must heed Jesus' warning: "Watch and pray that you may not undergo the test" (v. 38). But if Peter could be forgiven and restored after such abject failure and go on to heroic martyrdom for the sake of Christ, there is mercy for others as well. The scene may have had a familiar ring to Mark's first readers, some of whom may have denied their faith under torture or threats. Others had held fast, and had to forgive their companions who had failed but later repented.

The Crucifixion

Mark 15:1-47

Jesus' unjust condemnation by the leaders of the Jews (14:55–65) is followed by his unjust condemnation by a leader of the Gentiles (15:1–15). Mark sees all humanity as symbolically implicated in the rejection and mistreatment of the Son of God. Yet as he has stressed throughout the Gospel, the entire passion has been foretold in the Scriptures and willed by God to bring about his perfect plan of salvation. The crucifixion brings to a climax the mystery of Jesus, the suffering and glorious Son of Man. It is precisely in his moment of deepest pain, humiliation, and abandonment that his victory over evil is definitively accomplished and that he is revealed as Messiah and Son of God.

Jesus before Pilate (15:1–5)

¹As soon as morning came, the chief priests with the elders and the scribes, that is, the whole Sanhedrin, held a council. They bound Jesus, led him away, and handed him over to Pilate. ²Pilate questioned him, "Are you the king of the Jews?" He said to him in reply, "You say so." ³The chief priests accused him of many things. ⁴Again Pilate questioned him, "Have you no answer? See how many things they accuse you of." ⁵Jesus gave him no further answer, so that Pilate was amazed.

OT: Ps 2:2
NT: // Matt 27:1–2, 11–14; Luke 23:1–5; John 18:28–38
Catechism: the trial of Jesus, 595–96; Jews not collectively responsible for his death, 597
Lectionary: 15:1–47: Palm Sunday (Year B); 15:1–15: votive Mass of the Mystery of the Holy Cross

Mark returns to the account of Jesus' trial before the †Sanhedrin, whose de- **15:1** liberations have continued throughout the night. The text does not necessarily imply that there is a second meeting; **held a council** could also be translated "held a consultation" (RSV) or "took counsel." Since the Jewish leaders have no power to impose the death penalty, they have to formulate a plan for carrying out their verdict. As soon becomes clear, the strategy is to bring Jesus to the Roman governor with an inflammatory political accusation.

Since the Roman workday began at dawn, the **Sanhedrin** could execute its plan without delay. Although Jesus has offered no resistance, they bind him as if to imply that he is a dangerous criminal in need of physical restraint. The Greek verb for "hand over," *paradidōmi*, is the same verb translated "betray" when used of Judas (3:19; 14:10). There are overtones of betrayal here too, in that the Jewish leaders deliver a fellow Jew into the hands of a pagan ruler.

15:2   For Mark there is deep irony in the dialogue between Jesus and **Pilate**, as throughout the passion narrative. Jesus, the "beloved Son" of God (1:11; 9:7) who is destined to reign over the whole world (14:62; Dan 7:13–14), stands before an earthly procurator ruling over a small province. Yet it is Pilate who interrogates Jesus. He asks: **Are you the king of the Jews?** This title has not been mentioned before in the Gospel. Jesus did acknowledge that he was the †Messiah (Mark 14:61–62), a royal title. The implication is that the Sanhedrin has given that claim precisely the political spin that Jesus sought to avoid. Their own verdict of blasphemy would be useless with Pilate, since the Roman governor would have no reason to get involved in a religious dispute (see Acts 18:12–16). But the Roman Empire dealt harshly with any challenge to its authority. To claim to be king would be considered high treason, punishable by death (see John 19:12). But Pilate, a politically experienced ruler, seems to sense that the charge is invented (15:10).

Pontius Pilate

BIBLICAL BACKGROUND

Since the death of Herod the Great in AD 6 Rome had found it preferable to rule the tumultuous province of Judea directly through a military governor rather than indirectly through a client king. Pontius Pilate ruled as governor, or prefect, from AD 26 to 36. His headquarters were at Caesarea Maritima on the coast, but he came to Jerusalem to preserve order during major feasts, when there was heightened danger of riots and public disturbances. The first-century Jewish philosopher Philo describes Pilate as cruel, arrogant, and corrupt. After an incident in which his troops killed some Samaritans, he was deposed and sent back to Rome in disgrace.

Who Is the King of the Jews?
BIBLICAL BACKGROUND

The Old Testament is ambivalent regarding the institution of Israel's kingship. The Israelites had no king for generations after they entered the promised land, because God alone was King of Israel (1 Sam 8:7; see Isa 33:22). The people eventually demanded that God give them a human king, a demand that represented a rejection of God's kingship and a worldly desire to be just like other nations (1 Sam 8:4–22). God tells the prophet Samuel to grant their request, but warns of the greed and corruption of human kings. Nevertheless, God eventually provides his people with a king who is a "man after his own heart" (1 Sam 13:14) and who faithfully carries out his will: David. God promises David an heir who will reign on his throne forever (2 Sam 7:12–13).

The tension between Israel's desire for a human king and God's prerogative as the sole King of Israel is fully resolved in Jesus, the human heir of David (Mark 10:47; 12:35) who is also the beloved Son of God (Mark 1:11). God has fulfilled his people's desire in a way that far surpassed their expectations.

Jesus' reply to Pilate is enigmatic: **You say so.** It is neither an outright affirmation nor a denial. Indeed, Jesus is the King of the Jews, but not in the sense that Pilate understands it (see John 18:36–37). The title reappears throughout the passion narrative (15:9, 12, 18, 26), for the true nature of Jesus' kingship is revealed precisely in the laying down of his life for the redemption of his people.

Desperate to secure Jesus' condemnation, the **chief priests** heap other charges on him, which Mark does not specify (but see Luke 23:2). Jesus' refusal to **answer**, as earlier before the Sanhedrin (Mark 14:61), speaks more eloquently than any words of self-defense. He knows that the outcome is already determined—by the Sanhedrin on one level, but ultimately by God himself. The Jewish and Gentile rulers are unwitting instruments in God's plan of salvation. His silence again evokes the Suffering Servant, who "opened not his mouth" (Isa 53:7). But the prisoner's refusal to defend himself makes no sense to Pilate. Mark conveys not only surprise but a sense of awe with the phrase **Pilate was amazed** (see 5:20).

15:3–5

Jesus Is Handed Over to Be Crucified (15:6–15)

⁶Now on the occasion of the feast he used to release to them one prisoner whom they requested. ⁷A man called Barabbas was then in prison along with the rebels who had committed murder in a rebellion. ⁸The

crowd came forward and began to ask him to do for them as he was accustomed. ⁹Pilate answered, "Do you want me to release to you the king of the Jews?" ¹⁰For he knew that it was out of envy that the chief priests had handed him over. ¹¹But the chief priests stirred up the crowd to have him release Barabbas for them instead. ¹²Pilate again said to them in reply, "Then what [do you want] me to do with [the man you call] the king of the Jews?" ¹³They shouted again, "Crucify him." ¹⁴Pilate said to them, "Why? What evil has he done?" They only shouted the louder, "Crucify him." ¹⁵So Pilate, wishing to satisfy the crowd, released Barabbas to them and, after he had Jesus scourged, handed him over to be crucified.

OT: Gen 37:11
NT: Acts 3:13. // Matt 27:15–26; Luke 23:13–25; John 18:38–19:16
Catechism: the trial of Jesus, 595–98; Jesus handed over, 599–600

15:6–7   Mark tells of a custom whereby Pilate would grant amnesty to **one prisoner** on the occasion of **the feast**, that is, Passover (14:1). This practice is not recorded anywhere outside the Gospels, but it was not unusual in the ancient world to grant prisoner releases on festivals. Incarceration was not typically used as a criminal penalty in the Roman Empire; a prisoner would usually be someone awaiting either trial or punishment. Mark explains further that a certain **Barabbas** was then **in prison** among a group of **rebels who had committed murder**. Mark does not say whether Barabbas himself had committed murder (but see Luke 23:18–19), but he was probably a popular Jewish freedom fighter. Revolts and bloodshed were frequent in first-century Palestine as the Jews chafed under Roman rule.[1] Major feasts with nationalistic significance, such as Passover, only added fuel to the fire that constantly smoldered.

15:8   Mark does not tell us whether **the crowd** that comes forward to petition Pilate was recruited by the chief priests, or whether it had gathered in support of Barabbas or other political prisoners. It is very unlikely that it consisted of the same people who hailed Jesus at his messianic entrance to Jerusalem (11:7–10), who were mostly Passover pilgrims arriving from Galilee and elsewhere. More likely, this crowd is made up of Jewish nationalists who are there to lobby Pilate for the release of a prisoner, as well as the chief priests, their guards, and hired ruffians (see 14:43).

15:9–10   Pilate's question has a tone of sarcasm and contempt; he probably intends to taunt the Sanhedrin by referring to Jesus as a **king**. Jesus, bound and having suffered arrest, mockery, and beating, hardly looks like a royal figure. Why

---

1. Josephus, *Antiquities* 18.1.1; 3.2.

would Pilate offer to **release** him? Mark explains that Pilate **knew** that Jesus had been handed over **out of envy**. The chief priests are jealous of Jesus' popularity and see him as a threat to their power and influence. It would take no political genius to realize that they are not acting out of loyalty to Rome. Having decided to get rid of Jesus for reasons of their own, they hope to use the Roman governor as their henchman. But Pilate has interrogated Jesus himself and concluded that this "king of the Jews" presents not the slightest political threat. There is no reason to infer that Pilate is motivated by compassion or a keen sense of justice. Most likely he simply has no wish to be drawn into the Sanhedrin's scheming.

Pilate's attempt to escape the dilemma fails, since the **chief priests** incite the **crowd** to clamor for the release of **Barabbas instead**. This was probably no difficult task, especially if the crowd had gathered in support of rebel prisoners in the first place (vv. 7–8). Pilate's next move is unwise: he asks the crowd for its opinion on how to handle Jesus. It is not clear why Pilate would consult the crowd in determining the fate of a prisoner. But it may be that he hopes to play off the nationalists against the chief priests. Perhaps they would call for some milder punishment than the death penalty, or demand the release of Jesus as well as Barabbas. At the same time Pilate may wish to shift responsibility for the execution of an innocent man off himself and onto the crowd. | **15:11–12**

Pilate's negotiation tactics backfire. The crowd, which is becoming riotous, responds with the shrill cry: **Crucify him.** It is the first mention of crucifixion in the Gospel (the word for **again** would be better translated as "back" or "in response"). But Jesus had prophesied his death many times, and had hinted at the form it would take by characterizing a disciple as one who "takes up his cross" and follows Jesus (8:34). Crucifixion was Rome's standard punishment for violent criminals and insurrectionists, the most painful and ignominious form of execution known (see sidebar p. 168). Why would the crowd demand such a horrible fate for their fellow Jew? Mark does not explain, and leaves it as a question for the reader to contemplate. Perhaps the nationalists in the crowd regard Jesus as a threat to the release of their man, Barabbas. Perhaps they regard the kingdom of God that he preached (1:14–15) as a futile, pie-in-the-sky religious quest when what was really needed was violent, military action to liberate Israel. It is also possible that most people in the crowd did not know who Jesus was and were simply willing to go along with the chief priests' agitation. In either case, they demonstrate chilling indifference to the torments to which they expose him. The crowd's utter rejection of Jesus continues his progressive isolation throughout the passion narrative. But the reader of the | **15:13**

Gospel knows that it is even for this crowd who callously reject him that Jesus is about to lay down his life.

15:14–15   Pilate protests weakly, **Why? What evil has he done?** Readers of the Gospel know the answer: "He had done no wrong nor spoken any falsehood" (Isa 53:9). But the crowd, now more like a frenzied mob, can produce no answer and only shouts the louder, **Crucify him.** Pilate, fearing uncontrollable violence, placates the people by releasing Barabbas and sentencing Jesus to death. It is important to note that Mark in no way exonerates Pilate from blame for this decision. The Jewish leaders have taken the initiative in the proceedings, but the fate of the prisoner is in Pilate's hands. Although the governor is convinced that Jesus is innocent, he hands him over to death in a heinous act of cowardice and political expediency. He is no less guilty than was Herod Antipas for the death of John the Baptist (Mark 6:17–29). The "handing over" process—a progressive betrayal that began with Judas—is now complete: Judas handed Jesus over to the chief priests (14:10), who handed him over to Pilate (15:1), who hands him over **to be crucified** (15:15).

The name of the released prisoner is a clue to the symbolic significance of this scene. **Barabbas** means "Son of the Father" in Aramaic, and Mark has just shown Jesus addressing God as Abba, Father (14:36). Jesus, the true Son of the Father, is innocent but condemned to death, while a man guilty of rebellion— the antithesis of true sonship (see John 1:12; Gal 3:26)—goes free in his place. Jesus had prophesied that his death would be a "ransom," making atonement for

---

All Sinners Are the Authors of Christ's Passion

LIVING TRADITION

The Catechism teaches that "the Church has never forgotten that 'sinners were the authors and the ministers of all the sufferings that the divine Redeemer endured.' Taking into account the fact that our sins affect Christ himself, the Church does not hesitate to impute to Christians the gravest responsibility for the torments inflicted upon Jesus, a responsibility with which they have all too often burdened the Jews alone." Indeed, "our crime in this case is greater in us than in the Jews. As for them, according to the witness of the Apostle, 'None of the rulers of this age understood this; for if they had, they would not have crucified the Lord of glory.' We, however, profess to know him. And when we deny him by our deeds, we in some way seem to lay violent hands on him" (598, quoting the *Roman Catechism*).

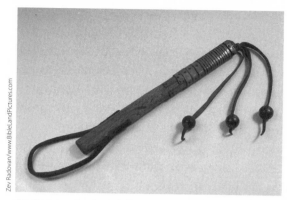

Zev Radovan/www.BibleLandPictures.com

Fig. 15. Reconstruction of a Roman scourge.

many who deserved to die (Mark 10:45). Barabbas is the first of many rebels to be ransomed by Jesus.

The typical prelude to a Roman execution was to be **scourged**, a terrifying punishment. Once sentence was passed the victim was stripped naked, bound to a post or pillar, and lashed until the flesh hung in shreds. The instrument was a whip of rawhide, braided with bone or metal. There was no limit to the number of strokes (unlike Jewish law, which set a limit of thirty-nine; see 2 Cor 11:24). Josephus records instances of flagellation until the prisoners' entrails or bones were visible.[2] It was not unusual for the victim to collapse and die from the scourging alone.

The Mocking of the King (15:16–21)

¹⁶The soldiers led him away inside the palace, that is, the praetorium, and assembled the whole cohort. ¹⁷They clothed him in purple and, weaving a crown of thorns, placed it on him. ¹⁸They began to salute him with, "Hail, King of the Jews!" ¹⁹and kept striking his head with a reed and spitting upon him. They knelt before him in homage. ²⁰And when they had mocked him, they stripped him of the purple cloak, dressed him in his own clothes, and led him out to crucify him.

²¹They pressed into service a passer-by, Simon, a Cyrenian, who was coming in from the country, the father of Alexander and Rufus, to carry his cross.

OT: Isa 50:6–7; 53:3–5
NT: // Matt 27:27–32; Luke 23:26; John 19:2–3, 17
Lectionary: votive Mass of the Mystery of the Holy Cross, of the Most Holy Eucharist, or of the Most Precious Blood of Our Lord Jesus Christ

For the second time during his passion Jesus is mocked, a humiliation that will be repeated again on the cross (vv. 29–32). The first to make sport of Jesus were the Sanhedrin and their guards (14:65); now it is Gentile **soldiers** under

15:16

2. *Jewish War* 2.21.5; 6.5.3.

Pilate's command. The soldiers were auxiliary troops recruited from among the non-Jewish inhabitants of Palestine and Syria to help keep the Jewish populace in line. They probably regarded Jesus as a welcome diversion from the tensions in the air in Jerusalem during a major Jewish holiday. **Inside the palace** probably refers to a large courtyard inside the **praetorium**, Pilate's temporary headquarters in Jerusalem. Archaeologists debate two possible sites for the praetorium: the fortress Antonia just north of the temple mount, or a palace built by Herod the Great near the western gate of the city. A Roman cohort was a detachment of about six hundred soldiers, one tenth of a legion; the **whole cohort** means all those who were on duty at the time.

15:17   The exhausted, bruised, and bleeding prisoner in their custody has just been sentenced to death on the trumped-up charge of claiming to be king. The soldiers probably take their cue from Pilate, who has used the title "king of the Jews" to taunt the Jewish leaders (vv. 9, 12), and they come up with a grotesque game of their own. In a charade of homage they clothe his naked body with the regalia of royalty, **purple** and a **crown** (see Esther 8:15; Sir 40:4; 1 Macc 10:20). Purple was a color of the wealthy because the dye was costly; the soldiers may have used a faded scarlet military cloak or a shabby blanket to serve as "purple." Spiky branches from a nearby shrub are woven together and shoved onto Jesus' head as an improvised crown. The **thorns** may have been a caricature of the sun rays emanating from the imperial crown portrayed on coins, signifying divine kingship.

15:18–19   In mock homage, the troops begin to salute Jesus: **Hail, King of the Jews!** mimicking the Latin salutation of the emperor, "Ave, Caesar!" The sarcasm quickly turns to physical abuse as the soldiers buffet Jesus' head with a **reed**, a farcical version of a kingly scepter. To ridicule his utter powerlessness they do what no one would dare to do to a king: spit on him (as in 14:65). Once again the Suffering Servant is in the background of Mark's account: "I gave my back to those who beat me, my cheeks to those who plucked my beard; My face I did not shield from buffets and spitting. The Lord GOD is my help, therefore I am not disgraced" (Isa 50:6–7). In a final parody of royal homage, the soldiers kneel before him. Viewed with the eyes of faith, the scene is profoundly ironic. Mark's readers know that Jesus is worthy of all homage as the "King of kings and Lord of lords" (Rev 19:16). It is precisely in his suffering and humiliation that he is crowned king.

15:20–21   Those condemned to crucifixion would typically be paraded naked through the streets to the site of execution, forced to carry the horizontal crossbeam and flogged along the way. That Jesus, a carpenter by trade who had probably lifted many a hefty beam, is unable to do so shows how severely weakened the scourging had left him. Roman soldiers claimed the legal right to press Jews into temporary service (see Matt 5:41), so they force the person nearest at hand **to carry his cross**. Mark identifies the man as Simon, a Jew from Cyrene in northern Africa (in present-day Libya), who may have settled in Jerusalem or traveled there for the Passover. Coming on the scene as a mere **passer-by**, he is suddenly brought into the center of the action and compelled to do what Jesus had described as the essence of discipleship: to take up the cross and follow him (Mark 8:34). Although Simon did not volunteer for the honor of carrying the Lord's cross, and perhaps even resented his sudden conscription into a death march, Mark gives a hint that this experience may have changed his life. The mention of his two sons, **Alexander and Rufus**, suggests that they became Christians and were known to the early Church (see Rom 16:13).

The Crucifixion (15:22–32)

---

²²They brought him to the place of Golgotha (which is translated Place of the Skull). ²³They gave him wine drugged with myrrh, but he did not take it. ²⁴Then they crucified him and divided his garments by casting lots for them to see what each should take. ²⁵It was nine o'clock in the morning when they crucified him. ²⁶The inscription of the charge against him read, "The King of the Jews." ²⁷With him they crucified two revolutionaries, one on his right and one on his left. [²⁸] ²⁹Those passing by reviled him, shaking their heads and saying, "Aha! You who would destroy the temple and rebuild it in three days, ³⁰save yourself by coming down from the cross." ³¹Likewise the chief priests, with the scribes, mocked him among themselves and said, "He saved others; he cannot save himself. ³²Let the Messiah, the King of Israel, come down now from the cross that we may see and believe." Those who were crucified with him also kept abusing him.

OT: Deut 21:23; Ps 22; Isa 53:12
NT: Gal 3:13; 1 Pet 2:24. // Matt 27:33–44; Luke 23:33–43; John 19:17–24
Catechism: Jesus' atoning sacrifice, 601–11

Everything Mark has written so far has prepared for the grim scene he now   15:22–23
describes. It is precisely here, at the moment of Jesus' deepest humiliation, that the titles expressing his exalted status—Messiah, King of Israel, builder of the temple, Son of God—come to light in their true meaning. Although hurled in insult, they paradoxically reveal the truth of Jesus' redemptive mission: that

it is accomplished through the pain and humiliation of the cross. Like every event in the Gospel, the crucifixion finds its meaning against the background of the Old Testament, and especially the figure of the just man in the Psalms and Isaiah, who suffers grievously but is finally vindicated by God.

The site of crucifixion was **Golgotha**, from the Aramaic word for **skull**— perhaps because of the rounded shape of the hill, or because of the many gruesome deaths that had occurred there. Those who **gave** Jesus **wine drugged with myrrh** were following a custom, based on Prov 31:6–7, of offering condemned criminals strong drink to lessen their torment. It was common to add myrrh to wine to enhance its fragrance and perhaps also its narcotic effects. But Jesus refuses this offer, in accord with his solemn pledge at the Last Supper: "I shall not drink again of the fruit of the vine until that day when I drink it new in the kingdom of God" (Mark 14:25). He is resolved to endure the passion without any alleviation of pain. The only cup he will drink is the cup of suffering given him by the Father (10:38; 14:36).

15:24   Mark narrates the climactic event of his Gospel in a stark phrase: **they crucified him**. In a Roman crucifixion, the victim's outstretched arms would be nailed or tied to the crossbeam, then the beam would be lifted with the body and fastened to the upright stake already set in the ground. Sometimes a block of wood was fixed midway up the stake as a kind of seat—only to prolong the agony. Although Jewish law had no provision for crucifixion, it did allow for the corpse of an executed criminal to be hung on a tree after death as a sign of being cursed by God: "God's curse rests on him who hangs on a tree" (Deut 21:23). The early Church sometimes described Jesus' crucifixion in this way (Acts 5:30; 10:39;

Golgotha

BIBLICAL BACKGROUND

Since the second century, Christians have traditionally venerated a small hill on the western side of Jerusalem as the site of the crucifixion. The site was probably an old limestone quarry, in which stood a hump of rock shaped like a skull. From the Roman point of view, the site was ideal because its location near a main road made crucifixions into a gruesome public display and frightening deterrent. Executions normally took place outside the city walls (see Lev 24:14; Num 15:35), and in Jesus' time the site was outside the walls, though the walls were later expanded to include it.

Another name for the hill of crucifixion, Calvary, comes from the Latin word for skull in the Vulgate translation of Mark 15:22.

Collection of the Israel Antiquities Authority, © Israel Museum, Jerusalem

Fig. 16. Heel bone of a man crucified in the first century, found in Jerusalem in 1968.

Gal 3:13; 1 Pet 2:24) to signify that Jesus willingly endured the curse of punishment for sin, so that we could be liberated from it.

The usual practice was to crucify the victim naked, although the Romans may have allowed a loincloth as a concession to Jewish sensibilities. By custom the execution squad claimed a right to the victim's belongings. Jesus' clothing probably consisted of an under and outer garment, a belt, sandals, and possibly a head covering.[3] Their **casting lots** for Jesus' **garments** evokes Ps 22:

> A company of evildoers encircle me;
> they have pierced my hands and feet—
> I can count all my bones—
> they stare and gloat over me;
> they divide my garments among them,
> and for my raiment they cast lots. (Ps 22:16–18 RSV)

For Mark this psalm, which Jesus himself will quote at the moment of his death (15:34), is an interpretive key to the crucifixion. It is the lament of an innocent man suffering unjustly, who is devoid of help or comfort, yet who so trusts in God that he praises God in advance for delivering him:

> You who fear the LORD, give praise!
> All descendants of Jacob, give honor;
> show reverence, all descendants of Israel!
> For God has not spurned or disdained
> the misery of this poor wretch,
> Did not turn away from me,
> but heard me when I cried out. (Ps 22:24–25)

Mark notes the time precisely: it was **nine o'clock** (literally, "the third hour") **when they crucified him**. The events of the passion occur in precise three-hour intervals (15:1, 25, 33, 34, 42), reminding the reader that nothing is happening   **15:25**

---

3. Lane, *Mark*, 566.

by mere chance; all is taking place "by the set plan and foreknowledge of God" (see Acts 2:23).

15:26   In Roman executions, a placard specifying the crime would be hung around the condemned man's neck or affixed to the cross. In Jesus' case the charge reads simply, **The King of the Jews**. Pilate intends this phrase ironically, as another jab at the Jewish leaders who had brought the charge against Jesus (vv. 9, 12; see John 19:19–22). At the same time it serves as a warning to other would-be messianic pretenders. But for readers of the Gospel, the phrase is weighted with a profound truth. Jesus is indeed King of the Jews, and he is enthroned on the cross because it is there that he exercises his dominion over sin, Satan, and death. He reigns through the act of love in which he gave up his life, and those who believe in him experience his liberating kingship.

15:27   **Two revolutionaries** (or "robbers") are **crucified** along with Jesus, probably two of those who had committed murder and were imprisoned with Barabbas (v. 7). The Greek word for robber or bandit (*lēstēs*) had also come to mean a political insurgent. Jesus thus dies, ironically, in the midst of Zealot-type rebels—exactly the false understanding of messiahship that he had distanced himself from during his whole public ministry. His association with sinners that began with his baptism in the Jordan (1:9) reaches its climax: Jesus takes his place in the midst of those who are separated from God because of their sin (Isa 59:2). Once again there is an echo of Isaiah's Suffering Servant poems: "He surrendered himself to death and was counted among the wicked" (Isa 53:12). The two revolutionaries are crucified with him, **one on his right and one on his left**; ironically, these are the very positions of royal honor that James and John had requested (Mark 10:37). Jesus had warned the sons of Zebedee that discipleship entails "drinking his cup"; now there is a graphic portrayal of what it means to be close to him.[4]

15:29–30   Jesus' utter isolation is intensified by the threefold mockery he now endures, a replay of the earlier mockery by the Sanhedrin (14:65) and the Roman soldiers (15:16–20). First, he is **reviled** (*blasphēmeō*) by those **passing by** on the road. The Greek verb can mean "blaspheme," "insult," "jeer at," or "verbally abuse" in any way. In blaspheming him they are blaspheming God, ironically the very offense for which the Sanhedrin had condemned Jesus (14:64; see 2:6–7). But for the readers of the Gospel it is a reminder of the fathomless mercy that is being poured out, for Jesus had announced in advance that "all sins and all blasphemies that people utter will be forgiven them" (3:28). The scoffers' **shaking their heads** evokes both the suffering just man of Ps 22:8–9 and the scorn

---

4. The NAB omits v. 28 because it is not found in the most reliable manuscripts.

heaped on Jerusalem after the destruction of the first temple: "All who pass by . . . hiss and wag their heads over daughter Jerusalem" (Lam 2:15; see Jer 18:16). The taunt also links Jesus with the temple by repeating the false accusation of Mark 14:58. Precisely by *not* **coming down from the cross** and saving himself Jesus is ushering in the end of the earthly **temple** (15:38) and the building of a new temple on the cornerstone of his crucified and risen body.

Second, Jesus is railed at by the religious leaders who had orchestrated his death (14:1, 55–65; 15:1–11) and who now come to gloat over their success. **He saved others** refers to Jesus' ministry of healing, which was regularly described with the verb *sōzō*, meaning both "save" and "heal" (5:23, 28, 34; 6:56; 10:52). But readers of the Gospel recognize a deeper sense to these words: Jesus saves people from eternal death. The scoffers taunt that despite his reputed wonder-working powers **he cannot save himself**. Yet it is precisely by refusing to "save himself" that Jesus saves others. From the beginning of his public ministry he had irrevocably committed himself to the Father's plan for a suffering Messiah in total solidarity with sinners (1:9; 10:45; 14:36). Indeed Jesus *cannot* save himself if he is to be obedient to that plan. As he had instructed his disciples, so it is for him: whoever loses his life will save it (8:35). Only by surrendering to death will he be raised up to life by the Father. Only by giving his body and pouring out of his blood can he renew once and for all the covenant between God and humanity (14:22–24).

The religious leaders intensify their derision with a demand for a miraculous sign, just as the Pharisees had done earlier (8:11). It is the final temptation of Jesus' life, the culmination of the testing that began with Satan in the desert (1:13). The temptation is to be a Messiah who gains adherents by stunning displays of power instead of by obediently accepting humiliation and defeat. Significantly, the title "King of the Jews" used up to this point (vv. 2, 9, 12, 18, 26) has been changed to **King of Israel**, a broader scope of kingship. "Jews" refers to members of the tribe of Judah, which was essentially the only remaining tribe since the eighth century BC. "Israel" designates all twelve tribes, long scattered among the nations, whom God had promised to restore and regather to himself at the coming of the Messiah (Jer 31:1; Ezek 37:19–22).

Finally, even the two insurgents **crucified with him also kept abusing him**. Jesus experiences only scorn, rejection, and incomprehension from those he came to save. It is the culmination of the biblical theme of the just man abused and insulted by the wicked, who does not cease to trust God. The scene evokes the psalm: "All who see me mock me; they curl their lips and jeer; they shake their heads at me: 'You relied on the Lord—let him deliver you; if he loves

15:31

15:32

you, let him rescue you'" (Ps 22:8–9). Mark may also have in mind the wicked scheming described in the book of Wisdom:

> Let us beset the just one, because he is obnoxious to us; . . .
> He calls blest the destiny of the just
>   and boasts that God is his Father.
> Let us see whether his words be true;
>   let us find out what will happen to him.
> For if the just one be the son of God, he will defend him
>   and deliver him from the hand of his foes.
> With revilement and torture let us put him to the test
>   that we may have proof of his gentleness
>   and try his patience.
> Let us condemn him to a shameful death;
>   for according to his own words, God will take care of him. (Wis 2:12–20)

Reflection and Application (15:22–32)

When we think of "the cross" Christians often call to mind the sorrow, agony, and injustice of Jesus' death. Or we may think of the crosses of suffering and trials in our own life. But for the eyes of faith, the cross—the whole paschal mystery of Jesus' suffering, death, and resurrection—has also become the source of a living power. St. Paul proclaimed "Christ crucified, a stumbling block to Jews and foolishness to Gentiles, but to those who are called, Jews and Greeks alike, Christ the power of God and the wisdom of God" (1 Cor 1:23–24). The cross is not only the means by which God reconciled humanity to himself two thousand years ago but also the means by which God works powerfully in our lives even now. How can we know and experience this power?

St. Paul explains that in a mysterious but real way our old self, captive to sin, has died with Christ on the cross. "Are you unaware that we who were baptized into Christ Jesus were baptized into his death? . . . Our old self was crucified with him" (Rom 6:3, 6). This is an objective truth, but it becomes our subjective daily experience as we *lay hold of it in faith*, believing in our hearts that "it is no longer I who live, but Christ who lives in me" (Gal 2:20 RSV). We do not have to do this on our own, since God has given us the Holy Spirit to reveal the love he poured out on the cross and to kindle the fire of that love within us. Jesus has taken upon himself and borne to the cross every one of our sins. When he rose from the dead, sin and Satan were crushed. We are no longer under the reign of sin (Rom 5:21; 6:11)! In this way the cross, a gruesome instrument of death, has become the tree of life.

The Death of Jesus (15:33–41)

³³At noon darkness came over the whole land until three in the afternoon. ³⁴And at three o'clock Jesus cried out in a loud voice, *"Eloi, Eloi, lema sabachthani?"* which is translated, "My God, my God, why have you forsaken me?" ³⁵Some of the bystanders who heard it said, "Look, he is calling Elijah." ³⁶One of them ran, soaked a sponge with wine, put it on a reed, and gave it to him to drink, saying, "Wait, let us see if Elijah comes to take him down." ³⁷Jesus gave a loud cry and breathed his last. ³⁸The veil of the sanctuary was torn in two from top to bottom. ³⁹When the centurion who stood facing him saw how he breathed his last he said, "Truly this man was the Son of God!" ⁴⁰There were also women looking on from a distance. Among them were Mary Magdalene, Mary the mother of the younger James and of Joses, and Salome. ⁴¹These women had followed him when he was in Galilee and ministered to him. There were also many other women who had come up with him to Jerusalem.

OT: Ps 22:2–3; 69:22; Amos 8:9–10
NT: Heb 9:11–12. // Matt 27:45–56; Luke 23:44–49; John 19:25–30
Catechism: Jesus' sacrificial death, 613–23
Lectionary: 15:33–46: Funerals for Children Who Died before Baptism; 15:33–39; 16:1–6: Mass for the Dead; votive Mass of the Mystery of the Holy Cross

The drama of redemption climaxes at the death of Jesus with its momentous **15:33** repercussions in both the cosmos and the temple. Mark has carefully structured his passion account in three-hour intervals. Now, during the last three hours of Jesus' agony, **darkness** envelops **the whole land** (or "the whole earth"), as if creation itself is mourning the abuse heaped on God's Son. The darkness cannot be explained with reference to a solar eclipse, because of its long duration and because an eclipse is astronomically impossible at Passover, which is always at full moon. In the Old Testament, supernatural darkness is a prominent sign of judgment on "the day of the Lord" (see Isa 13:10–11; Joel 2:10–11; 3:4). Three days of darkness preceded the death of the firstborn sons in Egypt, the precursor to Israel's liberation (Exod 10:21–23). Amos prophesied that "on that day" darkness would come at noon and God's people would "mourn as for an only son" (Amos 8:9–10). In his end times discourse Jesus had prophesied that the sun's light would fail at the climax of the great tribulation (Mark 13:24). Mark has given several signals that the great tribulation is being played out in Jesus' own passion: the arrival of "the hour," his trial and repeated handing over, and now the cosmic darkness. But the reader also knows that darkness is only the prelude to the glorious vindication and coming of the Son of Man (13:24–26).

15:34   The culmination of Jesus' sacrifice takes place at **three o'clock**, the customary hour of sacrifice. It is the hour when Elijah sacrificed to the true God on Mount Carmel in defiance of the prophets of Baal (1 Kings 18:36), and the hour when the paschal lambs were sacrificed in the temple. Later it becomes a traditional hour of prayer for Christians (Acts 3:1; 10:30). But for Jesus it seems to mark the point of utter defeat. Twice he cries out **in a loud voice** (15:34, 37). Elsewhere in the Gospel, a loud cry occurs only on the lips of those tormented by demons (1:26; 5:7). Jesus, who throughout his public ministry had been dismantling the powers of evil, now himself experiences the unbearable oppression of evil. Mark records Jesus' cry of anguish in Aramaic, *Eloi, Eloi, lema sabachthani?* before providing its translation: **My God, my God, why have you forsaken me?** These are the only words of Jesus on the cross recorded by Mark (and Matthew)—the most stark, astonishing, and scandalous words in the Gospel. Jesus, the "beloved Son" (1:11; 9:7), screams with the desolation of a human heart unable to fathom God's plan in its darkness and obscurity. What are we to make of this shattering cry?

It is significant that in his moment of supreme agony Jesus cries out not in his own words but in words taken from the liturgy of Israel. They are the opening verse of Psalm 22, a psalm of lament that plays a key role in the passion narrative (Mark 15:24, 32; 16:7). As commentators often point out, by citing the opening verse Jesus is implicitly invoking the whole psalm, which ends on a note of confidence in God's victory. But this interpretation, while true, cannot be used to soften the scandal of the crucifixion. Jesus' cry of abandonment is the climax of his progressive isolation throughout the passion narrative. He has been deserted by his friends, taunted by his enemies, insulted even by those crucified with him. He has been successively "handed over" by a disciple, by his own people, by humanity (represented by Pilate and the crowd), and now *by God himself.* It is the inexorable outcome of his stepping into the place of sinners at his baptism (1:4, 9) and his resolve to "drink the cup" of divine wrath (14:36). But there is a profound paradox in his cry. "My God" is the language of the covenant ("I will be your God, and you will be my people"),[5] expressing the perfect human attitude of trust in God. Yet the agonized question, "Why have you abandoned me?" expresses the anguish felt by those accursed by God,

5. Lev 26:12; see Gen 17:7; Exod 6:7; Ps 89:27; Jer 7:23.

320

The Splendor of the Cross

Theodore the Studite (ninth century) wrote, "How precious the gift of the cross, how splendid to contemplate! This tree brings not death but life, not darkness but light. This tree does not cast us out of Eden, but opens the way for our return. This is the wood on which Christ, like a king on a chariot, destroyed the devil, the lord of death, and freed the human race from his tyranny. It is the wood upon which the Lord, like a great warrior wounded in his hands, feet and side, healed the wounds of sin that the evil serpent had inflicted on our nature. A tree once caused our death, but now a tree brings life."[a]

a. *Sermon on the Adoration of the Cross*, PG 99:691.

who no longer belong to the covenant.[6] Jesus experiences the full force of the alienation from God caused by sin, yet precisely there, in that extremity of forsakenness, he confesses his filial confidence in the Father. It is the antithesis of his scoffers' taunt, "save yourself," for it is a decision to await salvation from God alone and not procure his own.[7] The cross has become the place of God's hidden triumph, where the covenant broken by humanity is reforged by the suffering Son of Man.

At the turning point of Ps 22, the lament turns into a song of praise. The sufferer begins to celebrate God's liberation, and vows to declare the greatness of God to his brethren in the midst of the assembly (Ps 22:23). Mark sees the psalm as fulfilled at the resurrection, where the women are told to proclaim God's mighty victory to the disciples (Mark 16:7; see John 20:17). It is also fulfilled every time Christians gather for worship, when Jesus proclaims the greatness of God in the midst of the assembly.

The misunderstanding that has plagued Jesus throughout his whole public   **15:35–36**
ministry continues to the end. Some of the **bystanders** mistake (or deliberately misinterpret) his cry as a desperate plea for the help of **Elijah**.[8] According to popular belief Elijah, who had been taken up to heaven in a whirlwind (2 Kings

6. To affirm that Jesus fully *experienced* this abandonment, according to Mark's account, is not to imply that God actually abandoned his Son. Jesus would have been aware that in many Old Testament passages God promises unconditionally never to abandon his people: Gen 28:15; Deut 4:31; 31:6–8; Josh 1:5; 1 Chron 28:20; Neh 9:17; Ps 9:11; Isa 42:16; 49:14–15; Hosea 11:9.

7. See Lorraine Caza, *Mon Dieu, pourquoi m'as-tu abandonné?* Recherches Nouvelle Série 24 (Paris: Cerf, 1989), especially 327–35, 408–23.

8. It is not implausible that "my God" (*Elohi* in Aramaic, *Eli* in Hebrew) could be confused with "Elijah" (*Eliyah* in Aramaic, *Eliyahu* in Hebrew), especially by nonnatives.

2:11), often came to the aid of the righteous in time of trouble. In response a bystander, probably a soldier, soaks a **sponge** in pungent sour **wine** (*oxos*) and holds it up on a **reed** for Jesus **to drink**. It is not clear whether this gesture is done in sympathy or in cynical mockery—or perhaps with cruel intent to prolong Jesus' last moments of consciousness so that he would see Elijah's failure to come. For Mark this detail evokes another psalm of lament: "for my thirst they gave me vinegar (*oxos*) to drink" (Ps 69:21 RSV). The suggestion, **Wait, let us see if Elijah comes to take him down**, displays the same error as those who taunted Jesus (15:30, 32): that Jesus' claims would be validated only if God would miraculously intervene to save him from the passion. But it is precisely by remaining on the cross, as the crucified Messiah and King of Israel, that Jesus reveals who he truly is (15:39).

15:37   Jesus' final breath is another **loud cry** of anguish, again evoking the psalm: "O my God, I cry by day, but you do not answer" (Ps 22:2 NRSV). With this cry he **breathed his last**, surrendering back to God the human life he had been given (see Gen 2:7). It is his final act of self-abandonment to the Father.

15:38   Jesus' death immediately results in two dramatic events, signaling the beginning of a new stage in salvation history. First, **the veil of the sanctuary was torn**. Two veils hung in the temple, signifying God's inaccessibility (see Heb 9:8): the outer veil at the entrance to the sanctuary (Num 3:25), and the inner veil curtaining off the most sacred chamber, the Holy of Holies (Exod 26:33; Heb 9:3–4). Mark is probably referring to the inner veil, beyond which only the high priest could go, and only once a year, on the Day of Atonement (Lev 16). That it was ripped **from top to bottom** signifies that God himself tore it, removing the barrier between himself and humanity. By his obedient death Jesus enters into God's presence as high priest on behalf of all humanity, opening access to the Father (see Eph 2:18; Heb 10:19–22). The ripped veil portends the end of the old covenant worship (Mark 13:2; see John 4:21–23), since the earthly temple would be replaced by a new temple "not made with hands" (Mark 14:58), with Jesus himself as the cornerstone (12:10).[9] This new temple, the Christian community, will truly be a "house of prayer for all peoples" (11:17), where Jews and Gentiles alike have immediate access to God. The temple veils were adorned with images of the stars, signifying that the temple was a microcosm of the universe. The tearing (*schizō*) of the temple veil recalls the tearing (*schizō*) of the heavens that occurred at Jesus' baptism (1:10), symbolizing that his death

---

9. Historically, there was an overlap of forty years (a "generation," 13:30) between the beginning of the new temple and the passing away of the old, during which time Jewish Christians continued to participate in the temple worship of Israel (Acts 2:46; 3:1; 21:26).

is the prelude to the end of the old creation, as he had hinted in the end times discourse (13:26–31).

Second, the **centurion** in charge of Jesus' execution, a Gentile, responds to Jesus' death with a confession of faith that is the climax of the Gospel: **Truly this man was the Son of God!** In contrast to the mockers who had demanded to "see" Jesus come down from the cross so that they may believe (v. 32), the centurion "sees" Jesus give up his life on the cross and believes. His exclamation may be prompted by Jesus' "loud cry," since ordinarily a victim of crucifixion died of asphyxiation or exhaustion, bereft of breath. Whatever the centurion may have meant, for Mark his acclamation is the full revelation of the mystery of the crucified Messiah. At the beginning of Jesus' public ministry, the heavens were torn and God the Father bore witness to his beloved Son (1:11). Now, at the culmination of Jesus' mission, the temple veil is torn and for the first time a human being acknowledges Jesus as the Son of God. The centurion's coming to faith is the first fruit of Jesus' sacrifice. The eschatological gathering in of the Gentiles, prophesied in the Old Testament (Isa 66:10–23) and announced by Jesus (Mark 13:10, 27), has begun!

15:39

For the first time in his account Mark speaks of **women** who had been accompanying Jesus during his public ministry. In contrast to the male disciples, who "all

15:40

Son of God

The revelation of Jesus as Son of God is central to Mark's Gospel. During his public ministry, the demons recognize Jesus' identity (1:34; 3:11), but are forbidden to speak because this revelation would not yet be rightly understood. For the Jews, son of God had a range of meanings. It could be applied to God's people (Exod 4:22; Deut 14:1; Hosea 11:1) and to the angels, members of the heavenly court (Job 1:6; Ps 29:1; 89:7). It became a royal title for the king of Israel (2 Sam 7:14; Ps 2:7) because of his special relationship to God.

But the New Testament confesses Jesus as Son of God in a sense that goes far beyond its previous meanings. Jesus is Son because of his unique relationship with the Father, sharing in his divine glory. Paradoxically, it is when he is stripped of everything and seemingly abandoned by God that Jesus is revealed in his divine identity as Son.

The Gospel of John deepens the understanding of Jesus as the Father's only-begotten Son (John 1:14; 3:16; 17:1). The early Church articulated this mystery in confessing Jesus as "true God from true God, begotten not made, one in being with the Father" (Council of Nicea, AD 325).

left him and fled" (14:50), they remain with Jesus in his hour of trial, all the way to Golgotha. But there is a hint that their discipleship too is hesitant: they look on **from a distance**, as Peter had followed "at a distance" after the arrest (14:54).

Mark identifies three of the women, perhaps because they were known by name to the early Church. **Mary Magdalene**, whom Jesus had delivered from severe demonic possession (16:9; Luke 8:2), was from the village of Magdala on the western shore of the Sea of Galilee. **Mary the mother of the younger James and of Joses** was probably a relative of Jesus' mother (see Mark 6:3), perhaps the wife of Clopas (John 19:25). **Salome** may be the woman Matthew identifies as mother of the sons of Zebedee (Matt 27:56).

15:41 These women exemplify true discipleship: they had **followed** Jesus (see 2:14; 10:21) and **ministered to** (*diakoneō*) **him**. Jesus had characterized his own mission as service: "the Son of Man did not come to be served but to serve (*diakoneō*)" (10:45). As he ministered to others through his teaching and healing, these women ministered to him. Their ministry may have included preparing meals, washing clothing, and other humble acts of service for Jesus and the disciples (see 1:31), faithfully carrying out his word that a disciple must aspire to be "the servant of all" (9:35; see 10:43). Mark concludes with a surprising comment implying that Jesus had as many women disciples as men. Their presence in his entourage is a sign of the dignity and esteem that Jesus accorded to women (see John 4:27).

The Burial of Jesus (15:42–47)

---

[42]When it was already evening, since it was the day of preparation, the day before the sabbath, [43]Joseph of Arimathea, a distinguished member of the council, who was himself awaiting the kingdom of God, came and courageously went to Pilate and asked for the body of Jesus. [44]Pilate was amazed that he was already dead. He summoned the centurion and asked him if Jesus had already died. [45]And when he learned of it from the centurion, he gave the body to Joseph. [46]Having bought a linen cloth, he took him down, wrapped him in the linen cloth and laid him in a tomb that had been hewn out of the rock. Then he rolled a stone against the entrance to the tomb. [47]Mary Magdalene and Mary the mother of Joses watched where he was laid.

OT: Deut 21:22–23; Isa 53:9
NT: // Matt 27:57–61; Luke 23:50–55; John 19:38–42
Catechism: Christ's burial, 624–30; we are buried with him in baptism, 1227

Jesus' Tomb

First-century Jews typically buried their dead in family tombs dug out of the limestone hillsides or the ground. According to custom, the corpse would be placed on a shelf in an outer chamber of the tomb for about a year, until the flesh decomposed. The bones would then be collected and placed in an ossuary or bone box in an inner recess.

Jesus' tomb, according to ancient tradition, was at a site less than two hundred feet from Golgotha, dug into the hillside just outside the western wall of the city. In the fourth century, when Christianity became legal, the Emperor Constantine built a magnificent basilica at the site, removing most of the hillside surrounding the tomb. Today the Church of the Holy Sepulcher, built over the traditional sites of both the crucifixion and the resurrection, is the holy place most venerated by Christians of both East and West.

Mark's account of the burial establishes two important points: that Jesus was truly dead and that, contrary to the usual practice for crucified criminals, he was given a reverent burial. Mark notes carefully that Jesus' death took place on Friday, the day when cooking and other tasks were done in **preparation** for the **sabbath**. Since burials were considered work prohibited on the sabbath, Jesus' body would need to be buried before the sabbath began at sunset. Moreover, it was against the law of Moses to leave a corpse hanging on a tree overnight (Deut 21:22–23), a law that was applied to crucifixions. **15:42**

Joseph of Arimathea is introduced as **a distinguished member of the council** (presumably the Sanhedrin). Mark does not indicate that he is a disciple of Jesus (but see Matt 27:57); he is simply a devout Jew longing for the fulfillment of God's promises. Normally the Romans would leave a crucified body to decay or be devoured by scavenging animals, so that the disgrace of execution would continue even after death. Thus it took courage for Joseph to approach **Pilate** requesting the body: he risked both the ire of the Sanhedrin who had condemned Jesus (Mark 14:64) and the danger of being associated with an enemy of the state. Joseph's deed of mercy is in the tradition of Jewish piety exemplified by Tobit, who also buried the dead at risk to himself (Tob 1:18–19; 2:8). **15:43**

Pilate is **amazed that he was already dead**, since victims often hung on a cross for days before expiring. Jesus' death after only six hours is an indication of the severity of the scourging and maltreatment he had already received (15:15–21). Pilate verifies the death by summoning the **centurion** who had **15:44–45**

The King Is Asleep

In an ancient homily for Holy Saturday, a bishop told his flock: "there is a great silence on earth today, a great silence and stillness. The whole earth keeps silence because the King is asleep. . . . God has died in the flesh and hell trembles with fear. He has gone to search for our first parent, as for a lost sheep. Greatly desiring to visit those who live in darkness and in the shadow of death, he has gone to free from sorrow the captives Adam and Eve. . . .

"The Lord approached them bearing the cross, the weapon that had won him the victory. He took [Adam] by the hand and raised him up, saying, 'Awake, O sleeper, and rise from the dead, and Christ will give you light. I am your God, who for your sake have become your son. Out of love for you and your descendants I now by my own authority command all who are held in bondage to come forth, all who are in darkness to be enlightened, all who are sleeping to arise. . . . I did not create you to be held a prisoner in hell. Rise from the dead, for I am the life of the dead.'"[a]

a. Epiphanius of Salamis, homily, from the Office of Readings for Holy Saturday, *Liturgy of the Hours* (New York: Catholic Book Publishing, 1976), 2:496–97.

witnessed it (v. 39), the most truthful witness to Jesus in the Gospel so far.[10] On the centurion's assurance he hands over the **body** (literally, corpse) **to Joseph**. Jesus had refused the demand to "come down from the cross" by his own power (v. 32); he will only be *taken down* in the utter passivity of death.

15:46–47   Only Mark notes that Joseph bought a **cloth** of **linen**, the fabric of the wealthy, in which to wrap the body. Joseph must have been a man of some means, who perhaps owned the nearby **tomb** (see Matt 27:60). The burial is apparently too hasty to allow for the customary anointing with spiced oils—but a woman had already lovingly done so just a few days before, in unconscious anticipation of Jesus' death (14:3–8). The burial again evokes the Suffering Servant, who was assigned a grave "with a rich man" (Isa 53:9 RSV). The **stone** rolled against the entrance to the tomb is for the sake of protecting the body from scavenging animals; it also emphasizes the finality of death. Mark makes careful note of the women disciples who witnessed the burial.

10. Moloney, *Mark*, 334.

The Resurrection

Mark 16:1–20

Throughout his Gospel Mark has been preparing his readers for Jesus' trium-phant victory over death, just as Jesus was preparing his disciples. But there is a sense in which no one could be prepared for the resurrection. Jesus' rising from the dead is no mere awakening of a corpse (like that of Jairus's daughter; 5:42). It is God's decisive intervention in time and history by which human existence is radically and forever transformed. The resurrection is the final stage in the one paschal mystery, God's mighty act of deliverance by which humanity is liberated from sin and restored to communion with him. The Gospel has only hinted (8:35; 12:26–27; 13:26–27) at what St. Paul develops in full: Jesus' resurrection is the source and principle of our own future resurrec-tion to eternal life. Mark's account of the resurrection is remarkably brief. But through his narrative he invites his readers to step into the story and allow the Holy Spirit to bring about the unshakable conviction of faith in the risen Lord that has transformed his own life.

The Resurrection (16:1–8)

¹When the sabbath was over, Mary Magdalene, Mary, the mother of James, and Salome bought spices so that they might go and anoint him. ²Very early when the sun had risen, on the first day of the week, they came to the tomb. ³They were saying to one another, "Who will roll back the stone for us from the entrance to the tomb?" ⁴When they looked up, they

saw that the stone had been rolled back; it was very large. **⁵On entering the tomb they saw a young man sitting on the right side, clothed in a white robe, and they were utterly amazed. ⁶He said to them, "Do not be amazed! You seek Jesus of Nazareth, the crucified. He has been raised; he is not here. Behold the place where they laid him. ⁷But go and tell his disciples and Peter, 'He is going before you to Galilee; there you will see him, as he told you.'" ⁸Then they went out and fled from the tomb, seized with trembling and bewilderment. They said nothing to anyone, for they were afraid.**

OT: Job 19:25; Ps 16:10–11; 86:13; Hosea 6:2; Jon 2:7
NT: // Matt 28:1–8; Luke 24:1–10; John 20:1
Catechism: Christ's resurrection and ours, 638–58, 992–1004; the first day of the week, 2174–77
Lectionary: Easter Sunday Vigil (Year B)

16:1–2   When Mark resumes his story, a full day has passed since the burial. He says nothing of Jesus or of the activities of the disciples during this time, leaving the mystery of Holy Saturday shrouded in silence. On Saturday evening, when the **sabbath** is over, the three women who had witnessed the death and burial are able to buy the **spices** or perfumed oils needed to anoint the body properly. Their devotion to Jesus moves them to perform one last act of kindness for him, heedless of any concerns about the onset of decomposition. The faithfulness of the women in associating with the crucified Jesus contrasts with the faithlessness of Peter and the Twelve (14:50, 66–72), who are conspicuous for their absence. At the earliest possible opportunity, at dawn on Sunday, the women come to the **tomb**. Mark's mention that **the sun had risen** is the first hint that the darkness accompanying the death of Jesus (15:33)—the apparent triumph of evil—has been definitively overcome. Mark may be alluding to a prophecy at the very end of the Old Testament: "for you who fear my name, there will arise the sun of justice with its healing rays" (Mal 3:20). It is **the first day of the week**, the day when God created light (Gen 1:3–5): the beginning of the new creation.

16:3   But the women are still thinking on an earthly plane. As far as they know, Jesus' life and mission have come to a tragic end, and there is nothing left to do but show their respect for his remains. Jesus' prophecy of his resurrection (8:31; 9:9, 31; 10:34) had completely eluded their grasp, just as it had for the male disciples. Their main preoccupation at the moment is a heavy **stone**. The women's inability to **roll back** the stone is symbolic of the utter powerlessness of human resources against death, the most inescapable fact of human existence.

Roll Away the Stone

LIVING TRADITION

St. Peter Chrysologus writes, "Is it from the door of the sepulcher, or of your own hearts? From the tomb, or from your own eyes? You whose heart is shut, whose eyes are closed, are unable to discover the glory of the open grave. Pour then your oil, if you wish to see that glory, not on the body of the Lord, but on the eyes of your hearts. By the light of faith you will then see that which through the deficiency of faith now lies hidden in darkness."[a]

a. *Sermon* 82, in Oden and Hall, *Mark*, 229–30.

But looking up (a biblical image for recognizing God's action),[1] the women see that the seemingly impossible has already been done. The **stone is rolled back**. God has entered the story, and has opened the grave (see Ezek 37:12–13)!

16:4

Not yet enlightened, the women enter the tomb to find only **a young man**—clearly an angel[2]—**clothed in a white robe**. This recalls the "young man" who had fled naked from Jesus' arrest (Mark 14:51–52), symbolizing the shame of the disciples who had abandoned Jesus in his hour of trial. The young man's heavenly attire (see 9:3; Rev 6:11; 7:9) is a hint that God has intervened to reverse the disciples' failure and restore their dignity (see on Mark 5:15).[3] At the sight of the angel the women are **utterly amazed**, filled with the wondrous awe that often accompanies biblical theophanies.

16:5

The angel reassures the women and gives the Easter proclamation that is at the heart of the Church's preaching: **Jesus of Nazareth, the crucified . . . has been raised**. This message stresses the reality of Jesus' passion: it is the same Jesus who truly suffered and died on the cross, who now is truly risen from the dead. **He is not here**: that is, he is not to be found in the tomb, the place of the dead. The passive verb "has been raised" means that it is God who raised him. Jesus' agonized question on the cross, "My God, my God, why have you forsaken me?" has received its answer. God has not forsaken his beloved Son but has vindicated him with a triumph far greater than any of his enemies could have imagined, an everlasting triumph over death itself. Jesus has not escaped death but *destroyed it from within*, "trampling on death by death."[4] His prophecy

16:6–7

---

1. See Gen 15:5; 22:13; Josh 5:13; Job 35:5; Zech 5:5.
2. See 2 Macc 3:26, 33; Tob 5:4–5; Acts 1:10; 10:30 for similar portrayals of angels.
3. See Moloney, *Mark*, 345–46.
4. Easter Troparion, a liturgical hymn sung in the Eastern churches.

has come true: he, the rejected stone, has become the cornerstone of a new and heavenly temple (12:10–11; 14:58; 15:29).

The women are told to confirm with their own eyes the reality of the empty tomb, the sign that Jesus' body is no longer bound by death. In itself the empty tomb is not a proof of the resurrection (see Matt 28:11–15) but a sign received in faith, confirming the testimony to the resurrection (see Acts 13:30–35; Rom 10:9; 1 Pet 1:21). The women are then given a solemn commission. In Jewish law women were ineligible to serve as witnesses because they were considered untrustworthy.[5] Yet the faithful women are called to become the first witnesses of the resurrection, the apostles to the apostles. The summons to **Galilee** recalls Jesus' promise that after he was raised he would go before the disciples to Galilee (Mark 14:28), the place where the gospel was first proclaimed and from which it would now go forth to the whole world. It is a reassurance that the disciples, and Peter in particular (see 14:30; Luke 22:31–33; John 21:15–17), have been forgiven for their failure and reinstated in their apostolic mission (see Mark 3:14–15). In Galilee the disciples themselves **will see** the risen Lord.

16:8   But the reaction of the women seems to thwart Jesus' promise. Just as the disciples had earlier fled in fear from the cross (14:50), the women flee in fear from the empty tomb and Easter proclamation. That they are **seized with trembling and bewilderment** suggests not just fright but a holy awe at the overwhelming divine power manifested in the resurrection. It is the reaction displayed throughout the Gospel to the disclosure of Jesus' divine dignity (4:41; 5:15, 33; 6:50; 9:6). Instead of carrying out the angel's commission, the women **said nothing to anyone**. The irony of the messianic secret in Mark's Gospel comes to a stunning reversal. Whereas Jesus had imposed silence on those he healed (1:44; 5:43; 8:26)—an injunction that was sometimes ignored (1:45; 7:36)—now it is time for the mystery to be fully made known, yet the response is silence.

The oldest and most reliable manuscripts of the Gospel of Mark end here, and record no appearances of the risen Jesus. This fact has occasioned much consternation. How could the Gospel end in such a disappointing and inconclusive way? Was the last page lost from the original manuscript, or did Mark perhaps die before he was able to complete his work? But when read in the light of his overall narrative purpose, the ending is not so surprising; indeed, it is purposeful. Throughout his work Mark has portrayed misunderstanding, fear, failure, and flight on the part of Jesus' chosen disciples. He has depicted the shortcomings of even the leader of the early Church, Peter, with relentless candor. He has brought his readers on a journey of discipleship as we too are confronted with

---

5. See Midrash *Rosh Ha-Shanah* 1.8; Josephus, *Antiquities* 4.8.15.

Jesus' startling words, astonishing claims, awesome deeds, and divine logic that overturns all human ways of thinking. Like the original disciples, we have had to come to grips with the mystery of God's plan for a crucified Messiah. Now, with his last verse, Mark has finally brought his readers right into the center of the story. We too are now face to face with the announcement of Jesus' victory over death—and how are we going to respond?

Mark writes knowing that his readers are well aware of how the story unfolds. Peter and the disciples did see the risen Lord, and their encounter with him becomes the bedrock of the apostolic proclamation of the gospel that resounded throughout the Roman Empire (see Acts 3:15; 1 Cor 15:3–8). The very existence of the early Christian community for whom the Gospel is written is testimony to the fulfillment of Jesus' promises (Mark 14:28; 16:7). In Mark's account they have been fulfilled not because the women succeeded in carrying out their commission, but by the power of God who is able to overcome every human failure. Mark has already shown that Jesus' word is utterly reliable.[6] Now every reader is invited to accept in faith the testimony to his resurrection. The story is not concluded because it continues in the life of every disciple of Jesus for all time.

Jesus Appears to Mary Magdalene (16:9–11)

---

[9] [When he had risen, early on the first day of the week, he appeared first to Mary Magdalene, out of whom he had driven seven demons. [10] She went and told his companions who were mourning and weeping. [11] When they heard that he was alive and had been seen by her, they did not believe.

NT: // Luke 24:9–11; John 20:11–17
Catechism: the resurrection appearances, 641–44

Verses 9–20, commonly called the Longer Ending, do not appear in the earliest manuscripts of the Gospel. Scholars are virtually unanimous in holding that these verses were not written by Mark but by a Christian of the late first or early second century who sought to fill out the abrupt ending of verse 8.[7] Yet the Church accepts this addendum as part of the †canon of inspired Scripture. The Holy Spirit's gift of inspiration is not limited to the original writer, but encompasses each biblical book in its final edited form.

---

6. See 8:31; 9:31; 10:32–34; 12:10–11; 14:17–21, 27–31.
7. A few ancient and medieval manuscripts of Mark insert other brief endings, which the Church does not accept as canonical.

16:9–11   The author of the Longer Ending was apparently familiar with all four Gospels (or with the oral testimonies on which they were based), and compiled these verses from the resurrection accounts in Matthew, Luke, and John. Verses 9–11 are an abbreviated version of Jesus' encounter with **Mary Magdalene** (John 20:11–17). Here, as in the other Gospels, it is clear that people do not simply "catch sight" of the risen Lord; rather, the Lord takes the initiative in appearing to whom he chooses. And significantly, the first person to whom he appears is a woman **out of whom he had driven seven demons** (Luke 8:2)—someone who by human standards might be considered the least reliable witness (like the healed demoniac of Mark 5:19–20). Mary goes to **his companions** with the news and finds them **mourning and weeping**, still limited to a this-worldly mindset in which the cross was the ultimate disaster. It does not yet enter their minds that God could have shattered the power of death itself. Predictably they fail to **believe** her testimony (see Luke 24:9–11).

Jesus Appears to Two Disciples (16:12–13)

---

¹²**After this he appeared in another form to two of them walking along on their way to the country. ¹³They returned and told the others; but they did not believe them either.**

NT: // Luke 24:13–32
Catechism: the doubting disciples, 643–44

16:12–13   Verses 12–13 seem to be drawn from Luke's account of the disciples who meet Jesus on the road to Emmaus (Luke 24:13–32). That the risen Lord **appeared in another form** suggests a mysterious ability to transform his bodily appearance. His risen body is such that he is not recognized until he makes himself known (see John 20:14; 21:4). In Luke's account the disciples do not recognize Jesus until he breaks bread with them at table, an allusion to the Eucharist. Once again an eyewitness report of the resurrection meets with only skepticism in the demoralized disciples.

The Apostles' Commission (16:14–18)

---

¹⁴**[But] later, as the eleven were at table, he appeared to them and rebuked them for their unbelief and hardness of heart because they had not believed those who saw him after he had been raised. ¹⁵He said to them,**

"Go into the whole world and proclaim the gospel to every creature.
¹⁶Whoever believes and is baptized will be saved; whoever does not believe
will be condemned. ¹⁷These signs will accompany those who believe: in my
name they will drive out demons, they will speak new languages. ¹⁸They
will pick up serpents [with their hands], and if they drink any deadly
thing, it will not harm them. They will lay hands on the sick, and they will
recover."

OT: Isa 40:9; 52:7; 66:19; Nah 2:1

NT: // Matt 28:16–20; Luke 24:36–49; John 20:19–23

Catechism: the apostles' commission, 2, 642; the Church's mission, 767, 849–56; miracles and
tongues, 2003

Lectionary: 16:15–20: Ascension of the Lord (Year B); Feast of St. Mark; Common of Pastors;
Anointing of the Sick; Mass for Ministers of the Church; For the Evangelization of Peoples;
Christian Initiation Apart from the Easter Vigil; 16:15–18: Conversion of St. Paul

Finally Jesus appears to the **eleven** remaining disciples as they are gathered **16:14**
together (see Luke 24:36–49; John 20:19–23) and reprimands them for their
unbelief and hardness of heart, familiar themes in the Gospel of Mark (6:52;
8:17, 33). With this reproach the author highlights for all his readers the crucial
importance of believing the testimony to the resurrection. Indeed, the distin-
guishing mark of a Christian is accepting the apostolic testimony: he is alive,
and we have seen him (see Acts 2:32).

Jesus' reproach does not invalidate the apostles' commission but rather pre- **16:15–16**
pares for it. Chastened by the recognition of their own slowness to believe, now
they are commissioned to **proclaim the gospel to every creature.** It is the same
charge given at the end of Matthew's Gospel (28:18–20; see also Luke 24:47)
and anticipated in the eschatological discourse (Mark 13:10). The good news is
no longer limited to God's chosen people, as it had been during Jesus' earthly
life (7:27; see Matt 10:6). It is destined for all the world, Jews and Gentiles
alike. The stakes are high: **Whoever believes and is baptized will be saved;
whoever does not believe will be condemned** (see John 3:18). Belief alone is
not enough; it must be expressed and ratified with baptism, an action of God
by which a believer is united with Jesus in his death and resurrection (see Rom
6:1–6) and incorporated into the Church. Whoever does not believe—that is,
whoever hears the gospel and refuses to accept it—forfeits God's gift of salvation (see Mark 8:35–36).

Jesus promises supernatural **signs** and wonders that **will accompany** not **16:17–18**
only the apostles but ordinary Christians (see John 14:12–14). Jesus had earlier
given his apostles authority to **drive out demons** (Mark 3:14); now this power
is extended to the faithful in general (see Acts 8:5–7; 16:18). They will **speak**

new languages, a reference to the gift of tongues given at Pentecost (Acts 2:4; 10:46; 19:6) and experienced in the early Church's worship (1 Cor 12:10; 14:1–28). They will be protected from deadly perils like venomous **serpents** (see Acts 28:3–6) or poisoned drinks. Finally, as the Twelve had done earlier (Mark 6:13), the believers **will lay hands on the sick** for healing. Just as Jesus always accompanied his preaching of the gospel with works of healing and deliverance (1:34; 3:10), so is the Church called to do. The preaching of the gospel is not merely a verbal activity but a demonstration of God's power.[8] For the early Church, healings were a major part of the credentials of the gospel.[9]

Reflection and Application (16:14–18)

In recent years, following the call of Pope John Paul II, there has been a worldwide effort to mobilize the Church for a new evangelization, bringing the gospel anew not only to mission lands but to the secularized post-Christian cultures of the West. The pope called Christians to rekindle the fervor of the beginnings and "allow ourselves to be filled with the ardor of the apostolic preaching which followed Pentecost."[10] Part of this impetus must include a renewed understanding of the role of healings and miracles in the work of evangelization. The testimony of Mark's Gospel underlines the importance of proclaiming the good news to unbelievers with expectant faith, asking the Lord to accompany the preaching of the word with signs and wonders that confirm its truth and demonstrate its power.

The Ascension (16:19–20)

[19]So then the Lord Jesus, after he spoke to them, was taken up into heaven and took his seat at the right hand of God. [20]But they went forth and preached everywhere, while the Lord worked with them and confirmed the word through accompanying signs.]

OT: Ps 110:1
NT: Acts 2:33–36; Eph 4:8–10; Heb 1:3; 12:2; 1 Pet 3:22. // Luke 24:50–51; Acts 1:9–11
Catechism: Christ's ascension, 659–67; accompanying signs, 156, 434

8. See Acts 14:3; Rom 15:19; 1 Cor 2:4–5; 2 Cor 12:12; Heb 2:4.
9. See Acts 3:1–10; 5:15–16; 8:7; 9:33–34; 14:8–10; 20:9–12; 28:8–9.
10. John Paul II, *Novo Millennio Ineunte*, 40.

The Longer Ending concludes with an account of Jesus' ascension, probably   **16:19**
influenced by Luke 24:50–51 and Acts 1:9–11. Jesus is now explicitly called **the Lord** (as he was obliquely in Mark 1:3; 5:19; 13:35), the Old Testament title for God himself. His resurrection has fully revealed his divine sovereignty. That Jesus is **taken up into heaven** and seated at God's **right hand** is the fulfillment of his prophecy before the Sanhedrin (14:62). The seat of highest honor, assigned to the king in Ps 110, belongs to Jesus who is now enthroned as King over all.

Jesus' enthronement in heaven does not at all entail his absence from earth,   **16:20**
but rather speaks of a new presence. As the disciples fulfill his mandate to bring the gospel to the ends of the earth (see Acts 1:8) the Lord works **with them** and confirms their **word** through the **signs** mentioned above (16:17–18; see Acts 2:43; 5:12; 6:8; 14:3). He remains present and powerfully at work in the Church until the end of the age (see Matt 28:20).

Suggested Resources

Note: commentaries by non-Catholic authors are marked with an asterisk (*).

From the Christian Tradition

The First Commentary on Mark. Edited and translated by Mark Cahill. New York: Oxford University Press, 1998. Probably written by an Irish monk of the seventh century. A delightful example of allegorical exegesis.

Oden, Thomas C., and Christopher A. Hall, eds. *Mark*. ACCS. Downers Grove, IL: InterVarsity, 1998. This series offers rich selections from patristic writings on every passage of the biblical text.

St. Thomas Aquinas. *Catena Aurea: Commentary on the Four Gospels, Collected out of the Works of the Fathers*. Vol. 2, *St. Mark*. London: J. G. F. and J. Rivington, 1842. Available online at www.ccel.org/ccel/aquinas/catena2 .html. A treasury of short patristic quotations on the Gospels compiled by St. Thomas.

Scholarly Commentaries

Donahue, John R., and Daniel J. Harrington. *The Gospel of Mark*. Sacra Pagina. Collegeville, MN: Liturgical Press, 2002. Succinct commentary; includes a lengthy and informative introduction.

*France, R. T. *The Gospel of Mark*. NIGTC. Grand Rapids: Eerdmans, 2002. Solid, thorough exegesis by a prominent evangelical scholar; designed especially for those who have knowledge of Greek.

*Lane, William. *The Gospel of Mark*. NICNT. Grand Rapids: Eerdmans, 1974. Older, but still a good resource for background information and sound, balanced exegesis.

*Marcus, Joel. *Mark 1–8*. Anchor Bible. New York: Doubleday, 2000. A detailed but engaging commentary written largely for scholars. The second volume is forthcoming.

Moloney, Francis J. *The Gospel of Mark: A Commentary*. Peabody, MA: Hendrickson, 2002. A relatively brief commentary full of theological insight.

Popular Commentaries and Study Bibles

Casciaro, Jose Maria, et al., eds. *The Navarre Bible: St. Mark's Gospel*. Dublin: Four Courts, 2003 (Spanish original, 1980). The biblical text with exposition and quotations from Church documents and the writings of popes and saints, especially St. Josemaria Escriva, founder of Opus Dei.

Hahn, Scott, and Curtis Mitch. *The Gospel of Mark*. Ignatius Study Bible. San Francisco: Ignatius, 2007. The biblical text supplemented with thorough and very informative footnotes, often citing the Fathers or Church doctrine.

Martin, George. *The Gospel according to Mark*. Chicago: Loyola, 2005. An easy-to-read exposition of the basic meaning of the text with helpful information about the world of first-century Palestine.

Perrotta, Kevin. *Mark: Getting to Know Jesus; A Guided Discovery for Groups and Individuals*. Six Weeks with the Bible. Chicago: Loyola, 2001. A good resource for a Bible study on selected passages of Mark for beginners.

*Wright, Tom. *Mark for Everyone*. Louisville: Westminster John Knox, 2004. Wright is the Anglican bishop of Durham, England, and a prominent New Testament scholar with a gift for communicating biblical insights in a vivid, anecdotal style.

Glossary

amen: a Hebrew term meaning "truly," "so be it," or "it is so," often said at the end of prayers (see 1 Chron 16:36). Jesus had a unique custom of saying "Amen" at the beginning of his solemn pronouncements, emphasizing their truthfulness and authority (see 3:28, etc.).

angel (Greek *angelos*, "messenger"): invisible spirit created by God, often sent by God to help human beings or to carry out his plan (see 1:13; 8:38; 13:27).

apocalyptic (from Greek *apokalypsis*, "revelation"): a distinctive type of ancient Jewish and Christian literature that professes to reveal mysteries of the future or the heavenly realm using symbols and strange imagery. Two prominent examples of biblical apocalypses are the books of Daniel and Revelation. There are also many nonbiblical apocalypses dating from about 200 BC to AD 200.

apostle (Greek *apostolos*, "emissary" or "one who is sent"): in the Synoptic Gospels, the twelve men chosen from among Jesus' disciples to share in his mission in a unique way (Mark 3:14; 6:7, 30). The term was also used more broadly in the early Church (Acts 14:14; Rom 16:7).

Aramaic: a Semitic language related to Hebrew, adopted by Jews after their exile in Babylon. It was the ordinary language spoken by Jews in first-century Palestine, including Jesus.

Caesar: the family name of the Roman emperors, which became their imperial title. See sidebar p. 241.

canon: the list of those books discerned by the Church as belonging to sacred Scripture.

Christ (Greek *Christos*): *see* **Messiah**.

covenant: a sacred kinship bond established between God and his people, involving a mutual commitment of love and fidelity. God formed a covenant with Abraham and later with his descendants, the people of Israel, through Moses. Through his passion, death, and resurrection, Jesus established the new and eternal covenant that fulfills the old (see Jer 31:31–33; Mark 14:24).

Decalogue: the Ten Commandments (Exod 20:2–17; Deut 5:6–21).

demons, unclean spirits: invisible, supernatural beings who tempt, oppress, and seek to destroy human beings, but whose power Jesus overthrows during his public ministry and definitively in his death and resurrection. See sidebar p. 47.

disciple: a follower of Jesus Christ, called to share in his life and destiny. All human beings are invited to become Jesus' disciples by denying themselves, taking up their crosses, and following him (see 8:34).

epiphany (Greek *epiphaneia*): an appearance or manifestation (see 4:39–41). *See also* **theophany**.

eschatology (from Greek *eschata*, "last things"): all that concerns the end of human history, the final tribulations, the coming of Jesus, the last judgment, and the resurrection of the dead (see 13:1–37). For the New Testament the end begins with Jesus' passion and resurrection, the transition from the former age to the new and final age of salvation history.

evangelist: one who proclaims the good news of salvation in Jesus Christ. **Evangelist** (capitalized) also designates an author of one of the four canonical Gospels.

Gentile: a person of non-Jewish descent. Much of the Gospel of Mark is concerned with the extension of God's blessings to the Gentiles, first in Jesus' own ministry and later in the Church.

gospel ("good news"): the joyful tidings that God has come to save us through his Son Jesus Christ, fulfilling all the promises he made to his people Israel. **Gospel** (capitalized) later came to mean one of the four canonical narratives of the life of Jesus, written to lead people to faith in him.

Herod, Herodians: Herod in the Gospel of Mark refers to Herod Antipas, ruler of the regions of Galilee and Perea from 4 BC to AD 39. He was a son of Herod the Great, ruler of Palestine at the time of Jesus' birth. The Herodians were Herod's supporters and appointees. See sidebar p. 119.

Judea: the southernmost of the three regions of Palestine (the other two being Galilee and Samaria), so called because it was mostly comprised of the area settled by the tribe of Judah.

kingdom of God: the experienced authority and reign of God that was at the center of Jesus' preaching (1:14–15). The kingdom is already present in the person of Jesus himself, grows mysteriously in the Church, and will be fully consummated at his coming in glory at the end of time (see Mark 4).

law, law of Moses, Mosaic law: *see* **Torah**.

Messiah (from Hebrew *mashiah*, "anointed one"): the descendant of King David promised by God, whom many Jews of Jesus' day hoped would come to restore the kingdom to Israel. See sidebar p. 30.

parable: a short, memorable story or image used to convey spiritual truths. See sidebar p. 82.

Passover, Pasch: the great holy day of the Jewish calendar, commemorating God's deliverance of his people from slavery in Egypt. Passover, or the paschal mystery, also became the Christian term for Jesus' passion, death, and resurrection. See sidebar p. 275.

Pharisees: members of an influential Jewish renewal movement that strictly observed Jewish laws and customs and maintained separation from Gentiles. See sidebar p. 60.

Pontius Pilate: Roman military governor of the province of Judea from AD 26 to 36. See sidebar p. 306.

prefigurement (or type): a person, thing, or event in an earlier stage of God's plan that displays in a veiled way the pattern of the *fulfillment* of his plan in Jesus Christ. The temple in Jerusalem, for example, prefigures the body of Christ, the true dwelling place of God. The many prefigurements in Scripture reveal the dynamic unity of God's plan of salvation. *See also* **typology**.

prophet: one called by God to speak God's authentic word to his people. The prophets often had to deliver a challenging message regarding sin, judgment, and repentance, and thus often met with persecution. Jesus fulfilled in himself the vocation of a prophet (see 6:4).

rabbi (Hebrew for "my great one"): a Jewish title of respect often used to address Jesus (see Mark 11:21). In later usage it designated those qualified to teach the Law of Moses.

repentance (Greek *metanoia*, "change of mind"): a wholehearted conversion or return to the Lord, acknowledging one's sin and need for his forgiveness. The call to repentance was a central element of Jesus' preaching (see 1:4, 15).

sabbath: the seventh day of the week, set apart by God as a day of rest and worship of God, and a sign of his covenant with Israel. The Church recognizes the sabbath as fulfilled in Christ's resurrection from the dead on the eighth day (Sunday); thus observance of the Lord's Day replaces that of the sabbath. See sidebar p. 47.

Sadducees: a party within Judaism in Jesus' time comprised of the priestly aristocracy, their families, and supporters. See sidebar p. 243.

sandwich technique: a literary device characteristic of Mark, in which one story is inserted in the middle of another so that each throws light on the other (see 3:20–35; 5:22–43; 6:7–30; 11:12–25; 14:1–11, 53–73).

Sanhedrin: the supreme judicial council of the Jewish people, consisting of seventy members, including elders, priests, and scribes. See sidebar p. 298.

Satan (Hebrew for "adversary"): in the Old Testament, a member of the heavenly court who accused or opposed God's people (1 Chron 21:1; Job 1:6–12). In the New Testament, Satan is the prince of demons, the invisible spirits who oppose God's plan and seek to destroy humanity. The Gospel of Mark presents Jesus progressively dismantling Satan's dominion (see 3:26–27).

scribes: men trained in the skilled craft of copying manuscripts, who were often experts in the law of Moses.

second coming: the coming of Jesus at the end of history when his divine glory will be fully revealed (see 8:38; 13:26; 14:62). Elsewhere in the New Testament it is often called the *parousia* (Greek for "coming" or "presence").

Septuagint (abbreviated LXX): an ancient Greek translation of the Old Testament. See sidebar p. 136.

Son of Man: Jesus' characteristic self-designation, drawn from Dan 7:13–14 and alluding in a veiled way to his vocation to suffer and be glorified by God. See sidebar p. 164.

synagogue (Greek *synagogē*, "assembly"): a local place of worship where Jews gather for prayer, readings, and instruction in the Law and Prophets. Synagogues arose after the destruction of the first temple in 587 BC; after the temple was rebuilt they continued to exist, and by the first century AD could be found in many cities of the Roman Empire. The Christian liturgy is in many ways modeled on the synagogue service.

Synoptic Gospels, Synoptics (Greek for "seeing together"): term applied to the Gospels of Matthew, Mark, and Luke because they contain much similar material and view the life of Jesus from a similar perspective.

theophany (Greek for "divine appearance"): a perceptible manifestation of God's holy presence, which causes human awe, fear, and trembling. *See also* **epiphany**.

Torah (Hebrew for "law" or "instruction"): the first five books of the Bible, attributed to Moses and thus also called the Law of Moses, the Books of Moses, or the Pentateuch. Torah is also used more broadly to refer to all God's teachings on how to live an upright life in covenant relationship with him.

typology: the recognition of how biblical persons, things, and events at an earlier stage of salvation history prefigure the way God would accomplish his future purposes, especially the culmination of his plan in Jesus Christ. *See also* **prefigurement**.

unclean spirit: *see* **demons**.

YHWH: God's holy name, revealed to Moses at the burning bush (Exod 3:14). According to ancient custom Jews refrain from pronouncing the divine name out of reverence; when reading the Scriptures aloud they substitute the title "the LORD" (Hebrew *Adonai*, Greek *Kyrios*) or another title for the divine name. The form YHWH (called the Tetragrammaton) is used because Hebrew script has no vowels; the form "Yahweh" is sometimes used to approximate the original pronunciation.

Index of Pastoral Topics

This index indicates where the Gospel of Mark provides material related to topics that may be useful for evangelization, catechesis, apologetics, or other forms of pastoral ministry.

Index of Sidebars

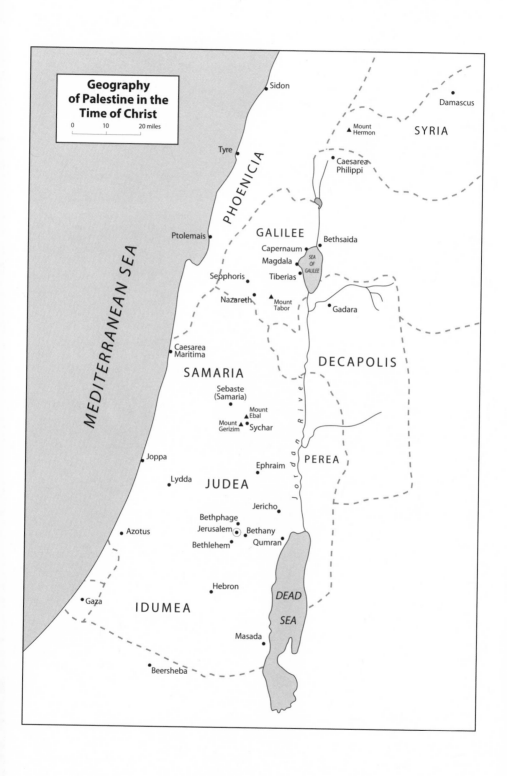

Geography of Palestine in the Time of Christ

0   10   20 miles

MEDITERRANEAN SEA

PHOENICIA

SYRIA

DECAPOLIS

GALILEE

SAMARIA

JUDEA

PEREA

IDUMEA

DEAD SEA

SEA OF GALILEE

Jordan River

Sidon
Damascus
Mount Hermon
Tyre
Caesarea Philippi
Ptolemais
Capernaum
Bethsaida
Magdala
Sepphoris
Tiberias
Nazareth
Mount Tabor
Gadara
Caesarea Maritima
Sebaste (Samaria)
Mount Ebal
Mount Gerizim
Sychar
Joppa
Ephraim
Lydda
Jericho
Bethphage
Jerusalem
Bethany
Azotus
Bethlehem
Qumran
Hebron
Gaza
Masada
Beersheba